Seeds of Knowledge

Seeds of Knowledge
The Beginning of Integrated Pest Management in Java

YUNITA T. WINARTO

With a Foreword by
James J. Fox

Monograph 53/Yale Southeast Asia Studies

Yale University Southeast Asia Studies
J. Joseph Errington, Chairman
Marvel Kay Mansfield, Editor

Consulting Editors
Hans-Dieter Evers, Universität Bielefeld
Hùynh Sanh Thông, Yale University
Sartono Kartodirdjo, Gadjah Mada University
Lim Teck Ghee, Institute for Advanced Studies, University of Malaya
Alfred W. McCoy, University of Wisconsin
Anthony Reid, University of California/Los Angeles
Benjamin White, Institute for Social Studies, The Hague
Alexander Woodside, University of British Columbia

Library of Congress Catalog Card Number: 2003-110894
International Standard Book Number: paper   0-938692-81-X
                                                                   cloth   0-938692-80-1

© 2004 by Yale University Southeast Asia Studies
New Haven, Connecticut 06520-8206

Distributor:
Yale University Southeast Asia Studies
P.O. Box 208206
New Haven, Connecticut 06520-8206
U.S.A.

Printed in U.S.A.

For my husband,
Vincentius Winarto

And my children,
Winastu, Winarnita, and Wijoyoseno

Contents

List of Illustrations
    Figures   ix
    Maps   ix

List of Tables   x

Foreword by James J. Fox   xi

Preface   xiv

Acknowledgments   xvii

Abbreviations   xx

1. Knowledge in the Making: An Introduction   1
2. The "Genuine" Rice Farmers in Their "Unbounded Niche"   36
3. Keep the Plants Healthy: Spraying "Medicines"   73
4. Spraying "Medicines" Is Old-Fashioned   113
5. "Now Our Way of Thinking Is Different"   162
6. Voicing for Freedom, Striving for Harvests   214
7. Recreating Knowledge and Persisting Paradigm   283
8. Seeds of Knowledge   340

Appendix 1—The brief history of the Green Revolution in Java   365

Appendix 2—Integrated Pest Management in Rice   367

Appendix 3—The Objectives and Organization of Integrated Pest Management Training   372

Appendix 4—Integrated Pest Management Program Competency Objectives   376

Appendix 5—The National Curriculum: "A Day in a Farmers' Field School"   *378*

Appendix 6—The Weekly Schedule of IPM Farmers' Field School in Ciasem   *380*

Glossary   *382*

Notes   *384*

Bibliography   *401*

Illustrations

Figures

1.1	The white rice stem borer's reproductive stages and its infestation of rice	6
1.2	*Apa ini?* What is this?	27
1.3	Structure and relationships among extension, plant protection, agricultural education and training systems	28
2.1	BIMAS operational units and farmers' institutions	59
4.1	The supervisors, trainers and farmers	117
4.2	The white rice stem borer's life cycle	158
6.1	Location of larvae during the dry season	231
6.2	Newly hatched larvae	264
7.1	Location of pupae and the emergence of a moth	330
Appendix 3.1	The organogram of the national IPM program of Indonesia	373

Maps

1.1	The province of West Java in the Republic of Indonesia	2
1.2	The regency of Subang and the district of Ciasem	5
2.1	Marga Tani and the centres of information	41
2.2	Marga Tani in the village of Ciasem Baru	43
2.3	Residential areas and the residents of IPM and some non-IPM farmers	47
2.4	The north coast region of West Java	53

2.5 The location of IPM and some non-IPM farmers' *Sawah*	55
Appendix 3.1 Location of IPM field training facilities in six provinces in Indonesia	374

Tables

2.1 Occupations of Marga Tani residents, 1992	49
2.2 *Sawah* ownership in Marga Tani, 1992	50
2.3 Total number and size of landholdings in Marga Tani, 1992	51
2.4 Distribution of land tenure agreements in Marga Tani, 1992	67
3.1 Fertilizers in the 1989–90 rainy season	91
3.2 The use of carbofuran in the 1989–90 rainy season	93
3.3 Frequency of spraying pesticides in the 1989–90 rainy season	106
3.4 Number of products in the mixture of pesticides	107
3.5 Rice varieties in the 1989–90 rainy season and the 1990 dry season	111
4.1 The IPM participants in Kampung Marga Tani	120
6.1 Diverse strategies in carbofuran application	238
6.2 Diverse mixtures of pesticides	246
6.3 Control strategies in the first and second moth flight	253
7.1 Rice varieties in the 1990–1992 planting seasons	289

Foreword

ON THE 6TH of November 1986, President Suharto assembled the governors of Indonesia's major rice growing provinces, regents from the main rice producing districts on Java and high-ranking officials from the Department of Agriculture. At this extraordinary meeting—called without advance explanation—the President issued an immediate ban on 57 widely used pesticides and announced his new national policy for the Integrated Pest Management (IPM) of rice. He also chided officials for covering up the extent of the damage caused by the spreading infestation of brown plant hopper, known as *wereng*, that had already devastated thousands of hectares of rice on Java.

In explaining how the outbreak had been induced by an excessive use of pesticides, the President was particularly critical of officials who concealed the truth on matters of national importance to preserve their personal careers. Suddenly and for several weeks, the *wereng* became the symbol of what government officials were hiding from the public. The popular singer, Iwan Fals, even composed a song about the *wereng* and its capacity for hidden damage. At the same time, steps were taken to reduce pesticide use and to allow the natural predators of the *wereng* to revive and to destroy this threat to the next season's rice crop.

With the threat to the rice crop reduced and the dissemination of a new resistant variety of rice, the Indonesian government set out to train farmers in methods of Integrated Pest Management. The FAO was invited to establish a training program that, compared with previous official extension efforts, was stunningly new and challenging. The program, based on a network of local "schools without walls," taught farmers to observe, experiment and then act. Instead of being instructed and guided from above, farmers were taught to think for themselves and do what they regarded as most appropriate for their field conditions. As it developed, the program was more than just a set of new lessons; it offered, in the context of the time, a subversive message.

By the mid-1980s, IPM scientists had worked out ways of dealing with the brown plant hopper as a pest and were confident in their methods, which proved to be effective. However, when pesticides were substantially reduced, a new pest emerged in the form of the rice stem borer—one of the main pests that Indonesian farmers had to confront before the introduction of pesticides. Developing the means and methods for dealing with outbreaks of these pests was a new challenge. Thus in the early 1990s, both farmers and scientists were involved in a similar IPM learning effort.

This, then, is the setting for this remarkable book, *Seeds of Knowledge*. It is a tribute to its author, Dr. Yunita Winarto, who seized the opportunity presented by the establishment of the FAO training program on Java to do basic anthropological research on how knowledge is acquired and transmitted.

Seeds of Knowledge has many facets. It is a unique document on a critical period in the history of Indonesian agriculture; it is an extraordinary examination of how local knowledge takes shape through the interaction of numerous individuals; but above all, it is a fundamental study in human learning.

There are increasing calls for greater attention to be paid to change and development that occur at the "grassroots" level. However, what actually goes on at this level is by no means clear and easy to follow. The process, if we may call it that, by which local views are formed, including contending contrary views, is not just a complex succession of events. It is a confusing and indeed a messy process. The great virtue of this book is the way in which it wrestles with this process of learning, unlearning and relearning. The efforts that Dr. Winarto has taken to provide an understanding of what went on among a small group of farmers is monumental. The narrative of this process, in all its details, is thoroughly engaging.

Hard-gained knowledge can be liberating and one of the effects of the "schools without walls" throughout Indonesia was their capacity to break the pattern of required acceptance by farmers of what they were directed to do from on high. When Indonesia first introduced the new rice varieties and embarked on its rice intensification program in the late 1960s, the name given to this national campaign was BIMAS, an abbreviation of *Bimbingan Massal*, the "Mass Guidance Program," to achieve self-sufficiency. Guidance (*bimbingan*) thus became the operative mode for all government activities directed to farmers. Initially, such guidance was probably of benefit but over time, guidance became ever more rigid, limiting farmers' ability to manage their own fields. Nowhere was this more apparent than in the days before President Suharto's change in policy on pesticides. Prior to this change, the army mobilised farmers to carry out saturation spraying in an ill-guided attempt to prevent the spread of the brown plant hopper. The establishment of the new field schools shifted responsibility to farmers for assessing the level of pest infestation in their particular fields and in the surrounding area, and to make judgements on what they ought to do as developments occurred. The knowledge gained from the use of these IPM methods enhanced farmers' self-confidence and at the same time it prompted an interest in knowing more than what local extension officers could provide. One of the most telling sections in this book is the description of the farmers' visit to the Sukamandi Agricultural Research Station to discuss pest management strategies with the rice scientists.

Seeds of Knowledge is an ethnographically rich account of a momentous period of change. Its setting is at the microlevel but its message and implications are of fundamental significance. Its cast of characters—Ayim, Rustam, Haji Ali, Idham, Iwan and the rest—lend a special flavour to a fascinating narrative of discovery.

JAMES J. FOX

Preface

ONE OF THE MOST exciting times during my fieldwork was listening to the farmers' conversations, either at the edge of their rice fields, at the verandah of their houses, or in front of the small food stalls (*warung*). This was the time when farmers shared their experience of how good or bad their paddy was and how successful their own or other farmers' strategies were. Also, they talked about what kinds of new pesticides they had heard about from the shop owner (*pemilik kiosk*) or other farmers, or what kinds of new rice varieties they had learned about. In such conversation, I learned how individual farmers interpret their own and other farmers' practices and the performance of their plants. Conversation means exchanging a bundle of interpretations. Many times I heard them correcting their previous assumptions about the ways of growing rice. Sometimes they came up with new propositions, confirming or falsifying their previous ones, challenging other farmers' propositions: arguing against or agreeing with their fellows' interpretations. Interpretation and reinterpretation went on and on, daily, weekly, and seasonally. It was during these conversations that they shared their feelings of joy and happiness if their plants had grown well. But this was also the time to grumble, to voice their disappointments, sorrow, and burdens of the many problems they had to encounter in farming and in daily life. The most frustrating thing was not being able to assist them. Hence, I feel very grateful to be able to publish this work. I hope this book will contribute significantly to the greater understanding of the farmers' struggles to reach prosperity.

For four planting seasons—from the 1990 dry season to the 1991/92 rainy season—I followed the farmers' efforts to cope with continuous pest and disease outbreaks, not to mention the economic pressures and burdens they had to overcome. In the 1989/90 rainy season farmers at my research sites in the district of Ciasem in the regency of Subang, West Java Province experienced a severe problem. A plague of white rice borer (*Scirpophaga innotata*) attacked thousands of hectares of rice fields. Farmers were still in great debt when they had to face more outbreaks of pests and diseases in the following seasons. At the same time, they were struggling against the persisting "top-down complete-credit-package." These occurred just after as many as 25 farmers in the 1990 dry season were completing their participation in an Integrated Pest Management (IPM) school, a "school without walls." Here they learned about the ideas and strategies of integrated pest management. This book is based on my experience following farmers' activities during and after they participated in that school, learning how they continuously modified and formed their existing knowledge. This book is thus a book about "knowledge in the making," particularly in relation to the integration of two modes of learning: the scientific and the local.

This work illustrates "the cultural in motion" phrase that Borofsky (1994b, 1994d) used in reference to the recent anthropological works that elucidate the dynamics of culture. In this vein, I would like to address the issue of how knowledge is formed and thus becomes a basis for action. Included will be how new ideas become a part of "local culture"; how variation contributes to the development of knowledge; how shared knowledge is formed; how shared and diverse knowledge are maintained; how changes in knowledge occur; and how previous knowledge endures. To understand these phenomena, one needs a consideration of why they exist and under what conditions they exist. What further consequences to people's knowledge, practices, and the growth of the plants do these phenomena have? The transmission of integrated pest management ideas to the local farmers is good grounds to examine these issues. It is also a case of local people struggling to survive in the circumstances in which those in power and authority have changed their environment. This is the story of how the local people tried to make use of the ideas introduced into their everyday form of struggle. Creativity instead of resistance underlines their daily struggle.

By understanding their story, a wider implication is expected to emerge. A very promising interface between different parties—the scientists, the bureaucrats, and the farmers—could in fact be created, hand-in-hand, to affect the existing condition at the local level, as well as to accelerate changes. Through a closer collaboration that cuts across boundaries between different worlds of expertise and farmers in different locales throughout the world, the sharp distinction between "scientists" and "practitioners," the "modern" and the "traditional," or the "global" and the "local," can be turned into a "dialectic" relation among various parties to foster the process of gaining a more sustainable and prosperous life in the future

The organization of the chapters in this book follows the sequential events of farmers' experience in knowledge formation and practices, i.e., from the period prior to the introduction of the Integrated Pest Management program in 1990 until the time I had to leave them in 1992. By presenting the story of farmers' struggles sequentially, preceded by a brief description of the setting, I aim to show how the details of the farmers' struggles in crop management continued from time to time.

Acknowledgments

THIS BOOK is based on my Ph.D. thesis submitted to the Department of Anthropology, Research School of Pacific and Asian Studies, The Australian National University in Canberra in 1996. Without the help of many people, this work would never have been published. I have incurred debts to all of them. For institutional support, I gratefully acknowledge the University of Indonesia for granting me a study leave to pursue my Ph.D. study at the Australian National University from 1991 to 1996 and to accomplish this work in 1998 and 1999. For financial support, my sincere thanks to the Equity and Merit Scholarship Scheme from the AusAID for providing a grant to finance my studies in Australia. The FAO National Indonesian IPM Program invaluably assisted me and financed my research in Subang, West Java from early 1990 until the end of July 1991. The Ford Foundation Regional Office in Jakarta agreed to provide me grants for my continued research in the 1991/92 rainy season. The International Student Office, Management Services, and the Disability Officer at the ANU provided great help when I needed to undergo treatments for health problems during my study. My gratitude also goes to the Department of Anthropology, Research School of Pacific and Asian Studies at the Australian National University, which offered me a visiting fellowship in August and September 1998 and again in June and July 1999. The FAO Global IPM Facility provided additional grants to enable me to prepare the manuscript of this book. The Australian National University in Canberra provided not only logistical and financial support, but also a favourable climate conducive to unhampered academic inquiry.

I wish to express my sincere gratitude to some special scholars whose support, attention, and encouragement have motivated me to pursue my study and see this work to completion. They have significantly influenced the course of my professional life: the late Koentjaraningrat, and Andrew P. Vayda, James J. Fox, Gordon R. Conway, Michael R. Dove, James Danandjaja, Parsudi Suparlan, S. Budhisantoso, Nico S. Kalangie, Kuswata Kartawinata, Iwan Tjitradjaja, Don S. Gardner, Lynette Parker, Penelope D. Graham, Peter Kenmore, Wolfgang Lindser, and Russell D. Dilts. Andrew P. Vayda stimulated my interests and inspired me with interesting ideas to do my work. James J. Fox, Don S. Gardner, Lynette Parker, and Penelope D. Graham have patiently read and supervised my Ph.D. thesis draft on the basis of which I developed this work. Michael R. Dove, Gregory Acciaicoli, and Paul Alexander gave invaluable comments on my thesis for the improvement of this work. The publication of this work would not be possible without their persistent encouragement and that of Peter Kenmore.

A large number of people assisted me from the beginning of my research until the completion of this work. My sincere thanks to the staff of the National IPM Secretariat in Jakarta and the IPM Field Training Facility in Jatisari, Karawang, and to my research assistants Chamiyatus Sidqiyah, Sri Widyastuti, Haryono and Sahnudin. My debt to those who provided invaluable help in computing and data processing: Ria van de Zandt, Daniel Fritsch, Charles C. Grimes and Jeanny; and to Gail Craswell, Norma Chin, Barbara Holloway, Amanda Scott and Robert Doxey for correcting and improving my English. Tony HS and friends, Margaret Tyrie and Kay Dancey assisted me in preparing and improving the maps and figures. Judith Wilson did meticulous work in reading my references. The International Rice Research Institute in the Philippines granted permission to reprint their slide production on white rice borer and some of the pictures published in Reissig, W.H. *et al.* (1986) *Illustrated guide to integrated pest management in rice in tropical Asia.* All the departmental staff, members, and fellow students of the Department of Anthropology, RSPAS, ANU will always be in my memory for their supportive assistance and friendships during the completion of my thesis and work.

Acknowledgments

Presenting the complex stories of farmers' daily lives and struggles in this book has not been an easy task. I gained great encouragement from the farmers. Their joy, curiosity, hopes, efforts, difficulties, disappointments and complaints always come to mind. For them, I had to accomplish this work. My greatest debts are to the farmers in Marga Tani and Kebon Cau (Desa Ciasem Baru) and in Desa Ciasem Tengah. Even though I was not able to incorporate the stories of farmers from this latter village into this book, their activities inspired my writing. More than once I had to interrupt their lives for so many days over four planting seasons. I learned from their struggle what life really meant. My sincere thanks to my "adopted parents," Haji Gojali and his wife in Marga Tani, Ciasem Baru and Haji Solichin and his wife in Marjim, Ciasem Tengah. My sincere gratitude to many other farmers who taught me a great deal about rice farming and the hardships of their life. To the assistance and help of the village leaders and staff, the hamlet leaders, the district agricultural official, the pest observers, the extension workers, and the BPP staff in Ciasem, I owe a great debt.

To my parents and my folk, and in particular to my family who went along with me through all the ups and downs, no words can express my debt and gratitude. I present this work especially to my husband, Vincentius Winarto and my children: Johannes L. Winastu, Monika S. Winarnita and Maximilian A. Wijoyoseno for their support, patience, love, and care.

Abbreviations

BALITTAN	*Balai Penelitian Tanaman Pangan* (Agricultural Research Station for Food Crops)
BAPPENAS	*Badan Perencanaan Pembangunan Nasional* (National Development Planning Board)
BIMAS	*Bimbingan Massa* (Mass Guidance)
BLB	Bacterial leaf blight
BPH	Brown plant hopper
BPP	*Balai Penyuluhan Pertanian* (Rural Extension Centre)
BRS	Bacterial red stripe
ETL	Economic threshold level
FAO	Food and Agricultural Organization
FTF	Field Training Facility
INMAS	*Intensifikasi Massa* (Mass Intensification)
INSUS	*Intensifikasi Khusus* (Special Intensification)
IPC	Integrated Pest Control
IPM	Integrated Pest Management
JALUR PANTURA	*Jatiluhur Pantai Utara* (the North coast region of Jatiluhur Dam)
KCl	Potassium Chloride
KELOTA	*Kelompok Tani* (Farmers' Group)
KTNA	*Kontak Tani Andalan* (The Contact Group of Prominent Farmers)
KUD	*Koperasi Unit Desa* (Village Cooperative Unit)
KUT	*Kredit Usaha Tani* (Farmers' Credit Package)
N	Nitrogen (Urea)
P	Phosphate

PERUM	*Perusahaan Umum* (Government-owned company)
PHP	*Pengamat Hama dan Penyakit* (Pest and Disease Observer)
PHT	*Pengendalian Hama Terpadu* (IPM = Integrated Pest Management)
POSKO	*Pos Simpul Koordinasi* (The Chain Post of Coordination)
PPL	*Petugas Penyuluh Lapangan* (Extension Worker)
RDK	*Rencana Kerja Kelompok* (The Farmers' Group Working Plan)
RDKK	*Rencana Definitif Kebutuhan Kelompoktani* (Definitive Plans of the Farmers' Group Requirements)
REC	Rural Extension Centre
RSB	Rice Seed Bug
SATPEL BIMAS	*Satuan Pelaksana Bimbingan Massa* (The Mass Operation Unit)
SATPEM BIMAS	*Satuan Pembina Bimbingan Massa* (The Mass Guidance Unit)
SLPHT	*Sekolah Lapang Pengendalian Hama Terpadu* (Integrated Pest Management Field School)
S.S.	*Saluran Sekunder* (Secondary Canals)
SUPRA INSUS	*Supra Intensifikasi Khusus* (Super Special Intensification)
TSP	Triple Superphosphate
USAID	United States Agency for International Development
WKBPP	*Wilayah Kerja Balai Penyuluhan Pertanian* (The Operational Region of a Rural Extension Centre)
WKPP	*Wilayah Kerja Penyuluhan Pertanian* (The Operational Region of Extension Service)
WRB	White rice stem borer
ZA	Ammonium Sulphate

1

Knowledge in the Making: An Introduction

ON THE FIRST FEW DAYS of my visit to Ciasem in the regency of Subang on the north coast of West Java (see maps 1.1 and 1.2), farmers complained about severe damage to their harvests. I entered their area in the first week of April 1990, less than two months after a severe white rice stem borer (WRB, *Scirpophaga innotata*) outbreak at the end of the 1989/90 rainy season. Early in the 1990 dry season, farmers told me the story.

> First, our paddy looked green and healthy. Suddenly, when the panicles appeared, they turned white, all stood up, ... wearing *Haji's* white caps (*pakai topi Haji*) .... There were thousands of white moths everywhere, but we did not know that these moths could damage our plants. This is our fate (*nasib*), ... a calamity (*musibah*), ... God's will.

Such was the farmers' understanding of the outbreak. They could do nothing but accept their misfortune. Up to the early 1990 dry season, the sporadic appearance of deadhearts and whiteheads was not an unknown phenomenon for the farmers. Deadhearts were reported as more common in the dry season than in the rainy season. However, farmers did not understand that larvae hatched from the egg-clusters that were laid by white moths caused these symptoms. The huge population of white moths in the 1989/90 rainy season was the first major experience of its kind for many of the farmers. Without any knowledge of the white stem borer's reproduction, farmers did not understand that those thousands of white moths would cause such severe damage to their plants.

By contrast, when I left the field at the end of February 1992, the majority of farmers considered the white moths the most devastating insects ("*kupu-kupu putih itu yang paling jahat*"), their major enemy. They acknowledged that these white moths were the source of

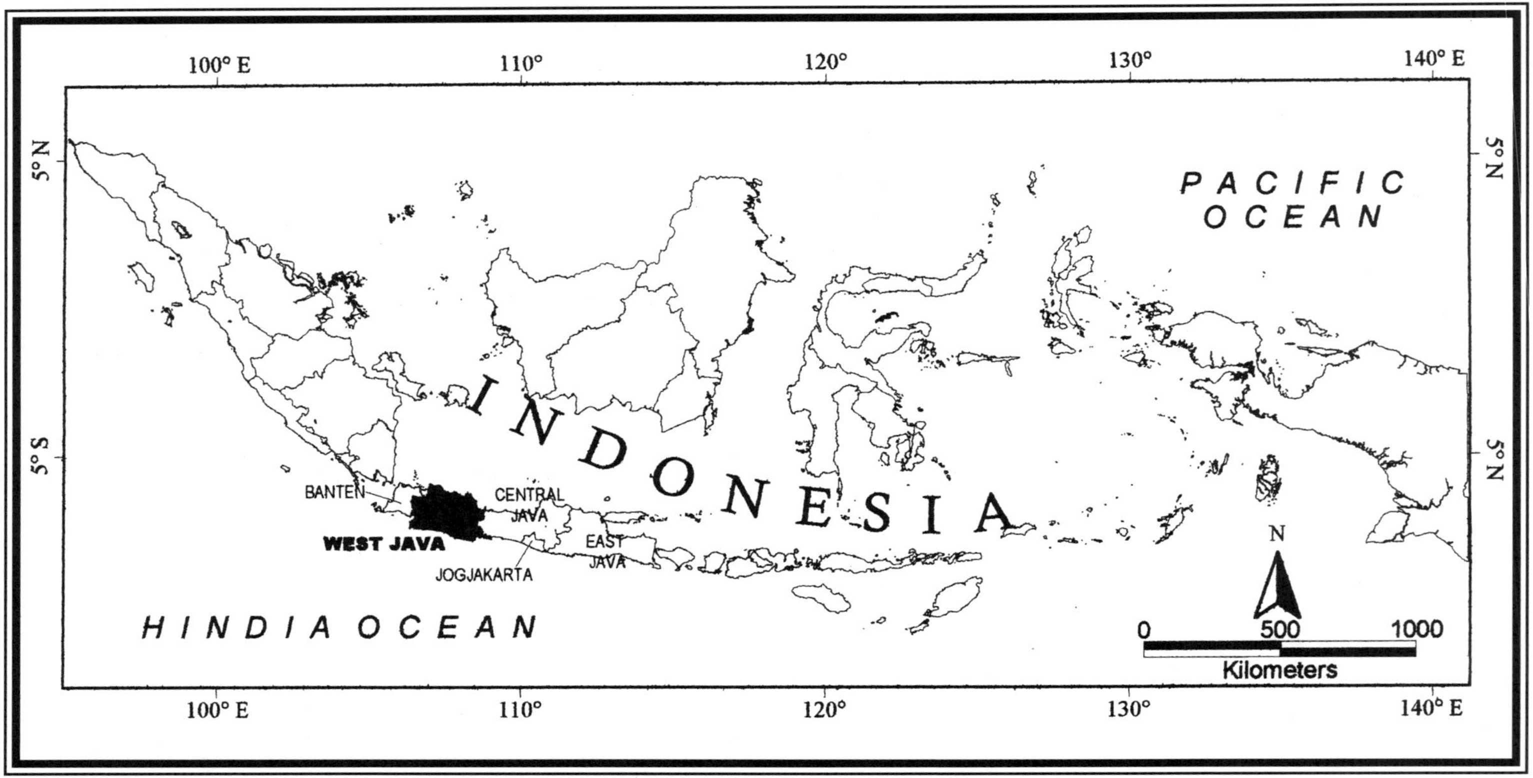

Map 1.1 The province of West Java in the Republic of Indonesia

larvae, which hatched from egg-clusters and bored inside the stems of their paddy (see fig. 1.1). This pest infests the paddy at two stages: the vegetative stage, which causes deadhearts (*sundep*), and the reproductive stage—when the paddy starts to form ears—which causes empty whiteheads (*beluk*, white panicles). The term *penggerek batang* (stem borer) had become familiar to the farmers as the cause of *beluk* or *bapuk* (*loba*: many; *empuk*: soft, many soft panicles). However, until early 1992, there were many diverse understandings about the cause of deadheart. Detailed knowledge of the pest's behaviour also varied.

In the 1990/91 rainy season, some farmers began to consider that spraying pesticide regularly—a common practice to protect plants or control pests/diseases—was not the most effective way to control the rice stem borer. In the last three decades since the introduction of the Green Revolution, farmers were used to regularly spraying pesticides on their crops. This practice was based on the earlier scientific belief in pesticides as the effective way of controlling pests/diseases. Farmers have been the subject of such propaganda and have indeed internalized that practice in their daily crop farming activities. After experiencing the outbreaks throughout the 1990/91 and 1991/92 planting seasons, they learned that a number of alternative strategies in pest control were more effective and efficient. Some farmers reduced the frequency of spraying pesticides, but until the end of the 1991/92 rainy season, the injudicious use of pesticides had persisted. Moreover, many farmers still metaphorically referred to pesticides as "medicines" whose function was to prevent or cure their paddy from "illnesses" (*penyakit*).[1]

Farmers gain their knowledge from observation, discoveries, experimentation and conversations over time (see e.g. Johnson 1972, Rhoades and Bebbington 1988, Rhoades 1987, 1989a; Richards 1986, 1989a). The time dimension is crucial, as only through time will the farmers obtain experience and understanding. Within this mode of learning, how could there be such major changes within two short years? How did these changes in their knowledge and practices happen? Did the changes occur only through the farmers' daily experiences within their mode of learning? In the 1990 dry season, the national government sought to introduce new scientific knowledge in the form of integrated pest management (IPM) principles to some farmer-participants. Some external ideas that turned over the earlier scientific belief about pesticides were introduced to the local farmers in a form of training. How significantly did these ideas contribute to changes? To what extent and how did these ideas become part of farmers' knowledge?

The IPM school introduced a new paradigm for using pesticides and a novel meaning of pesticide as poison. Until the end of my fieldwork, two years after the first introduction of these ideas, the old metaphor of pesticide as "medicine" and the conventional way of spraying pesticides in many cases still persisted. How and why was there continuity in the context of change? Variation in the farmers' understanding about the cause of deadheart and the reproductive cycle of the white rice borer reveals the fact that diversity is a reality (see Cancian 1967; Johnson 1972; Pelto and Pelto 1975; Vayda 1994). By considering the development of a common understanding of the pest's reproductive cycle, and its nature of infestation, it is still significant to examine how and why the diversity existed and why the convergence of understanding developed.

By examining these issues, this book presents the complex and dynamic nature of knowledge construction and the processes by which the interaction of people with different modes of learning and their responses to introduced ideas affect the production and reproduction of knowledge over time. This provides a detailed understanding of how the dialogue between two different perceptions and modes of learning—the scientific and the local—happens and leads to changes, modifications, and variations, or to the persistence of knowledge and practices.

Knowledge is Dynamic, Knowledge is Diverse

In a recent article, Barth (1994) has emphasised the value of studying human traditions of knowledge. Examining knowledge in its particularities, through the events by which people go about constructing meanings over time, presents an opportunity to examine

Map 1.2 *(opposite) The regency of Subang and the district of Ciasem*
Source: Reissig et al. (1986:130, 137, 139).

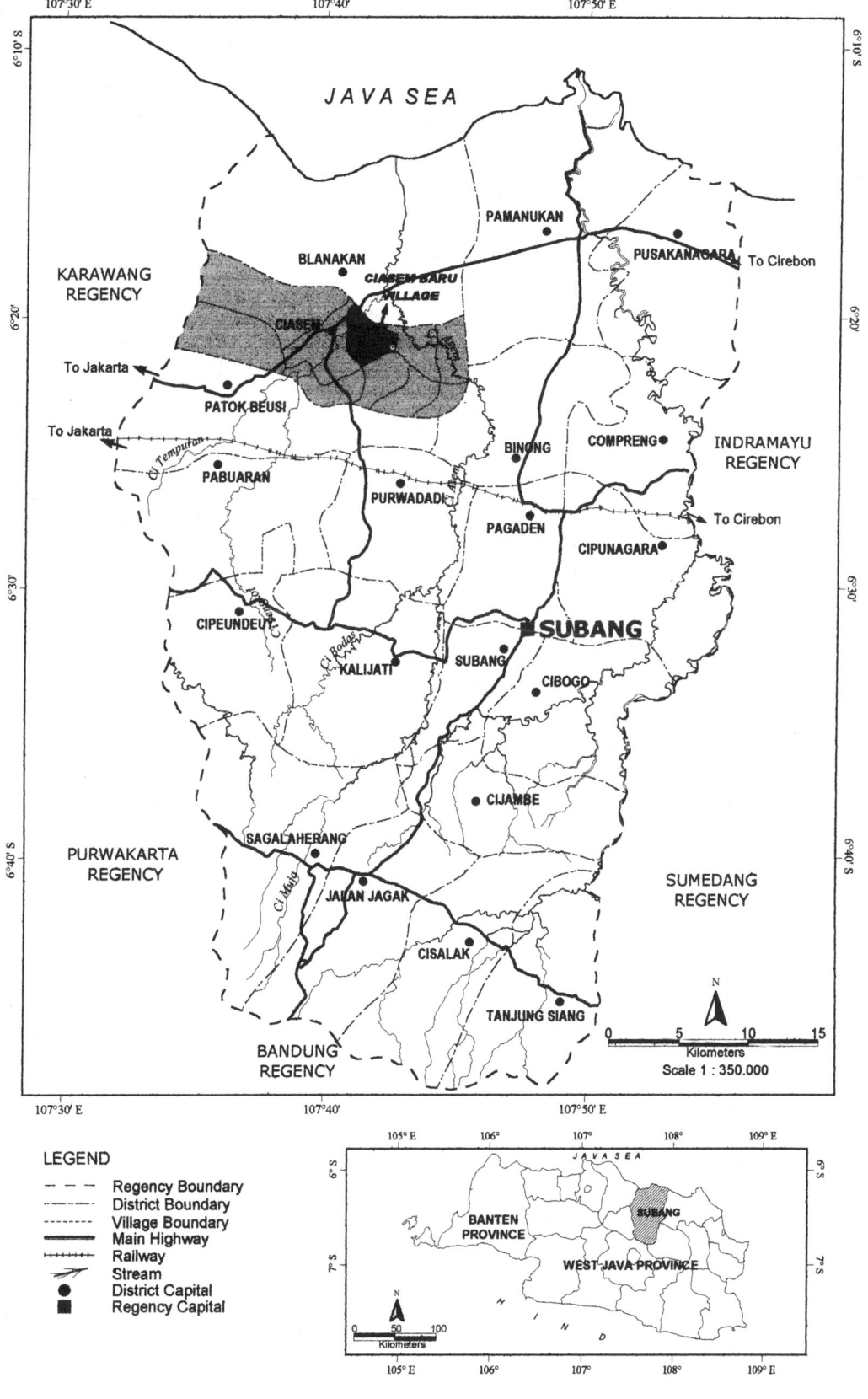

Figure 1.1 *The white rice stem borer's reproductive stages and its infestation of rice*

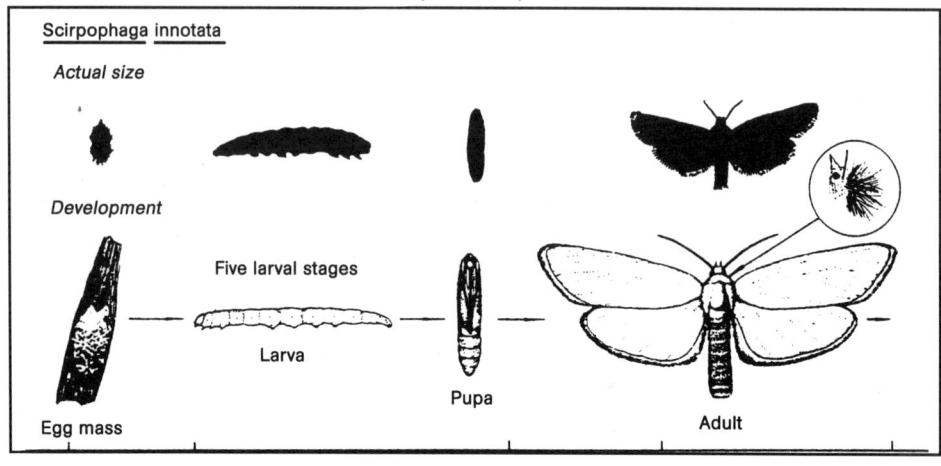

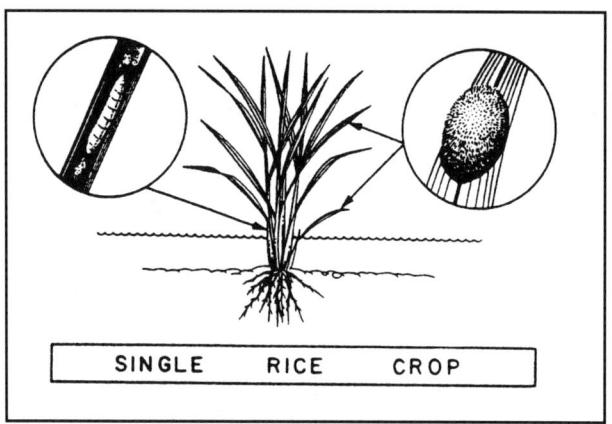

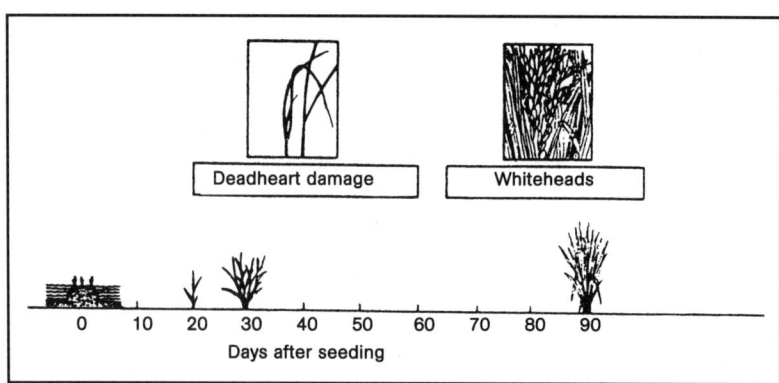

Source: Reissig *et al.* (1986:130, 137, 139).

variation and processes (Barth 1994:352). This approach, argues Barth (1994, 1995), has the advantage of moving us away from essentializing and homogenizing culture. Recently, warnings against essentializing have increased (see Keesing 1994; Vayda 1994). In the last two decades, various other scholars have emphasised the importance of looking at the dynamics and/or variability in a culture. Borofsky (1994d) has called upon the need to examine culture in its dynamic nature. He replaces the term "culture" with "cultural" to emphasise the difference between "culture" in its static form, and "cultural" as always in motion. Moore (1975, 1987, 1994) has also argued for a "processual approach" to ethnography that takes as its subject selected social-cultural phenomena seen over time. By arguing that "[T]ime is a constitutive dimension of social reality," Colson (1984:1–2) proposes the significance of examining people's experience over time. Through experiencing different challenges, people reorder their thinking and pursue different goals (Colson 1984:5).

In line with this perspective of examining the dynamic aspect of culture, Barth (1995) proposes recognition of knowledge as a major modality of culture. A focus on knowledge allows an articulation of culture in a more transitive and dynamic form. It also allows a greater recognition of other people's knowledge. Barth's (1995:66) approach sees culture as knowledge that

> ... abstracts it less and points to people's engagement with the world, through action. It acknowledges the fact of globally continuous variation, not separable into homogenized and mutually alien cultures. It alerts us to interchange and to flux.

In relation to this statement, knowledge cannot be seen as alienated from the actors. It is the product of continuous interaction, dialogue, negotiation and accommodation between specific actors and groups (Borofsky 1987, 1994d; Barth 1987, 1989, 1990, 1995; Lave and Wenger 1991; Arce and Long 1993; Long and Villareal 1994). Knowledge is also under continuous construction and transformation. It is always in the making as behaviour proceeds (Crick 1982; Goody 1987; Barth 1987, 1994; Keller and Keller 1993; Lave 1993).

By moving away from essentializing and homogenizing culture, Vayda (1994:320) has argued that variation should be the main object of study and not "mere accidents about norms." At an earlier stage,

Wallace (1970), Tyler (1969), Sankoff (1971) and Pelto and Pelto (1975) have posed the same argument. "Variations are not mere deviations from some assumed basic organization; with their rules of occurrence *they are the organization,*" argues Tyler (1969:5). It is also a reality that knowledge is diverse. Variation in individual repertoires and application of knowledge is widely distributed (e.g., Gardner 1976; Boster 1986; Brosius et al. 1986; Borofsky 1987, 1994b; Barth 1987, 1994; Long and Villareal 1994; Scoones and Thompson 1994b; Wassmann 1995). Long and Villareal (1994:43) have pointed out strongly that knowledge is "... multilayered ... and fragmentary and diffuse, rather than unitary and systematized." Knowledge remains contestable. It is not only contested from a diversity of individual positions, but also remains so through time (Barth 1993, 1994).

In her reviews on both cognitive anthropology and cognitive psychology, Lave (1988) raises the problems of both subjects in emphasizing cultural uniformity. As a consequence, major questions about

> ... social diversity, inequality, conflict, complementarity, cooperation and differences of power and knowledge, and the means by which they are socially produced, reproduced and transformed in laboratory, school and other everyday settings
>
> (Lave 1988:10)

would be left out. In line with this concern, Wassmann (1995) summarizes the changes in basic premises in cognitive anthropology. From a premise that culture is common ("shared") knowledge, the focus is now turning towards the study of individuals and the widespread distribution of knowledge. From the premise that knowledge is in the form of a "cultural grammar," as something static, organized into precisely defined fields in the form of lexemes subject to taxonomic rules, the move is now directing to one that focuses more on operationalization instead of categorization. Knowledge is defined as evident in everyday use by individuals. Many categories have no fixed boundaries (see Healey 1978/79), and are now grouped according to what a person can do in daily life. This involves a turning away from the perception of language as the only instrument that encodes knowledge (although it remains one of the focal points). Nonverbal actions also embody knowledge (Wassmann 1995:169–74; also see Bourdieu 1977; Holy and Stuchlik 1983; Dougherty and Keller

1985; Gatewood 1985; Harper 1987; and Keller and Keller 1993). As Barth (1995) says, knowledge also resides in "what people employ to interpret and act on the world" as feelings, embodied skills and other nonverbal actions. However, if language becomes the focal point, Wassmann (1995:173) argues to treat language "differently: no longer as lexicon, but in everyday use as 'discourse' from which inferences must be drawn as to the intended 'message.'"

In the ongoing review of cognitive anthropology, Vayda and Setyawati (1995:260–61, 1998) argued for the importance of examining practical activities or behaviour, as well as people's knowledge and ignorance concerning actual behaviour, regardless of whether the behavior is culturally appropriate, culturally influenced, or societally acceptable. Wassmann (1995) revised premises in cognitive anthropology from his examination of the individual knowledge of both the "omniscient informant" and "just plain folks" among the Yupno people of New Guinea. Although he was able to reveal how diverse individual knowledge is and how these variations relate to a range of variables (age, sex, context, personal experience, etc.), he did not examine how such diversity comes about. It has not been part of his objective to study how knowledge is acquired, retained, and transmitted or the processes that produce the diversity. On the other hand, Borofsky (1987) and Barth (1987, 1990), for example, have been able to show that the process of knowledge generation and transmission "contains the key to explaining variations" (Vayda 1994:324). In his study among the Pukapukan (Polynesia), Borofsky (1987) discovered that listening, observing, and imitating form the basic means of knowing. Extensive questioning was discouraged. Hence, diversity developed because people could differ in what they often observe or hear from others (also see Vayda 1994). He also found that public occasions, such as speeches at the feasts or public discussions where the elders displayed what they knew, provided an ideal opportunity for Pukapukans to acquire knowledge. Nevertheless, in the Pukapukan framework of challenges and counterchallenges, determining which information was correct was not easy. There was also great uncertainty and ambiguity regarding aspects of the cultural past. Not only were people's accounts diverse, but they also shared considerable creativity in transforming ambiguities of the past into plausible accounts of the present (Borofsky 1987:122). Through this mechanism, people created knowledge and history. In his study among the Mountain Ok people of New Guinea, Barth (1987) discovered that variations, modifications, and changes found in rituals and cosmological ideas were the result of re-creation from elements lodged in one or a few individual minds. Since the initiation rites were performed once every ten years or so, and through this period knowledge was kept in the care of a small number of experts, the reproduction of the rites is always a re-creation. The modification depends on the experts' memories, improvisation and borrowing from neighbouring groups (Barth 1987:24–29). In a later article (1990), which compares the interaction between initiators and novices in two different societies (Mountain Ok and Muslim Balinese), Barth (1990:640) shows how different styles of knowledge transmission generate deep differences in the form, scale, and distribution of knowledge. Such studies emphasise the discovering and explaining of the generative processes of knowledge construction and transmission.[2]

Even though diversity was not the prime focus in earlier studies on agriculture, some studies present evidence of individual differences in cultivation (see Johnson 1972:151). Johnson (1972, 1974), for example, argued strongly for the need to take individual differences in agricultural practice into account more seriously. From his study among swidden agriculturalists in Northeastern Brazil he found that "interpersonal conformity of *behaviour* in traditional agriculture is certainly the exception rather than the rule" (Johnson 1972:152). In an environment where the farmers had to face dilemmas, risks, and unexpected phenomena, the culturally transmitted rules underdetermined the practice. In such a situation, there were great disagreements in belief and practice among farmers. Johnson (1972) is able to distinguish at least three different kinds of individual variation as follows:

> First, the variation which inevitably follows from ecological differences such as soil type, degree of slope, aspect of slope, and so on; second, variation which results from differences in the qualities and capabilities of the individual producing unit, such as amount of food stored from the previous harvest or available household labor; and, finally, those differences which result from disagreement among indi-

viduals over the facts of the case or their meanings, such as whether certain crop mixes are superior to others.

(p. 152)

He also argues that the farmers' adaptation to local factors and problems is a creative one. Through this creativity, farmers transform the environment while they are adapting to it. The other significant aspect that—according to Johnson—is common and perhaps even the rule is experimentation. Hence, he concludes that:

> The variation and experimentation ... are of considerable theoretical relevance, for it is the basic stuff of which adaptation and evolutionary change are made.
>
> (Johnson 1972:153–54)

In recent studies on agriculture, many scholars have stressed diversity, experimentation, creativity, and dynamism as the main focuses of their studies.[3]

On the basis of these perspectives, I will address the dynamic nature of knowledge formation by looking at how people generate knowledge through time, how variable it is, and how diversity leads it to change. I argue that an examination of the process of knowledge formation needs to incorporate variation and the multilevel nature of events, acts, experiences, and to show how change occurs. A focus on these detailed processes provides the opportunity to examine: 1) how knowledge becomes a basis for action, 2) how particular events, actions and interactions between specific actors produce knowledge or affect aggregate behaviour, and 3) how changes occur at this aggregate level. Processes, according to Barth (1981:80), "provide the key conceptualizations for depicting how aggregation comes about, and explaining aggregate form." In her discussion about the growing interest among anthropologists and social scientists, Ortner (1984:146) also emphasises the need to "understand where 'the system' comes from—how it is produced and reproduced, and how it may have changed in the past or be changed in the future."[4]

In looking at knowledge as varied and as continuously reproduced through action and interaction over time, understanding the context in which specific action is performed, created or transmitted is of particular importance (see Rogoff 1984; Lave 1988, 1996; Thomason 1986; Borofsky 1987, 1994c; Bratman 1992; Vayda 1994). Rogoff

(1984) and Lave (1988, 1996) have pointed out that knowing is inherently embedded in contexts. "persons acting and the social world of activity cannot be separated," argues Lave (1996:4–5; see also her study on everyday arithmetic in Lave 1988). Since knowledge creation and dissemination involve specific actors and interacting individuals, Long and Villareal (1994:49) stress that we have to place it "fully in its social context, not as a disembodied process." By introducing the term "knowing," which refers to the fluid and flexible nature of knowledge as being different from the structured and rigid one ("knowledge"), Borofsky (1994b:335) argues that knowing varies with varying contexts. Strauss and Quinn (1997) also agree that it is important to look at situated cognition of the interaction between people and their material environment and human peers. Studies on agriculture also reveal that farming knowledge and practices are embedded in their social, political, and economic context. From his study among the Bwisha farmers in Central Africa, Fairhead (1993) concludes that farming knowledge and practices cannot be "elucidated, understood, or represented outside the social, political and economic dynamics of any community."

Understanding the generation and variability of knowledge in its particular context also leads us to question how and why consensus is reached. Besides examining the mechanisms for producing variation, Borofsky (1987) examines the mechanisms in generating common knowledge. Among the Pukapukan, not only context and repetition, but also critical remarks or challenges to what people say publicly play an important role in limiting the diversity of knowledge. Group discussion is also a way of resolving various issues, and hence, may bring about some resolution or consensus (Borofsky 1987:106). Lindstrom (1990) also found that among the Tanna in the South Pacific, shared knowledge is maintained through talking and conversational practice. From his study of manioc cultivation among the Aguaruna Jivaro, Boster (1985, 1986) concludes that consensus or agreement on the identification of manioc varieties is patterned according to the social contexts of learning and speaking about manioc. Hence, different modes and intensities of communication about manioc corresponded to different degrees of agreement (Boster 1985:193). These were patterned according to the sexual division of labour, individual expertise, and membership in kin and residential groups (Boster 1986:429).

This attention to how consensus and agreements are reached points to an issue raised by other scholars, namely the importance of looking not only at the processes that generate variation and changes, but also those that work toward the achievement of consensus in what people know (Sankoff 1971; Romney et al. 1986; Goodenough 1994:266). Barth (1994:354) also emphasises that one of the most important tasks of anthropology at present is to give a realistic account of how, under varying cultural conditions, "people achieve and reproduce a degree of conceptual accommodations and shared premises." Another issue in examining the social life as a process is the need to specify the nature of continuity in a sequence of change (Barth 1967). The kinds of ideas, knowledge and paradigms that have persisted throughout the process of knowledge formation, as well as how and why they remain, are interesting questions to pursue. Such centripetal and centrifugal tendencies in knowledge formation and transmission are the two properties of culture that are important to be accounted for (see Strauss and Quinn 1997). However, as Borofsky (1994a:247) says,

> Despite appearances to the contrary, it is not always easy to tell continuity from change. They tend to merge into as well as define one another.

It is significant therefore to examine further how consensus is reached where variation is profound, and how continuity exists when changes occur.

The Interface: Scientific Knowledge and Local Adoption

Various scholars have discovered that local knowledge is rich, detailed, and adaptive to its local environment, and also dynamic and changing constantly (e.g., Conklin 1957; Howes and Chambers 1979; Brokensha et al. 1980; Dove 1988; Chambers *et al.* 1989; Scoones and Thompson 1994a, 1994b). This knowledge is in continuous adaptation in a world of flux, where ecological, social and economic changes are normal and nowadays, often accelerating (Chambers 1992:1). Part of the cause for these changes is the implementation of development projects carried out within a framework of scientific knowledge and technology. In this era of development, as Hobart (1993:1) points out: "Not only are indigenous knowledges ignored or dismissed, but the nature of the problem of underdevelopment and its solution are defined by reference to this world-ordering knowledge." This represents the superiority of scientific knowledge over local people's knowledge. Chambers (1992) has summarized the complex situation of this interface between scientific and local knowledge and the role of power in this interface as follows:

> Invasions and colonisations from the cores of scientific knowledge generation and of political and bureaucratic power add to local knowledge, but also undermine and weaken it; they simplify, standardise and control conditions and environments, diminishing diversity and the local knowledge of managing and exploiting that diversity; and at the same time they provide new knowledge which is adopted and adapted in the dynamic of local knowledge.
> (pp. 1–2)

The Green Revolution in agriculture is an example of how the implementation of scientific knowledge in producing high yielding crops through the breeding of local plant varieties and related high-level inputs and infrastructure has simplified, standardised, and controlled the environment with external inputs. The implementation of this scientific knowledge in the form of technological packages has created further problems, often unintended by the external agents of development. Examples of problems created in rice crop production are the increased disparity between the rich and the poor, the expanding concentration of landholding, the replacement of women in traditional tasks by machines and male labourers, the replacement of traditional systems of irrigation with modern and technical ones, the loss of diverse plant genetic materials, the greater susceptibility of crop varieties to pests and diseases, and increased pest resistance and resurgence (Palmer 1978; Schiller 1980; Collier 1982; Hardjono 1983; Barlow and Condie 1986; Shiva 1988, 1991, 1993, 1997; Conway and Pretty 1991; Fox 1991; Chambers 1992; Pretty 1995). Nevertheless, a remarkable increase in crop production is evident, and in some cases there has been an improvement in the general standard of living (e.g., Collier 1982; Conway and Pretty 1991; Fox 1991; Pretty 1995).

Even though farmers have been subjected to the imposition of external knowledge and technology provided by extension agents and bureaucrats, or have become "...a cog in the agro-industrial machine..." as argued by Marglin (1996), they have continued to be creative (see Rhoades 1989; Maurya 1989; Pretty 1995; Warren et al. 1995). Rhoades and Bebbington (1995) affirm that farmers are creators of their own solutions, not merely adopters of introduced technologies. They are experimenters and innovators who are actively strategising and continuously processing, assessing and combining information—including information from external sources—to meet their needs and existing conditions. Since individual resources, production strategies, and experiences vary, there is evidence of intra-community variation in response to outside intervention. Pelto and Pelto (1975) found that the peasants and Indian communities in Latin America responded diversely to outside agents of change and other forces of modernisation. From his study of the relationship between social stratification and risk-taking among the Mayan Indians of Chiapas, Cancian (1967) discovered different segments according to wealth had different rates of acceptance of innovation. A great deal of variation within each segment exists as well. The incorporation of new ideas and modes of behaviour also entails a process of alteration according to farmers' own ways rather than according to scientists' preconceived ideas (see Rhoades 1989). As Arce and Long (1992:212) point out,

> when a new technology is introduced into an existing farming system, the technology acquires new meanings and uses, often other than those intended by the planners or implementers.

Farmers' efforts to rework introduced ideas represent their sense and understanding of their local dynamic conditions. In line with this, Richards (1994:166) reformulated a concept of local knowledge as:

> knowledge that is in conformity with general scientific principles, but which, because it embodies place-specific experience, allows better assessments of risk factors in production decisions.

However, as Fujisaka (1995:124) has stated, only recently has farmers' knowledge "been incorporated into agricultural research leading to the generation of new technologies."

Since science and technology have and will continue to transform the world, many scholars have argued for better collaboration and understanding between all the parties involved. Recent empirical findings reveal that the problems to be addressed are much more complex than appreciating and understanding local knowledge, finding solutions in the farmers' own capacities and priorities, or changing the conventional approaches of agricultural extension and research by involving farmers as active partners (e.g., Howes and Chambers 1979; Brokensha et al. 1980; Richards 1985; Chambers et al. 1989; Scoones and Thompson 1994a, 1994b). In *Beyond Farmer First*, Chambers (1994:xiv-xvi) and Scoones and Thompson (1994a:1–4) have argued that more complex issues have to be addressed relating to the complexity of knowledge, changes in the approaches and methodologies in agricultural research and extension, as well as changes in the institutions and policy. Sillitoe (1998) also argues strongly for the importance of providing a greater role for "indigenous" knowledge in development of the need to have meaningful communication between scientists and local people and to strengthen the interdisciplinary approach. He even thinks that a "revolution" is necessary to shift development practices, as well as research methodology in relation to the dynamism in the "indigenous" knowledge itself, and the need to develop appropriate facilitative methods. By criticizing the term used by Sillitoe (1998) and others, i.e., "indigenous knowledge," Dove (2000) argues that a dichotomy between the two knowledge systems (the scientific and the "indigenous") is unreal. Instead, "…all knowledge systems always represent a confluence of local and extra-local experiences" (Dove 2000:235). In agreement with Dove (2000) I perceive this confluence of experience as an ongoing process, which needs a thorough examination.

Knowledge formation and transmission are social processes (see Scoones and Thompson 1994b). Knowledge emerges as a product of continuous interaction and dialogue between different actors and a network of actors with different access to power and resources. It implies aspects of power, authority, and legitimation embedded in social relationships (Long and Villareal 1994; also see Lindstrom 1990). Chambers (1994:xv) notes that:

> The issue is not just "whose knowledge counts?", but "who knows 'who has access to what knowledge' and who can generate new knowledge, and how?"

By adopting this interactive and dynamic view of knowledge transmission, Long and Villareal (1994:42) argue that knowledge is an encounter of horizons and entails a joint creation of knowledge by both disseminators and users. Ortony (1993:2) has pointed out as well that knowledge goes beyond the information given. "It arises from the interaction of that information with the context in which it is presented and with the knower's preexisting knowledge." He differentiates the teaching-as-transmission or learning-as-reception metaphor from the learning-as-construction metaphor. The latter perceives human understanding as the result of the construction rather than direct transmission or reception of the introduced meanings (Ortony 1993:1–2; Mayer 1993:562–63). Moreover, the absorption or transformation of new ideas depends not only on the already existing network of knowledge and evaluative modes, but also on the accumulated social experience, interaction and dialogue between the actors over time and their interaction with the socioeconomic conditions and changing environments. As Hobart (1993:2) points out, a potentially useful task for anthropologists is "to discuss critically how the relationship between expert knowledge and local knowledge works out in practice, as we understand it." The main objectives of this book are not only to examine the interaction between those with differing modes of knowledge acquisition, but to investigate the subsequent processes in which knowledge is continuously formed and changed, and the extent to which action plays a part in the continuous knowledge formation.

In the last decade, studies of such interactions in agriculture have focused on the relationship between farmers and agricultural bureaucrats, scientists or extension officers, in particular on the methods and problems of interaction.[5] One form of interaction between farmers and scientists has been widely known as the Integrated Pest Management program where farmers learned from the scientists the various strategies of controlling pests and diseases. From their examination on such a program in Honduras (Integrated Pest Management in Honduras—MIPH), Bentley, an anthropologist, and

Andrews, an entomologist, show how technology was introduced using on-farm research comparisons and how farmers participated in that project. Bentley points out the weaknesses of this project, in particular the way farmers were viewed as experimental subjects, as just another organism in the environment. He also discovered that MIPH personnel overlooked the ways farmers were adapting the introduced technologies to meet their conditions. Despite these weaknesses, by learning that farmers' participation was an essential element of technological innovation, the project experienced changes and improvement.

On the other hand, Bentley and Andrews (1991:120–21) also note that farmers have limitations and incompleteness in their knowledge. In other articles Bentley and his colleagues (Bentley 1992, 1994; Bentley et al. 1994) argue that romanticizing farmers' knowledge and experiments must be avoided. Farmers' knowledge is uneven. There are a lot of things that they do not know or that they misunderstand. Both Richards (1980) and Bentley (1989, 1992) discovered that ease of observation played a role. Honduran farmers, according to Bentley (1989:25), knew more about plants that were generally large and stationary than insects that were generally small and mobile. They knew less about plant diseases that were usually caused by microorganisms. The southern Nigerian farmers comprehended the life cycle of *Zonocerus variegatus* (a variegated grasshopper) because the insect was large and visible. On the other hand, they did not understand the below-ground pests, which have complex life cycles involving extensive geographical spread and considerable time spans (Richards 1980:184). Many of the people's experiments had also been ecological failures. In relation to this, Bentley et al. (1994:179; Bentley 1994) implemented a project (between 1991 and 1993) on the basis of the motto:

> Find out what people know and explain what they don't know in a way that is compatible with what they do know.

In contrast to the MIPH carried out earlier, Bentley and his colleagues introduced ideas and principles of Integrated Pest Management (IPM), stressing especially natural pest control. They provided this knowledge in the form of short courses, accompanied by field experiments.[6] They drew the conclusion that scientific knowledge could fill the gap in farmers' knowledge. Through their study in the second year of the course, Bentley's colleagues (Bentley et al. 1994:180) discovered that new ecological ideas did stimulate farmers' invention. Although the project personnel followed the results of the farmers' learning process through giving exams and visiting farmers, the article does not discuss in detail how the farmers adopted and reinterpreted the new ideas over time.

Van de Fliert (1993) carried out recent studies of Integrated Pest Management in rice in Indonesia in Central Java in 1990 and 1992, and some undergraduate students from the University of Indonesia in Yogyakarta in 1990. One of the students returned to her study area in 1992 for a brief visit. She noticed some changes in the farmers' knowledge of prey-predator dynamics two years after the introduction of IPM (Vayda and Setyawati 1995). However, she did not follow up on how these changes took place. Van de Fliert carried out a comprehensive study at the village level before, during and after the introduction of IPM throughout five planting seasons in eight IPM and nonIPM villages.[7] She did a comparative study, looking at processes and effects taking place at these villages. She paid attention to how the trainers introduced IPM ideas, how the participants evaluated the trainers' activities, and how these farmers—in comparison with the nonparticipants—carried out their farming practices by relating these to the IPM program's competency objectives. Even though she examined the variations occurring in all villages and between the IPM and non-IPM farmers, she did not discuss in detail the variations emerging within these comparative groups in any particular place. Although she was able to present the differences the IPM training made to the participants in knowledge and practices, her study did not follow up in detail how the new ideas generated further notions and interpretations.

In the Philippines, studies evaluating the results of IPM programs were carried out by Rola et al. (1998) and Navarro et al. (1998). Changes in farmers' knowledge constitute part of their studies about the impact of IPM. Both used statistical analysis to score the knowledge gained by farmers (Navarro et al. 1998) and the common and differentiated knowledge farmers have (Rola et al. 1998). The statistical scores reveal improvement and changes in their knowledge.

Whereas Rola et al. (1998) assume that there is some "spilling over" of the newly learned ideas to non-IPM farmers, Navarro et al. (1998) do not say this. Unfortunately, the reports do not provide any understandings about how and why those changes occurred, not to mention how and why the "spilling over" of the IPM ideas to non-IPM farmers did or did not happen.[8]

These various studies imply that attention should be paid to how the learning process took place; how the new knowledge was disseminated to and adopted by other farmers; to what extent those ideas were diversely or uniformly adopted and which elements of previous knowledge persisted. This book will examine these issues, and complement the discoveries found by earlier studies.

Integrated Pest Management in the Rice-based Cropping System

Using Kuhn's (1962; 1970) term "paradigm," Perkins (1982:58) notes that the development of Integrated Pest Management (IPM) strategy in the 1960s to 1970s—together with another strategy called Total Population Management (TPM)—was perceived by entomologists as the articulation of new paradigms. Kuhn (1962:viii) defines the term "paradigm" as the "universally recognized scientific achievements that for a time provide model problems and solutions to a community of practitioners." In other words, a paradigm is "an accepted model or pattern" (Kuhn 1962:23) or a worldview shared by a group of scientists. The paradigm influences what scientists think of as reasonable problems and how they go about studying them (Kuhn 1970 in Kuznar 1997:52).

The IPM paradigms emerged as a reaction to the failure of the chemical control paradigm. From the early 1900s until the 1950s, the application of toxic chemicals had become the major tool for controlling insects, displacing previous nonchemical control approaches. Towards the end of the World War II, chemicals were predominantly used to control insect pests. Not only was the amount of chemicals increased and the threat to humans and other species found alarming, but also the contamination of the environment and the development of secondary problems caused further hazards. Examples of these were the elimination of natural enemies, the resistance of insects to the poisons, the resurgence of pests, and the outbreak of secondary pests (e.g., Smith et al. 1976; van den Bosch 1978; Perkins 1982). As a new paradigm, the IPM strategy developed not only as a control technique to keep pests below damaging numbers by integrating various methods, but also as a means of examining insect control (see Bottrell 1979; Perkins 1982). The ecological approach to pest management and the integration of various control techniques then became the bases of this strategy,[9] which also included the concept of economic threshold.[10]

The IPM concept, however, incorporates not only economic and ecological factors, but also the social ones by considering the minimal risks of pest control to humans and other beneficial nontarget organisms and the environment. Bottrell (1979), for example, formulates the definition of IPM as follows:

> Integrated pest management (IPM) is the selection, integration, and implementation of pest control based on predicted economic, ecological, and sociological consequences. IPM seeks maximum use of naturally occurring pest controls, including weather, disease agents, predators, and parasites. In addition, IPM utilizes various biological, physical, and chemical control and habitat modification techniques. Artificial controls are imposed only as required to keep a pest from surpassing intolerable population levels predetermined from accurate assessments of the pest damage potential and the ecological, sociological, and economic costs of the control measures (Bottrell 1979:v).

In relation to the implementation of IPM for agricultural crops, Smith et al. (1976:2) argue that this strategy is not only based on ecological principles, but also:

> ... integrates multidisciplinary methodologies in developing agricultural ecosystem management strategies that are practical, effective, economical, and protective of both public health and the environment.

Ironically, despite the emergence of this "paradigm shift" in pest control and the anxieties as a result of the hazardous impacts of pesticides (e.g., Carson 1962 *The Silent Spring*), the indiscriminate use of pesticides, in particular in agriculture, has persisted. Bentley et al. (1995:251) mention the claim of Gore (1992, cited in Bentley et al. 1995) that 13,000 times more pesticides are produced now than when *The Silent Spring* was published. The implementation of the Green

Revolution in agriculture involved extensive use of pesticides (e.g., Shiva 1988; Conway and Pretty 1991). In Indonesia, the implementation of such a package for rice intensification from the late 1960s achieved its goal in increasing crop production, but the pesticide component of this package produced disastrous effects on the environment, such as increased resistance and pest resurgence. Not only in Indonesia, but many other countries in Asia, the unprecedented outbreaks of brown plant hopper (brown plant hopper, *Nilaparvata lugens*), which had gradually increased its resistance and resurgence, damaged rice production (Bahagiawati and Oka 1987; Fox 1991, 1993a). These problems were similar to those that led to the development of IPM as a new paradigm in the 1960s to 1970s. From the mid 1970s up to recent times, however, scientists have tried to solve this problem by producing more resistant, high yielding varieties of rice (Bahagiawati and Oka 1987; Fox 1991).[11]

Since the introduction of the Green Revolution in the late 1960s, farmers have also become the subject of various intensification programs in the form of fixed and complete technological packages, along with extension services to assist and ensure that farmers implemented those packages (Hansen 1978; Sawit and Manwan 1991; see Appendix 1 for the brief history of the Green Revolution in Java). Since the 1980s, mobilizing farmers' groups has been considered a means to achieve the aims of the programs. However, assisting farmers in their needs to manage their own environment and resources better was not taken seriously into account until the National Integrated Pest Management Program was introduced in late 1989.

The IPM concept has been incorporated officially into the Indonesian national policy since 1979. Nevertheless, only after another unprecedented outbreak of brown plant hopper, a year after the proclamation of Indonesia's self-sufficiency in rice in 1984 was there a serious effort to implement IPM strategy in rice-based cropping systems. The initial aim was to overcome the recurrent outbreak of brown plant hopper. This pest had become resurgent due to the indiscriminate use of pesticides, which had eliminated predators. The Indonesian president at that time adopted the advice of his national scientific advisers to make a profound shift in the national policy of pest control (Fox 1991:75; Wardhani 1992), a move supported by the

FAO-Intercountry Program of Integrated Pest Management in Asia and its international network (FAO 1990:53–54), and those working for the Center for Policy and Implementation Studies in Jakarta. On 5 November 1986 a presidential decree (*Inpres* 3/1986) was issued. One of the prominent measures in this decree was the ban of 57 registered brands in a broad spectrum of insecticides for use on rice. The presidential decree also embodied a commitment to a national policy of Integrated Pest Management (IPM) to replace the method of pest control that depended on pesticides only (Oka 1991; Fox 1991). Another major improvement was the official instruction to improve the agricultural officials' and farmers' knowledge and skills in pest management (see Appendix 2) The decision in the declaration to give high priority to human resource development and biological and cultural controls in pest management—as opposed to largely chemical means of pest management—was of fundamental importance from the standpoints of international ecology (Fox 1991), sustainable agriculture (Conway and Barbier 1990) and human development (FAO 1991).

Seen in this history of rice intensification programs, IPM is thus only one moment in a longer relationship between government and farmers. Only through the establishment of the working relations between these two parties in the beginning of *Bimbingan Massal* (BIMAS) program, did farmers learn about the use of chemicals in pest control. Within the top-down technological package without appropriate explanation about the nature and impact of this foreign technology, farmers were forced to adopt this chemical weapon in their culture of growing rice. On the basis of the underlying assumption of the state moral economy to value the national economic profits over the country's social and ecological health, the use of chemicals was seen as appropriate. Only after the emergence of unprecedented consequences of the injudicious use of this chemical weapon, did the government correct its inappropriate pest management strategy. The problems thus lay more with those introducing and marketing pesticides than the guiltless farmers. However, through IPM—another form of relationship between those in authority and the farmers—the government aimed to change how farmers had previously controlled pests and diseases. In contrast to the Green Revolution, the government designed a program to transmit knowledge instead of transferring technological packages. By transmitting knowledge, the national and foreign experts intended to counter the core problems found in previous rice intensification programs. The ideal they put forward was to make farmers IPM experts and to empower them as a basis for creating a more sustainable agriculture. "Farmers as Experts in IPM" had become the distinctive slogan representing the goal of IPM in Indonesia. In adopting this slogan, the experts sought to differentiate their program from production-centered development. Their main aim was to achieve human resource development.

The experts again used the term "paradigm shift" to emphasise their objectives in changing farmers' knowledge. The unique feature of this paradigm compared to the earlier IPM paradigm was the incorporation of the human factor, that is the farmers, as the main agent in pest management. They were perceived as agents who had to be able to organize and observe, analyze, and make their own decisions (see Dilts and Hate 1996). The agricultural and government apparatus had to support farmers' creativity instead of forcing them to implement technological packages. Farmers were expected to change their beliefs and practices, i.e., from using pesticides to kill pests towards managing the ecosystem, growing a healthy crop, and preserving beneficial natural enemies (FAO 1990, 1991; The Indonesian National IPM Program n.d.; Kenmore 1992). Accordingly, planners expected farmers to use chemicals selectively only when frequent field monitoring confirmed an unfavourable ratio of natural enemies to herbivores (FAO 1990). To achieve this paradigm shift, improving decision-making skills based on agroecosystem analysis was crucial. The ecological approach of IPM became prominent rather than the mechanical instructions for field sampling and spraying based on centrally determined economic threshold levels (van der Fliert 1993:26). A kind of "experienced threshold" (*ambang rasa*, threshold based on farmers' experiences and feelings) based on the condition of the ecosystem in general, rather than relying on the "economic threshold," was what the planners wanted the farmers to gain (Dilts, personal communication 1992; Röling and van der Fliert 1994, 1998).

In such an approach, the experts' underlying assumption was that farmers were ignorant. Farmers were perceived as having an inadequate knowledge of the rice ecosystem, in particular of the "third trophic level": the predators and parasites. Training was thus perceived as the best means to introduce this knowledge (see Appendix 4). This evokes the image of scientists as the more knowledgeable outsiders helping the powerless and less knowledgeable farmers. As a consequence of this assumption, the question posed by the experts was how to improve farmers' knowledge. Changing farmers' mode of learning by urging them to go into the field and carry out detailed observations on the condition of their field's ecosystem was considered to be the main solution. With this objective, the experts designed training by involving farmers and agricultural officials in what they called a "learner-centred" discovery process. Led by the FAO, foreign experts from two major disciplines, adult education and entomology, the training modules were programmed on the basis of an adult learning process (andragogy) instead of lecturing (the "chalk and talk" method) as found in formal schooling (Program Nasional Pengendalian Hama Terpadu 1989).[12] The training program was based on "learning by doing" incorporating a set of modules on what the participants should do, followed by discussions and the writing of reports. Trainers provided explanations only if necessary, according to particular situations and problems. Throughout the learning process, questions and answers were thus expected to be held in a dialogical way (also see Röling and van de Fliert 1994, 1998) as presented in fig. 1.2. The question: "What is this?" or "*Apa ini?*" was made popular by the experts to differentiate their training program from the conventional one.

Such a training design is the hallmark of this program. This is the basic premise that differentiates it from previous rice intensification packages and other national development programs. In relation to the latter, Warwick (1986) mentions the similarities of the national family planning program with the rice intensification programs in its core strategy. Besides supplying contraceptive services as in the rice production packages, recruitment of clients in both programs, according to Warwick (1986:469), has been a combination of individual persuasion and community influence. In some cases, coercion was apparent as was applied to the farmers in the earlier rice input packages (see Palmer 1978:184). This external influence and pressure constitutes one of the major problems facing the Indonesian family-planning program. It relates directly to the basic problem of how the government should relate to its citizens (Warwick 1986:479; also see Robinson 1989). The relationship between government and the local people as the targets of any development program is crucial. How does the Indonesian government pursue its plan to transmit IPM knowledge to the local farmers by adopting the perspective different from the previous intensification programs?

Experts and farmers are, in fact, from two distinct worlds that seldom meet in direct communication. Local agricultural officials and extension workers are the usual intermediaries between these two parties. The planners thus set up a chain of knowledge transfer through the bureaucratic system. Improving the agricultural officials' knowledge and skills and changing their attitudes were also main aims of this program. The main trainers were selected not from among extension workers but from among pest observers—officials from the Directorate of Food Crop Protection—who had never before had direct communication with farmers (see fig. 1.3). The pest observers' main tasks were monitoring the conditions of pest populations and disease infestation on food crops and providing suggestions to local regional officials of the necessary management steps to take. The IPM experts saw that prior to the presidential decree when the "old paradigm" of IPM became the basis of pest management, the pest observers relied heavily on pesticide use in defining the control strategy. This viewpoint was the basis of their recommendations when, according to their observations, pest/disease control was necessary. The pest observers, therefore, became resource persons for pesticide use. Their training as pest and disease observers was also based mainly on the entomological aspect of food crops (Dilts, personal communication 1991). Few of them had ever grown their own crops, nor had the extension workers (The Indonesian National IPM Program n.d.). The extension workers were responsible for providing information and recommendations about governments' messages to farmers, and they are to assist farmers in implementing the government's rice intensification programs through the training and visit system. In this IPM program, the extension workers were appointed as the pest observers' assistants.

Initially, the international experts, in collaboration with national experts, trained a number of agricultural officials (from the Directorate of Food Crop Protection and Agricultural Extension) as the

Figure 1.2 *"Apa ini?" What is this?*

[Cartoon with speech bubbles:]
- LYCOSA PSEUDO ANNULATA ..... XCLIV..Q∑#!
- apa ini?
- ya.....itu jenis serangga yang makan hama ditemukan di mana, Pak? jumlahnya berapa? apakah sering terlihat?
- apa ini?

CARA BELAJAR PHT MANA YANG BENAR?

Source: The National IPM Program n.d.

Indonesian	English
Cara Belajar PHT mana yang benar?	Which ways of IPM learning is the correct one?
Apa ini?	What is this?
Ya … itu jenis serangga yang makan hama.	Yes … that is a type of insect which feeds on pest.
Ditemukan di mana, Pak?	Where do you find it, Sir?
Jumlahnya berapa?	How many?
Apakah sering terlihat?	Do you often see it?

Figure 1.3 *Structure and relationships among extension, plant protection, agricultural education, and training systems*

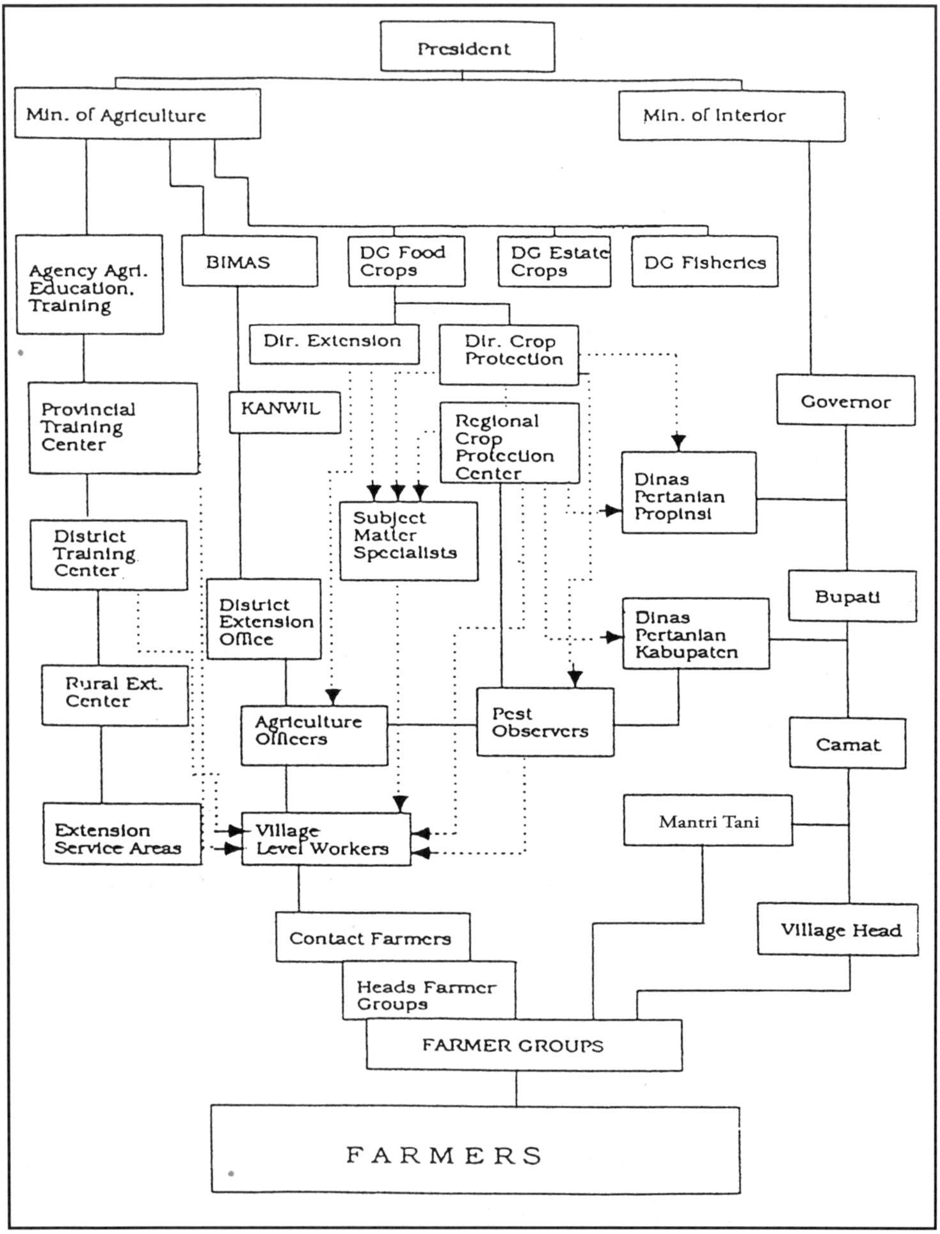

Source: FAO 1991: Annex 5:1.

core trainers during one season of IPM training. They were trained to cultivate rice on their own and develop the training modules designed by a foreign entomologist. The core trainers from the Directorate of Food Crop Protection (Field Leaders I) then trained other pest observers (Field Leaders II) in a shorter period of training focusing on "extension skills." The latter were expected to learn more about IPM and other problems in rice cultivation by assisting the core trainers in supervising a number of other pest observers. These pest observers, who were the main trainers in the IPM Farmers Field School, were recruited from six provinces in Indonesia and trained in a number of field training facilities. The training—held one season before supervising farmers in IPM Farmers Field School—consisted of growing rice, carrying out IPM field case studies, and group dynamics. Besides this field training, the pest observers undertook the secondary crop IPM training and courses to get diplomas in entomology. At a later stage, the extension workers were recruited and trained for a shorter period by following the pest observers in their practical training. These extension workers were expected to learn more about IPM by assisting the pest observers in training farmers (Rölling and van de Fliert 1994). Hence, the messengers and intermediaries between national/regional governments/experts and farmers were the extension workers who had the least practical and theoretical training.[13]

During one season before the pest observers carried out the secondary crop IPM training and took courses in the university, both the pest observers and the extension workers had to facilitate the learning of farmers in what the planners called The IPM Farmers Field School (*Sekolah Lapangan Pengendalian Hama Terpadu*, SLPHT).[14] To differentiate this type of school from formal schooling, the planners named it the "School without Walls." This was the setting where the trainers had to facilitate farmers' understanding of IPM principles and provide them with enough "basic knowledge" to enable them to make decisions on the basis of their fields' ecological condition (see Appendix 4 on the IPM program competency objectives and Appendix 5 on the IPM Farmers Field School's curriculum).

The attempted transmission of scientific knowledge in this way, with the objective of improving farmers' knowledge and changing their mode of learning, constitutes an opportunity to examine how farmers' knowledge and practices are (re)produced during and after such an intervention.

Discovering and Explaining Knowledge Formation

An examination of processes of farmers' knowledge formation during and after the introduction of IPM principles provides the opportunity to discover and explain process and variation. Some scholars have argued the need to apply or develop discovery procedures that explore these phenomena. With the increasing recognition that social processes are made of human actions or events involving human actions, they emphasise the importance of focusing on the empirical studies of events and actions so as to better understand processes (Moore 1987, 1994; Vayda et al. 1991:324; Barth 1994). It should be made clear, however, if the events we are observing actually constitute a process. As argued by Barth (1981) and Vayda et al. (1991) it is important to discern the empirical linkages between events. In their reviews of Moore's (1986, 1987) arguments that a particular event can evince or indicate process, Vayda et al. (1991: 324-325) argue that without producing evidence about how particular events constitute a process or how they are intelligibly connected, we cannot justify the claim that those events are part of a process. I agree with Barth (1981, 1994) and Vayda et al. (1991) that a study of process has to be able to reveal the intelligible, sequential relation of one event to another, with its embeddedness and linkages. Moreover, a causal explanation of processes must be sought not only "with respect to the events themselves, the linkages among events," but also to the "conditions under which the linkages do or do not obtain" (Vayda et al. 1991:328).

Events involving human actions in concrete everyday practice of knowledge transmission, creation, reproduction, or transformation are the focus of my study. I examined how the IPM knowledge and ideas were transmitted by the trainers, how the individual farmers received and interpreted these novel notions within and outside the setting of the IPM Farmers Field Schools, and in what ways they adopted or modified these notions in daily farming practices. Hence, my study stresses the importance of individual actors and their behaviour as "the reference point for understanding a particular unfolding of events, and/or understanding the processes involved in the reproduction or change of some set of structural features" (Ortner 1984:149).

To be able to discern recurrent sequences of these connected events, as well as their changes over time, I observed how the understandings and actions of individual actors produced further consequences—intentionally or unintentionally—for their practices, knowledge, and rice-farming performance, by following how the consequences affected actors' knowledge and actions over time. Hence, by following the sequences of these events I avoided relying simply on descriptions of these events at two points in time and on the extrapolation between these two states to indicate the course of change and continuity (Barth 1967:661). By following up the way that events were linked over time, I took into account seasonal ecological conditions and environmental problems, as well as the economic situation and the government's policy related to rice farming. I observed how individual farmers (re)interpreted and responded to these events on the basis of their understanding of IPM ideas. On the basis of their experiences, I followed how they reinterpreted those novel ideas and produced further actions and outcomes.

An understanding of why this process of knowledge formation works in a particular way with particular consequences should be based on a search that progressively relates these to contextual factors that can explain them. These contextual factors may include the actors' beliefs, knowledge, resources, aims and intentions, as well as the economic, cultural, social, political and environmental factors that affect actions and their consequences. In carrying out this attempt I agree with Vayda (1993:61; also see Vayda 1983, 1986) that we do not need to define in advance the factors that may be included (also see Tjitradjaja 1987, 1989). Hence, in tracing threads of influence we can move outward in space and backward in time and thus establish contextual factors empirically (Vayda 1983, 1993).

The advantage of taking individual actors into account is the possibility of seeing variability and heterogeneity in the adoption, interpretation, modification, and reproduction of knowledge and practices. It also gave me opportunities to: 1) observe the dynamics of knowledge formation, including processes of contestation, and 2) elucidate how variation and consensus are reached. In my research, I chose particular settings in which the IPM Farmer Field Schools were held. I did not, however, intend to study a particular community or culture in a bounded place and explain the processes of knowledge formation and transmission within a predefined spatial or temporal context. Instead, I focused my observation on the actions of the actors involved in IPM knowledge transmission—both the disseminators and the users—at a particular place. In following up the sequence of knowledge formation and transmission, I paid attention to who transmitted what kind of knowledge to whom, and who received what kind of knowledge from whom with what understanding. I examined further how and why these events happened, under what kinds of conditions understanding became a basis for action, and with what consequences. Even though I defined the individuals who belonged to my groups of informants (the IPM and non-IPM participants) and tried to follow their actions and understandings throughout the period of my research, the actors in a particular action and events at a particular time varied. Those involved included farmers from other places as well as nonfarmers (relatives, labourers, neighbours, government agencies, scientists, or chemical company officials, and shop owners). My efforts to understand the occurrence of particular events or the formation of particular meanings also led me to trace the contextual factors out of the setting and back to preceding events and histories.

This book is therefore intended to show that with these approaches, we can describe and explain critically the sequential events through which local farmers adopt and integrate the introduced knowledge within their own understandings and practices.

My Fieldwork

After carrying out my preliminary study in April 1990, I began my fieldwork in early May 1990, at the beginning of the 1990 dry season. I followed farmers' activities throughout three consecutive seasons: the 1990 dry season, the 1990/91 rainy season and the 1991 dry season, before coming to Australia to begin my course at the Australian National University. At the end of November 1991, I returned to the field to follow another planting season, the 1991/92 rainy season until the end of February 1992. After returning to Indonesia in August 1996, I briefly visited these villages in the period between September and December 1996, and again in 1998, and subsequently until 2001.

Following up my first visit to the district of Ciasem, I decided to observe two settings of IPM Farmer Field Schools. These "schools" were conducted by the same pest observer, but assisted by different extension workers in different villages. The two places were thus ideal to carry out a comparative study. The same pest observer introduced IPM knowledge to the farmers in those places. This and that he had a different assistant in each place provided a good opportunity to examine the extent of similarities or differences in the training and its follow-up stage. The "schools" were conducted in the hamlet of Kebon Cau belonging to the village of Ciasem Baru, and the hamlet of Marjim belonging to the village of Ciasem Tengah. I observed these two settings to examine whether differences in farmers' social and economic backgrounds would affect how knowledge was formed and transmitted. The number of large landowners in the first (Kebon Cau, Ciasem Baru) outnumbered those in the latter (Marjim, Ciasem Tengah). In this latter place, the number of small owners was greater than in the first. Unfortunately, after several weeks of training, I found that the IPM training in Kebon Cau would not reach its main objective. The nonattendance of IPM participants and their replacement with nonfarmer participants was high. I then moved to the other hamlet in Ciasem Baru, Marga Tani, which I had visited during my preliminary study. I moved between Marga Tani and Marjim in the course of my fieldwork. I also discovered that another IPM "school" held in the latter village, Ciasem Tengah, consisted of farmers living in different hamlets. Some of them were residents of the hamlet of Marjim. I then decided to include these farmers and those from other hamlets as my informants.[15]

Presenting the detailed stories of knowledge formation in the two places in a limited number of words for a Ph.D. dissertation was not an easy task. After a thorough consultation with my supervisor, my thesis—which forms the basis of this book—presented the findings of farmers' knowledge formation in one place only, Marga Tani in Ciasem Baru. With deep regret, this book does not present the farmers' stories from the other sites, Marjim and other hamlets in Ciasem Tengah. However, the comparison throughout the fieldwork gave me a rich understanding of the processes and the contextual factors affecting farmers' knowledge formation in both places.

In each place, 25 farmers were recruited as IPM participants. In Marga Tani, only 23 of them were real farmers. Two of these real farmers left the village after training, and two other participants decided to become labourers instead of cultivators. One of the latter decided to be a farmer-cultivator again during my last season there. Another farmer was absent in the 1990/91 rainy season to work in Jakarta (see chap. 4 and fig. 4.1). Besides these 19 IPM participants, I also included around 34 farmers, who were not recruited as IPM participants, in my sample. The number also varied seasonally. I tried to systematically follow their rice farming practices and knowledge acquisition throughout my fieldwork period, by also trying to keep myself alert to other actors emerging in the scene.

At the beginning of my research, the local agricultural officials perceived me as the one from "the centre" (*dari Pusat*). They perceived my job as observing the IPM "school," with the responsibility of reporting it to the "centre." Even tough I was an independent observer, in fact, I had the responsibility of submitting "daily field reports" of my activities to the National IPM Program.

> Once the pest observer consulted me for a decision whether to give permission to the head of the Rural Extension Centre (REC, *Balai Penyuluhan Pertanian,* BPP) to introduce a new brand of herbicide brought by a chemical company's salesman. This happened just at the opening week of IPM training in Marjim. At that event, before his introduction about the new brand of herbicide, the head of BPP asked me not to report this herbicide's promotion to those in the "centre."

On many occasions, the trainers and the BPP staff perceived me as a companion. They told me happy stories of farmers' enthusiastic responses, or grumbled about the problems they faced, for example, the absence of IPM participants in Kebon Cau and the hardships they had to go through in teaching farmers (see chap. 4). In the course of training, I did my best to be an "independent observer." In some cases, however, farmers' responses and difficulties in understanding the "teaching" slipped into my conversations with the trainers/BPP staff. Unexpectedly, this yielded further reactions that affected the training (see chap. 4).

Unavoidably, as introduced by the trainers/BPP staff, the IPM participants also perceived me as the one from the "centre," observing the training during the course of the IPM school. Farmers began to question the aim of my presence in the village when the training was over. They found that I did not leave them as the trainers did. Gradually, they accepted me as the one who would like to know and learn everything about rice farming. Telling me stories, informing me about the most recent pest/disease outbreaks, and grumbling about all the burdens were a reflection of how they perceived me as the only one left who would listen to their problems. In many cases, I received their questions and queries about the puzzling phenomena they encountered while responding to pest and disease outbreaks; questions that I was not able to answer. Learning of my activities in moving to various places which they themselves were not able to, several inquisitive IPM farmers asked my favour to find answers for their clues; for example, bringing specimens to the Centre for Pest and Disease Surveillance for examination; asking for books on rice farming and any information about pest/disease outbreaks, and assisting them in looking for information directly from the experts (see chap. 6). These were parts of farmers' requests that I was hardly able to refuse. When I was about to leave them, several farmers asked me: "Mom, who will replace you here? Who will accompany us to the field?" My dear friends, I also dedicate this book to you as part of my sharing with all your burdens.

2

The "Genuine" Rice Farmers in Their "Unbounded Niche"

THE IPM SCHOOL in Kampung Marga Tani was very lively. Before, during, and after the training, around 20 farmers chatted and talked about all the problems and issues found in their fields. Various questions and arguments were also raised in the discussions. A very different atmosphere characterized the learning process in this place from that in Kampung Kebon Cau where the number of IPM participants gradually declined.[1] This different circumstance made me curious to discover who the farmers were and their relationships to each other. In Marga Tani, the IPM participants are part of larger farmer communities spread in seven hamlets in the village of Ciasem Baru. Living within the community of practitioners (the farmers), provides a useful setting to learn the mastery of rice farming strategies. As Lave and Wenger (1991:35) have argued, "… learning is an integral part of generative social practice in the lived-in world." Not only mastering the skills, but also learning the knowledge and reasons for generating effective strategies can be acquired through daily experiences and communication. Resnick (1991) mentions that directly experienced events are only part of the basis for knowledge construction. She further states that,

> [P]eople also build their knowledge structures on the basis of what they are told by others, orally, in writing, in pictures, and in gestures. Our daily lives are filled with instances in which we influence each other's constructive processes by providing information, pointing things out to one another, asking questions, and arguing with and elaborating on each other's ideas.
>
> (p. 2)

Hanks (in Lave and Wenger 1991:15) also notes that "Learning is a process that takes place in a participation framework."

The first section of this chapter describes how the rice farmers in Marga Tani define their identities as participants of the community of practitioners and how they develop their network of communication and participation in daily life. In what forms of sociality were they enmeshed and to what extent did these contribute to their learning process? Farmers are, however, only part of a wider, complex society (see e.g., Redfield 1960; Wolf 1966). Referring to Kroeber's (1948) definition of peasants as part-societies with part-cultures, Borofsky (1994a:248) raises the difficulty of demarcating boundaries, "[C]ultural groups do not necessarily possess clear, distinct borders." Kemp (1988) also argues that villages and communities in Southeast Asia do not form closed units with distinctive boundaries. He further urges the need to contextualize local rural organization firmly within the framework of the wider society, including the state. In his work on *Reconceptualizing the peasantry*, Kearney (1996:2) argues that

> ... any genuinely anthropological approach to rural communities must theoretically situate them within global contexts and must attend to the history of the nation-state and to its position within global society.

This perspective can lead us away from the view that villages are bounded entities representing "closed corporate peasant communities" as echoed in Wolf's (1957) conception of peasant communities.

Following these arguments, I describe in the following sections how the farmers were linked to the wider society and acquired knowledge and information through various networks of communication. I also examine briefly how, within the framework of administrative and agricultural bureaucracies, they perceived their relations with these agencies, including those who conducted the IPM School, and how they collaborated with each other in this era of the Green Revolution.

Marga Tani and the Centres of Information

Marga Tani is located in a region crossed by a heavily used major highway that links Jakarta to other cities on the north coast of West and Central Java. Various means of transportation travel this road, day and night. A railroad track runs south of this highway linking

Jakarta to other cities in Java. On my way from Jakarta along this main highway, I passed several agricultural institutions before reaching my destination.

First is the Pest/Disease Surveillance Centre for Food Crops—22 km west of the district of Ciasem—where the IPM Field Training Facilities for the north coast region of West Java had been set up in the early 1990. The pest observers and extension workers from this region joined the IPM training there. The IPM farmers in Marga Tani called this centre "*Jatisari*," originating from the name of the district where it is located (*Kecamatan Jatisari* in the regency of Karawang). Since the introduction of IPM, they recognized this centre as the place where the IPM trainers were trained before they were.

About five km to the west of my research site, there is an agricultural research station on the southern part of the road. This research station: *Balai Penelitian Tanaman Pangan Sukamandi* (Sukamandi Research Station for Food Crops) is the responsibility of the Agricultural Research and Development Institute, a division of the Ministry of Agriculture. Farmers usually call this station by its acronym: BALITTAN or *Balai Pertanian Sukamandi*, where some Ciasem labourers have access to occasional work in the experimental rice plots. Farmers received information on rice varieties through these labourers. On the other hand, several research staff of this station own and cultivate land in the farmers' rice field areas. One IPM farmer in Marga Tani has an affinal relative working in this station. However, until the end of January 1992 when I accompanied some of them, farmers had no idea that they were free to visit this station. Aside from this visit, there had been no official communication between the experts at the station and the farmers. Through seed exchange, farmers also knew that there was another research station in a district east of Ciasem: Pusakanegara Agricultural Field Station.

Across from the BALITTAN Research Station, a large area of rice fields is cultivated by farmers who work on or rent fields from a government-owned company: PERUM *Sang Hyang Seri*. The older farmers in Marga Tani remembered the old name of this company as *Perkebunan Pé-èn-Té*. Officially its name was the *Pamanoekan en Tjiasemlanden* (Pamanukan and Tjiasem Lands), a plantation owned by the British for production of sisal/agave (*Agave sisalana Per*) and cassava (*singkong, Manihot utilissima* Pohl). The Subang region, according to Fujimoto (1986:84), was the private property of a British plantation company from 1811 to the end of the Second World War. After the period of the Japanese colonization from 1942 to 1945, the British again took over the plantation. From 1957 until 1971, the plantation was handed over from the British to the Indonesian people and government followed by several changes in the production goods. In recent times, the main objectives of this company are to: 1) produce, manage, preserve, pack, market, and distribute certified seeds; 2) train personnel in the production of seeds; 3) conduct research and training in these activities; and 4) carry out other activities supporting the improvement of seed production (PERUM Sang Hyang Seri n.d.).

Some farmers in Marga Tani have a rental agreement with the company, which is referred to as PERUM. They recognize this company as the agent responsible for producing certified, high yielding varieties. During the harvesting season, labourers from elsewhere in the northern coast regencies come to participate in harvesting activities, which they call *brandangan* (see the section on wage labour arrangement). Unlike the payment system in *sawah daerah* (farmers' rice fields), which takes the form of grain (*bawon*, shared-harvest), the harvest collected in *sawah* PERUM is paid in the form of cash. These labourers and farmers cultivating rice in PERUM are a source of information about rice varieties, fertilizer formulae, and pesticides to farmers in Marga Tani and other places.

Not far from these two centres of agricultural activity, some 122 km east of Jakarta is the capital of the district of Ciasem where the office and the official residence of the head of the district (*Camat*) are located. Moving east, there is an extension office for the district of Ciasem. Farmers know this office by its acronym BPP for *Balai Penyuluhan Pertanian* (Rural Extension Centre).[2] This is the office for the head of the BPP, extension workers, and staff. It is the centre for guidance and counseling in agricultural services. The head of the BPP has an official residence in this compound. A rice field cultivated by the extension staff is located at the back of the office. Even though farmers could reach this place by walking along the dikes of the rice fields (*sawah*) located between their hamlet and this office, they seldom visited it. Another route involves travelling through the village and along the main roads about 2 km from Marga Tani.

In contrast to the limited official communication between farmers and the experts in those agricultural insititutions, farmers had a close relationship with the owners of shops (*kiosk*) selling agricultural products. Two shops are located along the main road in front of the central market *Pasar Ciasem*, about 1 km from the BPP office. In these shops, farmers can find all they need for rice and secondary crop cultivation: seeds, fertilizers, pesticides, herbicides, rodenticides, fungicides or foliar fertilizers. During the early planting season, these shops are crowded with farmers from the early hours of the day. Dealers from the big chemical companies come to these shops to promote new products or assess sales. These and another shop across the junction to the village of Ciasem Baru have become the main source of information on products for the cultivation of rice, secondary crops, and fish. Not only have shop owners and their workers become the farmers' resource persons, but so also have the chemical companies' salesmen. They use these shops as a place to look for customers for their new products. In many cases, the shop owners also act as creditors to farmers who are unable to pay for their expenditures in cash.

When I entered the hamlet of Marga Tani, around 1.5 km from the main highway, the first building I found was the village office of Ciasem Baru. This office is the administrative centre at the village level for all the hamlets (seven hamlets) in Ciasem Baru. Messages from the central government in Jakarta and the various regional governments, from the province, regency, district, and the village pass to the farmers through this office. After passing this office and a state primary school, I came to the residential area of Marga Tani, which was built north and south of an irrigation canal along the village road. During my stay there, none of the houses had electricity from the government electric company. Through the village road passing this hamlet, people can go to and from other hamlets and villages and to the main Jakarta—Cirebon highway. Trucks loaded with bricks in the dry and fallow period or bags of grains in the harvesting season use this road, which can be very wet and slippery in wet

Map 2.1 *Marga Tani and the centres of information*

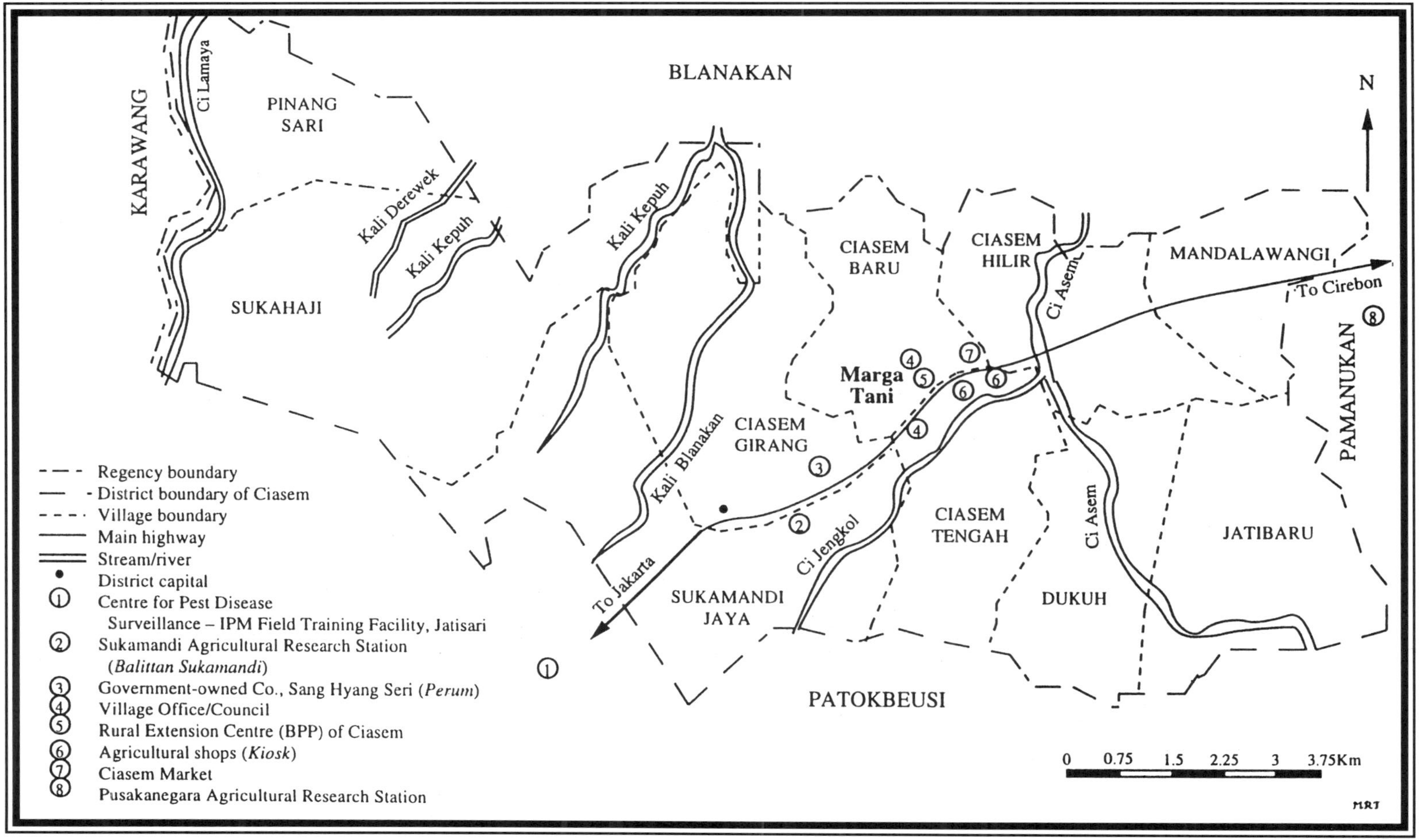

weather. Clay soils, sand and stones are the foundation of this road (see maps 2.1 and 2.2).

Surrounding this residential area are the rice fields, hundreds of hectares lying on very low, flat land with an elevation between 7 and 13 m above sea level. Rice field areas in the whole district of Ciasem have the same topographical features. Ciasem—together with several other districts—belongs to the north lowlands region of the regency of Subang. This northern region produces rice as the main crop. Its topography is different from the southern part of Subang, which resembles central West Java in the *Strata Priangan*. This area is a hilly, undulating, and mountainous region that produces various kinds of food crops as their product (Dinas Pertanian Tanaman Pangan Propinsi Jawa Barat 1991; Hussein 1986).[3] Approximately 48 km from the capital of Ciasem toward this hilly, mountainous region is the capital of *Kabupaten Subang*. Travelling further south, around 100 km from Ciasem, we reach the capital of West Java Province, Bandung (see maps 1.2 and 2.4).

The "Cabang" People

Marga Tani, the official name of the hamlet, is seldom used by the residents to identify their place or themselves. Originally, this hamlet was known as *Kampung Tjabang Sambirata*. *Tjabang* (*Cabang*) was the name of a river around which this hamlet was settled, and later—after the introduction of the technical irrigation scheme in the 1970s—became a secondary irrigation canal. Until recent times, however, the descendants of the first migrants who settled at this place referred to themselves as *Orang Cabang* (Cabang people) and called their hamlet *Kampung Cabang*. Even though every person refers to himself as a resident of *Kampung Cabang*, further identification occurs in relation to the original place from which a person came. Identification also relates to origin, either indigenous or migrant. Hence, the descendants of the original couples identify themselves as *orang asli Cabang* (the indigenous Cabang people) and refer to the recent migrants as *bukan asli Cabang* (nonindigenous Cabang people).

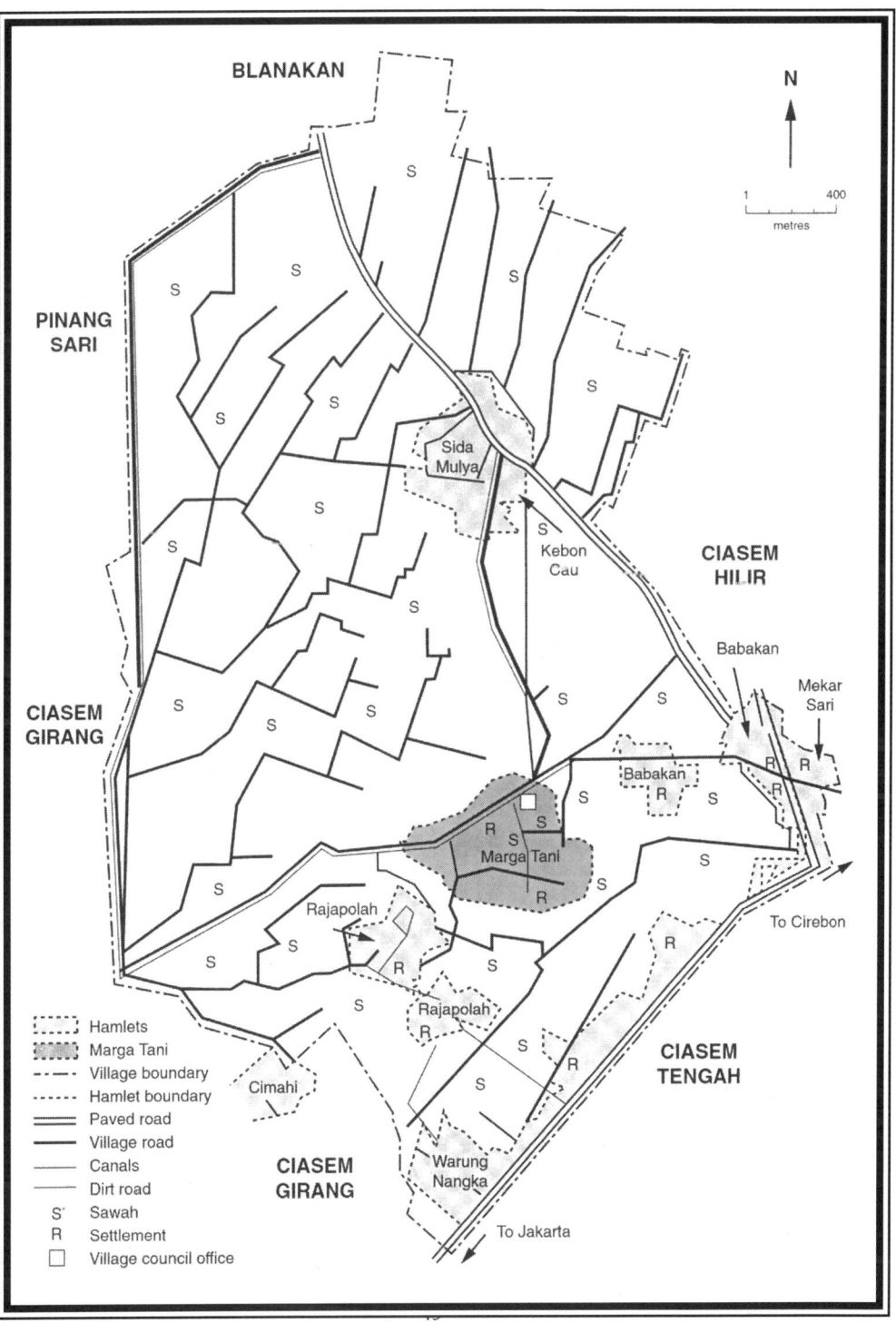

Map 2.2 *Marga Tani in the village of Ciasem Baru*

The majority of farmers living along the river, to the north and south of the secondary canal, are *orang asli Cabang* ranging from second to fifth generation descendants of the first migrants. Several older farmers named three persons as the first people who came to work as wage labourers on the British plantation that is now known as the area of PERUM Sang Hyang Seri. These people opened the forest adjacent to this plantation for residences and cultivation. Other migrants from various places on the north coast of West and Central Java came to work on the plantation, stayed in Cabang, and cultivated *sawah* they themselves established. The third generation farmers remembered that their parents owned and cultivated a large area of *sawah* surrounded by shrubs and bushes.

Even though recent generations of farmers speak Sundanese, they differentiate themselves from Sundanese who come from central West Java or *Priangan* (e.g., from Majalaya, in the regency of Bandung). "We are coastal people," is how they identify themselves as distinct from people in the central, mountainous region of West Java. Some said that they were Javanese, whereas others regarded themselves as a mixture of Javanese and Sundanese (*campuran*).

All the descendants of one elderly couple identify themselves as *satu keturunan* (one group of descendants). Many of them married each other and are related as bilateral kin. Some of them, however, married recent migrants from other hamlets in Ciasem Baru, various places on the north coast of West Java and Central Java (Brebes), and central West Java (Kabupaten Bandung). Through these intermarriages, affinal relations with kin in their natal villages have been maintained through occasional visits on both sides, in particular, for social and religious events, as well as rice harvesting and other cultivation activities. Through these networks of communication, the information on rice varieties and other rice-farming strategies flow in and out of Marga Tani.

Among those who identify themselves as "farmers," only a few consist of nonindigenous couples (*bukan asli Cabang*). They came from adjacent hamlets in Ciasem Baru (e.g., Rajapolah and Babakan). Hence, the majority of farmers in Marga Tani are consanguineally and affinally related to one another. Since they live along the both sides of riverbanks, communication between them is closely maintained through daily activities and other social and religious events. Examples of the events that brought these kin together are the life-cycle rituals (e.g., births, circumcisions, weddings, and deaths); family matters such as illness, building houses; celebrations at the end of fasting month (*Idul Fitri*) or other Islamic events, the Islamic prayers (*tahlilan*) and communal meals (*hajatan*) on particular events (*e.g.,,* after death and before/during a kin's pilgrimage to Mecca). Among those who still conduct agricultural rituals (e.g., on the first day of broadcasting seeds and transplanting, or before harvesting), the traditional rituals and *hajatan* are staged only by the members of the nuclear family or by the several nuclear families in one household/extended family without involving other kin. These events and daily communication in leisure time—during the day, in the evening, or fallow period (*masa bera*)—are significant settings in which issues, including problems in rice-farming practices, are discussed, argued over, and disseminated farmer-to-farmer.

Different networks of communication, however, exist on the basis of proximity, through adjacent residence or adjacent *sawah* (*batihan, tetangga nyawah*). In the farmers' perspective, neighbourhood does not refer solely to residential proximity as described by Jay for the rural areas of Modjokuto (1969:229–38). Rice fields' proximity also defines who are the farmers' neighbours in a block of rice fields. Only those who live close together or cultivate rice in neighbouring *sawah* engage in daily conversations. Farmers who are residential neighbours can also be *sawah* neighbours, but those who are close residential neighbours might not be close neighbours in the rice field areas and vice versa. One farmer may also have more than one *sawah*, and his neighbours in one *sawah* may either be the same or different from his neighbours in another *sawah*. One farmer thus can have several networks of communication. On the other hand, there are cases where farmers, who might be consanguineally/affinally related, seldom communicate due to distances in residence and rice fields. The other factors that bring them together, or make them stay apart, are similarities or differences in their interests in carrying out particular activities, or in social status in terms of the "rich" and the "poor." In farmers' perceptions, "rich" farmers are those who own a large area of *sawah*. Thus, not all neighbours or close relatives have intimate relationships or occupy their time with conversations on farming practices.

These farmers are, however, only some of the residents in Marga Tani. The other Marga Tani residents, i.e., those who live in the southern part of the hamlet and came from the north coast of Central Java (Tegal and Brebes), are called by the farmers *orang bataan* (brick makers), or *orang dari wètan* (people from the east) (see map 2.3). These are the later migrants who came to Marga Tani in the 1980s to earn a living. Most of them are engaged in brickmaking. The north coast Javanese dialect is the daily language of these *bataan* people. During my stay in the period from 1990 to 1992, these two groups seldom engaged in daily communication and conversation, as if they lived in different worlds and places. There were no intermarriages among them either. However, some farmers had business relations with the brick makers. Both groups are Moslems, but the Moslem leader and all of those who went on the pilgrimage (become *Haji*) were farmers. These people gained respect from others because of their higher status in religion.

The "Genuine" Rice Farmers

"We are the genuine farmers ..., original farmers and [we] only farm [rice]" ("*Kami ini petani tulèn, petani asli ..., melulu tani*"), state some farmers, referring to their main occupation in rice cultivation. By identifying themselves as genuine rice farmers who carry out full-time rice farming activities, they differentiate themselves from farmers in other places who also cultivate secondary crops (*palawija*). It does not mean, however, that these farmers do not have secondary jobs. Nevertheless, of the total farmers, only 14.9% were engaged in other occupations during the period from 1990 to 1992 (see table 2.1, note). One farmer's primary occupation was as a teacher outside the village (in the regency of Cirebon), but he still cultivated rice. Those who had secondary jobs driving motorcycles (*tukang ojèg*), trading rice (*bandar beras*), raising cattle, selling soybean cakes or furniture, as well as those who cultivated rice in other areas all traveled in a wider region. Through this mobility they had the opportunity to

Map 2.3 *Residential areas and the residents of IPM and some non-IPM farmers*

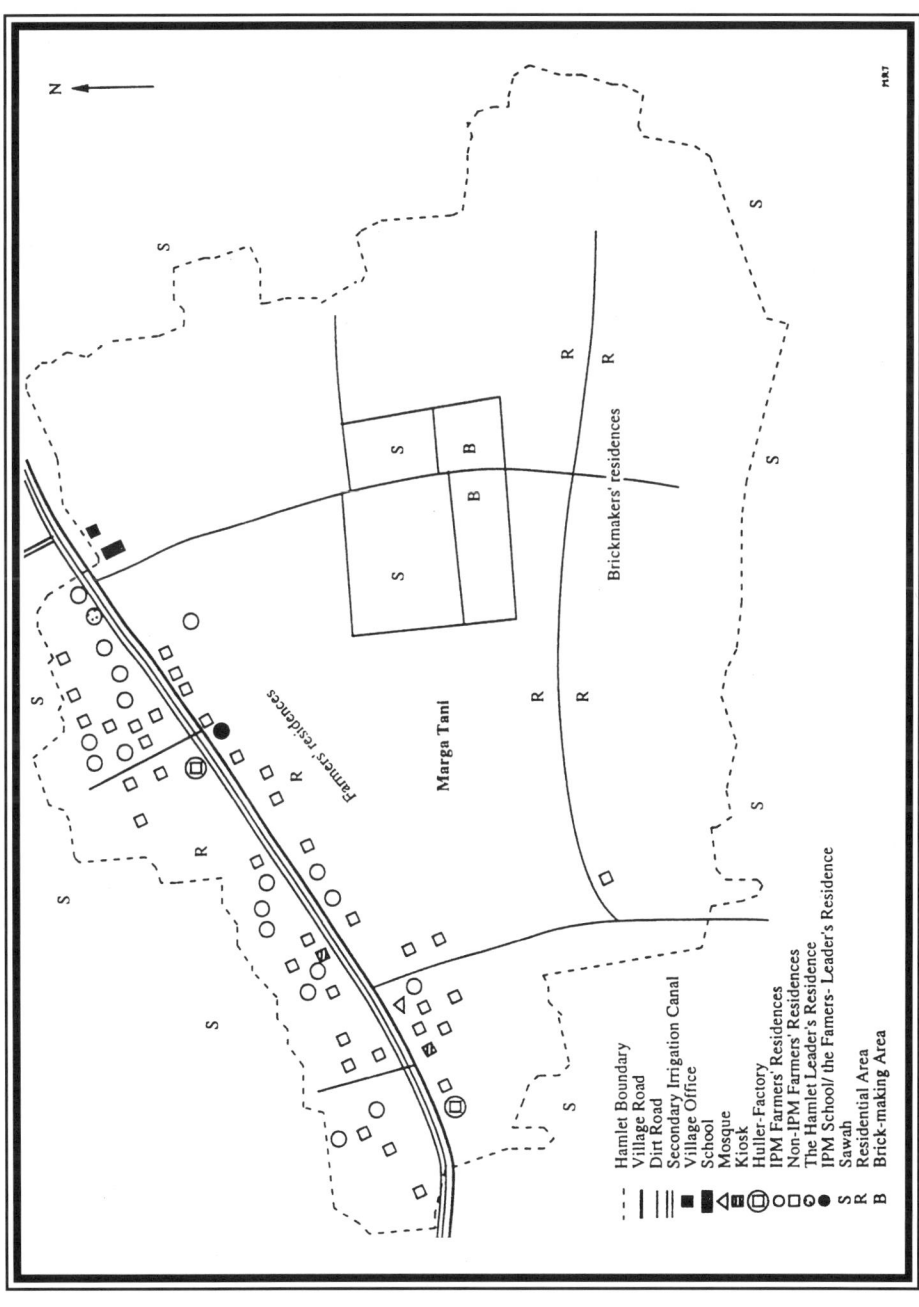

observe, compare, and acquire information on rice cultivation strategies and plant performance from various places.

Although these secondary jobs were off-farm activities, they perceive themselves as farmers who, at present, dedicate their time, mind, and orientation only to producing rice. White and Wiradi (1989) also discover that despite a high degree of economic diversification, paddy was still the largest single source of income in nine Javanese villages they had been studying. For some farmers in Marga Tani, being "genuine" rice farmers did not only mean a dedication to cultivating rice, but also implied their rice-farming background. Some farmers, however, had long years of off-farm work experience in Jakarta, either as pedicab drivers, motorcycle, or tricycle drivers, harbourside workers and in other occupations. After the banning of pedicabs, motorcycles, and tricycles from the main roads of Jakarta in the mid-1980s most returned to Marga Tani to pursue rice cultivation.

My own census indicated that from 74 of the total 255 households, only 32.4% (or 9.4% of the total households) were owners, whereas 67.6% (or 19.6% of the total households) were landless (see table 2.1). As found by Pincus (1996), there was an exceedingly high incidence of landlessness in North Subang villages. Farmers themselves were aware that even though they are the descendants of the original owners in this area, most of them are now landless because of the increased demands on *sawah*. Several older farmers told me that before the 1960s, *Orang Cabang* owned through inheritance all *sawah* surrounding their hamlet. The demands on land increased after the period when migrants and evacuees from central West Java or nearby places purchased land in Ciasem Baru.[4] *Sawah* became a commodity, and the price of land increased. Farmers then perceived that selling land was a way to get sufficient funds to go on a pilgrimage to Mecca, build a new house, or invest in some other undertaking. The number of landless farmers gradually increased (see Pincus 1996:40 on the history of villages related to the selling of lands in North Subang). For landless farmers, owning *sawah* in the current economic situation where the price of *sawah* always increases over time is remarkable. It should result from hard work in accumulating resources. However, farmers who have small *sawah* or are landless can have "a lot of capital" (*kuat modalnya*) if they are able to accumulate resources from cultivating a number of *sawah* and other sources. Farmers also differentiate those who own *sawah* through their own efforts from those who were already "rich" because they inherited *sawah*.

In contrast to the size of *sawah* owned by farmers in the neighbouring village (Ciasem Tengah), owners in Marga Tani have larger sized *sawah*.[5] The number who own more than one ha *sawah* are also greater (58.8% of the owners: 17 out of 24 farmer-households) than those who own less than one ha (41.2% of the owners, see table 2.2). Among the latter, only three own *sawah* less than 0.5 ha.

Table 2.1 *Occupations of Marga Tani residents, 1992*

Occupation	Household			
	Number	%	Number	%
Farmer[a]:			74	29.0
Owner (*petani pemilik*)	24	32.4		
Cultivator (*petani penggarap*)	50	67.6		
subtotal farmer	74	100.0		
Merchant/trader			10	3.9
Labourer[b]			143	56.0
Civil Servant:			4	1.6
Teacher	2	0.8		
Village officer	2	0.8		
subtotal civil servant	4	1.6		
Pensioner			2	0.8
Driver (car and motorcycle)			11	4.3
Out of town			11	4.3
Total households			255	99.9

Source: My own survey, February 1992.

[a]The total number of farmer-households was 74 (29.0%) of the total households in Marga Tani. Seven (29.2%) of the 24 owners were also cultivators. One cultivator was a teacher (a civil servant). Those who had other occupations (including the teacher) amounted to 14.9% of the total farmer-households.

[b]Labourer signifies wage labourers in rice farming (*buruh tani*) and brickmakers.

Table 2.2 *"Sawah" ownership in Marga Tani, 1992*

Total area (ha)	Number	% of total	Number	% of total
Ownership:			17	32.1
<1	7	41.2		
1–2.5	5	29.4		
2.6–5	4	23.5		
>5	1	5.9		
subtotal ownership	17	100.0		
Nonownership:			36	67.9
Total number of cases[a]			53	100.0

Source: Data from *Pajak Bumi Bangunan* in Desa Ciasem Baru, Kabupaten Subang in combination with my own survey, February 1992.

[a] Number of cases represents 53 from a total of 74 farmer-households consisting of 19 IPM farmer-households and 34 non-IPM farmer-households (see ch. 1).

In a situation where owning land is a limited opportunity, how do the landless farmers have access to land to grow rice? A complex set of land-tenure and working arrangements was found in Marga Tani as in other places in West Java and the regency of Subang (*e.g.*, Hayami and Kikuchi 1982; Wiradi and Manning 1984; Fujimoto 1986; Pincus 1991, 1996). Not all landowners (*petani pemilik*) from distant places (*guntai*) or Marga Tani operate their own lands. These owner-nonoperators transfer their responsibility in cultivation to other farmers through various land tenure agreements. The types of agreements found in Marga Tani consist of share tenancy or sharecropping (*maro*),[6] sharecropping on a rotation basis among siblings (*maro bergilir*), renting (*nyewa*), pawning or mortgage (*gadai*), subleasing (*alih garapan*), working on relatives' land (*nggarap*), or a combination of these possibilities.

Through one particular arrangement or a combination of several types of arrangements from different *sawah*, each farmer can have access to land for cultivation. However, not all farmers have access to a number of *sawah*. Once a farmer has sharecropping tenure, he can maintain that tenure for quite a long time and hence, reduce the opportunity for tenure for other farmers. Renting land requires cash in advance, another constraining factor. The number of landholdings each farmer can have and the total area in each season can vary—according to the opportunity he/she can have and his/her decision to reduce or enlarge his/her landholdings.

Table 2.3 indicates that almost half (49.0%) of the informants cultivate two or three *sawah*, and only 30.2% rely on only one *sawah* to grow paddy. Three farmers hold rights on six to eight *sawah* spread over the region within and across administrative boundaries. Looking at the total area, only 28.3% of farmers cultivate less than 1 ha. Many farmers (34.0%) have a total area between 1 ha and 2.5 ha. Those who hold *sawah* of less than 1 ha cultivate lands between 0.29–0.43 ha, whereas the largest is around 6.2 ha.[7] The other option for earning income for the landless cultivators and those with no access to a *sawah* to cultivate is through working as wage labourers for other farmers, either permanently (*kuli matok*) or occasionally (*kuli harian*).

In a situation where it is difficult to have access to cultivate land, becoming a labourer is the only alternative. Once a farmer decides to be a labourer only, other people will call him a "labourer" and no longer a farmer or a cultivator (*petani, penggarap*), and vice versa. This distinction—between farmer and labourer—is significant in relation to who makes the decisions in rice cultivation. The decision makers

Table 2.3 *Total number and size of landholdings in Marga Tani, 1992*

Number of Landholdings	Size of landholding (ha)				Totals	
	<1	1–2.5	2.6–5	>5	Number of cases[a]	% of all cases
1	12	4	0	0	16	30.2
2–3	3	14	8	1	26	49
4–5	0	0	6	2	8	15.1
>5	0	0	1	2	3	5.7
Totals						
Number of cases[a]	15	18	15	5	53	
% of all cases	28.3	34.0	28.3	9.4		100.0

Source: Data from *Pajak Bumi Bangunan* in Desa Ciasem Baru, Kabupaten Subang in combination with my own survey 1992.

[a]Number of cases refers to 53 from a total of 74 farmer-households consisting of 19 IPM farmers and 34 non-IPM farmers.

are those who have to think out a strategy to achieve their aims, as well as to cope with constraints and problems in rice farming. Sharing or discussing knowledge of rice farming strategies with labourers—who do their tasks without reflecting on them—is perceived by farmers as an unequal exchange of knowledge. In farmers' views, even though labourers are sources of information on rice varieties and fertilizers, pesticides, and herbicides, they do not have the same degree of knowledge as cultivators in terms of developing strategies. Permanent wage labourers who assist their landlords in the decision-making process are exceptions, and so are those who have ever been cultivators. However, years of experience and expertise in rice-farming strategies are the indicators of how extensive their knowledge is. In the context of knowledge exchange, farmers appreciate this knowledge more than ownership or size of landholdings. Hence, the experienced cultivators and owner-operators gain confidence as farmers with more knowledge than owner-nonoperators who seldom go to their *sawah*, and cultivators who rely more on their labourers (not industrious or lazy farmers, *kurang rajin, malas*; like to walk only on dry land, *suka jalan darat saja*), and those who have just begun their rice farming activities. On the other hand, farmers appreciate those who were originally labourers, but who have been able to become experienced owners due to their industriousness.

"Sawah," the "Open" Environment

Their world of rice farming, in the farmers' perspective, is only a part of the whole region of rice activities in JALUR PANTURA, along the north coast of West Java Province. A blanket of synchronous rice fields covers 260,817 ha of irrigated lands in ten river basin areas, spreads from the regency of Bekasi in the west to the regencies of Karawang, Subang and Indramayu in the east. Only roads, dikes, and canals separate these areas without clear-cut boundaries. This large blanket of rice fields is the place where farmers learn and evaluate plant performance and each other's cultivation strategies. This whole region receives its irrigation from a large multipurpose dam, Waduk/Bendungan Ir. H. Juanda, which is well known as Waduk/Bendungan Jatiluhur (Jatiluhur Dam). It began its operation in 1967.

Map 2.4 *The north coast region of West Java*

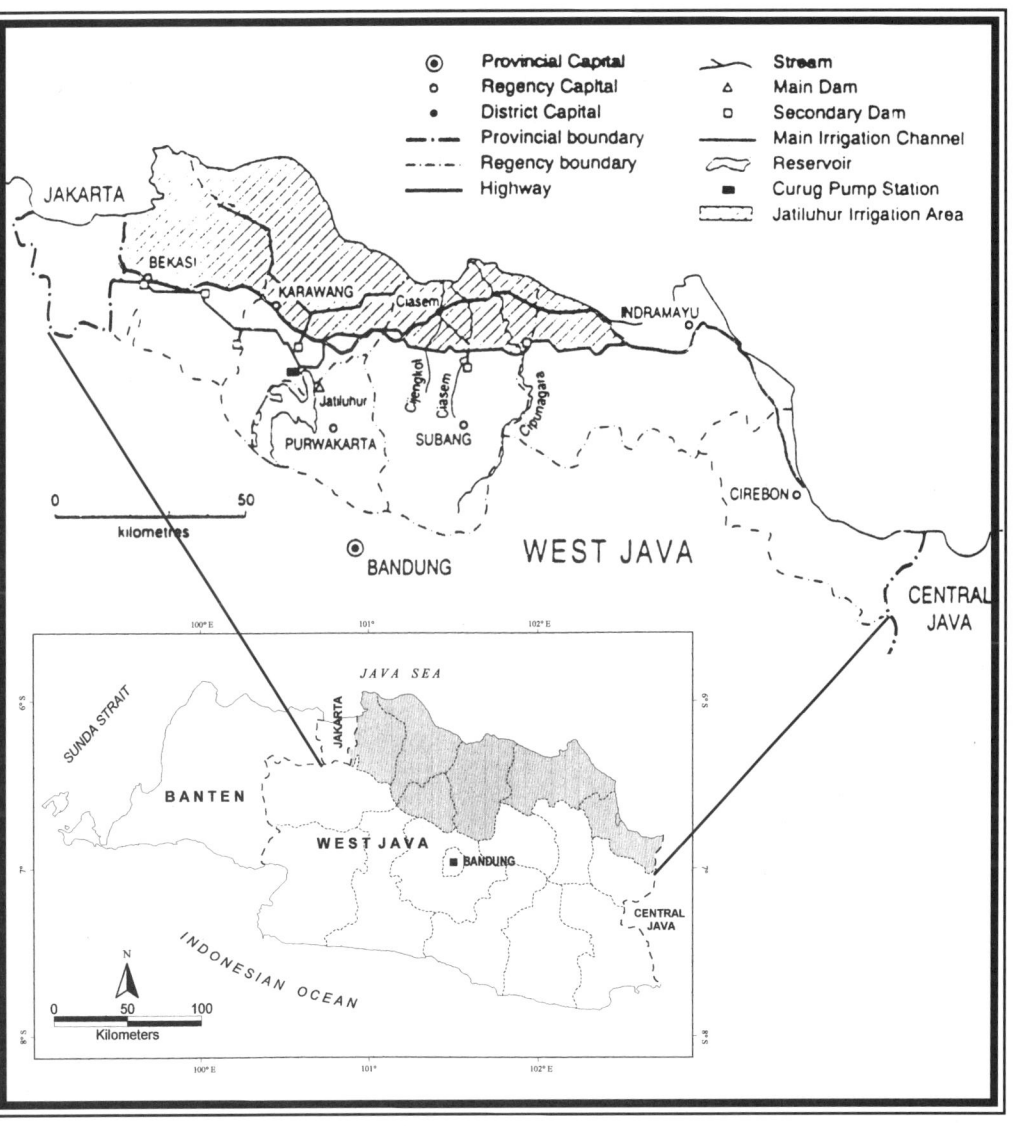

This dam is located in the district of Jatiluhur in the river basin of Sungai Citarum (southwest of the regency of Subang). Its main functions are to generate high capacity hydroelectric power and irrigate the north coast areas of West Java (PERUM *Otorita Jatiluhur* n.d.) (see map 2.4).

JALUR PANTURA is a major "rice basket" area in West Java that contributes significantly to Indonesian national rice stocks.[8] Since 1968, with the completion of the Jatiluhur Dam, various rice intensification programs have been introduced in this area. This region is thus a very important "rice basket" area for the Indonesian government. Farmers have not only been subjected to the various rice intensification programs, but also to the marketing activities of large companies producing various agricultural products. Since 1987, the district of Ciasem has been included as one of the areas for the implementation of the Super Specialized Intensification Program (SUPRA INSUS, see Appendix 1). As many as 7,100 ha of rice fields are included in this program, including the area of PERUM Sang Hyang Seri. Farmers are aware that their rice fields are part of this important rice production zone. The success or failure of their harvests will affect the production of rice in the wider context.

The blanket of rice fields in the regency of Ciasem receives the irrigation water of the Jatiluhur Dam from the main irrigation canal (*saluran induk*) Bangunan Tarum Timur (BTT) no. 30, through the secondary dam, Bendung Jengkol. The older farmers recall this dam as an old one built during the period of Dutch colonization. Bendung Jengkol diverts irrigation water to several secondary irrigation canals in Ciasem Baru through a water gate at the south-west borders of Desa Ciasem Baru, west of Marga Tani: *Pintu Cadas*. The canal to the east, *Saluran Sekunder Jengkol* (S.S. Jengkol), is the one that was previously known as *Kali Tjabang* and divides the residential area in Marga Tani into two parts. From this secondary canal, the water is diverted to farmers' *sawah* surrounding Marga Tani through tertiary canals. There are several other secondary canals irrigating *sawah* in Ciasem Baru and its neighbouring villages (see map 2.5).

Farmers who cultivate *sawah* in a particular block receiving water from those canals appoint a person as *ulu-ulu*. The *ulu-ulu* is responsible for water management and control of the tertiary canals that divert water from the secondary irrigation canals to each *sawah*. He also has the task of solving problems and conflicts among the water users. Conflicts among neighbours often exist, in particular at the times when every plot of *sawah* badly needs water. As a payment, the *ulu-ulu* receives harvest shares from the farmers. An enclave of

Map 2.5 *The location of IPM and some non-IPM farmers' "Sawah"*

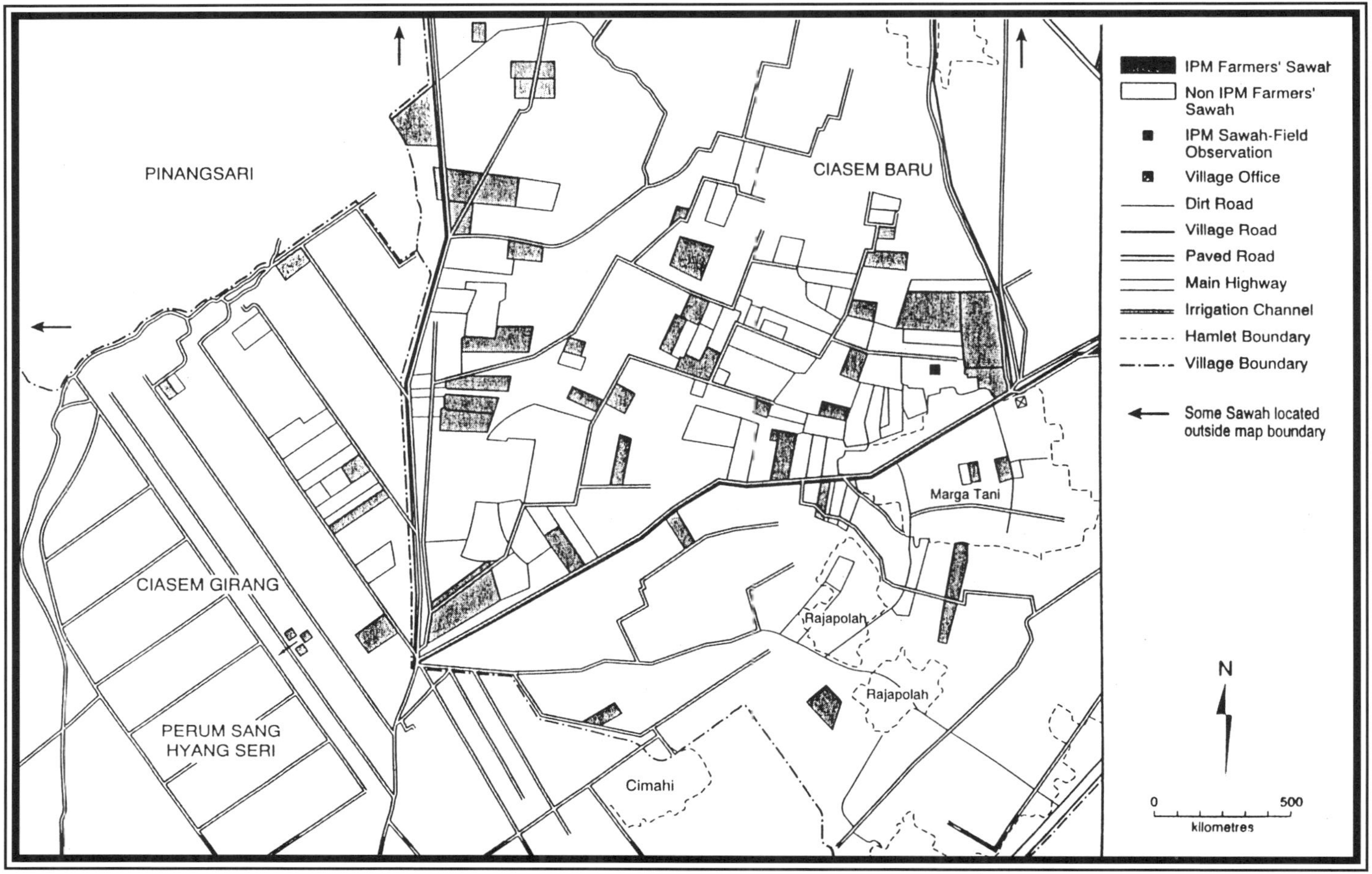

rice fields that does not receive water from the irrigation scheme is located between the farmers' and the brick-makers' residences at the southern part of the secondary canal. Farmers call these fields *sawah tegalan* since they can only be cultivated in the rainy season. These are converted *sawah* on dry land or on land that has been quarried for making bricks. None of the *sawah* in this area is allocated for the local government officials for their payment. On the other hand, these officials receive harvest shares from the farmers in the form of cash (*suksara desa*, donation for village expenses).

"Kampung" and the State, Farmers and the Authorities

Kampung is the daily term farmers use to refer to a hamlet, their place of residence. Officially, it is known as *dusun*. *Dukuh* is another term for hamlet. The farmers used to call their hamlet *Kampung Cabang*. As an administrative unit, a hamlet is divided into several neighbourhood areas. Each area has its leader (*kepala rukun wilayah* and *kepala rukun tetangga*), coordinated by the head of the hamlet, *kepala dusun* or *kepala kampung*. He is elected by the hamlet residents and becomes their representative, acting as the intermediary between them and the village officials. The Marga Tani people call their hamlet leader *wakil* (representative). In the views of the people, he is their leader as well as their representative to the higher authorities in the administrative bureaucracy. As a *kepala dusun*, he is responsible for the administrative affairs of the people in his hamlet and for delivering messages or implementing the government programs directly to the people. Once a week, together with the religious leader known as *amil*, he attends the weekly meeting at the village office. There he receives the government messages and programs from the head of the village.

The head of the village is known as *kepala desa*, or in people's terms, *lurah*. He is a local person, elected by the villagers. *Balai desa* or *kelurahan* is the name for his office. He has the same responsibilities as the *kepala dusun*, but with a larger area to be managed—a village. In Desa Ciasem Baru, there are seven hamlets under his responsibility. He is also responsible to the head of the district, *Camat*, who is appointed by the government. Once a week he attends a meeting held in the *kecamatan*, the district office, a day before he usually conducts the village meeting in his own office. By doing so, he has the time to deliver to his staff and all the *kepala dusun* in his village the messages he has earlier received from the *camat*. In the farmers' eyes, he and his staff are the government officials who are responsible for governing and leading them to prosperity. Farmers expect that the village head and his staff will always be alert to their problems and hence provide assistance in coping with any hazards in daily life, including rice farming. "We are only ordinary people" (*Kami ini hanya rakyat*), is an expression used by some farmers when referring to their position as ordinary citizens. They often complained to me that during times of hardships, none of the village officials visited or assisted them *in situ*.

Farmers also recognize the higher levels of authority: *camat* as the head of the district and *bupati* as the head of the regency. The *camat* is responsible to the *bupati*, and the *bupati* is responsible to the head of the province, the governor (*gubernur*) of West Java. Through these lines of command and responsibilities, all the programs and messages from the national government in Jakarta come down to the people at the lowest level of the administrative hierarchy: the *kampung*. One of the main programs is rice intensification. Under the formal institution, the Mass Guidance Program (*Bimbingan Massa*, BIMAS), each leader from the provincial level to the village level (*gubernur, Bupati, camat* and *lurah*) is responsible for the implementation of this intensification program in each region. Although the governor has overall responsibility for providing guidance, other leaders act as the heads of the implementation unit of the Mass Guidance Program (*Kepala Satuan Pelaksana Bimbingan Massa*, SATPEL BIMAS). In these positions, they have additional tasks as the leaders of the coordinative channels, known as the POSKO (*Pos Simpul Koordinasi* or the Chain Post of Coordination). Hence, they are also responsible for managing collaboration between all the related government agencies and the farmers' institutions in each region (Sekretariat Badan Pengendali BIMAS 1990:82–3) (see Fig. 2.1).

Under the BIMAS intensification program, the government defined the role of the Rural Extension Centre (BPP) as the provision of guidance and extension services to the farmers. During my fieldwork in 1990 and 1991, BPP pursued its work in coordination with the agricultural officer at the district level (*Kepala Cabang Dinas Pertanian Kec. Ciasem*). However, the head of BPP—known as *kepala* BPP (*Kepala Balai Penyuluhan Pertanian*)—was responsible directly to the head of the Regency of Subang as the head of the Mass Intensification Unit at the regency level. At the end of my fieldwork, the rural extension services were in the process of being transferred to the responsibility of the agricultural officer at the district level (under the Ministry of Internal Affairs). Each BPP had its region of agricultural services (*Wilayah Kerja Balai Penyuluhan Pertanian*, WKBPP) in the same area as the district region. This area was further divided into smaller units: the extension services area at the village level (*Wilayah Kerja Penyuluhan Pertanian*, WKPP) with its boundaries similar to village boundaries. Each WKPP had its own extension worker (*Penyuluh Pertanian Lapangan*, PPL). All the farmers in Ciasem Baru had one extension worker to assist them with any problems in rice farming. On the other hand, the extension worker also acted as the intermediary between the higher level agricultural officials and the farmers, as well as the messenger of all recommendations in rice intensification programs. Besides providing assistance and services to the farmer-fishermen and their families, extension workers were responsible for the accomplishment of the regional and national objectives (Departemen Pertanian 1987).

In 1987, when a female extension worker took up this position, farmers in Marga Tani became acquainted with their extension worker for the first time. In their eyes, this female extension worker was very industrious, visiting them in their homes and *sawah*. This experience became their reference every time they complained about the absence of an extension worker. Until 1992, farmers had experienced three extension workers, and the latter two were male. Quite often I heard the farmers' complaints when they badly needed somebody to solve their problems: "... they earn a government salary to assist us ..., their main job should be visiting us, to be with us in the fields, not just sitting in the office ...." Even though the extension worker had the responsibility to visit and train farmers bi-weekly, they seldom did this in the period after the IPM training. Besides training and visiting farmers, the extension workers had many other administrative jobs, as well as attending meetings, implementing crash programs in various aspects of agriculture and accompanying visitors.

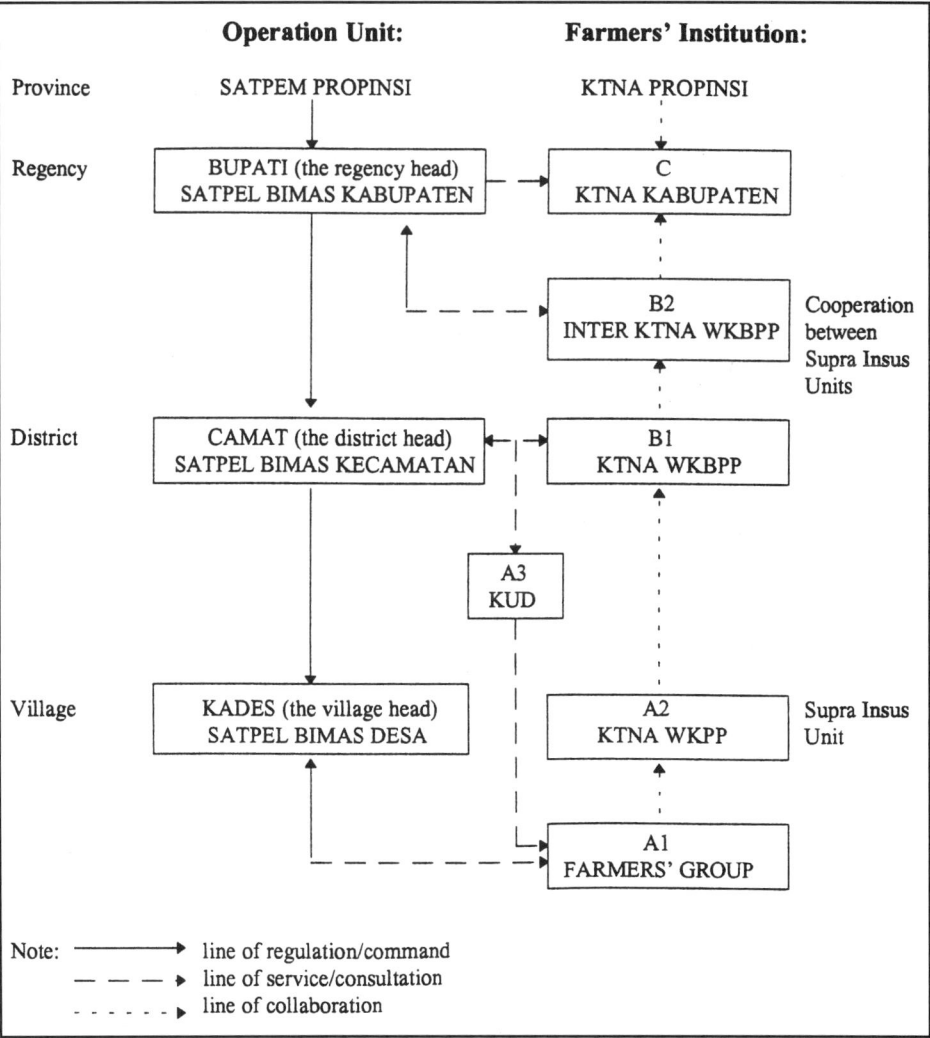

Figure 2.1 *BIMAS operational units and farmers' institutions*

Adopted from: Sekretariat Badan Pengendali Bimas 1990.

To express their position in this kind of power relation, farmers described themselves metaphorically as "a flock of ducks or buffaloes" and the government as their "herder." Their life would be prosperous if the "herder" led the "flock" well. But, the "flock" would become unmanageable if the "herder" did not lead them properly. Farmers are also aware that in the contemporary environment, they cannot rely only on their everyday knowledge to cope with and solve unexpected problems. Scientific knowledge is necessary, and the proprietors of this knowledge are those in power and authority to deal with rice cultivation.

Thus, farmers perceived the implementation of the IPM school as the government's effort to assist them, to enable them to cope better with pests and with disease problems in rice farming.

> "The government felt pity for us," said Idham, a talkative IPM participant. "The government was serious in assisting us, spending so much money to help us cope with the pest problem," said Ayim, another IPM farmer.

In their view, the visits of central government officials, the officials from Jatisari, a foreign official from the FAO during training, and my presence in their area following the IPM school, were all evidence of how serious the government was. When they spoke about these government officials, they referred to them as people from the "centre" (*dari pusat*). Hence, all the regional and local level officials are those in the "middle," acting as the intermediaries between them and the central government in Jakarta.

Collaboration in Rice Farming

The rice-farming situation I discovered in those early years of the 1990s—during and after the introduction of IPM—was a portrait of how farmers coped with the current demands and constraints of the Green Revolution. In this section I briefly describe how they collaborated with one another to have access to resources and knowledge.

Rice-farming unit

The nuclear family of man, wife and children is the autonomous unit of production and consumption as discovered by Jay in the rural areas of Modjokuto (Jay 1969). Jay (1969:9) further describes that such a unit "... typically occupies its own house, jointly works the land to which its members have rights, and disposes of its crop and its profits independently. It maintains itself and controls its own resources." It is on the basis of this that the farming unit is developed. The manager of this unit is automatically the head of the nuclear family, either a man or, in some cases, a widow. The man's wife and growing sons assist the head of the family in carrying out farming practices to the extent that the man is not able to hire wage labourers for performing some particular jobs. In some cases, the man's assistance also consists of his married sons or sons-in-law, in particular if they have not been able to form their own households. For them, this is a period of learning how to grow rice more intensively than in their youth.

In cases where local men marry migrant girls and stay in Marga Tani, they belong to their own parents' households. This rule also implies to all the migrant men who marry local girls and decide to become Marga Tani residents. As part of their parents'/parents-in-laws' households, they have the obligation to assist their parents/parents-in-law in rice cultivation. In this position, they do not have the right to pursue their own decisions without consulting their parents/parents-in-laws, unless the latter give them their consent. The obligation to provide a house and a *garapan*, a piece of *sawah*, on the other hand, lies in the hand of parents/parents-in-laws. This *sawah* functions as capital to develop their sons'/sons-in-laws' own enterprise in the future. Once a man has a piece of land to be cultivated, his career as a farmer begins. It marks a change in his status from "just a helper" to his parents/parents-in-law to a full participant in the world of rice farming. He will be known as a *penggarap* (cultivator), having his own *garapan* (cultivation). He will be the manager and/or cultivator of his *sawah*. This is when he finds himself an independent decision maker of his own resources. He has the freedom to accept, reject, or innovate with various external schemes and information of input packages. In reality, a son/son-in-law can hold more than one position at once: be a helper at his parents'/parents-in-law's *sawah* and a manager of his own.

If his parents/parents-in-law are landless, he can only inherit or obtain a share of the right to cultivate a sharecropped or permanent sharecropped *sawah*. In some cases, he acquires the cultivation right through renting or pawning. In these right transfers, no particular agreements between parents and children or in-laws are made about the sharing of costs and yields. If he is allowed to earn all the income, he and his wife are responsible for all the expenses. If not, they will only earn wages as assistants or labourers.

Farmers' group

Before 1987, there was no formal collaboration in rice farming. Formal farmers' groups—*Kelompok Tani* (KELOTA)—began in 1987, when the first extension worker led the farmers to form several groups and choose a leader for each group. The formation of those groups was part of government efforts to mobilize farmers in the implementation of the rice intensification program. Officially, a farmers' group—as stated in the decree of the Minister of Agriculture (1989)—is,

> ... a non-formal group which grows and develops from, by and for farmers with its role as a production unit learning class, and a vehicle to collaborate in rice farming and accommodate the socioeconomic aspirations of farmers and their families in order to achieve the collective goal of the improvement of productivity and income (my translation; Sekretariat Badan Pengendali BIMAS 1990:64).

This ideal goal underlying the formation of the farmers' group was new to Marga Tani farmers.

One form of such a group is supposed to consist of farmers cultivating *sawah* in one adjacent area (*kelompok tani hamparan*). This was the type of group suggested by the extension worker in 1987, which resulted in the formation of several farmers' groups. However, the farmers' groups in Marga Tani resembled residential farmers' groups (*kelompok tani domisili*) because they consisted of farmers who reside in one hamlet. Farmers in the rice fields surrounding this hamlet come from many other places (*petani guntai*). During my fieldwork, only one group was still in operation, the *Kelompok tani Jayabakti I*, led by Haji Ali, a rich farmer and a migrant from central West Java who married a local woman (Haji Nafi's daughter) in 1973. The other groups did not function anymore. Farmers in Marga Tani—excluding *petani guntai*—considered themselves part of the sole remaining group and mentioned Haji Ali as the farmers' leader in Marga Tani.

Farmers recognized that the main activities of the group were to register those who had the intention of applying for a credit package (a government subsidized scheme consisting of all commodities supporting the implementation of the rice intensification technology), distribute the package, and collect farmers' payments after the harvest. In the first three seasons since its formation in 1987, the majority of farmers in Marga Tani made use of the package. Even though taking the package constrained their choices in determining the types and amount of inputs (fertilizers, pesticides and herbicides), having credit was beneficial for farmers who had difficulties in accumulating cash for capital. After the occurrence of a serious debt in the local Village Cooperative Unit (*Koperasi Unit Desa,* KUD) in 1989–90 and the disappearance of farmers' savings, the number of farmers applying for the credit package (*Kredit Usaha Tani,* KUT) declined.[9] Farmers also learned that within the group, they should take a collective decision at the beginning of the season on the type of rice variety to be planted and when to begin their planting. The extension worker formerly led the farmers in conducting this meeting. Another function of this meeting was to transfer messages about the new technology or recommendations from the government to the farmers. The farmers recognized no other activities as part of the group's objectives.

Haji Ali told me that he was appointed as the head of the group at the request of the previous extension worker when farmers' groups were being formed. He considered his job as mainly taking responsibility for the distribution of the credit package, whereas any initiative on farmers' mobilization for collective action was supposed to be in the hands of the hamlet leader rather than his. However, he was the only farmers' leader in Marga Tani known to the local agricultural/village officials. Hence, he was always the first contact person whenever the extension worker or other agricultural/village officials had to deliver messages about rice cultivation to the farmers, not to mention the promotion of new brands of pesticides. His residence was also the centre of farmers' activities, including farmers' meetings at the beginning of the planting season and the IPM training in the 1990 dry season.

Land tenure

Various land tenure agreements not only provide ways for landless people to earn income from growing paddy, but also give them the opportunity to acquire knowledge of both farming skills and *sawah* ecological conditions. Ecological conditions of particular fields can vary due to elevation, soil or the availability of water supply to those fields. Variation in the right to make decisions and the duration of access to a particular *sawah* affect the depth of knowledge a farmer can gain from his experiences in cultivating that particular field.

SHARECROPPING

Sharecroppers are those who pay rent in the form of a share of the season's output (Pincus 1991:59). In Marga Tani, the costs for fertilizer, pesticides, and the output are divided in half (*maro*), whereas the costs for cultivation tasks, i.e., plowing, hoeing, weeding, and transplanting, are the responsibility of the sharecroppers (also see White and Wiradi 1989; Pincus 1996:153). Owners are responsible for paying official taxes and donating money for the village's expenses. Recently, farmers reported some cases where sharecroppers had to share the burden of paying taxes. They do not have power to determine the shares, in particular where the owners refuse to reimburse extra expenses in the course of a pest/disease outbreak.

In this type of agreement, the extent to which the sharecroppers are responsible for decision-making in cultivation depends on the degree to which the owners transfer that responsibility to the sharecroppers. However, all the cultivation practices are left to sharecroppers. Since the majority of landowners in the areas surrounding Marga Tani are *petani guntai* (*e.g.*, 81.1% from 180 *sawah* in Block Cadas),[10] the sharecroppers only make a report to the owners and calculate the costs and benefits after the harvest. In some cases, the sharecroppers rely on the owner's resources if they do not have capital left. These expenses will be counted later.

As long as the owners are satisfied with the results of their sharecroppers' work, the agreement can last a long time. The farmers name this type of agreement *maro matok* (permanent sharecropping). These sharecroppers thus can gain knowledge about the particular agroecological conditions of their rice fields over a longer period of time.

SHARECROPPING IN ROTATION

Another type of sharecropping agreement is *maro bergilir* (sharecropping in rotation). Sharecroppers in this type of agreement are mainly children/children-in-law of the owners (men or women). The owner-nonoperators transfer their rights to cultivate lands to their own children (men and women) on a rotating system, one in each season, so as to enable them to earn additional income. The number of children and the size of *sawah* determine the number of sharecroppers in one season and the area they cultivate.

In the case of daughters who have the right to sharecrop, either their husbands or married children-in-law act as the cultivators. In the latter case, the owner and the cultivator arrange the sharecropping agreement. Since the owners themselves are residents of Marga Tani, the extent to which the sharecroppers have the right to make decisions depends on the degree to which the owners transfer the choice and decisionmaking to the sharecroppers.

RENTING

In renting agreements, the cultivators pay the rent in cash in advance of the planting season. The amount of rent covers the payment for two seasons only. With the rent payment, the owner transfers his cultivation rights to the cultivator, and the renter incurs all the productivity expenses himself. On the other hand, he earns the income. Observation and decision-making processes are entirely in the hands of the renters. The shorter term of renting and the possibility of renting other fields in the future provide opportunities for the renters to assess the different agro-ecological conditions in various *sawah*. Renting agreements are also a means to cultivate lands in PERUM Sang Hyang Seri.

As in sharecropping, renting lands from a particular owner can extend over a long period of time (*sewa jaga* or *sewa matok*, permanent rent agreement). In several cases, the younger generation inherits the right to rent the owner's lands from their parents. As in the case of permanent share tenancy, the renters thus have the chance to gain experience about the same *sawah* over a long period of time.

PAWNING (LAND MORTGAGE)

Under the *gadai* (pawning) system, landowners turn over cultivation rights in exchange for a cash loan. The term of pawning and the amount of loan depend on the agreement between the owner and the pawner. The cultivator retains rights to the land until the loan is repaid in full, which can extend beyond the period agreed upon (Pincus 1991:66, 1996; also see White and Wiradi 1989). The pawner may choose to cultivate the land himself and gain experience in farming, or he may transfer it to others through another agreement (another pawning or sharecropping contract).

SUBLEASING

Subleasing or *alih garapan* is a transfer of cultivation rights from those who gain rights through a particular type of agreement (either *gadai*, *nyewa* or *maro*) to others in another agreement (one of the above agreements). This provides the opportunity for landless farmers who do not have access to land through direct agreements with the landowners to earn income and thus gain experience in farming. This type of agreement occurs among relatives or between parents and newly married children/children-in-law.

Table 2.4 shows the composition of various land tenure agreements. One farmer can have more than one type of agreement. The figures indicate that the highest percentage of landholdings is operated through renting agreements (33.8% of renting and permanent renting). Second is the sharecropping agreement (27.4% of sharecropping and sharecropping on a rotation).

Wage labour arrangements

Even though farmers do not perceive labourers as equal partners in knowledge exchange about farming strategies, labourers are in fact sources of information through their observations and experiences in particular activities. Various types of labour arrangements exist in Marga Tani, i.e., daily wage labour (*kuli/buruh harian*), permanent labour (*kuli matok, kuli tetap*), wages paid on the basis of contract per task, e.g., preparing the ground, pulling seedlings and transplanting (*borongan*), wages paid in the form of a share of the harvest (*ceblokan*), and harvest share for the reapers (*brandangan*) (see various wage labour arrangements in Pincus 1991, 1996; also see Hayami and Kikuchi 1982).

DAILY WAGE LABOUR

Daily wage labour is the form of arrangement for daily tasks when the owners/cultivators are not able to carry out the tasks themselves.

Table 2.4 *Distribution of land tenure agreements in Marga Tani, 1992*

Land Tenure	Number	% of total
Owner-operated	35	25.2
Not owner-operated:		
Operated by relatives	4	2.9
Worked by relatives[a]	1	0.7
Sharecropping:		
Sharecropping	36	26.0
Sharecropping on a rotation	2	1.4
Renting:		
Renting	41	29.5
Permanent renting	6	4.3
Pawning	1	0.7
Subleasing:		
Pawning—pawning	1	0.7
Pawning—sharecropping	3	2.2
Renting—worked by relatives	1	0.7
Others:		
Working on relatives' land	6	4.3
Operating on relatives' land	2	1.4
Total number landholdings[b]	139	100.0

Source: My survey conducted in 1992.

[a] I use different terms: "operating" and "working" (by relatives or on relatives' land) with the intention of differentiating two kinds of working arrangements between relatives. In operating, the owners/landholders transfer the right to cultivate and make decisions in rice farming to their relatives. In the second (working), the owners/landholders ask their relatives to work on their behalf. The owners/landholders still preserve the right to make decisions.

[b] Each farmer can hold more than one plot of land (see table 2.3). Among 53 farmers, the number of landholdings amounted to 139 *sawah*.

Examples of these tasks—all done by men—are dike preparation (*mopok*, making dikes from mud and *namping*, final touches in making dikes), seed bed making and broadcasting seedlings, fertilizing and herbicide, pesticide and foliar fertilizer spraying. Farmers use daily labourers (including women) to weed when they do not contract labourers in the *ceblokan* system.

Even though the labourers are paid on a daily basis, the owners/cultivators might use the same labourers throughout the season. In this situation, not only do the labourers gain experience in carrying out tasks, but also—in some cases—the owners/cultivators acquire information and reports about the conditions of their fields from the labourers.

PERMANENT LABOUR

Some owners use permanent labourers as their assistants in cultivation, either to carry out the tasks themselves, or by hiring other wage labourers. Permanent labourers (*kuli matok*) are responsible for all types of daily tasks as performed by daily labourers as well as water management and observations, which are usually carried out by the farmers themselves. How much responsibility labourers take on depends on the extent to which the owners themselves participate in cultivation practices. The owner-nonoperators mostly rely on their permanent labourers' activities. Even though these labourers' activities merge into a managerial role, people still call them labourers who have their landlords (*dunungan*, *majikan*) to serve. In some cases, the labourer makes the observations and reports to the landlord and provides him with strategic suggestions, e.g., in pesticide spraying. By doing this, the permanent labourer may obtain feedback from his decisions and experiments. The permanent relationship between them provides the opportunity for mutual experiences gained by both parties.

CONTRACT LABOUR BY TASK

Contract labour is confined to particular tasks such as ground preparation, pulling seedlings and transplanting. With the use of tractors in plowing, the farmers then draw up a contract with a particular tractor's owner through a sponsor, an intermediary between the owner and the farmers. The sponsor not only acts as a spotter for customers, but also determines the time schedules for plowing and receives the payments. In Marga Tani, the sponsors carry out the plowing activities themselves. The farmers perceive them as labourers of the tractors' owners in this particular task and call them *kuli bota* (tractor's labourers). Since their task is mainly to deal with plowing, which largely depends on the availability of water, the *kuli bota* have the advantage of obtaining detailed information about water and soil conditions in dispersed rice field areas and their particularities in different seasons (wet and dry seasons).

Taking up seedlings and transplanting are also carried out through contract labourers who organize themselves in planting groups, each with its own leader and specialization in transplanting types, e.g., in using bamboo sticks (*rèng*) or wooden tools (*taplak*) to measure the spacing for transplanting. In these groups, women are predominant in taking up seedlings and transplanting. Men are responsible for carrying the seedlings into the fields and doing the measurements using a wooden tool (*taplak*). In these activities, they can acquire knowledge about the growing condition of seedlings if the farmer is experimenting with a new rice variety. Other events, such as pest infestation during the period of transplanting, also provide labourers with new information. They can thus be a source of information to other farmers.

CEBLOKAN

Under the *ceblokan* system, preharvest tasks such as weeding and fertilizing are performed without pay in exchange for the exclusive right to harvest a given area of *sawah* (Pincus 1991:42, 1996:106–7; also see Hayami and Kikuchi 1982).[11] The payments the labourers receive are thus in the form of a harvest share (*bawon* with the common share of 1:6, one part from the six parts the harvesters are able to reap) from the total yields. The main preharvest task is weeding, which is carried out by the *kuli ceblokan* and his/her family. Hence, men, women and children are involved in weeding and harvesting. Through weeding, they gain knowledge of various types of weeds and herbicides as well as the impact of different types of herbicides on the growth of weeds. A more permanent relationship between them and the farmers can also give an advantage to the latter in the case of reports made by the *kuli ceblokan*.

"BRANDANGAN"

Farmers, who prefer not to use *kuli ceblokan* for landholdings that are located in distant places, have to hire wage labourers to perform the weeding tasks. In harvesting, every cultivator and labourer is allowed to harvest under the *brandangan* system. In this system, there is no particular right given to particular people in harvesting the field. Everybody has access to a portion of the field to carry out the harvest and grain threshing. Each harvester receives payment in the form of *bawon*, sometimes a smaller amount of *bawon* compared to *kuli ceblokan* (1:7 compared to 1:6).[12] Harvesters in both the *brandangan* and *ceblokan* system gain knowledge of the relation between the yields and the particular rice variety through the amount of *bawon* they receive. Experiments made by farmers in planting new types of rice varieties as well as differences in rice varieties planted by different farmers provide an opportunity for them to make comparisons and thus enrich their knowledge. The *brandangan* activities are practised in distant *sawah* areas, including the area of PERUM Sang Hyang Seri and BALITTAN Sukamandi, and provide the means to gain knowledge from other places.

Seasonal Cultivation Practices

Two main planting seasons, the rainy (*musim rendeng*) and the dry season (*katiga, musim gaduh*), constitute one calendar year of rice planting. A fallow period (*bero*) of two to three months (August/September-October/November) follows these two planting seasons. This calendar year of rice farming follows the annual wet and dry seasons along the north coast of West Java. The climate of Indonesia is primarily governed by the wet northwest monsoon from October through March and by the dry southeast monsoon from April through September. On the basis of the length of the wet and dry seasons, and the quantity of monthly rainfall during those seasons, the major areas along the north coast of West Java belong to the D3 agroclimatic zone. In this zone, the wet season, with a rainfall of more than 200 mm lasts for three to four months/year, whereas the dry season with less than 100 mm rainfall lasts for five to six months/year (Oldeman 1983).[13]

The low rainfall during the dry season indicates the dryness of the coastal areas in the absence of westerly winds. At this period, the dry winds come from the southeast. The daily air circulation contributes to this situation when the cool, dry winds from the mountains at night pick up moisture and do not lead to precipitation. In the wet season, on the other hand, the wet monsoon comes from the northwest and arrives first in northwest Java (Oldeman 1983). The schedule to begin the rainy season planting, however, depends entirely on the schedule of water supply from the Jatiluhur irrigation scheme.

Throughout the entire JALUR PANTURA region, the supply of water is managed through five divisions (blocks) with half month intervals for the starting period in each division. Officially, the water management supply for division I starts on the first of October. Two weeks later, the water management supply for division II starts in mid-October. The third water management supply starts on the first of November, and so on. Between the 1989–90 and the 1991–92 rainy seasons, Ciasem Baru (S. S. Jengkol, Talangsari, Cadas, and Laban, in the south of Ciasem Baru) received water from division II. This means that officially, the planting season begins in mid-October. In reality, the schedule can be delayed due to factors such as minimum rainfall and the bad condition of canals and water gates. If there are not enough rains in the early planting season and there are leakages of water from damaged irrigation facilities, the process of ground preparation can be slower. The alluvial type of landform in most rice field areas in Ciasem Baru consists of clay and conglomerate or tufaceous sandstone (Tim Survei Tanah Pusat Penelitian Tanah dan Agro Klimat 1990). During the very dry fallow period, deep cracks form in most of the dry soils. Without sufficient rainfall, the flooding of each *sawah* can take longer than scheduled. The process of ground preparation could thus take several weeks from the initial date of water supply as regulated in the irrigation scheme. In the last decade, tractors have replaced the use of buffaloes in ground preparation. Broadcasting and pulling out seedlings, transplanting, water management, weeding and/or spraying herbicide, fertilizing and spraying pesticide are the regular activities of every season. A calendar-based system of spraying insecticides with an interval of one to two weeks throughout the season was a common practice before the introduction of IPM in the 1990 dry season.

The harvesting time depends on the initial date of broadcasting seedlings and the maturity period of the rice varieties. If the rainy planting season begins late (late November or December), farmers will harvest their paddy some time in March. Without any disruption of water supply from the irrigation scheme, farmers have the opportunity to make decisions on the date to begin the dry season's ground preparation. Farmers in Marga Tani prefer to begin the dry season planting by referring to the occurrence of the common dry season's "illness": the "May illnesses" (*penyakit keMeian*). Their decision is based on calculating the critical growth of young plants and the period in which the "May illnesses" usually occur. If they begin their dry season planting in April, then they will harvest their yields in August. In the fallow period that follows, all the irrigation canals will dry up. This is the season where farmers usually perform the activities such as *hajatan* (feasts and ceremonies) and house construction.

THE CLOSE COMMUNICATION and collaboration among individual farmers as described in this chapter indicates how they are able to maintain their life as "genuine" rice farmers in a situation where land has gradually become a scarce commodity. Alleviating problems in rice farming becomes their main concern. By perceiving their position as "people" under the governance of those in authority, they positively responded to the government's efforts to help them through IPM training. This chapter also indicates how farmers with a strong identity to place of origin and rice farming live in an unbounded world. Marga Tani is a case of a "niche" for farmers within the horizontal and vertical webs of linkages with diverse sources of information. Various networks of communication provide means to acquire knowledge from elsewhere. This reality confirms the arguments that peasant villages and communities are not closed entities with distinctive boundaries. The following chapter examines in detail how these farmers within such a niche pursued their cultivation practices during the Green Revolution era, and how, through daily activities, farmers learned and acquired knowledge in rice farming.

3

Keep the Plants Healthy: Spraying "Medicines"

> When we were planting our "long-stem" rice varieties, rice farming activities were entirely in our own hands. Now, the government makes the regulation: when to plant, what to plant, and how to plant. It is true that we can now obtain a much higher yield and income than before, but the recent condition makes me more anxious and worried since the more 'medicines' we have … the more 'illnesses' attack our plants.
> (Haji Nafi)

> Now, I always feel restless at home. What is happening in my field? Will there be any pests or "illnesses" that attack my paddy?
> (Haji Ali)

> The farmers have to use "theory" if they would not be left out. Nowadays, cultivating rice needs "theory," "politics," "thoughtfulness."
> (Arman)

THESE STATEMENTS reflect the increased risks and anxieties in rice farming as a consequence of the Green Revolution. The farmers admit the truth, however, that changes in rice farming have allowed them to earn more money than previously and to improve their living standards. Yet, there are costs. Their life is now "restless." They have more problems to overcome, and more thought is necessary to sustain their farming activities. One main problem is the emergence of more pests and diseases despite the increased availability and use of pesticides. The farmers' complaint that "The more 'medicines' (*obat*) we have … the more 'illnesses' (*penyakit*) attack our plants …," reveals the nature of risks that the farmers themselves confront. They did not knowingly take on the risks they now face (see Douglas and Wildavsky 1983). They were ignorant of the underlying phenomena. As Bentley (1992:10) found, in Honduras, farmers " … noticed that the number of insect pests increased the more they used agrochemicals, but they were ill equipped to understand why."

Increased pest/disease attacks derive from the farmers' own practice of "over-killing the pests" (Shiva 1988:247). These practices have, however, been developed as the farmers' responses to the introduction of a reductionist technology in the Green Revolution. The approach underlying this technology has failed to "... recognize that pests have natural enemies that have the unique property of regulating pest populations" (Shiva 1988:248). Moreover, the state apparatus has introduced in the form of "technological packages and messages" without transfer of comprehensive knowledge of the ecology of pests, insects' reproduction, or pests' resistance to pesticides. In such a situation, the farmers have to cope with the unintended consequences of their own efforts. "Nowadays cultivating rice needs 'theory,' 'politics,' 'thoughtfulness' ..." is an expression of how they have to struggle, to think, and develop strategies to survive in such a complex situation. Coping with unexpected risks and experimenting with new agricultural inputs are significant means to acquire and improve knowledge. The farmers' knowledge is thus concerned not only with the skills of rice cultivation, but also with how to cope with problems in growing rice better.

In this chapter I describe how the farmers' knowledge derives from experience in daily rice farming practices. Rice cultivation is carried out by individuals. Experience, however, develops within social, cultural, and ecological settings. These settings consist of other farmers' actions, perceptions, their common ways of knowing and perceiving, and their interaction with one another and the immediate environment. In the first part of this chapter I examine the farmers' objectives in cultivating rice, how they assess their strategies and what their perspectives are in dealing with daily phenomena. The second part deals with the ways the farmers learn in everyday situations of rice farming. On the basis of this knowledge, how do they interpret the outbreak of pests and disease and maintain the growth of their paddy? The final part of this chapter discusses these issues and, in particular, the farmers' responses to the severe unforeseen white rice borer outbreak in the 1989–90 rainy season.

Rice Cultivation: Objectives and Assessments of Performance

Bentley (1992:10–11) argues that knowledge is largely built on two principles: ease of observation (or conspicuousness) and cultural importance (or perceived importance). Cultural importance determines what people choose to observe, whereas conspicuousness determines how well people can observe something. The farmers' ways of looking at nature, their priorities and values determine what properties are seen in their rice environment. Their objectives and values in assessing the performance of plants and cultivation strategies have developed on the basis of their experiences throughout the period prior to and during the Green Revolution.

Prior to the Green Revolution, the farmers used to select traditional long-stem varieties through trial and error. Their aim was to select paddy with the best yields and tastes (*padi yang "ngejodoh"*). These were the two dominant criteria in choosing rice strands. In the early period of the Green Revolution, the introduction of the very unpalatable, high-yielding varieties led the farmers to diversify their strategies. They planted long-stem varieties for their own consumption and short-stem or "government" rice varieties (*padi pemerintah*) for sale. Rice became a commodity and a source of income. Gradually, the government improved the palatability and productivity of high yielding varieties. The history of pest attacks and the introduction of various high yielding varieties improved the farmers' knowledge of rice varieties that were resistant to pests, in particular to brown plant hopper (BPH, *Nilaparvata lugens*). Avoiding harvest failure by planting these varieties became one of their objectives. In 1976 there was an unexpected outbreak of brown plant hopper. This outbreak severely damaged their traditional long-stem varieties and *Pelita*, the dominant high yielding varieties at that period. Understanding the greater risk of planting these susceptible varieties and to avoid recurrent damage, the farmers stopped planting traditional varieties. *Pelita* was gradually replaced by other high yielding varieties.

These common experiences contributed to the development of the farmers' shared objectives: having palatable rice for consumption and achieving high productivity and income in a sustainable way.

Risk avoidance had gradually become part of their objectives. At present, the farmers value these objectives equally. They ascribe high priority to both risk avoidance and profitability (see Winarto 1997a). The "safety-first" principle, as argued by Scott (1976), was not the only primary concern. According to Scott's (1976) thesis, the profitability of investment and yield per unit of land were secondary concerns rather than primary ones. Both types of concerns affect the ways the farmers assess the growing conditions of their plants. The plants' "good performances" in healthiness and productivity have become the main criteria in evaluating their own and other farmers' strategies. The farmers' expertise in rice farming is assessed according to their ability to grow healthy paddy and produce high yields.

Metaphorically the farmers perceive the condition of paddy as similar to that of their own body. The biological process of the human body and healthiness underlies their perception of the growth of paddy. The growing stages of paddy are seen as stages in human life.

The farmers perceive the period when the seedlings have been transplanted as the most fragile stage when the plants are not able to stand up firmly (*encan ngelilir*). The growing period (*masa tumbuh*) begins after this fragile stage is over (*enggeus ngelilir*, after the plants wake up) when the number of stems and leaves grow (the tillering stage). In this period, the farmers have to do the weeding (*ngarambèt*) twice. When the paddy reaches the reproductive phase, the leaves have grown to the same height (*enggeus rampag*). This stage is named *mapak anak*, the beginning of the pregnancy period (*meteng, reuneuh*). After flowering (*masa berbunga*), the panicles come out one by one. This is equated with "birth" (*bijil*). The ripening stage is called as *mratag* when the grains are formed (*keur ngisi*). If all the stems are fully formed and are bowed over (*tungkul*), the harvest time comes. If the harvest labourers have brought home all the paddy (in the case of *ceblokan*), the farmers usually say that all "the paddy has come home" (*padi enggeus dugi ka imah, padi sudah pulang*) (see Prawirasuganda 1964).

In addition to this paradigm of biological growth, the farmers view the performance of paddy in terms of its healthiness. Again, this view is an analogy of the human body. A person can be healthy, unhealthy, or sick and so can a paddy. Farmers often mentioned three conditions of paddy:

- First, paddy that is "healthy" (*padi nu sehat, saé, mulus*). A healthy paddy has an even height with a lot of stems, green leaves at the vegetative stage, good flowering and grain formation, a long panicle-stem, a lot of panicles, full-size unhusked grains (hard and yellow), transparent white husked grains, and is free from pests or disease from the tillering stage up to the harvest stage.
- Second, paddy that is "unhealthy" (*padi nu kirang sehat*).
- Finally, paddy that is "sick" (*padi sakit, padi nu geuring*). These paddy have uneven height, a small number of stems, red or yellow colour of leaves at the vegetative stage, green coloured leaves at the generative stage, green coloured panicles at the mature grain stage, and not all of the panicles are "fully formed" (flat and thin).

Another measurement the farmers use to assess plants' performance is the weight of grain after harvesting. "How many tons/*bahu* (0.71ha)" or "how many *kuintal* (100 kg)/*bahu*" are questions the farmers ask of one another's yields. This is a critical assessment in evaluating the performance of a variety, particularly during the trial-and-error stage. The other criterion is rice palatability. The farmers have two opposing terms to assess rice palatability: *pulen* (palatable, good-tasting) or *bèar* (unpalatable). The farmers will not plant unpalatable rice for their own consumption.

In the farmers' view, the performance of paddy is related not only to the inherent quality of particular varieties, but also to their own practices and natural conditions. These aspects underlie the farmers' explanations of their *sawah*'s daily condition.

Ecological Perspectives and Supernatural Belief

The FAO-IPM experts have seen the farmers as a fundamental resource and not as a factor that impedes development (Dilts and Hate 1996:2). This is one of the basic premises underlying the IPM program. They perceive, however, that prior to IPM training, the farmers did not have appropriate knowledge of their rice ecosystem. In the midterm review of IPM in a rice-based cropping system, the FAO experts mention that:

> Farmers and their national agricultural support system operated without adequate, often fundamental, knowledge of the rice ecosystem.
>
> (FAO 1991:6)

Examples of basic ideas that are considered absent from the knowledge base of many farmers are insect reproduction and the role of predators and parasitoids (FAO 1990, 1991:6). Bentley (1989; 1992) also found that Honduran farmers lacked detailed knowledge of insect reproduction. He argues that the farmers' ignorance stems from the impossibility of observing some aspects of the ecosystem without microscopes and other special equipment, and so too for the Marga Tani farmers. However, the farmers' own experiences are also significant. Prior to the Green Revolution, knowledge of predators and parasitoids on small insects did not constitute part of their knowledge. They did not consider them crucial to the control of pests and diseases, except in the case of animals preying upon rats. Their traditional pest controls could—in their view—effectively cure the "illnesses," except in a severe condition of pest outbreak.

> The farmers' traditional pest control included practices such as: putting a wrecked painted-paper-made umbrella or "red bottles" at each edge of the field or canal if deadhearts (*sundep*) occurred. Also, spraying water of a particular leaf (*dringo benglé, Acorus calamus*) around the field while casting a spell; drying the field; or taking no remedial action at all. In the case of leaf folder attack, the farmers had to renovate their silos—the place for storing grain—as a preparation for having a good yield.

Throughout the Green Revolution era, the increased use of pesticides and pest resistance led the scientists to assume that knowledge of predators/parasitoids and insect reproduction are significant as a basis of pest management control. This knowledge has become part of scientists' knowledge, but not the farmers.

The farmers' ignorance of recondite biological facts does not mean that they do not have adequate knowledge of other domains of their rice ecosystem. Various scholars have also examined the farmers' detailed knowledge of their crops and the environment (see, among others, Freeman 1992; Conklin 1957; Brewer 1979; Richards 1985, 1986). The farmers take into account various components of the crops' ecosystem that—according to their understanding—significantly affect the growth of crops. In answering "why my plants look unhealthy," the farmers look not only to the natural conditions, but also to their own practices, from the stage of selecting varieties right through to harvesting. Their rice environment is constituted by nature and their own making (Watts 1983:14; Richards 1989b).

The following are examples of how the farmers explain phenomena by referring to both natural condition and human practices:

> Armin (a middle-aged IPM farmer and the hamlet leader), Tarmi (an old non-IPM farmer) and many other farmers explained that the best planting time in the rainy season was at the end of the "tenth month" (*bulan sepuluh*, October), or in the "eleventh month" (*bulan sebelas*, November). "If possible, do not plant rice at the end of the 'twelfth month' (*bulan duabelas*, December) or in the 'first month' (*bulan satu*, January). The paddy is still small when the wind from the west comes." Arman (a young IPM farmer) and Idham (an old IPM farmer) described the effects of the west wind on their own body as if they had a fever (*merinding*), similar to the effects of the wind on paddy. Thus, the "young" paddy could not grow taller and would not be resistant to the attack of rice gall midge (*ganjur, kelèb*). This "illness" is perceived to be closely related to weather, although the cause is not always apparent. "Rice gall midge is caused by a kind of animal, but the presence of this animal is caused by the west wind ...," said Armin.

This account indicates how the farmers explain the occurrence of several phenomena at one period of time. They related their planting schedule to weather, the growing condition of paddy, and pest attack. Another example is their explanation of the growth of paddy and the condition of harvest in relation to weather, fertilizer application, and pest population:

> In the farmers' view, if planting is started earlier, the paddy will grow well. These farmers believe that rains in the early month of the rainy season—that come from the south, the mountains—carry nutrition. This perspective is shared by many. Arpan (a middle-aged IPM farmer) described the colour of this rain as "a green-rain." In Armin's view this rain can fertilize their paddy. It is as if they received additional "... 'money' ... because the paddy grows well." Chemical fertilizer could, thus, be reduced or applied only once instead of twice. Yudi (a middle-aged IPM farmer) mentioned that an excessive fertilizer application could lead to flourishing of paddy and increasing brown plant hopper's population. If there are strong winds and high

rainfall in the "second month" (*bulan dua*, February)—during the Chinese New Year period—their paddy can easily lodge and collapse. If the grains have not fully formed, they would face a decline in yields. Some farmers try to avoid this risk by delaying their planting schedule up to the "twelfth month." By doing so, they will harvest their paddy in the "third month" (*bulan tiga*, March) when the rains decline. According to their own perspectives, they cannot always follow an ideal planting schedule.

Even though the farmers have the ability to relate various aspects affecting the growth of paddy to each other, the mechanisms that are beyond their ability to observe are not part of their understanding. The farmers can only guess what the source of the symptoms is for rice gall midge in their plants. The increase of the brown plant hopper's population is explained in relation to humidity, the fertile growth of paddy, and fertilizer applications without any recourse to the ideas about the decline in the population of the brown plant hopper's predators.[1]

The farmers' ignorance of the unobservable reality leads them to refer to the supernatural power at the time they are not able to explain the puzzling phenomena. Some farmers explain a huge number of rats and their severe attack on plants, for example, as the coming of "ghosts" (*siluman*), or as originating from the "north sea." Parts of the Javanese belief become the basis of their explanation. In the case of the severe white rice borer outbreak in the rainy season of 1989 and 1990, several farmers referred to the Javanese calendar as the underlying reason. One year in that calendar, the last in the cycle of eight years, usually brings bad luck to people. As Moslem followers, however, many refer to "God's will" (*kehendak Pangeran*) to explain the calamity. The farmers have to do their best to pursue their life, but God is the Almighty who decides everything. As those who inherit parts of the Sundanese culture, the farmers, in some cases, perform rituals at the time they are about to broadcast the seedlings, transplant them, and harvest the grains. Their intention is to ask help of God and various other spirits: their ancestors and the goddess of paddy to give them luck in the future rice planting, or to thank them for the yields they are going to harvest. In the latter, the farmers perform the rituals to worship the goddess of paddy, *Nyi Pohaci* or *Dewi Sri*.

Some farmers in Marga Tani still hold the belief that paddy is an incarnation of a goddess known as *Nyi Pohaci* (*Dewi Sri*). According to the legend, after *Nyi Pohaci* died, from her grave grew various kinds of plants including paddy. The highest God sent the seeds of these plants to the earth to be grown by the people of Padjadjaran kingdom in West Java (see Ki Umbara 1973). When the farmers start to sow seeds and transplant the seedlings, some of them still practise rituals to ask the spirits to take care of *Nyi Pohaci*. Before harvesting, the farmers make an offering to *Nyi Pohaci* in a ritual (*mipit*) to make her happy and to ask her permission to be harvested. The first five stems cut with the *ani-ani* (the traditional hand-knife) are perceived as *indung* ("mother") for future seeds and are not allowed to be consumed (also see Wessing 1974; Adimihardja 1989).

Apart from this belief, an ecological perspective underlies the farmers' view of their *sawah* as only part of the larger ecosystem consisting of other *sawah*. The practices of neighbours in adjacent *sawah* would, to some degree, affect a farmer's own plants. If a neighbour sprays pesticide, for example, it could force him to take similar action. If not, "the pests could migrate to my own *sawah* and cause damage to my paddy." A farmer wanting to avoid rat attacks would delay making a nursery if his neighbours had not started broadcasting seeds. "*Patunggu-tunggu ...*," each waits for others to go ahead.

The farmers' decisions cannot thus be seen in isolation from those of others. As Watts (1983:17) says: "Some people's productive choices constitute other people's productive constraints." According to Schelling (1978:14):

> People are responding to an environment that consists of other people responding to *their* environment, which consists of people responding to an environment of people's responses.

A similar perspective underlies the farmers' perception of their neighbours' social activities. Infrequent visits by neighbours who are preoccupied with secondary jobs and social activities or who do not take care of their paddy is believed to create an unfavourable habitat for growing rice. Their industriousness and willingness to share responsibilities for collective actions, on the other hand, could form a favourable habitat for growing a healthy crop.

The farmers' world of rice cultivation also extends beyond their immediate surroundings. For example, the continuous planting activity by PERUM in the neighbouring village is perceived by the farmers as a storehouse for rats (*gudang tikus*). They are also aware of the interdependencies between their farming and the larger world of agricultural development programs and modern technology. As part of the large JALUR PANTURA region, their planting activities in each rainy season are regulated by the government's irrigation schedule. Water supply is only one factor. If there is sufficient water to make seedbeds, they face questions related to technological devices. Will there be enough tractors for a large area of rice fields? Will all the tractors be in good condition? Dependency on a high level of inputs also forces the farmers to rely on the provision of credit packages, landowners, fellow farmers or money lenders, inside and outside their village, for debts and loans. Information on price also forms a significant part of the farmers' decisions in rice cultivation.

Factors that affect the growth of paddy do not stop at the boundary of their fields. All are closely related without clear-cut boundaries. This perspective, which is gained through various ways of learning and believing, becomes the basis of their action, evaluation, and explanation.

Learning from Experience

Two dominant ways of learning that constitute the main mechanisms of knowledge formation are observation and experimentation (Johnson 1972; Richards 1986; 1989a; Rhoades 1987; Rhoades and Bebbington 1988; Bentley 1989; 1992; Bentley and Andrews 1991). These are supplemented by conversations, consultations, receiving messages and information from various local and external sources (e.g., Arce and Long 1992; Long and Vilareal 1994; Shiva 1988; Richards 1992), as well as exchanging materials, e.g., seeds (Richards 1986; Boster 1986). The extent to which each farmer acquires knowledge through a particular way or several ways of learning is related to the situation a person encounters in daily farming practices, access to information, the social networks in which he engages, and the source of knowledge with which he deals.

Observation and asking questions

At the end of the 1989–90 rainy season, Ardi (a young IPM farmer who had graduated from a high school in agriculture) and Eka (a middle-aged IPM farmer) went travelling to PERUM. After the severe outbreak of white rice borer, they were looking for a substitute variety for *IR64*. From their observations they found a particular variety that was promising. The panicle stems were long, the form was good, and the panicles were plentiful. They discovered from the cultivators what the variety was. Its name was *Cisanggarung*.

Observation is a way to assess plants' performance, gather further information on new, promising varieties and other farmers' strategies, e.g., the application of fertilizers and pesticides. Observation is also an important way to interpret the effectiveness of one's own practices.

> When I followed Kus (a permanent-wage labourer) for the second time to his field to observe the growth of the seedlings, he pointed out the dead animals spread around his seedbed after spraying *Thiodan*. I saw a dead fish one metre away from the seedbed, then one snake and another fish near the dikes. These dead animals confirmed Kus' belief that "... *Thiodan* is the strongest pesticide. See, everything was killed by *Thiodan*." Win (an IPM farmer) also mentioned the effectiveness of the "boiled-granular" after spraying this insecticide, because of his observation that "everything was killed."

Kus and Win are examples of farmers who, through observation, gain confidence in the effectiveness/ineffectiveness of a particular strategy. A strategy will not be repeated if—in their views—the result is ineffective. Observation is thus a way of being certain, of being confident that some phenomena are real (see Berger and Luckmann 1966:13; Holy and Stuchlik 1983:43).

The objectives of rice farming and the way the farmers assess plant performance affect not only what they observe but also how they observe. Prior to IPM training, the farmers used to observe their paddy from the dikes while controlling their *sawah* or carrying out some activities. If they found their plants grew well, they rarely went out of their way into the field. "Previously I did not care (*dulu sebodo aja*)" was the remark by Awi (an old non-IPM farmer). They decided to go into the field only if something strange in the plants attracted them to know more, such as changes in the colour of the leaves. Armad said,

> I only went into the field if I saw that the leaves had turned red. If I noticed some changes, I went in a rush to find money, to borrow it from other farmers to buy "medicines."

Formerly, the farmers tended not to look deliberately for insects but to notice them as part of carrying out their normal work (Bentley 1992:11). An individual farmer might observe insect behaviour unintentionally. The results of individual observation can thus vary one from the other. The farmers' knowledge of insect behaviour, however, can be a result of an intentional examination of unhealthy plants. Win, for example, made detailed observations of his unhealthy paddy by pulling out the stems to see what was inside. Hence he said: "I knew that there were some larvae inside the stems." Win gained this knowledge prior to IPM training. So did some other farmers.

> When I followed Ujan (a permanent wage labourer) to his seedbed that had been sprayed with *Baycarb* (to control brown plant hopper) the previous day, he showed me the stems that had been attacked by stem borer (*sundep*, deadhearts). While observing the rice hill he found that some new stems were growing. He interpreted this as the effects of the spraying he did yesterday. He then pulled out the stems that were attacked by *sundep* and found larvae inside.

Once the farmers discover new information, farmer-to-farmer transmission follows.

> At that time his neighbour, Arkam (a young non-IPM farmer) came. Ujan showed the larvae to Arkam who had never seen them. By referring to his practice Arkam advised Ujan to spray his seedlings again: "After spraying twice, my seedlings are now growing healthily." Ujan was in doubt about what to do next, whether to sow new seeds or to transplant the seeds. On the way home, he found that the seedlings of another farmer (Haji Dali) that were going to be transplanted also looked "sick." The leader of the transplant labourers (Haji Dali's son-in-law) told Ujan that the paddy was attacked by green leafhoppers. In his view, many green leafhoppers were found after spraying. Ujan, however, went straight away to pull out the stems. He found that in every stem there were some larvae inside. In a rush he went back to his field, met his other neighbour, Idrus (a middle-aged non-IPM farmer), told him about his finding, and asked Idrus to inspect the stems of his paddy. After doing some more observations of Idrus's seedlings, Ujan came to the conclusion that the condition of his seedlings was better than the others. He drew up a comparison: the seedlings of Haji Dali were the worst affected—1:1 (each stem had larva inside), second were Idrus's seedlings—3:1 (the larvae were found in every three stems), and the third were his own seedlings—5:1 (only one larva was found among five stems). Later, Ujan decided to spray his seedlings and so did Haji Dali.

This story reveals how observation of plant performance in different places leads the farmers to make comparisons. Very often and unintentionally, farmers make comparisons on the basis of observation. Comparison is thus an integral part of farmers' learning on the basis of which they acquire new understandings. The way Ujan interpreted the infected seedlings and did the comparison shows his creativity. At this stage, spraying was still considered the best cure for plants.

In many cases, additional information is necessary to complement observation. The main mechanism is through asking questions. The sources of information can vary, including labourers.

> Haji Nafi explained the ways of learning about various rice varieties in the period prior to the Green Revolution. "If I saw paddy that looked good in appearance, I asked the transplant and harvest labourers what the yields/*bahu* were. Of the transplant labourer, I would ask how many *sangga* he received, and of the harvest labourers, how many *ikat* he received. The labourers might know exactly the share of the harvests they received and the differences they got from harvesting this new variety as compared to the previous one. They would not tell a lie. At present, we use kg/*bahu*."[2]

Labourers are the main source of knowledge relating to particular practices, types of rice, or types and amounts of fertilizers, herbicides, and pesticides.

Experience and experimentation

A better understanding of what has been observed, testing previous assumptions, and gaining confidence that phenomena are real and possess certain characteristics are achieved through experience and experimentation. For the farmers, the validity of information received from other sources has to be empirically proved through experience (*pengalaman*) and experimentation (*percobaan*). In the farmers' views, the former refers to the direct experience they receive through daily farming practices. The latter refers to an intentional or unintentional action in carrying out experimentation.

EXPERIENCE THROUGH PARTICIPATION

The skills involved in cultivating rice—e.g., flattening soils after plowing, building and making the dikes neat, or making seedbeds (men); transplanting, weeding and harvesting (men and women)—

are acquired through imitation and direct practice. "Copying" or "mimesis," according to Bourdieu (1977), is fundamental to the acquisition of habitus. This learning takes place by assisting parents as teenagers before getting married or as sons/sons-in-law before having their own households. The farmers also learn the reasons for practicing these skills by listening to what their parents tell them about what, how, and why to carry out these activities in certain ways.

Knowledge can also be gained through working as wage labourers. Win reported that "Being a wage labourer, I have had a lot of experience in learning diverse practices performed by many other farmers." The degree of knowledge and understanding acquired by this means may, however, differ from that acquired from cultivating one's own field. First, a wage labourer is hired to carry out a task without knowing the cultivators' reasons for carrying out a particular strategy. Second, the job is terminated when the wage labourer has accomplished his work at a particular time. He does not follow the impact of his work on the growth of plants. A time dimension, a strategic plan and an ecological perspective do not underlie work as a labourer.

Win's position as a day labourer is, however, different from that of Kus and Ujan, who have positions as permanent wage labourers. Kus and Ujan have to perform all the tasks that a cultivator should. Knowledge gained from performing their activities is similar to that gained by a cultivator. By contrast, Umid (a middle-aged IPM farmer)—Haji Ali's permanent wage labourer—only follows his master's decision. Haji Ali is an owner-operator. In this position, Umid has the opportunity to follow sequentially the results of his master's strategies. Observing plants before or after treatment, interpreting and reporting the results to Haji Ali, and discussing the findings with his master for future actions all enrich his knowledge. Haji Ali is an example of a landowner who improves his knowledge through direct observation, interpretation, and experience. Unlike him, Haji Arie (a landowner and Haji Ali's brother-in-law) rarely goes to his own fields and trusts Acing (an old non-IPM farmer and a permanent wage labourer) to make decisions. His knowledge improves on the basis of Acing's reports. He does not gain knowledge from direct observation of his own strategies. Differences in the degree of participation in rice cultivation determine differences in knowledge gained.

EXPERIMENTATION

Johnson (1971; 1972) notes that systematic experimentation is a common practice, even among poor sharecroppers with a security orientation. Many other anthropologists and scholars have also found that farmers experiment spontaneously (Richards 1985, 1986, 1989a, 1989b; Rhoades 1987, 1989; Rhoades and Bebbington 1988; Maurya 1989; Bentley 1989). Although farmers do intentionally conduct experiments (Rhoades and Bebbington 1988),[3] experimentation can also occur unintentionally (Richards 1986, 1992).

Intentional experimentation. The objective of obtaining better yields and better income provides a basic motivation for the farmers to improve strategies. Success in rice farming is the main aim. The increasing complexity of rice technology leads the farmers to experiment with a wider range of practices. Experimentation is an important way of testing their own ideas and the information received from other farmers. Quite often they intentionally try a new strategy to test its effectiveness. Comparison between the treated and untreated plots is a common way to prove it. Further trial aims to validate earlier results. Experimentation is thus a way of building up confidence in the appropriateness of a particular strategy. However, the farmers live in an open environment where various variables may affect their experiments. The situation with which they are dealing in their experiments is a highly complex one, not as controlled as the scientists have. The followings are examples of the farmers' experimentations with rice varieties and fertilizer.

RICE VARIETIES. As among the Mende farmers of West Africa (Richards 1989a:19), experimentation with rice varieties is a long established tradition in Marga Tani, dating back to the period when the farmers planted their long-stem traditional varieties.[4] The "exotic" performance of new varieties—e.g., number of stems, form of grains, and healthy growth—provided attractive incentives for the farmers to know more about the plants, in particular their yields. Exchange of seeds and trials with new seeds—planted directly in *sawah*—followed. The decision to replant the new varieties in the following season was based on whether those varieties provided a palatable taste and the expected yield. A number of rice varieties were planted as a result of the farmers' trials and decisions to plant more than one variety. This diversity further provided an opportunity for the farmers to make comparisons. The farmers continued their trials with the introduced government varieties (the high yielding varieties).

> In 1989, Apri (a middle-aged, non-IPM farmer and a motorcycle driver) went to Kuningan, another regency in the eastern part of West Java. After being attracted by the good performance of a strange variety, *IR41*, he asked for nine kg of seeds from the local farmer. He and his brother shared the seeds and planted them for the first time in the 1989–1990 rainy season. At that time the majority of the farmers were still planting *IR64*, the favourite HYV (high yielding variety). Although his plants were also attacked by white rice borer, he decided to replant *IR41* in the 1990 dry season. He gained confidence with the more promising yields of this variety rather than *IR64*. He found that *IR41* had fewer panicles than *IR64* but produced a heavier weight. The formation of the grains was good and reached a full size. In the 1990 dry season, when many other varieties were attacked by the bacterial leaf blight (*krèsèk*) at the maturity stage, his plants were in a "good condition." From his evaluation of the yields, the amount of inputs (fertilizers and pesticides), and its resistance to disease, he came to the conclusion that *IR41* was a "strong" variety.

Apri is not alone in experimenting with a new variety. The promising performance of a new variety is, however, not the sole motivation to experiment. The other aim is to avoid the declining quality of a variety that has been planted consecutively in several seasons. Ayim explained his experience in trying out a new variety:

> When there was a severe outbreak of brown plant hopper in 1976, my paddy, *PB30*, was not attacked by this pest, not like the other variety, *Pelita*, that was severely damaged by brown plant hopper. Many other farmers were still planting that variety. I got two tons/*bahu* yields of rice when other farmers were only able to harvest three *kuintals* (300 kg)/*bahu*. This was the evidence that changing rice varieties was necessary. Possibly declining yields were due to the decline in soil nutrition or the increase of pest attacks if we planted the same variety continuously.

Through trying new varieties, the farmers adopted *IR64* widely. The government introduced this variety in 1987. In the 1989 and 1990 rainy season, *IR64* was planted in 70 out of 81 *sawah* (86.4%) cultivated by 34 farmers (see table 3.5). In a much smaller number of *sawah*, a range of other varieties were grown, resulting from individual decisions to adopt particular varieties. These varieties consisted of *Way Seputih, Cisadané, Muncul* (*Dèlis* or *Jègger* in local terms), *Poso, IR41,* and a glutinous variety, *Ketan Sumatera*.

FERTILIZER. Experimenting with fertilizer is a very dynamic element in rice farming. Every individual farmer is involved in this activity. First, it is related to the different stages of introducing various kinds of chemical fertilizers by the state apparatus.[5] Although the farmers received instruction and information about the use and advantage of the introduced substance, experimentation was the best means to assess whether the claimed advantages of the substance to the growth and yields of paddy were true. Second, the farmers had to adjust the recommended amount of fertilizers to the resources they had, as well as to the particular soil condition of their *sawah*. Third, they continued to experiment with new varieties. Each variety may respond differently to a particular substance and amount of fertilizer. Experimenting with fertilizers is also a means of coping with changes in plant performance due to changing conditions of weather, soil, water, or the attacks of pest/disease in different seasons and *sawah*. If they are not satisfied with plant performance, they continue their experiments until they find the most appropriate formula.

There are different ways of conducting experiments. Some farmers tried the formula they received from other farmers through consultation and asking questions, whereas others tested their own procedures, a modification of the government's recommended formula. The following two cases show differences in sources of information.

> When Haji Arie (the owner-nonoperator) did his own cultivation for the first time, he asked his father, Haji Nafi—a knowledgeable farmer—for the appropriate fertilizer formula. After receiving the formula, he made a trial in his own field by asking his permanent wage labourer to apply it. He felt satisfied with the formula and stuck with that regardless of the differences in seasons or rice varieties.
>
> After the introduction of urea (N) in the early 1970s, Ayim tried to determine what amount of urea was appropriate. He carried out similar trials for the amount of urea and triple super phosphate (TSP)

when the agricultural officials introduced TSP. He remembered how he increased the amount of these two components at a time when the Indonesia rice production increased dramatically in the early 1980s.[6] After the introduction of potassium chloride (KCl), he adopted this component in his experiment until he gained confidence in the amount he used, i.e., 150 kg of urea, 100 kg of TSP for the first application/*bahu*, 25 kg of TSP and 25 kg of KCl for the second application/*bahu*.

Conducting experiments in the rice plots was common. There were a few farmers who conducted experimentations in a small plot.

> Wira (a young IPM farmer, a junior high school graduate) discovered the formula: 150 kg of urea and 100 kg of TSP/*bahu* by first conducting an experiment in one plot of 5 m². In this plot, he broadcast 6 kg of urea and 4 kg of TSP. In the rainy season, he found that his paddy lodged, fell on the ground. In his interpretation, he had applied too much fertilizer (without differentiating whether urea or TSP was the cause of lodging). Hence, he reduced the formula in the next dry season up to 8 kg consisting of 6 kg of urea and 2 kg of TSP. The paddy was still lodged. He then made a decision to reduce it to 6 kg in the following rainy season: 4 kg of urea and 2 kg of TSP. Without an understanding that the cause of lodging was an excessive amount of urea (N) rather than TSP (P), he first reduced the amount of TSP instead of urea. When the paddy still lodged he decided to reduce the urea instead of TSP. At last he found that the growth of his paddy was good. Then he calculated this amount to get the sum of fertilizers for one bahu. He never used KCl or ammonium sulphate (ZA) in the application.

Wira made changes in several experiments successively. Once he found that the result of his trial was good, he stuck to his formula as Haji Arie did. Like Wira, Rustam (a young non-IPM farmer, a senior high school teacher who graduated with a degree from university) made experiments in six successive planting seasons. Each experiment was based on his evaluation of the growth of rice in the previous season. His objective was to gain a better understanding of the appropriate proportion. In his trial, he adopted KCl at the later stage without adopting ZA. An understanding of rice environment is thus achieved through successive experiments. Furthermore, the dynamics of the environment stimulate them to make successive trials, even in a known environment. The incorporation of KCl in the latter trial by Rustam is a case of how the farmers test the information received from other sources. It was also a test to examine the advantages of the new technology. KCl application is a relatively recent technology, but is not a completely unknown one. Other farmers had adopted this substance earlier.

Table 3.1 *Fertilizers in the 1989–1990 rainy season*

Fertilizer Application	Insecticide component	Number of cases[a]	Totals Number of cases[a]	Totals % of all cases
Once:				
	Urea	1		
	Urea-TSP	6		
	Urea-TSP-KCl	6		
	Variation[b]: Urea-TSP-KCl; Urea-TSP-ZA	1		
	subtotal, Once		14	41.2
Twice:				
	Urea-TSP; Urea-TSP	1		
	Urea-TSP; Urea-TSP-KCl	3		
	Urea-TSP; Urea-KCl	4		
	Urea-TSP; KCl	2		
	Urea-TSP; TSP-KCl	3		
	Urea-TSP-KCl; Urea	1		
	Urea-TSP-KCl; Urea-TSP-KCl	2		
	Urea-TSP-KCl; Urea-TSP	1		
	Urea-TSP-ZA; Urea-KCl	1		
	Urea-TSP-ZA; TSP-KCl	1		
	Variation[b]:			
	Urea-TSP-KCl; Urea-TSP-KCl			
	Urea-TSP; Urea-KCl	1		
	subtotal, Twice		20	58.8
Total numbers of cases[a]			34	100.0

Source: My survey, conducted in 1991 and 1992.
[a]Number of cases refers to the number of farmers (34) on which data about fertilizers in the 1989–90 rainy season were available. Three farmers included in this account stopped farming in the following seasons. The rest were part of the original 53 sample (see table 2.2).
[b]The fertilizer formula applied in different *sawah* varied.

Through trials, each farmer can come up with his own "formula." As a result, there is great diversity in fertilizer application, both in the number of applications, the component-mixture, and the amount of each component (see table 3.1).

In the 1989–90 rainy season, 41.2% of farmers preferred to apply fertilizers only once to avoid the damage of excessive amounts of fertilizer on plants and a late application in the second sowing. If there was a delay in the first sowing, the late application could retard the growth of paddy (*padi jadi muda lagi*).[7] The rest (58.8%) applied the fertilizer twice, as recommended in the rice technological package. Variation was also found in the adoption of the components of the fertilizer used. All farmers adopted urea, only one farmer did not apply TSP. Although four farmers (11.8%) did not apply KCl, only three farmers used ZA (8.8%). If we look closer at the "formula" (the fertilizer mixture and the amount of each component), a great variation prevailed. Among those who applied fertilizer once, there were various combinations. In other cases, the same mixture (e.g., a mixture of urea and TSP used by six farmers) was applied in several different combinations. Greater diversity was found in the two-time fertilizer application with variation between the first and second application (see table 3.1). In several cases, the farmers varied their formula in different *sawah*.

How did the farmers perceive the function of each kind of fertilizer?

- Urea: increased the fertility of the crops
- TSP: there were diverse views of the function of TSP. Some farmers believed TSP loosened and fertilized the soils. Others interpreted the advantage of this fertilizer for making the stems healthy, improving the weight of grain, strengthening the roots, or prolonging the green colour of the leaves.
- KCl: many farmers gained an understanding about the particular function of KCl in strengthening the stems and making the paddy healthy. However, they did not find this component a crucial element in increasing the yields when compared with the costs they had to incur (see van de Fliert 1993:85–6).
- ZA: farmers did not understand the differences ZA could make in the growth of plants.[8]

The farmers made up these inferences on the basis of their interpretation of plant performance following up the application of a particular fertilizer formula.

From the extension worker, the farmers knew that they were supposed to mix the granular insecticide, carbofuran, with fertilizer. They learned that this insecticide—known as *obat dasar* or *obat tabur* (basal "medicines" or broadcast "medicines")—was a preventative "medicine." It also functioned as a "medicine" for pests at the bottom of plants. However, not all farmers applied this pesticide in a mixture with fertilizers (44.1% of the total number of cases, consisting of those who applied carbofuran once and twice in either one or two applications of fertilizer, see table 3.2). The advantage of using this insecticide in relation to its costs, they thought, was unconvincing. Among those who applied granular insecticide in a mixture with fertilizers in the 1989–1990 rainy season, the majority used *Furadan*,

Table 3.2 *The use of carbofuran in the 1989–1990 rainy season*

Application	Component-mixture	Number of cases[a]	% of all cases	Totals Number of cases[a]	% of all cases
Once:					
	Carbofuran	4	11.8		
	Kerosene	1	2.9		
	No carbofuran/kerosene	9	26.5		
	subtotal, Once			14	41.2
Twice:					
	Carbofuran: once	6	17.6		
	Carbofuran: twice	5	14.7		
	Kerosene : once	1	2.9		
	No carbofuran/kerosene	8	23.5		
	subtotal, Twice			20	58.7
Total numbers of cases[a]		34	99.9	34	99.9

Source: My survey, conducted in 1990 and 1992.
[a]Number of cases refers to the number of farmers (34) on which data about fertilizers/carbofuran application in the 1989–90 rainy season were available (see table 3.1).

a well-known brand of carbofuran. To reduce costs, a few farmers used kerosene instead of carbofuran.

Unintentional experimentation. As Richards (1992) found among the Mende, the farmers in Marga Tani also carry out experiments unintentionally. The farmers may conduct experiments by accident. In many cases of seedlings shortage, I found that the farmers would try to find seedlings wherever they could, for example, through begging from other farmers who had excess amounts of seedlings after transplanting. The transplant labourers could find seedlings elsewhere on their own initiative. Such supplementary seedlings might be different from the initial ones. Unintentionally, the farmers would grow a strange variety. They then had the opportunity to follow the growing conditions of different varieties in one plot of *sawah*. The farmers could sometimes receive incomplete or incorrect information. For example, Arman received incomplete information about the maturing period of one variety he recently adopted. Following an attack of rats in his paddy, Arman learned by accident that a difference in maturation time could induce a rat attack. Unintentional experimentation can also be found in other practices, such as fertilizer application.

> Rustam had three plots of *sawah* and two of them had already had a complete treatment of fertilizer when suddenly he realised that there was no more KCl left. The latest plot was then planted without KCl and this situation provided an opportunity for him to make a comparison between the two different fertilizer treatments.

These cases reveal how through experience and experimentation, the farmers gain knowledge and thus become the producers of rice-farming strategies. If through continuous experimentation, a farmer can design an appropriate strategy and maintain a good appearance in the growth and yields of his rice, other farmers perceive him as a "model" farmer (*petani teladan, jègger*), an "expert" in rice farming. If a farmer has long experience in rice cultivation, he will be known as a "knowledgeable" and a "well-experienced" farmer (*petani yang sudah pengalaman*). Knowledge gained in these ways is accumulated individually. Other farmers can only observe the results of his strategy in plant performance without knowing what his strategy is, unless he communicates it. Conversation is the means to communicate and circulate knowledge, so that—to some extent—the farmers' findings become shared cultural knowledge.

Conversation and listening

Before the introduction of IPM, only a few farmers consulted written materials, i.e. agricultural textbooks, news, and articles in newspapers or magazines. These were the farmers who had a higher level of education, e.g., Rustam, Ardi, and Iwan (a young IPM farmer, and a graduate from junior high school). The farmers seldom take notes of their own activities, except in the harvesting period. At that time, they have to measure the weight of their yields and count the harvest share for each harvest labourer. The farmers' leader takes notes; he is responsible for counting the farmers' debts and payments. If the farmers take notes, as was done by Iyub (a young IPM farmer, a graduate from senior high school) during an attack of rats in his field, they keep the notes for themselves. The circulation of the agricultural books owned by Ardi was also limited to particular farmers, e.g., Rustam (Ardi's brother) and Iwan (Ardi's brother-in-law). Knowledge is not generally circulated through written materials, but through verbal communication (see the "oral" traditions of circulating knowledge among the Pukapukan, Borofsky 1987; the Mountain Ok people, Barth 1987; or the Tanna, Lindstrom 1990).

Conversation is a way of exchanging knowledge during leisure time, both in the fields and neighbourhood. Exchanges of knowledge in conversation are stimulated by several factors. For example, the introduction of new resources and technologies and their related problems, the evaluation of the farmers' trials and strategies, the infestations of pests or diseases, natural hazards, and a range of information received from external sources. These issues and the farmers' aim to obtain a good harvest and avoid risks are the basis of serious conversational exchange. This is not only the means to share and receive new ideas, but also to make comparisons with others' strategies and others' plant performances. Information from other farmers can be used as a basis for validating or invalidating their own findings, and to argue for or against others' strategies. Although experience and experimentation are significant ways to ascertain the validity of a particular phenomenon or strategy, conversation is a means whereby the farmers acquire a greater confidence in their own strategies. New ideas received through conversations can also affect their decisions to make adjustments and changes in future strategies. Conversation can thus significantly contribute to the reproduction and or modification of knowledge (Lindstrom 1990:11).

The extent to which knowledge is distributed through conversation will depend on who is involved in particular conversations through work or social networks. Although the farmers freely engage in conversations, not all cultivators will share their findings. Not all have an equal opportunity to converse or to have others appreciate what they want to say. Differences in occupational status and ability can lead to an uneven distribution of knowledge. However, there has been no regulation of who can have access to knowledge through this means of communication.

Conversation in the field is common when the farmers are working in their *sawah* during peak seasons or carrying out daily observation and control. In many cases, however, the farmers are not able to meet their own neighbours if they have a different time schedule, or if their neighbours come from distant places and employ labourers to carry out the jobs. To converse with them is perceived by many farmers as inappropriate. Hence, exchanging knowledge tends to be restricted to the farmers who are owners and cultivators, or permanent wage labourers who act as the owners' assistants. Wage labourers, however, can share their experience as presented in the following case:

> In the 1990 dry season, Haji Ali decided to make an experiment by mixing kerosene with fertilizer. The day before, Haji Ali had listened to other farmers' conversation about the use of kerosene in the IPM training (see chap. 5). When Haji Ali and I arrived in his field, his neighbour, Arman, was also in his *sawah*. He was observing the work of his wage labourers and his own brother, Akim (a young IPM farmer), applying fertilizers. While watching Umid, Haji Ali's permanent wage labourer, mixing the fertilizer, *Furadan* and kerosene, Haji Ali and Arman were talking about the experiment. Arman told Haji Ali that this experiment would not be effective since he also used *Furadan*. "You used *Furadan* and also used kerosene, how can you measure the results? You should not use *Furadan* if you would like to know the effectiveness of kerosene" (on the yield of rice and for preventing pest/disease attacks). Amran's criticism is based on the logic of

scientific method in an experiment, i.e., by testing a single agent and controlling for others. Haji Ali then realised that he had made a mistake, but Umid was already mixing and applying the fertilizer. While watching Umid working, Haji Ali and Arman discussed many things about rice farming. Every time Umid came out from the *sawah* to fill the basket with fertilizer, he told us that his hands became dry. The fertilizer did not melt in his hands, so it was much easier to apply the fertilizer than usual when he did not use kerosene. Haji Ali and Arman agreed with Umid about the advantage of kerosene in applying fertilizer. Akim, who later joined us in the conversation, told of his experience in using kerosene. He told us about the source of information of using kerosene, the way he poured the kerosene into the water, and the result of his experiment. He perceived that kerosene was effective in driving the pests away from the plants because of the "smell." So, he did not need to spray pesticides, and his paddy was not attacked by rice stem borer. Arman also told us about his other brother's experience in using kerosene in the last three seasons. His yields were always good.

Haji Ali gained knowledge of his own experiment from direct observation, other farmers' comments and experiences in conducting similar experiments, and his own wage labourer. Through conversations, new ideas are spread, such as the use of kerosene as a preventive measure against pests. Even though the main issue discussed in daily conversation is the most current problem, the conversation can cover a wide range of issues from various sources and places.

When I joined several farmers in a *warung* (food stall) run by Aming's (a middle-aged, IPM farmer) wife in the 1990 fallow period, the discussions mainly focused on yields and disease infestation. The conversation, however, also covered various other issues raised in the last season. For example, the different characteristics of various rice varieties, the harvest failure of several farmers—including those from another district—its relation to rice variety and the attack of rice seed bugs, the control strategy of rice seed bugs, the pesticides used by the farmers in controlling this pest, the plan of planting rice varieties in the next season, and many other topics. An old farmer, Arjan (Aming's father-in-law who lived in another hamlet) dominated the talk. Others (Arman, Akim, Iman [a middle-aged non-IPM farmer], and Oyid from Blanakan) were sharing their interpretations of their own or others' strategies. Arjan talked while the others (Akim, Arman, Oyid) made comments and sometimes raised questions for Arjan who then answered on the basis of his experience. Iman did not talk much, but Aming joined the conversation later. Aming's and Akim's wives were there, listening to their talk while continuing their own work serving the customers or looking after the children.

In many discussions in which I participated, several farmers (cultivators) dominated the talk regardless of differences in age or length of experience. Other farmers (cultivators or labourers) and their wives listened and made comments if they felt this was necessary. Not all cultivators however, had the same talent or willingness to participate in a discussion. In many conversations when several farmers such as Arpan and Eka were present, I noticed that they were always quiet. They listened to the conversations, but made comments rarely. Not all farmers would spend the time to make visits to neighbours for a conversation. Haji Ali, who did not like going out without a particular purpose, never visited his neighbours for a talk. Recognizing his position as a leader and a respected person because of his wealth and religious status, he welcomed everybody to come to his own house to watch television or just to have a chat.

Listening to conversation is also a significant way to acquire knowledge or to stimulate experimentation.

> Armad learned for the first time about the "May illness" from his own father while his father was talking about this illness with other farmers. As a young farmer, he not only listened to their conversations but also remembered the ideas. When he became an independent farmer, he noticed that his father's talk was true. In each dry season he found that his paddy would be attacked by "the May illness" if he started to plant too early or too late.

> Rustam learned about the way to trap rats with birds' nests from listening to those who were chatting together in his house. In the following season in 1989 he tried his first experiment to trap rats in his own *sawah* by using birds' nests.

These two cases show the importance of listening in the reproduction of knowledge.

Consultation

Young farmers usually consult with older ones and those with less experience consult with more knowledgeable farmers, not vice versa. Haji Nafi and Romi (Rustam's and Ardi's father, a non-IPM farmer) are examples of the farmers who have become a source of knowledge for beginners or others who seek information. Adma, in a younger age group than H. Nafi and Romi, is a "model" farmer who is appreciated by others for his "best" strategy in rice farming.

Conversations and consultations are the means to learn about his strategies for a particular event and season.

Consultation is also a common way to gain knowledge from external sources or from more authoritative sources such as extension workers and shop owners. Since the introduction of various rice technological packages, the farmers regularly acquire knowledge from authorized sources in the rice intensification programs. In this context, the extension worker acts as the messenger to these people. Direct contact between the farmers and the extension worker in Marga Tani was introduced in 1986 and 1987 when a female extension worker was allocated to this village. Transferring "messages" as well as answering the farmers' questions about their problems were her main activities. The new male extension workers who replaced her seldom visited the farmers. The farmers experienced a change from frequent visits and face-to-face communication to a one-off farmers' meeting at the beginning of the planting season (see Sawit and Manwan 1991).

In such a situation, the farmers learned about new technologies and inputs from further external sources, e.g., radio, television, relatives, and other farmers, workers in PERUM and BALITTAN Sukamandi, shop owners, and chemical company dealers. Shop owners are sources of information who—like "pharmacists"—can advise the farmers on how to "cure" their paddy. The shop thus has a double function: as a "pharmacy" (*toko obat*) and as a source of advice. More than that, to keep the farmers as their "permanent customers," the shop owners allow them to purchase inputs on credit if they have difficulties making cash purchases.

> Several years ago Asma (a middle-aged IPM farmer and a religious leader) went to *kiosk* Syafi in Ciasem. He consulted Syafi for the best "medicine" he could use to cure his paddy that looked "sick." Syafi told him to use *Thiodan*: "Use this, this is a good 'medicine.'" That was the first time Asma learned about *Thiodan* and how to spray it regularly.

While Asma consulted the shop owner himself, Wira (a graduate of junior high school) gained knowledge of pesticides by spending his time in the shop, reading the labels on every new product. That was how Wira learned about pesticides before making a decision on what new product he would use in pesticide spraying. In this context, the farmers are the active agents who seek out information.

On the basis of these various ways of knowing, how did the farmers interpret the infestation of pests and diseases on their paddy?

"Illnesses" on Plants: Pest or Disease?

The farmers' perception of pest and disease is closely related to how they perceive plants and their growing condition. All strategies are oriented towards getting the paddy to grow well and healthy, as if they are treating their own body with care and nutrition. What the farmers think of plants further influences what they do with plants, and vice versa (see Sillitoe 1983). The farmers perceive pests and diseases primarily in terms of their effect on plants: the emergent symptoms of "illnesses" (*penyakit*). Just as they would treat the illnesses in a human body, their further activities are intended to cure the "illnesses" on plants, or if possible, prevent them from becoming ill.

The farmers use the term "illness" to indicate the symptoms of both pest/disease and the pest/disease themselves. When I asked what caused "illness" in paddy, some farmers could make a distinction between illness that was caused by animals (*satoan* or *binatang*) and illness in which "... there is no animal," or "... the animal is unseen." This difference then functions as the basis for classifying pest and disease. Pest (*hama*) refers to the first (the animal is seen) and disease (*penyakit*) refers to the second (the animal is unseen). Some farmers, however, were not able to specify the difference. In other cases, the farmers use the term "illness" to refer to the "unhealthy" condition of their paddy due to other factors, e.g., lack of nutrition or weather. The categories the farmers use to classify entities in their natural world are in some degree overlapping and are not mutually exclusive as found by Healey among the Maring in New Guinea. Healey (1978/79) argues against the tendency in ethnoscience to present folk taxonomies as if

> they are structured on the assumption that no taxon may simultaneously be included in two or more higher order taxa, which are themselves contrasted or mutually exclusive.

He further argues that "This assumption is dubbed 'the principle of taxonomic rigidity' (Healey 1978/79:361)." The Maring, on the other hand, recognize and encode in their taxonomy, several crosscutting, nonexclusive categories.

There is also a range of variation in the farmers' ability to identify animals or insects. Ease of observability plays an important role here (Bentley 1989, 1992; Bentley and Andrews 1991). Observable animals and insects are easily identified. These are rats, brown plant hoppers (*wereng coklat*), rice seed bugs (*lembing, kungkang*), cutworms (*ulat grayak*), black bugs (*lembing batu*), and mole crickets (*gaang, blalangan*). Not all farmers are able to identify the cause of rice gall midge and rice stem borer. Since the insects are inside the stems, not all farmers classify these symptoms as caused by "pests." They use the term "illness" for deadheart (*sundep*). They refer to the symptom of rice gall midge as a form of onion's leaf (*kelèb*) or a tire valve (*pèntil*).

An individual's interest in knowing more about a particular phenomenon can lead him to seek its cause through detailed observation.

> Sukim (a middle-aged non-IPM farmer and a "model" farmer), could identify the cause of deadhearts (*sundep*) and whiteheads (*beluk*) as larvae (*uler* or *ulat*) by pulling out the "infected-stems." Due to colour differences, Sukim perceived these larvae as different, even though they derived from the same origin (white moths). He was also able to identify the white moths that laid eggs in the leaves, but he never observed the hatch of the larvae out of the eggs and how the larvae got inside the stems (before the attack of white rice borer in 1989–90).

The insects' reproduction is a rarely observed phenomenon for Sukim and many other farmers, unless they observe it accidentally. Their observations might focus on a particular stage only, e.g., larvae that cause deadhearts or whiteheads, without a comprehensive knowledge of the complete cycle of their reproduction.

The farmers have almost no knowledge of parasitoids and microorganisms. These organisms are beyond a farmer's ability to observe. If the difficulty of observation causes them to know less about insects than about plants, it leads them to know much less about plant diseases (see Bentley and Andrews 1991; Bentley 1989). The farmers always refer to *krèsèk* as a type of "illness" where the "animals are unseen." They use this term to describe plants that become dry at the reproductive stage, and thus make the sound: *"krèsèk, ... krèsèk ..."* when the wind blows. Up to the 1989–1990 rainy season, only a few farmers knew the possible cause of the disease. However, they did not have a clear idea of the difference between a fungus and a bacterium as the possible cause.

On the basis of their degree of damage to plants, the farmers classify animals and insects in the rice environment into three categories:

1 harmful to paddy (*sato nu ngarusak paré*, or *binatang yang merusak padi*), such as rats, brown plant hopper, rice seed bugs, black bugs and cutworms.
2 disturb paddy but do not cause severe damage (*sato nu ngeganggu paré, enteu ngarusak*, or *binatang yang mengganggu padi, tidak merusak*), such as caterpillars, mole crickets, green leafhoppers (*walang daun*), crabs (*yuyu*) that used to make holes in the dikes, and mosquitoes (*rembetug*).
3 neither harm nor disturb paddy (*sato nu enteu ngarusak jeung enteu ngeganggu paré* or *binatang yang tidak merusak dan tidak mengganggu padi*), such as snakes, eels, fish, frogs, earthworms (*cacing*), dragonflies (*kinjeung, capung*), grasshoppers (*simeut*), and spiders (*gonggo, lancak*).[9]

The first category of "dangerous pests" reveals the farmers' historical experience with the attacks of those pests that led to a decline or a failure in a harvest (see van de Fliert 1993, 96–97 for similar findings in Central Java).

Pests that are classified into the second category are not perceived as severely damaging plants. The "white disease or white pest" (*hama putih* or *hama bodas*: leaf folder or rice caseworms) was even recognized by the farmers as bringing luck according to the "old people." But, it is not any longer now.

> "The 'ancestors' said that *hama putih* was a sign of good fortune and so we had to repair our silos. But now everybody sprays the pest though it is not quite damaging," an explanation I commonly heard about this pest.

Prior to IPM training, the farmers did not have any idea that there were two kinds of "white pest" (*hama bodas*): leaf folder (*hama putih palsu*) and rice caseworm (*hama putih*).

Formerly, deadhearts and whiteheads were also common, particularly in the dry season, but they never damaged the plants as severely as in the 1989–90 rainy season. Moths are also common in fields, but the population had never been as high as in that season. Since there was no understanding about rice stem borer reproduction, the farmers had no idea that the moths laid eggs and that the larvae from these eggs were the destructive insects. Aming reported,

> ... We knew that there were many moths and eggs in the last rainy season. Moths were everywhere: in the fields, from the bottom to the top of paddy in the fields, at home, and along the streets. The numbers were up to thousands .... But, we did not know that these were pests and caused the harvest to fail. The paddy still grew well and green. Suddenly ... when the panicles came out, all were white ... *bapuk*.

In the 1989–1990 rainy season, 61,556 ha of *sawah* (23.6% of the whole irrigated area) in JALUR PANTURA were heavily damaged by white rice borer (WRB, *S. innotata*). In Ciasem Baru, 578 ha (76%) of rice fields were affected by this outbreak, of which 251 ha (32.9%) were severely damaged (*puso*) (Balai Desa Ciasem Baru 1990). Severe damage was found in plants that were transplanted in late November and December, following the schedule of water supply for division III (1–15 November) and division IV (16–30 November) (see chap. 2).

Since the early 1900s, *S. innotata* has been a major and eruptive pest in the lowland areas of Java (to a height of 200 m) that had a pronounced dry season with rainfall below 200 mm during October/November (e.g., the north coast of West Java and several places in Central and East Java, Kalshoven 1981; Oka 1991). On the north coast of West Java, there had been nine outbreaks in the period between 1900 and 1940 with the last outbreak in 1937. The infestation of WRB in 1989–90 occurred 53 years after the last outbreak (Rauf 1990). Rauf (1990) asserts that the major outbreaks in the period of 1900–1940 occurred when the previous dry season was too dry and the rainy season came late (see chap. 6). Throughout this period, the position of WRB as the major pest had been usurped by the yellow rice borer (*Scirpophaga incertulas*). *S. incertulas* became dominant after the construction of the Karawang irrigation scheme in 1931 and the Jatiluhur irrigation scheme in 1968 (Rauf 1990). Only the oldest farmer, who was 90 years old in 1990 and lived in Kebon Cau, the neighbouring hamlet of Marga Tani, remembered the severe attack of WRB before the 1930s. The infestation in the 1989–1990 rainy season was the first experience of WRB outbreak for many farmers who began their farming activities after the 1940s (Winarto 1995).

The third category covers other animals (insects, vertebrates, reptiles, and birds), some of which are natural enemies or predators of rice pests. Although most farmers perceive these animals in terms of their effects on plants, they have some knowledge of prey-predator relationship: "… an animal that eats another animal." The most common example of these predators is rats, whereas the others are spiders (particularly the orb spiders), frogs, birds, salamanders, and dragonflies (see van de Fliert 1993, 97; Bentley 1992, 10). When the farmers discuss the problem of rat attacks, they cite the extinction of many rat predators as the main cause.

> "When we were planting long-stem varieties, rats were not as common as today. Many animals preyed on rats: snakes, civet cats, … at that time there was grass and many bamboo trees. Now the snakes are gone, they were hunted for the market. So are the civet cats. When there were still many trees in PERUM, many birds also preyed on rats such as the sparrow hawk (*alap-alap*) and eagle (*elang*). I saw myself how the sparrow hawk caught the rats in the field. After the trees were cut and especially after CIBA did the aerial pesticide spraying from the aeroplane (late 1960s), all birds and red ants in the trees disappeared. Now, the only enemies left for rats are man and dogs," said Tarmi (an old farmer). Tarmi's wife who was listening to Tarmi's story added spontaneously: "The enemy of rats now is 'medicine.'"

The farmers understand that changes in habitat lead to changes in prey-predator dynamics. That understanding, however, does not include prey-predator dynamics among smaller insects. "I thought that all insects were pests," said Aming and many other farmers. The farmers tend to view small insects as their enemies. Given this attitude and the farmers' aims to keep their plants free from damage and sickness, they like to see a dramatic die-off of insect populations (see Bentley 1989:27). The common method the farmers used to "kill all the pests" up to the 1989–1990 rainy season was to spray pesticides.

Keep The Plants "Healthy": Spray "Medicines"

To keep plants healthy, both to prevent them from catching any "illnesses" and to cure them if they become "sick," the farmers spray "medicines." Spraying "medicines" is also the way to keep pests far away from their plants through the "smell" of the medicines left on paddy. This is the preventative measure the farmers used to carry out. These strategies are an analogy of treating their own bodies when they are ill. Through primary health care programs carried out by the national government, the farmers have been used to getting medical treatment by taking pills and injections for both preventative and curative measures. One aim of the primary health care program, as stated by Haliman and Williams (1983:1449) is "... initiating community-based health services of a curative, disease-preventative and health-promotive nature ...."

To strengthen the need to protect their plants from "illnesses," the farmers refer to the proverb: "*Sedia payung sebelum hujan*" ("Have an umbrella ready before it starts raining").[10] Although this proverb has become part of their own knowledge in using pesticides, it originates from the agricultural officers who introduced the use of chemical pesticides as a way to control pests. Information received from diverse sources of knowledge has strengthened the implementation of this strategy. This information is focused on which "medicines" are the best and strongest for killing pests, which medicines protect or cure plants, and the methods of using the "medicines." Very seldom is information circulated among the farmers about the toxicity of the chemicals to their own health and environment, the unexpected consequences of the decrease in natural enemies or the increase in resistance and the resurgence of pests. The perceived effects of spraying pesticides or broadcasting granular insecticides are dizziness, vomiting, and headaches (*mabok*). Although the farmers notice the extinction of eels, fish, snakes, and frogs as an effect of pesticide spraying, this killing is beyond their expectations. "We want to kill the pests, and not those animals."

The farmers learned the prophylactic use of pesticides in a calendar-based system in the variety of ways outlined above. Some farmers prove that after a couple of weeks, the insect population recuperated. Not all farmers, however, spray pesticides regularly without a preceding observation of the condition of the plants. They also experiment with the frequency of spraying season to season. As a result of individual experience and decisions, there was a great diversity in the frequency of spraying and in the mixture and brands of pesticides used. Table 3.3 shows that in the 1989–1990 rainy season, the range of spraying was up to seven times a season. Only one farmer did not spray at all, because he raised fish in his *sawah*. Three farmers varied the number of sprayings in different locations, each with a different range of sprayings (see note to table 3.3). The largest percentage consisted of those who sprayed three times (29.4%) followed by four times (20.6%) and twice (17.6%) a season. The total sprayings from 34 farmers in 81 locations amounted to 279 sprayings. On average, each location was sprayed by pesticides 3.44 times in one season. Almost 65% of farmers sprayed their fields three or more times (see table 3.3).

The farmers' understanding of the function of each pesticide varies. Even though most have a false impression of its purpose,

Table 3.3 *Frequency of spraying pesticides in the 1989–1990 rainy season*

Number of sprayings	Number of cases[a]	% of all cases
Zero	1	2.9
Once	2	5.9
Twice	6	17.6
Three times	10	29.4
Four times	7	20.6
Five times	2	5.9
Six times	2	5.9
Seven times	1	2.9
Combination[b]	3	8.8
Totals	34	99.9

Source: My survey, 1990–1992.

[a]Number of cases refers to the number of farmers (34) on which data about pesticides in the 1989 and 1990 rainy season were available (see table 3.1).

[b]Three cases of farmers who varied their frequencies of spraying in different *sawah*. They sprayed a different combination: once and twice; three and four; five and seven times.

some farmers could identify the function of a particular pesticide to control a certain pest, e.g., *Applaud*, (a juvenile hormone retardant) to control brown plant hopper,[11] or *Bassa* (BPMC) to control brown plant hopper and leaf folder. Many farmers are able to differentiate only the overall effectiveness of each product. *Thiodan* (endosulfan) was very popular as the "strongest medicine" that could kill any pest. A mixture of more than one "strong medicine" was considered best to get a more effective result. "Making a cocktail" (*campuran* or *oplosan obat*) from several products is a common practice. One reason for making a "cocktail" consisting of the expensive and cheaper pesticides is to reduce costs and yet still achieve an effective result (*murah tapi ampuh*, cheap but powerful). Figures in table 3.4 show that 38.2% farmers used only one product, whereas the rest (58.8%) made a "cocktail" of more than one for a single spraying.

The combination of ingredients used in the "cocktail" also varies. Each farmer has his own formula in mixing different brands of both the banned and permitted pesticides. Romi—who used to carry out experiments by mixing several products—made a "cocktail" consisting of: *Thiodan, Sumithion, Sevin*—all belonging to the group of banned insecticides—and two permitted insecticides: *Applaud* and

Table 3.4 *Number of products in the mixture of pesticides*

Number of products	Number of cases[a]	% of all cases
Zero	1	2.9
One	13	38.2
Two	7	20.6
Three	3	8.8
Four	4	11.8
Five	1	2.9
Variation[b]	5	14.7
Totals	34	99.9

Source: My survey, conducted in 1990 and 1992.

[a]Number of cases refers to the number of farmers (34) on which data about pesticides in the 1989–1990 rainy season were available (see table 3.1).

[b]Five cases of farmers who diversified the number of products in different *sawah*: one farmer used one, two and three sorts, each in different *sawah*; four farmers used one and two sorts, each in different *sawah*.

Indobas. Even though the presidential decree to ban 57 insecticides for use on rice was declared in 1986, in the 1989–1990 rainy season most farmers still did not know about the ban. They did not receive this information from the extension workers or from the shop owners. One shop owner in Ciasem knew about the ban, but he did not tell the farmers so that he would not lose customers. Hence, the farmers kept using the banned insecticides. *Thiodan* was the pesticide most frequently used by the farmers in the 1989–1990 rainy season (78.1% sprayings from the total 279 sprayings in 81 *sawah*). There were seven other banned insecticides used. Some farmers sprayed boiled carbofuran, which is extremely hazardous and was strongly discouraged. Only a few farmers used the permitted insecticides without mixing them with the banned insecticides.

When the farmers identified the increased population of white rice borer moths in the 1989–90 rainy season, some farmers applied granular insecticides in the first application of fertilizer. Not all farmers applied these insecticides in the second application. When deadhearts appeared, only one farmer (Armad) practised what "the ancestors said," i.e. drying the fields, but he also sprayed insecticides. Other farmers kept spraying insecticides preventatively, until the unexpected indication of whiteheads occurred. In a panic, some farmers increased the frequency of sprayings at the ripening stage, whereas others did nothing. In their view, no action would effectively "cure" whiteheads. Since the farmers had already sprayed pesticides and some farmers had applied granular insecticides, they were not able to explain what caused the ineffectiveness of their own practices. Given this situation, a strong rumour derived from external sources concerning the distribution of false pesticides (*Thiodan* and *Furadan*, a granular insecticide) proved effective in changing the farmers' practices.[12] In a quick response, the farmers replaced the false product (*Furadan*) with the newly released one (*Indofuran*) in the following 1990 dry season (Winarto 1995).

Several farmers who did not experience severe damage gained confidence in their own strategies. Another phenomenon was the severe damage by WRB to *IR64* that was transplanted in mid- or late December 1989. From this outbreak, the farmers gained knowledge of the plants' susceptibility to pest outbreak.

Risk-Avoidance and Risk-Spreading Strategy: Towards a Diversity in Rice Variety

The WRB outbreak destroyed the image of *IR64* as a profitable and reliable variety. The fact that *IR64* had been planted for three successive years reinforced and extended the understanding that rotating and varying rice strands was beneficial in avoiding risks. The range of WRB impacts on different varieties provided an opportunity for the farmers to make comparisons. They interpreted the diverse outcomes of WRB outbreak in relation to their own practices. One conclusion drawn from this comparison was the declining quality of *IR64*. The farmers' discovery that other varieties had stronger qualities than *IR64* motivated them to explore the characteristics of those varieties. The farmers also referred to the planting schedule, the time of outbreak, and the growth-stages of the crop to their previous knowledge of rice gall midge outbreaks in relation to planting schedules; then, they interpreted the novel phenomena (WRB attack) in relation to established understandings and thus gained additional knowledge.

Despite this improved knowledge, the farmers' experience of the WRB attack increased their understanding of persistent high risks in rice cultivation. A great worry spread among many farmers that future harvests would again fail. It was a great shock for those who could not harvest at all or could harvest only a small amount because of low yields (less than one ton/*bahu*). In the 1989–90 rainy season, there was a great range in yields, from zero to average rainy season yields (3.5–5 ton/*bahu*). All *sawah* producing less than 1.0 ton/*bahu* were planted with *IR64*. Only a small number of *sawah* cultivated with *Cisadané* and *Way Seputih* had yields of 1.0–2.0 ton/*bahu*. The rest were *IR64*.

The loss or decline in yields had a great impact on the farmers who cultivated only a small piece of land, rented fields or share-cropped their harvests. They not only lost their earnings, but also could not get enough rice for their own subsistence. The only way to sustain their life was to look for more credit for consumption and future capital. In such a situation, the major issue at the beginning of the 1990 dry season was how to avoid risks (see Wharton Jr. 1971;

Scott 1976 for the "safety-first principle"). Some farmers decided not to continue cultivating since no cash was available to pay rent. The majority chose to change and/or to diversify rice varieties. Diversifying rice varieties was perceived as a way to spread the risks in case a similar outbreak occurred. As Johnson (1971) found among Brazilian peasants, the sharecroppers spread their agricultural efforts over several varieties of land and crops as a way of "maximizing security in the face of risk." A few who had gained confidence in *IR64* did not alter their decisions or planted *IR64* only on some parts of their *sawah*. As a result, there were eleven (11) nonglutinous rice varieties and two (2) glutinous varieties planted by the farmers in the sample (see table 3.5).

Although only five farmers (14.7%) diversified rice variety in the 1989–1990 rainy season, the number increased to 20 farmers (58.8%) in the 1990 dry season. Two farmers diversified rice variety within one location. On the other hand, two farmers who previously had not planted *IR64* decided to plant this variety in the 1990 dry season. They were confident that a different season would not yield a similar outbreak of pests. Seeds of new varieties were acquired by exchange or purchase from diverse sources.

This diversification in rice variety occurred in a situation where the farmers had flexibility in their exercise of individual decision making. No collective decisions or coercion from local authorities (the farmers' leader or the local agricultural and administrative leaders) constrained the farmers' choice. In contrast, members of one farmers' group in the neighbouring village, Ciasem Tengah, led by a respected farmers' leader and the local extension worker planted only one variety, *Cisadané*, in the 1990 dry season. The role of the leader in one farmers' group in this village was prominent, because the members had a high degree of understanding that planting a uniform variety in one rice field area was significant to avoid pest attacks. In such a situation, the individual's choice was constrained by the group's decision and respect for following their leader's decision. Changes occurred in both places, but did so according to different mechanisms of decision making.

Table 3.5 *Rice varieties in the 1989–1990 rainy season and the 1990 dry season*

	% of variety planted in *sawah*	
Variety	1989–1990[a]	1990[b]
IR64	86.4	22.4
Cisadané/Cisadané Super	3.7	27.1
IR42	0.0	21.2
Way Seputih	2.6	10.6
Muncul	4.9	3.5
Others[c]	1.2	11.8
Glutinous varieties	1.2	7.1
Combination:	0.0	3.7
IR42—*Way Seputih*		
IR42—PN70		
IR42—*Cisadané*—IR64		
Totals	100.0	107.4

Source: My survey, conducted between 1990 and 1990.

[a]The number refers to the percentage of the variety in a total of 81 *sawah* cultivated by 34 farmers in the 1989–1990 rainy season. In this season, each *sawah* was planted with one particular variety.

[b]The number refers to the percentage of the variety in a total of 85 *sawah* cultivated by 64 farmers in the 1990 dry season. The total number of *sawah* changed following the changes in the number of cultivated landholdings and the cases of farmers who stopped or began farming in this season. Three *sawah* cultivated by two farmers were planted with more than one variety.

[c]Examples of other varieties that were absent in the 1989–1990 rainy season but were planted in the 1990 dry season were *Ciliwung*, *Cisanggarung*, IR36, IR42, IR99, and PN70.

THIS CHAPTER SHOWS how knowledge is constructed in the lived-in world of daily, rice farming activities. The learning process the farmers have gone through is ubiquitous. As Lave (1996:8) says, the learning process is "… an integral aspect of activity in and with the world at all times." The world of farmers consists of the complex structure of persons acting in a setting, i.e., in the relationships among the farmers themselves and with other parties in diverse positions, within and outside administrative boundaries (see Bentley and Andrews 1991; M. Brookfield 1996); with their own and other farmers' work; a range of production inputs; and their "open-dynamics" rice environment. Diversity in learning and knowing, despite a shared knowledge and common ways of learning, is an apparent phenomenon. In addition to this, the farmers' underlying knowledge and perceptions of growing plants and treating them with care and attention, their explanations of the plants' performance and unforeseen phenomena reveal the viewpoints as raised in the theories of situated activity in learning. In favour of these theories, Lave (1996:7) argues that the theories of situated activity: "... do not separate action, thought, feeling and value and their collective, cultural-historical forms of located, interested, conflicted, meaningful activity."

The farmers' doing and perceiving reflect their responses and learning within the historical process of improving rice production in Java, and its unintended consequences. The economic and ecological perspectives, even though with some limitations, become the basis of evaluating and explaining their strategies. A mixture of other perceptions and values is also influential: for example, the metaphorical introduction of chemical inputs, the Moslem and traditional beliefs of both Javanese and Sundanese, the analogical perception of both human and plant biological processes, and medical treatment for illnesses in both of them. On the basis of these interlinking variables and perceptions, as well as the constraints they have in understanding and explaining daily phenomena, they have to continuously respond to pest and disease outbreaks. The unprecedented white rice borer outbreak in the 1989–1990 rainy season prior to IPM training was an example of how, with their knowledge, perception, and leftover resources, the farmers were struggling to survive.

At the time the farmers were planting diverse rice varieties as a strategy to avoid further hazard, the IPM trainers began the IPM school's activities at the period of transplanting in the 1990 dry season. The following chapter examines how the learning process took place.

4

Spraying "Medicines" Is Old-Fashioned

The weather was hot and dry when—during the 1990 fallow period—I joined some farmers who were watching the building of an IPM farmer's house. Following my talk with the father of the IPM farmer, the builder of the house, Akim (a young IPM farmer) confidently explained why there had been a severe attack of WRB in the last season: "The problem was that, at that time, we did not understand that the white moths (*kupu-kupu putih*) were the cause of the deadhearts (*sundep*) and empty whiteheads (*beluk*). Now we understand that the white moths can lay eggs. The most dangerous thing, however, is not the moths but the egg clusters (*kelompok telur*). From one egg cluster can hatch 150 larvae (*ulat*). Imagine that." One non-IPM farmer who was listening to the conversation raised a question: "Can we spray the moths with *Thiodan*?" Ucup (a middle-aged IPM farmer) answered: "Now, the government bans the use of *Thiodan*. That 'medicine' (*obat*) can eradicate or kill not only pests, but also insects' natural enemies (*serangga-serangga musuh alami*). If the natural enemies are killed, there will be nothing to prey (*memangsa*) on the moths."

IN THIS CONVERSATION, some words that had not previously existed in the farmers' language were evident in the IPM farmers' vocabulary, i.e., "egg clusters," "natural enemies," or "insects' natural enemies." This dialogue also illustrates how the IPM farmers were able to use their own words in the new understandings of WRB reproduction and the negative impacts of spraying pesticides. Some of them were also able to phrase the new ideas as introduced by the trainers. "*Sekarang petani itu harus teliti, harus mengamati dulu* (Now, farmers have to examine, have to observe first)," reported Ayim. Most of them now understood that observing the condition of pests and natural enemies was necessary before making decisions in pest control. In some conversations between the IPM and non-IPM farmers I also heard how the IPM farmers used the new notion: "*Sekarang kalau enggak ada penyakit, nyemprot obat itu kuno* (Now, if there is no illness, spraying medicines is old-fashioned)."

These statements are in contrast to the farmers' perspective in the use of "medicines" prior to the training and their ignorance of the WRB reproductive cycle and its control strategies. Their responses to the severe outbreak of this pest in the 1989–1990 rainy season prove what Bentley says that "What farmers don't know can't help them." (This is the title of Bentley's 1989 article, p. 25). How did the IPM training contribute to this improvement in the farmers' understanding? What forms of interactions occurred in the course of training where the trainers and farmers encountered one another? The IPM "school" is a means by which farmers, as expected by the IPM experts, learn "... the language of field ecology that will allow them to read and understand the book (Dilts and Hate 1996:2)." What the IPM experts saw as the "book" was the farmer's rice field. Self-learning about their own fields is the underlying premise of this "school." Nevertheless, the IPM principle and strategy originate from a body of scientific knowledge with its particular scientific vocabularies, meanings, and discourse structures. Even though the national IPM experts had stipulated that the IPM trainers avoid the use of foreign terms, the trainers used many new words in their communication with farmers. These terms were already part of the trainers' vocabulary but not of the farmers' (Winarto 1994, 1999). Examples of these terms are:

> *ekosistem* for ecosystem, *ambang ekonomi* for economic threshold level, *musuh alami* for natural enemies, *predator* for predator, *parasit* for parasite/parasitoid, *siklus hidup* for life cycle, *intensitas serangan* for the intensity of pest attack or damage symptom, *populasi* for population, *jaring makanan* for food web, *gulma* for weeds, *nimfa* for nymphs, *pupa* for pupa, *larva* for larva, or *diskusi* for discussion.

An IPM farmer complained that: "... Many words could not be understood." The trainers and farmers in Marga Tani are bilingual, speaking both the Indonesian and Sundanese (local) languages. Understanding messages in both languages should not be a problem. In reality, the farmers did not easily understand some alien terms.

Despite that the IPM farmers were able to incorporate the newly introduced terms into their language and discourse, their understandings and usage of these ideas varied. The majority of IPM farmers understood some new terms quite clearly, such as "natural enemy" (*musuh alami*) or "farmers' friends" (*teman petani*). Other terms were interpreted with diverse meanings and degrees of understandings. An example of this is the economic threshold level (*ambang ekonomi*). One term that is basic for the unit analysis of field ecology, the "ecosystem" (*ekosistem*), was also vaguely comprehended. The IPM farmers never cited this term in their daily conversations. How can this diversity of interpretation and understanding of different concepts be accounted for? Diversity was also found among individual participants. Some farmers could recall and use several new terms in their conversations, whereas some could neither remember these terms nor understand their meanings. Variations in individual understanding are common in any learning process. This chapter describes how such variations in understanding occurred by examining the manner in which the trainers introduced these terms and the ways the two parties interacted. My description of the IPM farmers and how they were selected will follow in the first section. How the "school" was accepted and implemented in the local setting of power and authority will be discussed in the second part.

"We, the 'Schooled Farmers'"

The role of actors, the learners, in the situated activity of learning is central (see e.g., Lave 1993; Chaiklin 1996). The extent to which new ideas in a learning process are reinterpreted, modified, adopted and used in daily life and lead to further changes will depend mostly on the learners' responses and actions. An understanding of who the actors were as the participants in the IPM "school" and how they were selected is significant to later examine the further impacts of the IPM "school" on the participants themselves and the community. Only a small proportion of farmers were selected as participants in each "school." In Marga Tani alone, the 25 participants amounted to only one-third of all owners and cultivators in this hamlet. In combination with the IPM farmers in the other hamlet, Kebon Cau, the total number of participants consisted of only a small fraction (5.6%) of a large number of farmers (around 900 owners and cultivators,

Balai Desa Ciasem Baru 1990). By being selected as IPM farmers, they have the privilege of obtaining a particular body of knowledge. They are expected to be the "change agents" in their community. The IPM planners have the intention of not making IPM a "body of knowledge" owned by only a small distinctive group within the local community. The IPM participants are expected to disseminate what they learned to other farmers. A set of criteria about the participants and the rules of attendance were set out by the planners to attain the aim of this "school."

The IPM planners aimed to transfer learning skills and knowledge about the field's ecological conditions. Regular attendance at the full sessions of IPM training was considered necessary. By attending all sessions, the participants were expected to master the ecological understanding gradually (Gallagher, personal communication 1991). The limited number of farmers and the small size of the group for discussions—five farmers in each group—were designed by the IPM experts to allow each farmer to participate (R. Dilts, personal communication 1992). Four criteria were set up to select participants: ability to disseminate new ideas; own or operate *sawah* as "real farmers' (*petani murni*); ability to read and write; and agree to attend the training regularly (also see van de Fliert 1993:130). Only local knowledgeable persons can select the participants on the basis of these criteria. The main trainer, the pest observer, did not have direct access to farmers. The responsibility of selecting the participants was transferred to the extension worker. He/she had the access to and was assumed to be knowledgeable about his/her area. One extension worker was responsible for recruiting 50 farmers from two farmers' groups: 25 farmers for one IPM "School" (see fig. 4.1).

In reality, each extension worker approached the local leaders, either the hamlet or the farmers' leader, to assist his/her selection of the participants. In Marga Tani, the extension worker approached both. However, the hamlet leader had a more dominant role in selecting participants than the farmers' leader. As seen by the farmers' leader, the hamlet leader had more power in dealing with matters related to hamlet residents. He did not dare to object to the hamlet leader's choice, even though he was not happy with the list. Some participants did not belong to the category of "real farmers." Among

Spraying "Medicines" Is Old-Fashioned

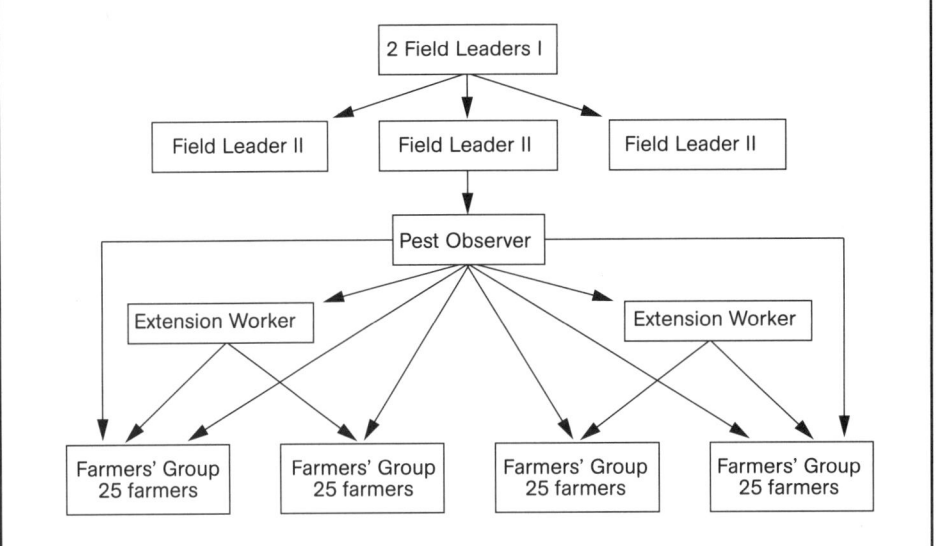

Figure 4.1 *The supervisors, trainers, and farmers*

these were the village security officers, non farmer-operators, and the "nonactive" farmers.

Another significant variable that may affect the learning is how the participants get acquainted with the aims and objectives of the "school." The extension worker left this problem in the hands of the local leaders. Without distinguishing the forthcoming "school" from the previous extension programs, the local leaders circulated the invitation to the participants just to "attend a meeting" (*datang kumpulan*), "an extension" (*penyuluhan*), or a "school about farming" (*sekolah pertanian*). This was the kind of information spread by the selected participants to their friends to join the "meeting," without knowing the purpose. After the first session of the training was held, some of the selected farmers, including the respected ones, decided to quit. These model farmers preferred to take care of their several dispersed *sawah* at the peak season of work in the fields. Some of them perceived themselves as too old to attend the "school" in the formal sense. They preferred the younger farmers to replace them.

As a result, in the first three weeks of training, the number of participants declined to around 14–15 farmers. The number increased again in week four and in the following weeks (up to 22–23 farmers each week). Some new participants replaced the drop-out farmers on the basis of the farmers' leader's and farmer-to-farmer's invitation. In addition to the late participation of some farmers, not all IPM farmers attended the full ten weeks of training. Among the 25 participants in the final list, there were 23 "real farmers" who were the decision makers in their own *sawah*, consisting of seven landowners and 16 cultivators. From this list, Haji Ali named only a few farmers who were likely to be listened to by other farmers in daily conversations (see table 4.1).

In relation to the participants' existing knowledge prior to training, the amount of experience a rice farmer has is significant. The younger the farmer, the fewer years of experience he has. However, the farmers' own history and number of years engaged in rice farming is a significant factor as well. Of the 25 participants, 14 (56.0%) were between 31 and 40 years of age, four (8.0%) were older than 40 but less than 50 years old, and seven (28.0%) were considered as "young" with ages between 25 and 30 years (in 1990). Not all farmers belonging to these age categories had similar years of experience in rice farming.

One criterion for IPM participation is the ability to read and write. This requirement is related to the training method uses writing and counting. All participants met this criterion though they had varying amounts of formal schooling. Six of the seven young farmers had secondary schooling (four had graduated from senior high school: Ardi, Asmid, Diloh and Iyub; and two had graduated from junior high school: Iwan and Wira). Ardi was the only one who had attended the agricultural senior high school. Of the 19 middle-aged and older farmers, only two had ever been to secondary school (Haji Ali to junior high school and Usin to senior high school). The rest of the participants had been to primary school (68%), but only two of them had graduated from the primary school (Adma and Arman) (see table 4.1).

Although attendance in the second and third weeks of training declined, the percentage of attendance from week IV onward was constant and high (around 90%). By comparison, the other field school, in Kebon Cau, had a lower percentage of attendance. Several factors seem to explain the high level of attendance at Marga Tani. First, the participants were mostly farmer-operators (92%), though some had secondary jobs. Second, they had arranged to have the training in the afternoon, ordinarily leisure time. Third, they were attracted by the incentives to earn Rp.1,000 or 50 cents/weekly (see van de Fliert 1993). Even though the participants in Kebon Cau had the same motivation, the IPM participants in Marga Tani had a greater commitment to attending the sessions themselves. Only for some sessions did some participants ask their relatives to substitute for them. The participants were also closely related to one another as kinsmen and/or neighbours.

Of the 25 farmers, only three were not related consanguineously or affinally to other participants. A local resident adopted one of them (Ayim) as a son. Of the 22 farmers, 12 were the descendants of the first settlers in Marga Tani and 10 were migrants from close and distant places. Their local wives were all related consanguineously to the 12 farmers (see table 4.1). Of the 23 farmer-operators, only Ayim did not have *sawah* in Blok Cadas. The rest of them cultivated rice fields in the area of Blok Cadas and other areas. All the IPM farmers thus had criss-crossing relationships, either as kinsmen or neighbours in the hamlet and rice field areas. This social network provided a way to share and keep the new ideas in use in their daily conversations. At this stage, the new words received in the training (e.g., "natural enemies," "economic threshold," "egg clusters") could only be used by and communicated among themselves (see Philips 1982 on her study of the law students). Gradually, a sense of solidarity and identity developed in the course of training. Some farmers referred to their trials for nonspraying as one way to show the IPM strategy to the "lay-farmers" (*petani awam*). Hence, after week V of training, these farmers began to criticise several participants who were still spraying pesticide in the absence of pest attack, because this action showed "a lack of solidarity (*kurang kompak*)."

Gradually, the group developed an identity as the receivers of a particular body of knowledge in the context of a schooling system. They recognized the distinctiveness of their knowledge from that of

Table 4.1 *The IPM participants in Kampung Marga Tani*

Ownership[a]	Age-group	Tenancy[a]	Area of land-holdings (ha)[a]	Education	Relation-ships
Landowner					
Adma	31–40	owner-operator renter pawner	5.05	completed primary school	consanguine
Aming	31–40	owner-operator renter sharecropper	3.68	primary school	affine
Ayim	31–40	owner-operator	2.19	primary school	non-kinsmen
Eka	31–40	owner-operator sharecropper	1.18	primary school	affine
Haji Ali, farmers' leader	31–40	owner-operator	5.26	junior high school	affine
Idham	41–50	owner-operator sharecropper on pawned land wage labourer	1.09	primary school	consanguine
Iyub	25–30	owner-operator sharecropper renter worker on relative's land	4.50	completed senior high school	affine
Landless					
Akim	25–30	sharecropper renter	2.29	primary school	consanguine
Amid, *ulu-ulu*	31–40	sharecropper permanent wage labourer	0.71	primary school	affine
Ardi	25–30	sharecropper wage labourer	0.68	completed senior high school	consanguine
Armad	31–40	permanent sharecropper renter	4.43	primary school	consanguine
Arman[b]	31–40	sharecropper	1.21	completed primary school	consanguine
Armin, hamlet leader	31–40	permanent renter	5.29	primary school	consanguine
Arpan	31–40	operator on relative's land worker on relative's land	2.67	primary school	consanguine

Table 4.1 The IPM participants in Kampung Marga Tani (continued)

Ownership[a]	Age-group	Tenancy[a]	Area of land-holdings (ha)[a]	Education	Relation-ships
Landless (cont.)					
Asma, *amil*	31–40	sharecropper, renter	1.47	primary school	consanguine
Asmid[c]	25–30	assisted his brother		completed senior high school	consanguine
Diloh	25–30	sharecropper renter assisted his father-in-law	1.78	completed senior high school	affine
Iwan	25–30	worker on a pawned land renter	1.43	completed junior high school	affine
Onol,[e]	41–50	not a farmer, a village security officer	0.0	primary school	non-kinsmen
Ucup	41–50	permanent sharecropper	2.0	primary school	consanguine
Umid[d]	31–40	renter permanent wage labourer, wage labourer	0.36	primary school	non-kinsmen
Usin[c]	31–40	worked on relative's land		junior high school	consanguine
Win[d]	31–40	renter wage labourer, permanent wage labourer	0.43	primary school	affine
Wira	31–40	sharecropper	0.57	completed junior high school	consanguine
Wahyu	41–50	sharecropper renter	1.71	primary school	affine

[a] subject to change

[b] moved out of Marga Tani to work in Jakarta in the 1990–1991 and 1991 planting seasons and returned to Marga Tani in the 1991–1992 rainy season

[c] moved out of Marga Tani (to other village/Jakarta) in the post IPM training (from the 1990–1991 planting season) and did not return to Marga Tani

[d] decided to become wage labourers only in the post IPM training (from the 1990–1991 planting season)

[e] cultivated rice for the first time in the garden of the village office in the 1990–1991 planting season and ceased cultivating afterwards

the other non-IPM farmers. Hence, a new category of farmers emerged gradually in their daily conversations: "We the 'schooled-farmers' (*kita, petani yang sekolah*) and those the 'unschooled' (*petani yang tidak sekolah*) or the 'lay' farmers." Through interaction and conversation, the IPM farmers repeatedly used these words when different practices and arguments between these two parties emerged in their daily rice farming activities. As Philips (1982:199) says, "Segregated learning also heightens awareness of the aspect of one's social identity that is associated with the knowledge being acquired." Lave and Wenger (1991:53) also mention that

> Learning ... implies becoming a different person with respect to the possibilities enabled by these systems of relations, ... learning involves the construction of identities.

Formerly, the majority of IPM farmers were not respected either as "knowledgeable-expert-model" farmers or as prominent community figures. Their new identity as "farmers who were schooled" now gave them more confidence as "those who have more knowledge" than those who were "unschooled."

An IPM School in The Local Setting of Power and Authority

The introduction of IPM is only a part of a longer relationship between government and farmers since the time the Green Revolution was implemented in Indonesia. As with similar mechanisms of introducing rice intensification packages, the IPM was introduced to the local farmers through the bureaucratic apparatuses. In the earlier times of the Green Revolution, the local-regional bureaucrats played a determinant role in making the programs work (see Palmer 1978; Hansen 1978). Exercising their power over the local farmers was dominant. IPM, on the other hand, aims to empower farmers. How then was such a program placed in the local setting of power and authority? How did the local bureaucrats play their roles in this program?

The major actor in this setting of introducing an entirely new type of program was the pest observer, the official from the Directorate of Food Crop Protection. He was the main trainer in the four IPM Farmer Field Schools in one district and thus was the pest observer in the district of Ciasem. He had power in making decisions on where, how, and what to do in implementing IPM training. An example of how he exercised his role was the selection of the IPM field experimental plots. These plots were the main resources for observation and comparisons throughout the entire period of training. Because the training was intended to be a "school without walls," other training activities were supposed to be carried out close to the training plot. The pest observer, assisted by the extension worker, made some modifications to meet the local situation. The rice fields in Marga Tani extend continuously without sufficient space between fields to accommodate a large number of people. The trainers thus decided to use the farmers' leader's residence as the place for training. They then chose the nearest *sawah* owned by the parents of one of the IPM farmers to be the IPM field plot.

    The plot was divided into two: one-half received the current technological package (SUPRA INSUS), and the other received IPM (PHT = *Pengendalian Hama Terpadu*) treatment. The SUPRA INSUS plot—treated with the rice technology package—received a preventive carbofuran granular application, whereas the IPM plot was to be treated on the basis of pest control measures after group decisions based on observations (Program Nasional Pengendalian Hama Terpadu n.d.; van de Fliert 1993). In Marga Tani, the cultivator himself carried out the treatment regardless of the decisions made by the IPM groups' discussion. The IPM farmers met only once a week and the discussion about the plot was held in a "formal" training session, whereas daily farming activities were still carried out by the cultivator himself. At the time the IPM trainer asked the cultivator to use his *sawah* for IPM training, the cultivator had already applied the first fertilizer in a mixture with granular insecticide and had sprayed pesticides once. The trainer asked him not to tell anybody about the granular application and pretended it had not been applied. Covering up the reality is an example of how the local agricultural officials exercised and pursued their work. This is also an example of how the ideal plan designed by the national experts was modified by the actors at the implementation stage according to the local situation.

    In relation to the use of this plot, the IPM experts had decided to compensate the owner for possible yield loss as a result of trampling and pest damage in case wrong control decisions were taken (Gallagher, personal communication 1991; also see van de Fliert 1993: 127). In reality, the trainer decided not to provide the money to the owner. An interest to gain some economic benefits overrode the consistency of implementing the rule.[1] The trainer's decision created a further unintended consequence. Later, at the reproductive stage, the cultivator was anxious about the destructive impact of 25 farmers trampling on his paddy. He was then reluctant to have all of them in his field. Another example of the trainer's modification was replacing the making of "Insect Zoos" (*Kebun Serangga*) with a session called "Imitating Predator's Behaviour." Gallagher (personal communication, 1991), on the other hand, strongly argued that the "Insect Zoo" was the most important session to allow farmers to observe the reality of the prey-predator relationship, and it should not be replaced by any other session. The late arrival of the materials needed to make the "zoos" was the trainer's reason for replacing it.[2]

Under the coordination of the National IPM Program, technical supervision was provided by Field Leaders I and II. They had the responsibility of supervising and assisting the trainers, distributing materials, receiving and evaluating the trainers' reports and monitoring the implementation of the program. Field Leader II directly supervised the pest observer. During the training, he came only once to Marga Tani as did Field Leader I when accompanying visitors from Jakarta. The extension officials came more often than the Field Leaders to assist the extension worker and monitor the training. Both the head and the senior extension officer of the BPP in charge of food crops also served as coordinators and supervisors of this program. The local farmers, on the other hand, were under the authority of the village and district administrative officials. Coordination with all these government agencies was thus necessary so as to place this national program within their jurisdiction.

The exercise of power by the local authorities was first revealed in the decision of the BPP's head to hold the opening ceremony in only one place, at Kebon Cau in Ciasem Baru. The administrative officials from the village and district levels were invited by the BPP staff to come to only one IPM School's official opening ceremony, instead of events in each of the four locations. Financial support was, in fact, provided by the National IPM Program to conduct the opening and closing ceremonies in all places. Again, an economic interest was the underlying reason for the BPP staff's decision. For them, IPM was financially the best supported of all other agricultural programs in their area. In front of the farmers, however, the BPP staff gave their reason of not placing too much of a burden on the head of the district (*Camat*) to open the IPM "schools" in four places.[3]

At this ceremony, *Camat Ciasem* symbolically opened the IPM schools in his district. As a consequence, not all IPM farmers attended this ceremony. Only some IPM farmers at Kebon Cau and representatives of those in the other three places in Marga Tani and C. Tengah were invited to come. The closing ceremony was also held in one place, at Marjim, C. Tengah. Hence, no single official ceremony attended by the local bureaucrats was carried out in Marga Tani. Later on the farmers complained that the trainers introduced the school without permission, coming and going without any decency.

It was into this official hierarchical setting of IPM training that the third party entered: the local agricultural extension and administrative officials. The local officials, as Hobart (1993:12) says, "... also have distinctive powers and forms of enshrined knowledge, with their concomitant closure." As in many other development projects, several discourses about development coexist. Hobart (1993:12) mentions the coexistence of at least three discourses: the discourse of developers, of the local people being "developed," and of the national government and its local officials.[4] The existence of these different discourses in the context of IPM training first came into play when the local officials and IPM trainers addressed their messages to the local farmers at the opening ceremony. Through these messages, the IPM training was not only placed in the context of the national agricultural policy, but also in the context of the current local interests, objectives, and problems. The local authorities used several new phrases and pieces of jargon to explain the aims of the training and contrast the new practice of spraying pesticide with the old one.

> It was 9:15 am when the head of BPP Ciasem began his speech. He was the first speaker at the opening ceremony of IPM School at the residence of the hamlet leader of Kebon Cau. About 30 farmers attended the meeting plus a number of local bureaucrats from the district and village levels. The head of BPP mentioned that the objective of this

school was "... to make farmers IPM Field-Experts, at least in their own rice-fields (... *untuk menjadikan petani Ahli Lapang* PHT, *sekurang-kurangnya di sawahnya sendiri)*"; but he did not expand any further. He also asked the participants to continue attending for the next 10 weeks of training and said that they had to own *sawah* (the owners, though cultivators were okay too). The next speaker was the Field Leader II who was responsible for supervision of IPM training in the district of Ciasem. After explaining the nature of IPM training, he mentioned the term economic threshold *(ambang ekonomi)* as a criterion by which decisions about pest control should be made, but he did not explain the term. He also introduced the new slogan of spraying pesticide: "*Kalau sekarang itu yang 'getol nyemprot itu kuno'* (At present those who spray pesticide diligently are old-fashioned)."

The first speakers gave only a brief description of the training without a detailed explanation of the new terms they used. The head of the district agricultural office (*Kepala Cabang Dinas Pertanian Kecamatan Ciasem*), the third speaker, elaborated upon the meanings of IPM. When presenting a new slogan for spraying pesticide ("If unnecessary, don't bother"), he explained why there was a change in the use of chemicals by referring to the nature of technology, which, according to him, was always changing.

> The district agricultural officer explained IPM as a way to control pests in an integrated way, and not by only eradicating pests. Spraying pesticides would be carried out only if necessary and based on the results of observation. He also asked farmers not to use *Thiodan* because it was "too strong" and killed all animals. In fact, not all animals were "farmers' enemies" (*musuh petani*). As a consequence, one day, pests could not be controlled. He gave an example of farmers' malpractice in controlling leaf folder (*hama putih palsu*). Further, he also introduced a new slogan in contrast to the old proverb of spraying pesticide: "... *Kalau dulu: 'Sedia payung sebelum hujan,' sekarang 'Kalau tidak perlu tidak usah'*." (If previously 'Have an umbrella ready before it starts raining,' now 'If unnecessary don't bother.') He explained the reason for this change in relation to the nature of technology and cited the changes in fertilizer application as an example. Technology, according to him, "... always developed, as happened with fertilizer. It was not a technology if it did not develop. So, farmers do not need to be afraid." At the end of his speech, he expressed his hope that in the future the authorities would not visit this district because of a "failure" (like the recent harvest failure), but because of a "success."

His explanation about the common nature of the changing technology was a reason to give legitimate grounds for the changes the government made in their own policies. In his speech, he introduced several new terms, such as "integrated" (*terpadu*), "observation" (*mengamati*) and "farmers' enemies" (*musuh petani*). He also related this training to the recent experience of harvest failure.

In the following speech, the *Camat Ciasem* (the Head of the District of Ciasem) highlighted again the farmers' injudicious use of pesticide in relation to the recent harvest failure. He related this failure to farmers' inappropriate use of pesticides by using the farmers' own metaphor: pesticides as "medicines." He emphasised that preventing pest attacks should be the main objective for farmers to avoid another harvest failure. He also asked farmers to implement the current rice technological package, the SUPRA INSUS technology. One of the components in this technology was the implementation of integrated pest management strategy. His emphasis was a warning for farmers' own defects in rice cultivation while introducing again the new slogan about spraying pesticide.

> The *Camat* said that controlling pests was not part of the government's task anymore, but was the duty of every individual farmer. He asked farmers to avoid carrying out activities improperly (*jangan sampai salah kaprah*). He further said that "... For instance, if somebody has a stomachache, he buys *aspirin* and *bodrex* (medicines to cure cold and headache) instead of medicines to cure stomachache. For farmers, the important thing is to control pests. There is no sense being furious following a pest outbreak. If it (your paddy) fails, it has failed (*Kalau sudah paèh, paèh baé*). The important thing is to do the best to prevent pest attacks. How? It depends on farmers' industriousness: be diligent in controlling pests, don't surrender to God's will ("... *aktif mengendalikan hama, jangan sampai diserahkan pada Takdir Allah SWT*")." He then mentioned farmers' negligence in observing their fields and their "ignorance" of the "ten points of SUPRA INSUS technology." The control of pests was one of the points in this technology. He urged the farmers again to implement all ten points of this technology so as to avoid the previous disaster in which farmers became aware only after the occurrence of "illness" (*Petani tahunya setelah ada penyakit*). The farmers agreed by answering: "Yes." (*Ya*). He also asked farmers not to blame the extension worker as they had in the case of WRB outbreak, since the extension worker would not be able to control 500 ha of *sawah*. Their own reporting to the Farmers' group was necessary. The *Camat* repeated the new phrase to "control" and not to "eradicate" pests; that farmers who diligently sprayed pesticides were "old-fashioned," and that "... Observation first was necessary before taking any action, and do not take action without first observing (*Ngawaskeun heula, baru ambil tindakan, jangan tindakan heula*)."

The speech of the *Camat* illustrates how the local authorities used this opportunity to exhort farmers to maintain the high rice production in their regions. Similar messages were also transmitted by the extension officers to farmers in the other three places where they themselves "opened" the training officially. A BPP staff member for food crops made a correlation between the declaration of INPRES 3/86, the injudicious use of pesticides, and the current harvest failure. After mentioning the name of the two brands of banned insecticides (instead of the 55 other banned insecticides), he asked farmers to follow the presidential declaration to avoid another "hazard" and "harvest failure." It was clear that the local officials used the current "harvest failure" to again warn the farmers to follow the forthcoming program. This was the common way of enforcing farmers to follow their commands in implementing rice intensification packages. The local bureaucrats thus placed IPM training in the context of their aims to avoid the re-emergence of any disaster in the future that could further affect their own prestige.

"School Without Walls": Learning Scientific Knowledge

The IPM weekly sessions in Marga Tani and other places followed the opening ceremony in Kebon Cau. For four to five hours a week, the participants got together to learn new ideas. The processes the farmers went through involved learning new terms and concepts, skills, as well as the ways of discovering phenomena and seeking out the logic behind them. These included the learning of these new terms, concepts, and skills by being trained in their use, not only by looking at or pointing to actual objects or samples of the kind pictured, but also by understanding the whole context of their use.

The regularity and agreement of the usage, the uniformity of the context, and the praise, judgment, or punishment accompanying the use of new concepts, and skills may significantly affect the whole learning process (see Bloor 1983 on Wittgenstein's ideas of learning a language game; also see Wittgenstein 1958). In a communicative event where trainers and learners interact, however, prior experience, information, and the expectations of both parties significantly contribute to the interpretation and understanding of the new meanings (see Saville-Troike 1987, 1989). The extent to which the new words have counterparts in the existing body of the learners' knowledge is also significant (Winarto 1999). The following section examines how these factors contributed to the varying receptions of the new IPM concepts by the participants.

Natural enemies and their role in rice environment

"Natural enemies" (*musuh alami*) was the best understood term. This is an example of how an introduced concept was gradually adopted by all participants in a common understanding as "those that prey on pests." Hence, they are "farmers' friends" (*batur petani, teman petani*), or "farmers' helpers" (*pembantu petani*). Formerly, farmers only understood the prey-predator dynamics for rats. Through training, farmers came to understand that the term also stood for insects. All small insects were formerly classified as "pests." They also gradually understood that animals belonged to the farmers' category as "animals that neither harm nor disturb paddy" were in fact, natural enemies. This introduced term, thus, had its counterpart in the farmers' own vocabulary.

Farmers' adoption of the terms "natural enemy" and "farmers' friend" shows how the training, as well as farmers' own experiences and expectations, led to an agreement about what those terms meant. The trainers' introduction of complementary terms: "farmers' friends in preying upon pests" contributed to the relatively quick adoption of this term. The understanding underlying this term was practical, i.e., that by controlling pests, natural enemies were helping farmers to secure their yields. By understanding this, farmers perceived natural enemies as beneficial and not merely as animals that neither harm nor disturb paddy. The enrichment of the schema or model the farmers already had had occurred: the classification of insects/animals according to their impacts on paddy and the predation of rats. In relation to the first, the farmers modified their own classification by involving the criterion of predation and the benefits to their own well-being. The preservation of natural enemies in the context of growing rice was also an enrichment of their schemas or models in interpreting the ongoing events of rice farming (Winarto 1998). These shared and enriched understandings occurred gradually through repetition in various ways of learning during 10 weeks of training.

IDENTIFYING INSECTS: BALLOT BOX PRETEST AND "APA INI?" ("WHAT IS THIS?")

In the first week of training, farmers had to take a preliminary test called the Ballot Box Pretest. In this test, farmers had to put their answers into box A, B, or C according to their choice for each question on top of the boxes. The pest observer had made small boards to write down the questions. The questions had a multiple-choice type of answer. For several questions, the pest observer put the objects being asked about under the boxes, e.g., insects or symptoms of damage on plants. The questions included the identification of natural enemies and pests, rat attacks, diseases, age of seedlings, and those related to the current stage of rice cultivation. This was the first event where farmers encountered the term, "natural enemy" (*musuh alami*), written on several boards. During this session, farmers were not given any explanation about *musuh alami*.[5]

Surprisingly, some farmers commented that questions about the identification of pests and natural enemies were easy. Their answers were based on the differentiation of insects to the category of "pests" and of "animals that were not harmful to paddy." If the insects were not pests, they would thus be natural enemies. Without narrative explanation, farmers made guesses based on their previous experiences. Unknown natural enemies, however, were not easily identified. For instance, when Wira examined a spider in one of the plastic bags, he knew it was not an orb spider (it was in fact a wolf spider, *laba-laba pemburu* or *Lycosa pseudoannulata*). However, Wira did not know whether to categorize it as a pest or a natural enemy.

The same difficulties occurred when the farmers were asked by the trainers to engage in a dialogue about particular insects in the session called "*Apa Ini?*" ("What is this?"). In this session, two farmers in turn were asked to communicate—to raise questions and provide answers—about a particular insect. The trainers put the insect in a small plastic bag. The farmers were supposed to pose questions about what the insect was, where they found it, how many were found, whether it disturbed paddy, and what the farmers should do next in dealing with it. The farmers had no difficulty identifying orb spiders and dragonflies as "natural enemies." Since the trainers tried not to provide a prior explanation, farmers used their own prior knowledge:

> Haji Mur (a middle-aged IPM farmer who was a farmers' leader in Kebon Cau) told his partner, Fadli (a middle-aged IPM farmer) that the insect was found in the stem of paddy while making webs. Fadli asked: "Does it disturb paddy?" Haji Mur answered: "No, it does not disturb paddy." Fadli: "Does making a web disturb paddy or not?" Haji Mur: "It does not disturb paddy or people, so it is a natural enemy." Fadli: "Should it be eradicated?" Haji Mur: "No."

At this stage, the IPM farmers assumed that their own term for animals that do not disturb paddy was "natural enemies." Then, the Field Leader II introduced the appropriate way to treat natural enemies, i.e., by not spraying them.

> Spiders should be preserved, do not disturb them. They are mostly killed by "medicines." So, do not spray them (*Laba-laba kudu dilestarikan, ulah diganggu, paehna teh lobana ku obat. Jadi, moal disemprot*).

For smaller insects such as the *kukuyakan* (*kumbang kubah*, ladybird beetles, *Coccinalidae*), the farmers could not correctly state their place in the rice field nor their effects on plants, for they had no prior knowledge of them. Their conversations were thus a made-up story concerning the insect's behaviour.

> Ujan told his partner, Aim (a middle-aged IPM farmer) that he did not know what the insect was, but that it came from the field (*sawah*). Aim asked: "Where is it found?" Ujan (guessing): "In the grass, canals, disturbing." Aim asked again: "Where?" Ujan: "In the grass, making the grass short (*Suket. Jadi prindil*)." Aim: "Where in the canals?" Understanding farmers' incorrect dialogue, the Field Leader II intervened in the conversation by explaining that the insect's place was in the leaves of paddy. The farmers then continued their conversations. Aim asked: "Does it disturb leaves or paddy?" Ujan (correcting his previous answer): "Leaves, the paddy's leaves, so buy 'medicines.'" Aim asked: "Spray with what 'medicines'? (*Semprot obat apa?*)." Ujan could only answer: "Spray it." The Field Leader II corrected their dialogue by mentioning that the insect preyed on pests, so it did not need to be sprayed.

This was also the first time that the Field Leader II mentioned the role of natural enemies, i.e., preying on pests, and hence, they should not be sprayed. At the end of the session he stated the meanings and objectives of IPM. According to him,

There are three objectives of IPM (PHT), namely: 1) to make the paddy healthy (*agar tanaman sehat*); 2) to optimize production (*supaya produksi optimal*); and 3) to conserve the environment (*lestarikan lingkungan*). If you use "medicines," the costs will be high. The better way is having a smaller cost but gaining optimal yields. Farmers have to be certain whether these animals are pests or "natural enemies." Don't mix them up.

In the following week, the trainers still placed emphasis on training farmers to distinguish natural enemies from pests.

COLLECTING INSECTS AND DRAWING THE ECOSYSTEM

An important means used in IPM to make farmers understand the differences between insects and natural enemies was by collecting insects in plastic bags. While collecting insects, the farmers discussed and argued about the insects they found, their names, and whether they belonged to the category of pests or natural enemies. This provided an opportunity for farmers to pose questions directly to the trainers, e.g. about insects' identification and behaviour. The pest observer assisted the extension worker if necessary. Returning from the field, the trainers asked the five farmers in each group to draw and write down what they had found in the field. This was the first time they had been asked to do so.

The trainers helped the farmers to draw a rice hill in the middle of a sheet of paper surrounded by the insects. The farmers had to place the insects as they were found in the plants, draw the damage caused by rats or white rice borers and provide other information, e.g., the condition of water and sunshine. They had to write the names of pests on the right and natural enemies on the left. While working, they discussed how to draw the animals, what the names of the insects were, which ones belonged to which categories, or how many insects they had found. Arguments occurred over "strange" insects, such as: *cocopèt* (*Euborellia stali*), *bobotolan* (*kumbang tanah, Ophionea nigrofasciata*), *kukuyakan* (*Coccinelidae*) and *lalat daun* (*laleur daun, Hydrellia sasakii*).

The pest observer introduced these new names while pointing to the insects. Besides insects, the farmers also found eggs (*telor*). This finding led to a further understanding about spiders' eggs, which were in fact farmers' friends. The IPM farmers' participation in this activity varied: some took an active part in drawing, writing and arguing; some only watched and had nothing to say; and others asked questions of the pest observer or extension worker. "While spraying pests, we have to preserve 'our helpers' (*pembantu kita*). How can we do that?" This is an example of farmers' queries. The trainers then led the farmers to draw conclusions about what they had to do next.

Each group might collect different insects. In the group's presentation, information about these diverse "strange" insects was introduced and shared with other farmers. Questions and arguments about the insects were raised by farmers and followed with the trainers' explanation. Presentation was thus a mechanism to share knowledge.

THE ROLE OF NATURAL ENEMIES: "PREDATOR" AND "PARASITE"
By substituting the "Insect Zoo" session with another session: "Imitating Predator's Behaviour," the farmers could not observe directly the fact that natural enemies prey on pests. The pest observers thus explained the role of natural enemies by introducing new terms: *predator* and *parasite*. All farmers in the IPM school in Kebon Cau when I did my observation said: "No," when the pest observer asked them whether they understood the meaning of "predator." The pest observer explained the meaning of those terms:

> A predator is a natural enemy, its task is to prey. An example of a predator is the spider. Its task is to prey on pests. There are two kinds of natural enemy: the predator and the parasite. Let us use the example of the stem borer. If formerly you made an observation of the stem borer's egg clusters ... (the pest observer referred to the previous white stem borer outbreaks and if—at that time—farmers had made an observation) .... Collect the egg clusters and put them in a plastic bag. If these eggs hatch, it is uncertain yet that from these eggs will hatch only larvae. Maybe some of them will be like ants (*simeut*). They are black but small; they are named "parasites." Those are ... natural enemies. (By using his hands, he showed the place of egg clusters and parasite.) This is the place of the parasite, and this is the egg cluster. If the moths lay eggs (*ngendog*) ... the parasite will come nearby. When the moths lay the eggs on the leaves, the parasite puts in its needle. It is a small needle ....Thus if the moths lay eggs and the eggs have not been covered by smooth hairs, the parasite comes, puts its needle into the eggs and lays eggs there. Nine days later when the eggs hatch, the parasites will come out rather than the larvae. The parasite has the character of living on others. Like ourselves, live on others, but we do not make our friends suffer; that is the parasite (*Sami jeung urang,*

numpang hidup di batur ... bari urang enteu nyusahkeun ka batur ... itu namina parasit). What we are going to learn here is not about the parasite, but the predator. For instance, this *bobotolan* (ground beetle) preys on *wereng* (brown plant hopper), and this spider preys on moths. Thus, anything that has the function to prey is a predator (*Berarti kalau yang sifatnya memakan itu berarti predator*). The predator usually has a bigger body than its prey. An example is a frog. A frog is a predator, a natural enemy. Usually it preys on smaller things.

For the first time, in explaining the role of the parasite, the pest observer used the white rice borer as an example. He also mentioned the predator of WRB moths. This verbal explanation was followed by exercises. First, the farmers had to draw four kinds of predators on a piece of paper, and second, write down what each predator preyed upon. Third, the representative of each group had to imitate the predators' behaviour: how they walked and how they preyed on pests.

Without direct evidence on prey-predator relations, the farmers became confused when they had to write down what preys on what. The majority of them did not know what to write. They asked questions: "... Spider preys on what?" "... *Bobotolan* preys on what?" "... *Kukuyakan* preys on what kinds of pests?" For some new natural enemies, the farmers had no prior knowledge of their prey. Even for spiders, they could only identify the prey after being led by the trainers:

> "Spiders prey on what? Would the moths be preyed upon or not? (*Laba-laba makan apa? Kupu-kupu dimakan enggak?*)." "Eaten (*Makan*)," answered the farmers. Then the pest observer led them again, "What kind of moths? (*Kupu-kupu naon?*)." "*Aprel* (white stem borer moths)," answered the farmers again. "Now, write it down: *kupu-kupu aprel*," said the pest observer.

For most of the time, the pest observer had to lead the farmers to identify the prey, e.g.: *Bobotolan* preys on small brown plant hopper, or *nimfa* (nymphs); the *kukuyakan* also preys on small brown plant hopper and WRB eggs. Although the farmers had to carry out exercises and both parties were involved in a dialogue, the interaction in this communicative event relied heavily on the trainer's narrative explanation. In this event, the pest observer also explained about the differences between "pests" (*ada satoanana*) and "diseases' (*tidak ada satoanana*). In the next stage, the trainers introduced the effects of pesticides on natural enemies.

EFFECTS OF "MEDICINES" ON NATURAL ENEMIES

Mengenal Pestisida (Knowing about Pesticides) was a session in which the IPM farmers could directly observe the impacts of pesticides on natural enemies. The farmers had to count within how many minutes the natural enemies died. The experiment used two kinds of pesticides: granular (*furadan*, carbofuran) and liquid pesticides (*azodrin*, monokrotofos) put in two different cups. In each cup the farmers had to put different kinds of natural enemies, i.e., spiders and *bobotolan*. After noting the time the first spider died followed by the second and third, the farmers had to count the average time; and so with the other natural enemy. The trainers asked them to write down the results and draw a conclusion about what was going to happen if pesticides killed the natural enemies, what would be the effects on pests and other aspects of environment.

Through the experiment, the farmers were able to observe directly that natural enemies were killed by pesticide. The question posed to them was, however, a difficult one to answer. The linkage between the killing of natural enemies, pests, and environment was something beyond their empirical world. Hence, they had to think and imagine things that had never been observed empirically. The IPM farmers in one group were guessing that the impacts might be dangerous to the environment, but how? The pest observer helped them by stating the results of their own experiments. Arguments among themselves occurred without any agreement. Understanding the difficulties the farmers had, the pest observer led them again:

> "... The spiders and *bobotolan* were sprayed by carbofuran and *azodrin*. First, what are the impacts on the environment, the environment will be ... more or less ... damaged or not? (*Ayeune kieu. Disemprot ku carbofuran jeung azodrin, kana lingkungan kumaha pertama, lingkunganana kira-kira, rusak enteu?*)." Farmers answered: "Damaged (*Rusak*)." Pest observer: "Now, from the viewpoint of the environment, it will be damaged, polluted. Then by spraying spiders and *bobotolan* automatically, what will happen to the pests? Now if the natural enemies have died, ..., more or less ... what will happen to the pests? (*Nah, kalau musuh alami itu mati, terhadap hama itu bagaimana? Sekarang kan musuh alaminya mati, ..., kira-kira yang akan timbul itu bagaimana, untuk hamanya itu? ...*)" Farmers then answered: "Harmful (*Merugikan*)." Gradually they came to a consensus that: "If spiders and *bobotolan* died, the plants will be damaged, so ... so ... the pests will damage the

paddy (*Apabila laba-laba dan bobotolan mati, padi akan rusak, maka ... maka ... hama-hama tersebut akan merusak tanaman padi*)."

After being led by both the pest observer and the extension worker, all groups arrived at similar conclusions—with some slight variation—that the environment would be damaged and that the natural enemies would disappear, so the pests would multiply out of control. On his own initiative, the extension worker explained further:

> ... Thus if the spiders and the *bobotolan* are sprayed with *azodrin* and *furadan*, they are killed. Second, the natural enemies will disappear and there will be a pest outbreak, because the paddy is not in balance (*padi tidak seimbang*).... When the natural enemies are extinct, the pests exist, so the pests' life is free, and thus they can multiply. Like ... the outbreak of white rice borer. This outbreak occurred because the natural enemies were out of balance (*musuh alami tidak seimbang*) ... the paddy was destroyed. The damage occurred because other natural enemies were killed. Our environment was polluted, the water was polluted, and so were the lives of others. If the environment is continually sprayed, it will be polluted. Like fish, if they are continuously sprayed, their life will be hampered. Maybe they will be killed as well.

In this narrative, the trainers provided a story about the damage to the paddy if the populations of pests and natural enemies were not in balance by citing the example of the white rice borer outbreak. They also told the farmers about pollution and its further impact on water and fisheries. At the end of the session, the pest observer expanded the story by using the example of pest outbreaks in their own area, the JALUR PANTURA region. Through this verbal statement, the farmers received the trainers' propositions imaginatively. However, through a repetition of exercises and the use of farmers' experience of the WRB outbreak as the example, they gradually understood the concept of natural enemies and their role in the rice environment.

Conversations about insects—both pests and natural enemies—and diseases continued throughout training, not only within the formal sessions but also before and after training. Several farmers brought insects in plastic bags and asked the pest observer about their names, behaviours, effects on plants and how to control them if they were pests (e.g., the larvae of seedlings flies or *lalat bibit*, the eggs of spiders, or the eggs and larvae of white rice borer). In week VI, Idham brought a rice hill infected by "red disease" (*penyakit beureum*) to have the pest observer explain the disease and its causes, and how to control it.

Pesticides: their use, costs and consequences

Changing the farmers' perspectives in the use of pesticides needs a great effort to make them understand and believe that the new idea is significant for growing healthy crops. On many occasions the trainers had to respond to the farmers' expectations and perspectives that were based on their previous understanding of the use of pesticide. To convince them the trainers had to introduce and repeatedly explain the new idea throughout training. An analogy as found in interpreting the concept of "natural enemy" was not the case here. The farmers were even asked to twist around their perception of pesticides from "medicine" to "poison." A paradigm shift in the use of pesticide was the main focus of this training. Throughout the whole ten-week sessions, the farmers gradually learned to use the symbol of a different paradigm: the killing of insects and the prey-predator dynamics, not merely the prevention of crop illness. Preventing the crops from illnesses was the old dominant paradigm in the use of pesticides. Changing the representation of the learners, as mentioned by Petrie and Oshlag (1993), was what happened in this event of learning.

PESTICIDE: "OBAT," "NYEMPROT," AND "PESTISIDA"

The IPM experts aimed to change the farmers' views of pesticides from that of medicine, *"obat,"* to something poisonous (*racun*). The IPM farmers were not only expected to change their definition of pesticides, but also to replace the word "medicine" with "poison." The meaning of a word is, however, contextually defined. It depends on its use in the speakers' language. Farmers have used the word *"obat"* since the first introduction of pesticides in the Green Revolution era. This word has become part of their daily language in rice farming and designates a substance to cure or prevent illnesses on plants. The other terms are *"nyemprot"* as the abbreviation for *"nyemprot obat"* (spraying "medicines") and *"pestisida,"* a direct borrowing from pesticide. Until the end of training, no one changed the term *"obat"* to *"racun."* The following is an example of a dialogue between farmers and the pest observer using the terms *"obat"* and *"disemprot,"* a passive form of *"nyemprot"*:

> Idham (asking about the ways to control WRB): "... for the control of *penggerek*: what is the *'obat,'* Sir? Is there any medicine for destroying the eggs, or do we let the eggs hatch? Or, if we see the moth for the first time, do the moths have to be sprayed (*disemprot*), so as not to allow them to lay many eggs, Sir?" Pest observer: "Now, we are learning IPM. In my own view, if it is the moth, according to the recommendation from there (referring to the national agricultural officials) ... [the moths do not need to be sprayed]. It is true that if we go to the field quite often and if in the evening there have been many moths, it means that there will be many eggs in our *sawah*. How to control it? As I said, the moth does not need to be 'sprayed' (*Yang* untuk *dewasanya tidak usah disemprot*). This is according to the instruction from there, *pak*. What we have to pay attention to [are the eggs] ... because the moths are not dangerous. The dangerous ones are the eggs. It is true." Idham: "But, if there are no moths, no eggs." Another farmer gave his comment: "If the moths are not being killed ... [they will lay eggs]." Another farmer (Usin) mentioned the possibility of overlooking the eggs laid at a later stage. Idham continued: "If we 'spray' [the first egg], the other eggs will not be killed by the 'medicine,' Sir. (*Disemprot itu kan [yang lain-lain] enggak mati kena "obat," pak*). When the strength of the 'medicine' lessens, the eggs hatch again, live again." Pest observer: "The egg is not to be 'sprayed,' Sir." Idham: "Yes." Usin: "We mean that the 'medicine' is that from below: *obat butiran* (granular insecticide)." Pest observer: "Yes, but the 'medicine' persists for a long time." Idham: "For how long does the 'medicine' work?" Pest observer: "Up to twenty days, Sir."

Since the farmers used to say *"nyemprot"* or *"disemprot"* as an abbreviation for spraying "medicine," they often also used this word for broadcasting granular insecticide. In this dialogue the pest observer corrected the misused words. While he convinced them of the need to appropriately control WRB, he used the term *"obat"* for the granular insecticide as well. This dialogue suggests that although the two parties use the same word (*obat*), they communicate different expectations and perspectives. After gaining some knowledge about the WRB's reproductive cycle, the farmers expected to get an answer about the appropriate pesticide to "kill" WRB moths. The pest observer, on the other hand, tried to correct their perceptions with the instructions for controlling WRB as received from "above," the national government (the Directorate of Food Crop Protection, the Ministry of Agriculture). He did this from a position of authority.

Since the trainers themselves did not change the old terms for pesticide to "toxin" or "poison," the terms *obat* and *disemprot* persisted. In their duties as agricultural officials, the trainers themselves seemed to have been used to applying the old term when speaking to the farmers. As in the *Camat*'s speech in the opening ceremony, "pesticide" was presented as the real "medicine," used to cure illnesses in people. When explaining the meaning of IPM, i.e., the use of "medicine" as a last resort (*pakai obat merupakan jalan yang terakhir*), the pest observer made a reference to "people who got sick" and "took medicine as the last resort (*Seperti orang yang sakit dan minum obat merupakan jalan terakhir*)." Later on (in the middle of training) in his comments on farmers' talk about the use of pesticide, he repeated the analogy used by the *Camat* in his speech.

> Once, an IPM farmer reported: "There was somebody who sprayed the paddy with *Hopcin, pak* (*Ada yang disemprot maké Hopcin* [to control brown plant hopper], *pak.*)." Pest observer: "*Nah*, that is it. Thus, like a person who gets stomachache, but buys Bodrex [medicine to cure a cold instead of medicine to cure stomachache]. Thus, it is inappropriate (*Nah itu. Jadi, seperti orang nyeuri beuteung, meuli obat Bodrex. Jadi tidak tepat sasaran*)." Another farmer gave his comment: "... he is given medicine to kill worms (... *diberinya obat cacing*)." The other farmers laughed.

Besides providing examples of using medicine inappropriately, the trainers tried to convince the farmers of the need to avoid the use of the "strong medicine." In his explanation in the session on "Knowing Pesticide," the extension worker asked them to use pesticides wisely and not "to use the strong medicine (... *penggunaan pestisida ini harus secara bijaksana, jangan menggunakan obat yang keras-keras ...*)." Then he gave examples of the "strong medicines" such as: *Thiodan, Dursban, Elsan,* and *Sevin*. He told the farmers that:

> The recommended pesticides are only ten, *pak: Darmabas, Kiltop, Baycarb, Basa, Indofuran, Carbofuran* and *Curater*. Another one is *Darmafur*. The government recommended these.

An incomplete list of pesticides banned in the presidential instruction was relayed and of those, only *Thiodan* was repeatedly mentioned in various conversations.

THE USE, COSTS, AND CONSEQUENCES OF PESTICIDE

In many instances of verbal communication, the trainers gradually introduced three main propositions about the use of pesticide:

1. "medicine" as the last solution (*obat atau pestisida merupakan jalan terakhir*);
2. "medicine" is costly (*obat itu mahal beayanya*); and
3. "strong medicine" kills natural enemies that prey on pests and pollutes the environment (*obat yang "keras" membunuh musuh alami yang memangsa hama dan mencemari lingkungan*).

The other propositions stressed by the trainers were the effect of pesticide on pests' resistance (*obat membuat hama jadi kebal*), the need to use the appropriate pesticide and pay attention to farmers' own health.

In the early weeks up to the middle of training, however, the farmers still had the tendency to see killing or eradicating pests as the best response to their presence in the paddy when the number of pests outweighed the number of natural enemies. Only through the repeated explanations by the trainers did the farmers gradually understand the need to use pesticide judiciously. The following sections are examples of how these communications occurred.

"Medicine as the last solution." In the first week of training, the pest observer introduced the idea of "using 'medicine' as the last solution" in the context of explaining the meaning of IPM. He repeated this proposition again in his evaluation of the farmers' weekly presentations. In week VI, the farmers argued about the application of carbofuran in controlling WRB eggs. The pest observer used the idea of using "medicine" as the last resort in contrast to the preventative application of carbofuran according to the government package. The farmers, who gained knowledge that the only alternative to applying carbofuran was mixing it with fertilizer, still referred to this government recommendation in their discussions. On the basis of this knowledge, Idham argued against the pest observer's explanation about the working time of carbofuran (between 14 to 20 days). According to Idham,

> The moths used to come at the later growing stage of paddy, more than 15 days after the application of carbofuran with fertilizer. If we

have to apply carbofuran again and again, our 'pocket' [money] will be finished," argued Idham. Understanding the farmers' habit of mixing carbofuran with fertilizer according to the "package," the pest observer answered: "I myself will take this position, *pak*. Because this is PHT *ya pak,* I am implementing PHT. It is true that for us, the situation is difficult because the recommendation has been "packaged." The regional government recommended us to apply carbofuran. The field has to be "*Indofuran*" (referring to a brand of carbofuran). But I argue that carbofuran can only be applied if there are WRB eggs in the field. Carbofuran can be applied if the outbreak has occurred. Around 10% or above 10% [of the economic threshold level for *sundep*], we can apply carbofuran. But, if according to Pak Idham ... [to apply carbofuran with fertilizer], why we apply carbofuran while there is no outbreak ... maybe [there will be no outbreak] up to ... the "end of the world" (*paneuri kiamat teh*). Nah, that is why. According to PHT, we have to observe the field first. If there is an outbreak, start to apply carbofuran.

The pest observer also mentioned the appropriate amount of carbofuran to use if necessary. The farmers, by contrast, could not easily accept this novel idea. Iyub, for example, commented that "If we have to apply fertilizer without carbofuran, the condition of paddy would be similar to the situation when attacked by the mole cricket (*gaang*). It would be dangerous for the roots." Although Idham did not agree with Iyub's argument about the attack of *gaang*, he mentioned again his anxieties that the migration of pests would be a problem if carbofuran were absent, in particular under conditions where the transplanting schedule was not uniform. Knowing that the farmers had not been convinced by his explanation, the pest observer told them again:

> ... We are learning PHT, *Pengendalian Hama Terpadu* (Integrated Pest Management), *bapak* can use insecticide or carbofuran or others, if there has been no other way to take.... If later on there will be some moths, or eggs, ... we have to be careful. That is why with this PHT we have to go to the field often. Thus we know the conditions of the field, so that our paddy will not be attacked by pests without our consent. Thus, it is not right that we start reporting when there has been an outbreak .... [W]e have to observe first. If, for example, *bapak* feels that it is ... difficult to decide what kind of "medicine" to apply, you can consult the extension worker. Nah, we learn here to study the PHT problems. It does not mean that you are not allowed to use "medicine." However, please only use "medicine" if the other ways cannot solve it. So that is it, *pak*. As a last solution. It is not the same as the situation in which *bapak* knows there are moths, but without any

knowledge of what type of moths are there, you already apply *Thiodan*. What is the cost of *Thiodan*? Maybe 0.5 l per can. Rp.9,000.- per 0.5 l ....[6] And what are the pests? The moths, but you do not know yet what kind of moths there are. If you count the expenses, you will "lose" (*rugi*). Nah, ... that is why we are now learning, so that *bapak* knows about the life cycle (*siklus hidup*) of the moths, or learning about the *sawah* system. If we want to "spray" we have to take many things into consideration first (*harus banyak pertimbangan*). Whether this decision will make a loss for you (*merugikan*). And about the "medicine," if you spray with *Thiodan*, whether the environment will be damaged so that the natural enemies will die, so that there will be an explosion of pests. At the end, the moths will be plenty and cannot be controlled by their natural enemies.

In this explanation, the pest observer mentioned all the new ideas and perspectives on pesticide including the costs and the negative consequences on the environment and natural enemies. The pest observer had, however, to repeat it every time the farmers expressed their anxieties. The farmers' statements about WRB reflected again their orientations to eradicating pests, based on their previous experience of severe harvest failure. The visitors, the national and regional agricultural officials, also raised this proposition—to use pesticide as the last resort—during their visits to observe IPM training in Marga Tani (week VIII). After answering the farmers' questions about the ways of controlling pests and diseases, the team leader told them about various alternatives besides using pesticide, i.e., rotating rice varieties; cropping patterns; sanitation (e.g., cleaning up weeds from dikes); drainage intensity; and mechanical control such as handpicking WRB's eggs.

In the dialogue between the farmers and pest observers, or the farmers and national agricultural officers, the officials are in a strong position to influence and change the views of the farmers, the learners. The relationship of the officials as the authority and the farmers as the subordinates still dominantly underlay the communication between these two parties.

"Medicine is costly." Prior to IPM training, the farmers acknowledged the high price of pesticide and developed various strategies to reduce costs. For instance, Haji Ali decided to reduce the number of times he sprayed in the rainy season of 1989–90; the other farmers mixed an expensive pesticide and a cheaper one to produce the same amount

of liquid, or boiled a much lesser amount of granular insecticide than that recommended by the government. However, they could find ways to purchase pesticides even if they did not have any more capital. Armad reported that he decided to borrow money or purchase pesticide on credit to be able to buy pesticide to cure the "illnesses" of his paddy. Throughout training, the trainers convinced the farmers of the high costs of purchasing pesticides. The following is an example of the extension worker's suggestion:

> Continuously using pesticide means that we increase our costs, because the price of pesticide is now high .... For one litre only, the price can be up to Rp.18,000.- to Rp.20,000.-. With PHT we can reduce our expenses ... and the yields would still be high ... but without additional expenses ya ... Nah, with PHT we can reduce costs. First, we can reduce costs and then we conserve the environment. Because, if natural enemies are continuously eradicated, ... the growth of pests will accelerate.

The farmers' anxieties about the damage caused by pests or diseases to their plants, however, could not be eliminated at once. For two decades they have been accustomed to eradicating pests so as to secure their yields. They have also faced great risks and uncertainty in protecting their harvests. These anxieties were reflected in the IPM farmers' questions about controlling pests and diseases in front of visitors: the national agricultural officials. Ardi asked about the appropriate "medicine" to control seedling-flies (*lalat bibit*). Idham raised the issue of "red-disease" (bacterial red stripe) and asked for the effective medicine to prevent or cure the plants. The head of the Subdirectorate of Pest and Disease Control answered that the "medicine" was not available on the market yet, and that the price was very high, up to Rp.50,000/litre. She and the team leader (the director of the Extension Directorate, *Direktur Direktorat Penyuluhan*) advised the farmers to make early and continuous observations and remove the infected plants. On this occasion she told them to consider the costs of "medicine." Under conditions where they could not obtain high yields and earn high profits, using "costly medicine" would be a burden for them. The costs of production would be high. However, Idham expressed again his anxieties about attacks on plants that had already reached maturity. The official from BIMAS explained that there was another way to prevent this disease, i.e., by applying the recommended fertilizers. Idham still expressed his anxieties about the possible attack of another pest: rice gall midge. The director of the Extension Directorate then told the farmers again that using pesticide should be the last alternative.

As indicated by various conversations throughout training, verbal statements were the predominant means used by all parties to convince the farmers about costly pesticides and about possible alternatives to them in the control of pests/diseases.

"Medicine kills natural enemies, pollutes the environment and increases pests' resistance." The proposition that "medicine kills natural enemies and pollutes the environment" was introduced in the early weeks of training. The farmers learned about this message through the trainers' narrative explanations, the exercises and discussions in the sessions "What is This?" and "Knowing Pesticides." The only concrete example the farmers had was the killing of natural enemies by pesticide. The trainers thus repeatedly used the farmers' own experiences as examples. The pest observer referred to problems of pest attacks in the JALUR PANTURA region while evaluating the farmers' presentation in the session on "Knowing Pesticides." He explained all the damage that had been caused and might occur if the farmers continuously used pesticides injudiciously. The pest observer then pointed to their own experiments of how fast the natural enemies died from pesticides. The situation would be worse if they applied an excessive dosage of pesticide. He cited again the example of *Thiodan* as the most expensive and damaging pesticide, in particular if they did not apply it according to the recommended dosages. Then he asked the farmers to use the recommended dosage without providing any examples.

The pest observer emphasised the importance of paying attention to the farmers' own health during the exercise of spraying pesticide appropriately (week VII). He reminded them of the importance of filling the sprayer correctly, the need to use protective devices and to look at wind direction. At the end of this session, the pest observer introduced the consequence of spraying *Thiodan* on pests' resistance (*hama jadi kebal*). Again, *Thiodan* was cited as the example without mentioning the other banned insecticides. He also asked them to avoid the use of "strong medicines" (*jangan pakai obat yang keras*) and the same "medicines" continuously (*jangan memakai obat yang sama terus menerus*). This abstract statement was again presented verbally—followed by instructions—without any elaboration of how pesticide could increase pests' resistance. Another main exercise to change the farmers' perspectives was the weekly field monitoring in the session on agroecosystem analysis.

Field observation and agroecosystem analysis

Weekly field observation and analysis of the agroecosystem is the core of the IPM training. This is a session where the farmers are trained to analyze the ecosystem, to carry out weekly observations and make their own decisions. The farmers are observers, experimenters and strategisers in assisting their paddy to grow well and be healthy. However, methods needed for detailed, systematic observation: using diagonal random sampling, writing, drawing and counting were not part of their strategies. Mastering these skills took time. Accordingly, the interaction between the trainers and the learners—for most of the time—focused on learning these foreign methods. In addition, the issue of pest/disease control was emphasised rather than the overall agroecosystem analysis.

FARMERS' PARTICIPATIONS

Although the IPM experts had aimed to keep groups as small as possible, so as to allow each farmer to participate, the farmers' involvement in this session on agroecosystem analysis varied. Several factors seemed to contribute to this variation. The IPM farmers who took an active role in the group's activities were those who had the initiative to learn, who felt confident practicing these skills, or who dared to talk in front of many people in the group presentation. Another factor was the division of labour in the group's activities. The degree of participation also varied according to the type of activity.

Field observation was the first session and lasted from week two to week nine. Farmers had to go into the field to look at and note down the number of stems, insects, damage symptoms and natural enemies found in the sample. There were 15 samples of rice hills for each plot: the SUPRA INSUS and the PHT. The trainers put three bamboo sticks (*ajiran*) at each plot to identify the samples. Around each single stick, farmers had to make observations on five rice hills.

In the first exercise, the trainers asked everybody to collect whatever insects or animals they found. When the trainers asked them to start counting and taking notes in the following week, the group decided on who did the counting and who took the notes. The trainers instructed the other participants to collect whatever insects they found and put them in plastic bags. This division of labour persisted until the end of training. In week VII, the cultivator of the IPM plot—who did not receive any compensation—raised an objection to trampling in his field. The pest observer convinced him that the observation was to be carried out only once each week and only two farmers in each group were allowed to enter the field for the rest of the training. As a result of this modification, not all participants did the observation within the plots. The pest observer gave orders to the other farmers to do weeding or to collect insects in other fields. Many of them only stood at the dikes, watching their friends or conversing about the conditions of paddy. Back from the field, not all of them participated in drawing, counting, and writing up their conclusions. A varied degree of the participants' involvement in this session was a common phenomenon throughout the training. Only around 14 farmers out of 25 (56%) were active participants.

Other participants, however, were also involved in informal discussions while drawing, calculating and writing up their conclusions. They raised questions and comments about their findings. The following is an example of Adma's group's discussion about the reduction in the number of stems, and the population of natural enemies in different plots:

> Ardi: "... last week there were 30 stems in that rice hill, now there are only 28, it is reduced. Adma: "It is reduced because the fertilizer's application was too late. So, after [the stems were] growing, they became retarded." Then Adma asked Arpan how old the paddy was at that time. Arpan said that the age of the plants was 15 days. Idham in the other group listened to the discussion in Adma's group and gave his comment about the growth of stems. Another farmer then said that the reduction was also caused by the excessive number of seedlings transplanted at each place. According to Adma "... there were too many seedlings during transplanting: five to six seedlings." Answering my question Adma said that to be able to obtain the best result, the number of seedlings should only be two or three at each place. While drawing, the discussions continued about the spraying of pesticide at the SUPRA INSUS plot. One farmer reported that one plot

was sprayed and the other one was not. Arpan said that only one plot was sprayed, the SUPRA INSUS one. Arpan raised a question about the condition of natural enemies they found. "At the SUPRA INSUS plot there were many natural enemies and no pests. Here, at the PHT plot that was not sprayed, there were only a small number of natural enemies." Answering my question Arpan told me that he sprayed the SUPRA INSUS *plot* yesterday by using *Basa* in a mixture with other pesticides (*campur-campur*). ... After a while, Adma mentioned his findings: "There are five spiders at the PHT plot, while there are seven spiders at the SUPRA INSUS plot." Ardi: "It is strange, *bu* (speaking to me). At the plot that was sprayed there are many natural enemies, at the other one that was not sprayed, only a small number of natural enemies are found." Another farmer also expressed his confusion: "That is the 'peculiarity,' *bu*" ("*Itu yang aneh, bu*") ....

This conversation reveals the farmers' perception of the plants' conditions on the basis of their own understanding of fertilizer application and transplanting. The same perspective was used when they were discussing their findings about natural enemies, i.e., in relation to their new understanding about the impact of pesticide and their own practices in spraying pesticide. Why they found the reverse from what the trainers said should be found (more natural enemies in the plot treated with pesticides), they did not know. They did not ask the trainers either. Their analysis was, however, focused only on the results of their findings in the samples and not on the whole condition of the field, as was usual.

If every farmer felt free to express his opinions or to raise questions in the group's discussion, only a few farmers used the opportunity to engage the trainers after the groups' presentations. Idham was the most persistent, whereas the other farmers kept listening or raising comments. The diverse degree of farmers' presence and participation affected—to some extent—their understanding and ability to recall the new messages.

"EKOSISTEM": THE ECOSYSTEM

The ecosystem and the related components of a rice environment formed the basic unit of analysis in weekly monitoring. Throughout training, the trainers mentioned the term "*ekosistem*" many times. In practice, the farmers did the analysis of their fields in accordance with the experts' definition of ecosystem. Nevertheless, this term was entirely new. They had no prior knowledge of what it meant.

This term did not exist in their daily language, unlike words such as *sawah*, *petak*, and—a more recent word—*lahan* (all stood for "rice field"), or the names for what they found in the field. The farmers had no idea of the relation of these words to ecosystem. The trainers, on the other hand, never gave a verbal explanation about its meaning. Instead, the pest observer gave instructions only about what the farmers had to do and about what they had to consider in the discussions and conclusions. The introduction of this term was an example of how a foreign word, representing an abstract notion, was transmitted as just a word without a context to explain it.

In using this term, the pest observer or the extension worker pointed to various activities. For instance, the pest observer's instruction to carry out field observation: "*Sekarang kita akan melakukan pengamatan ekosistem dulu.* (Now, we will first carry out the ecosystem observation ...)." He repeated this instruction every week as he opened the training. Drawing the ecosystem was another activity related to this term. The trainers told the farmers to write down the word as the title of their drawing: "*Tuliskan di atas sini Ekosistem Minggu III* ... (Write down above here the Ecosystem of Week III ...)." So, the farmers repeated the writing of these words every week when they started to draw. They changed only the number of the week: week IV, week V, etc.

On some occasions, the pest observer mentioned the word "ecosystem" while directing the farmers on what to draw, or evaluating farmers' presentations. In the early weeks of training he told them not to think too much about spraying pesticide, because:

> "This discussion is the discussion of ecosystem (*Ini diskusinya diskusi ekosistem di sini*) .... It is too much to think of the problems of spraying pesticides .... Please, explain the results of your observation: what are the natural enemies, what are their 'illnesses.' Then, make conclusions, that it (the ecosystem) is like this, it should be treated like this."

On another occasion, the pest observer mentioned the meaning of ecosystem as the relation between paddy and natural enemies, or between pests and natural enemies. These examples reveal how the pest observer used a varied combination of words while stating the term "ecosystem." He pointed to diverse objects or conditions for the farmers' focus of attention without any verbal or any constant definition for those varied objects. The farmers' concept of the term thus varied. If Ucup thought about the place of insects in the paddy, Haji Ali imagined that the word stood for the schedule of observation (*jadwal*): week III, week IV, (*Minggu III, Minggu IV*) etc. The other farmers also had similar ideas.

The extension worker carried out similar ways of training—by using direct exercises and without detailed explanations—during his one-week IPM training at the FTF Jatisari. When I asked the two extension workers, they guessed that ecosystem stood for the relation between various components of the rice environment. One extension worker told me that he had never heard this term in his previous training and work. Since he just learned this term in the IPM training, he thought: "*Mungkin itu bahasa hama* (Maybe it is pest language)," the language used by those dealing with pests and not by the extension officials.

THE ECOSYSTEM ANALYSIS AND THE ECONOMIC THRESHOLD LEVEL

Instead of looking at and analyzing the whole plot as the farmers usually did, the trainers led the farmers to focus on the samples of rice hills. Despite interpreting the agroecosystem conditions of the plot, the trainers' emphasis was most often narrowed down to answering simple questions. For example, whether the plants needed to be sprayed, or whether the pest population had reached the economic threshold level (ETL) (also see van de Fliert 1993:139).

> While leading farmers to draw their conclusions on what they found in the field, the extension worker said: "Now, what is the conclusion. There have been some leaf folders already, nah, maybe *bapak* can draw a conclusion about how to treat this plant: Does the plant need to be sprayed or not? If not, what are your reasons; draw a conclusion." Again the extension worker led the farmers with a similar question: "*Apakah tanaman ini perlu disemprot atau tidak*? (Does this plant need to be sprayed or not?)"

The farmers, then, focused their answers on the need to spray the plants based on the number of pests and natural enemies. Looking at the farmers' orientations to the comparison between the average number of pests and natural enemies as the basis for making decisions, the pest observer told them to expand their analysis. He asked them to consider first what kind of pests and natural enemies were found and whether the pests would be preyed on by the natural enemies.

> The pest observer gave his comments on farmers' presentations (in week III): "... we do not need to focus only on the large number of natural enemies and the small number of pests. We have, however, to look first [at the other factors]. The natural enemies are spiders, *nya pak*, then, the pests are leaf folders. It is true that the leaf folders are preyed upon by the spiders, but are these [leaf folders] effectively preyed upon by these [spiders]?, so, don't first compare it with the natural enemies."

Second, the pest observer asked the farmers to look at the degree of attack or damage symptoms on plants.

> Let's look, however, at the "attack" only (*Kita lihat aja serangannya*). This is leaf folder *nya pak*. The leaf folder's attack on plant is too small if the population is only 0.06. Nah, for example, the leaf folder attacks one leaf of paddy. For instance, one leaf is completely finished by the leaf folder, so it means that for one rice hill the value or the score is four (4). If only half of the leaf is attacked, the value is two (2). Thus, from 15 rice hills, the attack is only slight (*hanya juruna wungkul*). Thus, you are right that it does not need to be sprayed. I think, however, that you do not need to compare it with the natural enemies. You can do this, but only if the attacks are bigger.

Although the pest observer tried to expand the farmers' analysis, he also led them to focus on the intensity of the pests' attack. Later on, the pest observer introduced the term *ambang ekonomi* (economic threshold) without a clear and detailed explanation of what it meant.

The introduction of the economic threshold level (ETL) focused on the type of pests found by the farmers in a particular week, for instance, the introduction of the "value (score) of leaf folder damage symptoms" (10% for deadheart symptoms) in week III, and the ETL of WRB eggs ($0.3/m^2$) in weeks IV and V. The farmers differed in their memory of these numbers. In Marga Tani, the participants referred to 25% damage symptoms of *sundep* (deadhearts), while those in Kebon Cau referred to 0.03% damage symptoms of *sundep*. In the following week, the pest observer corrected their mistakes. This is an example of how information received by the farmers deviated on the basis of what they remembered.

Memorizing a particular number is difficult for the farmers to do. Understanding this difficulty, in week VII, the pest observer dictated a list of the ETL for a number of pests. He asked the farmers to write them down in their notebooks. This process resembled the way teachers in a formal school dictate lessons. The IPM experts, on the other hand, do not favour this method. Some farmers who brought their notebooks (given by the trainers) wrote in them, but the other farmers just listened. The pest observer told them that what he meant by *batasan* (ceiling or limit) was:

> "... what number of pests need to be controlled" (*berapa hama itu yang harus dikendalikan*). Thus, the economic threshold was the ceiling to control pests (*Ambang Ekonomi ialah batas pengendalian hama*). He, then, mentioned the economic threshold of a number of pests one by one.[7] At the end of his statements, the pest observer told farmers to implement PHT if the condition of pests was below these economic thresholds. "If the attacks are small and you spray the pests, then it is not PHT practice (*Kalau di bawah ambang batas tersebut gunakan PHT. Kalau serangannya sedikit lalu disemprot, itu bukan PHT*)."

In this explanation, the pest observer equated the practice of IPM with a simple proposition for not spraying pests below the economic threshold levels. The participants' focus on control of fields on the basis of economic threshold levels became more common than the ecosystem analysis for field management. This perspective could be found in weekly presentations as shown in the week IX's group presentation:

For the first presentation, Iwan presented the conclusion of Group III as follows:

> SUPRA INSUS:
> "In the SUPRA INSUS I counted that the average number of stems per rice hill were 23. The natural enemies were *bobotolan*, 0.2/rice hill and spiders, 0.2/rice hill. No pests were found; but we found the attacks of rat, 10 stems from the total number of stems: $10/345 \times 100\% = 2.9\%$. The conclusion: rats have to be controlled by using poisons (*diumpan*) or by pumping the smoke of Zinc (*dikompos*)."

> PHT:
> "The average of stems were 17 stems. The natural enemy was *bobotolan*, 0.5/rice hill. No pests were found. The conclusion was similar to the other plot: no need to control it."

The farmers' understandings of the economic threshold level thus focused on the number of pests, the level of pest attack and damage symptoms, above which they had to take action. The trainers did not provide an explanation of ETL in relation to the costs, the yields, or any other factors. As van de Fliert (1993) found in Central Java, the pest observers in her research settings did not seem to be comfortable with explaining the many factors that have to be considered in the economic analysis of a farm. Hence they "fled back to their old, straightforward knowledge when they had to explain it to the farmers" (van de Fliert 1993:139) by which she meant the pest observers' knowledge prior to being trained at the IPM field training facilities. Since the ability to recall numbers relied heavily on memorization, the farmers' statements about the ETL numbers varied.

By contrast, in week IX, the trainers asked the farmers to draw their conclusions by referring to several factors of the rice ecosystem without any counting. In the session called *Ambang Ekonomi dan Tindak Lanjut* (Economic Threshold and its Follow-Up), the pest observer divided the five groups into three, each with a different insect pest to examine. He then gave a list of factors found in the field such as natural enemies, rice variety, weather, the incoming insect pests (immigrants), the age of insects, diseases, and rats. He also gave the farmers two lists of different conditions for each factor. One list, under the heading of the "odd" (*ganjil*), and the other list under the heading of the "even" (*genap*). The choice of odd or even was made by the farmers by calculating the date of birth of one farmer in each group. Finally, each group had a name of a pest and a list of variables and their conditions to be analyzed to reach a decision on whether a control action was necessary. In this case, farmers had to think—using their own imagination—about the relation of these variables. Farmers' reference to their own experiences became dominant as the discussion in Iwan's group suggests.

> Iwan's group had rice seed bugs (*walang sangit, kungkang*) as the pests found in the field. The field's conditions were defined as follows: no natural enemies, a resistant rice variety, cloudy weather, a small number of immigrants and mature insects. Farmers repeated these conditions several times in the process of imagining what the real conditions looked like before being able to find any answer. Iwan mentioned all the factors above, followed by Arman: "The rice seed bugs are relatively few." Haji Ali repeated it again: "In the *sawah* there are *nyak*, rice seed bugs, no natural enemies, the rice variety is resistant." Arman mentioned about the weather: "The weather is a bit dark (*mendung*), cloudy, so does it need to be controlled or not *teh*?" Haji Ali then

gave his conclusion: "No need to control it, no need." Amid, however, mentioned the condition of natural enemies: "No natural enemies, so the rice seed bugs have to be controlled." Arman agreed with Amid. Haji Ali, then, changed his mind: "It must ... (*Harus*)." Iwan led the farmers to draw their conclusions. "The rice seed bugs have to be controlled, because ... (and then he stopped, asking the other farmers) What are the conclusions?" The discussion continued until another farmer raised the condition of the weather, the small number of immigrants, and the age of the insects. When they discussed the age of the insects Haji Ali mentioned the age of the plants: "If the plants have not been flowering yet, no need to control it. The rice seed bugs do not disturb the plants." Iwan raised the question of the plants' age: "What is the age of the plants?" Iyub, then, asked the trainers about the age of the plants. Without waiting for the trainers' answer, Arpan said: "No need to consider the conditions of the plants ... there are rice seed bugs." Iyub: "It means the plants are at the flowering stage." The extension worker (from another village) approached the farmers and posed a question: "If the plants are at the flowering stage, what is your opinion?" Haji Ali seemed still in doubt. The extension worker stimulated the farmers again: ""Gradually, gradually the rice seed bugs will .... While there are no .. " In the end Iwan said that the pests should be controlled. Arman agreed because there were no natural enemies: "They will be preyed on by what?" "By rats ..." replied Iwan laughing. Asma and Iwan asked again whether the pests needed to be controlled. Haji Ali then said firmly, changing his mind again: "They have to be controlled, it should be (*Wajib pisanlah, kudu-kudu pisan gitulah*)."

After considering various factors, they found the most significant factor in relation to their own experiences: the mature rice seed bugs that were usually found at the plants' flowering stage. By considering the other significant factor, i.e., the natural enemies—though the number of pest immigrants was small—they were able to reach consensus on what they had to do with this pest. At this stage, farmers were able to incorporate the role of natural enemies into their analysis. The discussion in the other groups was also lively, although Idham's group had difficulties in understanding the game. Several words were also strange for them, such as *faktor* (factor) and *imigran* (referring to migrant insect pests).

In contrast to the previous conclusions, in this session the farmers drew their conclusions without any counting or reference to the economic threshold level. Ayim presented the conclusion of Group I with brown plant hopper as the main pest.

First, Ayim mentioned the conditions of the field: "The rice variety is resistant, there are no natural enemies, the weather is hot, the immigrants are few, the insects are at the mature stage ....Our conclusion: brown plant hoppers do not need to be controlled, because the variety is resistant and the weather is hot." Answering Iwan's question Ayim said that in the hot weather, the brown plant hopper cannot grow fast, whereas the rice variety is resistant. "… Ya, if the condition is hot like this, which [plants] are attacked by brown plant hoppers? None. There are some [BPH] in the fields, one or two, but they cannot grow fast," explained Ayim again. "How if suddenly bad weather occurs?" asked another farmer. Ayim replied: "It is okay if it comes only once, unless the bad weather comes continuously."

Ayim was very confident of his answer through referring to his own experience and the empirical fact of brown plant hopper's population in such hot weather. The farmers were, in fact, able to relate various relevant aspects of the rice ecosystem as they usually did. The emphasis of training on the calculation and the ETL, however, led them to focus only on the need to control pests or diseases rather than on an overview of how to manage the field and to grow a healthy crop.

Throughout training, the pest observer had, in fact, raised the importance of looking at various other field conditions during group discussion and analysis, for instance, water, weeds, sunshine, soil, age of plants, or timely fertilizer application. In week V, the farmers' conclusions incorporated the need to control weeds after receiving guidance by the pest observer to think about the weeds found in the field. During observation, the farmers overlooked the weeds by focusing more on counting and taking notes. On another occasion, the pest observer praised one group's conclusion that they should make observations as the appropriate way to proceed if they found an early indication of pests. This would allow them to follow the development of the pest population. When Idham brought a sample of plants infected by "red disease," the pest observer also mentioned various alternatives to consider besides spraying "medicine." Although the trainers had mentioned these other factors elsewhere, the emphasis on the economic threshold level led these trainers to put emphasis on training farmers to master the skill of calculation.

CALCULATION: STEMS, INSECTS AND DAMAGE SYMPTOMS

> Observation of the pest population density in the field is very important to be able to decide whether a pest control action is necessary or not.
>
> (my own translation, Program Nasional Pelatihan dan Pengembangan Pengendalian Hama Terpadu 1991a:83)

This is the fundamental reason why the calculation of pest density and damage symptoms was emphasised strongly throughout the training. For the farmers, calculation was not an easy skill to master. Counting yields and expenses were part of their daily and seasonal activities. However, drawing, counting and writing as practiced in training were not an important part of their traditions in cultivating rice. In most of the agroecosystem analysis sessions the trainers had to assist farmers in mastering these skills. Only through trainers' corrections of errors week-by-week, did the farmers gradually master this skill. The farmers' ability, however, varied due to the varying degree of participation and their ability to grasp and memorize such an abstract concept. Although counting the average number of stems was not difficult to master, i.e., n stems/n rice hills; it was not easy for farmers to differentiate the calculations for insects from damage symptoms:

For insects: $\dfrac{\text{n insects}}{\text{n-rice hills}}$;

For damage symptoms: $\dfrac{\text{n stems damaged}}{\text{n stems in n-rice hills}} \times 100\%$.

This confusion persisted up to week VI.

In response to the farmers' difficulties and my feed back on how confusing the calculation was for the farmers, the trainers, in cooperation with the head of the BPP, designed a game as a way to stimulate their motivation to understand this method. The trainers and the BPP staff provided the winners with money and a pack of cigarettes. Nevertheless, in the following week (week VIII), one visitor from the national agricultural officials' team who visited Marga Tani still found mistakes in the farmers' counting. The head of the BPP told him that they had already given explanations about this problem many times, and yet the farmers still made mistakes. When one of the national agricultural officials commented on Idham's questions about the disease on plants, he warned them not to make mistakes in their calculation:

> To count pests find the average per rice hill; do not put a percentage. This counting is important because the conclusion from this calculation will indicate the economic threshold: whether paddy needs to be sprayed or not.

The economic threshold was, once again, stated as the criterion to spray paddy based on the results of calculation. Calculation was, thus, a significant factor in the ecosystem analysis as perceived by many parties: the local trainers, the head of the BPP, as well as the national agricultural officials. The IPM experts, on the other hand, perceived that the "experience threshold" was more important than the "economic threshold" (Dilt, personal communication 1991).

In the last session of the Ecosystem Analysis (week IX), the trainers still found the farmers' mistakes in the use of percentages. As soon as the training was over, they forgot the counting formula. *"Tidak ingat lagi"* (I cannot remember it anymore), or *"Repot, pakè itung-itung segala* (It is troublesome to do the countings)," were the answers I got from Arman, Ucup, and many other farmers.

Farmers' questions and conversations

Local ecological conditions became the main reference in carrying out the entire training. Accordingly, the experts had designed some particular topics from which the trainers could select those which were significantly related to the problems *in situ*. Knowing pesticides, predator and parasite, spraying pesticides and health aspects, agroecosystem analysis and follow-up were examples of those topics. In Marga Tani, the pest observer decided to provide the farmers with several other topics: life cycle and food web, rat population, rodenticides and some group dynamics. The once-a-week IPM training was also a good opportunity for the farmers to raise questions derived from everyday problems and experience. The pest observer welcomed their questions while he was still visiting them.

For the 25 participants, the training session was an opportunity to meet together. Before and during training they could converse about their daily problems and practices. What questions and problems were raised by the farmers in each school and when they were raised varied according to the diverse conditions in each school. As a result, the explanations received by the farmers about pests/diseases and the ways to control them in each school varied. A modification in the training session was also carried out by the trainers as their responses to particular ecological conditions.

Questions were also raised by the farmers repeatedly through several weeks of training followed by observations and practices as taught by the trainers. The following are examples of their queries on WRB.

> In week V, Idham, Ayim, Usin, and the pest observer were talking about WRB before the training. Idham asked the pest observer about the life of WRB moths, how long they would stay alive. The pest observer's answer stimulated Idham to raise further questions about the life of the eggs and the moths. For the first time they learned that the moths died after laying eggs four or five times. "... So, if the mother died, how could the eggs hatch (referring to the chicken's life cycle)?" asked Idham. The pest observer gave an explanation about when and how the eggs hatch. Idham then mentioned the need to eradicate the moths. The pest observer replied that there would be a new "pesticide" released: *Karpos*, but it was still in the testing process. He continued his explanation about the eggs and asked farmers to collect the eggs and make an observation. If larvae came out, similar things would happen in the field. So, farmers could apply *Furadan*. Idham replied that it would be better to eradicate the moths rather than let them lay eggs.

In his evaluation of the farmers' presentations in week VI, the pest observer told them again to remember the economic threshold of *sundep*. He said that,

> "If it reaches 10%, *bapak* can apply carbofuran." One farmer corrected the pest observer's explanation by referring to the previous information received from the other pest observer, i.e., 25% (see above). The pest observer again corrected farmers' mistake. Responding to farmers' questions, the pest observer told them the ways to count *sundep*. He tried to convince farmers by referring to the "white book's recommendation." "That is the economic threshold—the limit at which the pests have to be controlled. This is by looking at the recommendation in the white book." Again, the "white book" as published by the national agricultural officials was cited as the only correct source of information. After answering farmers' questions about red disease, which he referred to as the "bacterial leaf streak" (*bakteri daun bergaris*) and the way to control it, the pest observer drew the WRB life cycle as his response to farmers' questions (see fig. 4.2).

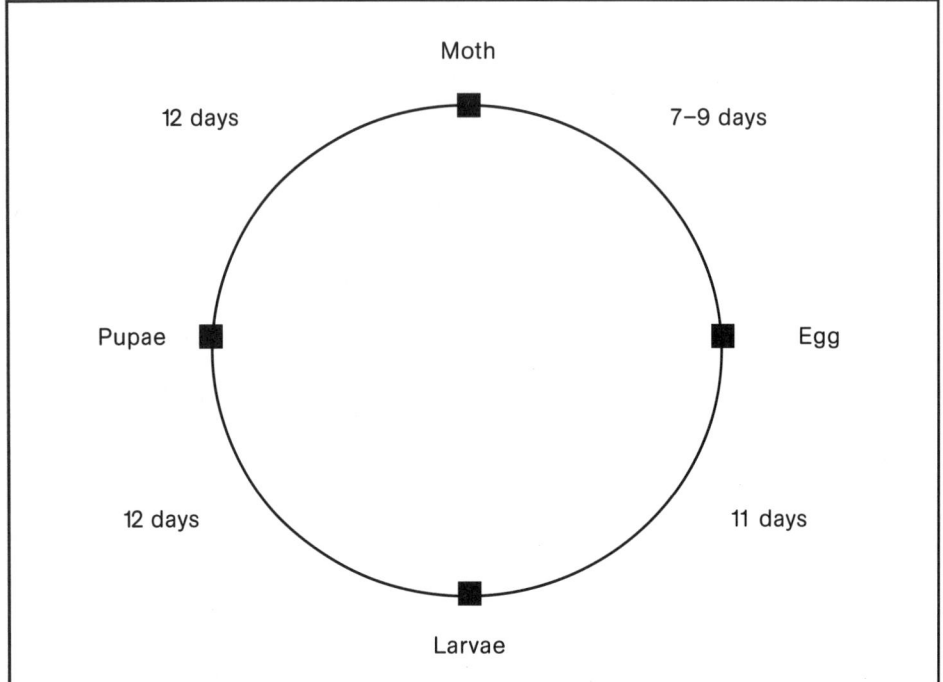

Figure 4.2 *The white rice stem borer's life cycle*

After drawing the life cycle, the pest observer mentioned the length of each stage: 7–9 days for the life span of moths; 11 days for the egg's incubation; 12 days for the larvae to grow and then reach the pupal stage; and 12 days for the pupa to stay alive before changing into moths. He also told the farmers the length of the diapause period (*masa diapause*)—the pupa's resting period—in the previous years and in the fallow period that could reach up to four months until the rain came. In recent times, it only lasted up to 12 days. Questions and answers continued.

> Adma raised a question about the number of larvae hatched from one egg cluster. The pest observer told them that between 50 and 150 larvae could hatch from one egg cluster. "*Buset...* (dear me!)," replied a farmer. Farmers grumbled about the number of the larvae. Idham tried to count: "50 up to 150, five times." Arman: "It could be up to one trillion." Idham counted it again: "... It only happened within one

month. From one moth could hatch 650 larvae. If there are five moths, how many larvae could hatch from the eggs within one month. Five times 650, it reaches 3000 already. The 3000 hatch again, so it becomes how many millions." The discussions still continued about the WRB, and about the appropriate way to control this pest by using carbofuran, the appropriate amount of carbofuran and the working time of carbofuran, etc.

In weeks VII and VIII, the farmers (Iwan, Arman, Ardi) brought the samples of larvae hatching from the eggs they had been collecting. These farmers carried out their own experiments by collecting the egg clusters, putting them into the plastic bags, and observing what hatched out from the eggs.

> The farmers discussed these findings and identified them as larvae, the differences between larvae and parasites, when the eggs hatched, what the farmers did following the results of their own observations, etc. The pest observer confirmed their findings that it was the larvae and not the parasites that hatched from the eggs. In week VIII the farmers borrowed the extension worker's magnifying glass (*kaca pembesar*) to observe closely what the larvae looked like. The farmers also found several egg clusters during field observation. Asma, for example, learned for the first time the form of the WRB eggs. Other farmers tried to identify the differences between WRB eggs and spiders' eggs.

Gradually, the participants received information about the WRB from verbal statements, a drawing of its life cycle, and their own findings through collecting and observing the hatching of the eggs. Several farmers did the carbofuran application after knowing the results of their own observation as taught by the pest observer, i.e., by discovering that larvae instead of parasitoids hatched from the eggs. Their initiatives in bringing samples of larvae to training contributed to the spread of this knowledge to those who did not make observation, and to the spread of other information, such as the farmers' own experiments with kerosene in a mixture with fertilizers, a practice that was not recommended. The IPM training thus became an arena for farmer-to-farmer transmission. This was also the setting where the IPM farmers learned for the first time about the WRB reproductive cycle and strategies for its control. They already had knowledge of a simpler reproductive cycle, such as in a chicken, without having the special term for the cycle they just learned (*siklus hidup*). Also, they had not incorporated this notion into a pest control strategy. Combining these two domains: the life cycle of an insect and the pest control strategy in rice farming was an improvement in their knowledge repertoire. The IPM "school" thus significantly contributed to the understanding of these novel ideas.

THE IPM "SCHOOL" IS AN EXAMPLE of transmitting scientific knowledge and strategies to the local people by incorporating the people's actual participation. The case of the IPM "school" in Marga Tani is a mirror of how the national plan and design were implemented at the local level by local government officials. The stories in this chapter reflect their efforts to adjust the national design to local conditions; to implement the ideal "discovery-experiential learning process" by changing the learners' perspectives and behaviours; and to use and explain the scientific terms in actual conversations with the learners. A combination of introducing new concepts and ideas in narrative explanations and stimulating the participants to learn and discover on their own was what I found in the course of training. The learners' reactions, difficulties, understanding or misunderstanding fed back to the trainers. In many cases, the trainers slipped back to the conventional way of providing extension or teaching students as if in a formal school. In the whole process of learning, the farmers were in fact interpreting the newly introduced ideas within their own existing schemas or models of interpretation in rice farming (see Sweetser 1987 on the people's simplified world of areas of particular experiences). Moreover, they learned by practice how to enlarge the range of references as well as to change their perspectives in pest management. The active engagement of the participants in this transmission of knowledge resembles the kind of "learning-as-construction metaphor" mentioned by Ortony (1993: also see Mayer 1993; Petrie and Oshlag 1993).

Convergence in the farmers' understanding of the various ideas can be attributed to the consensus the farmers were able to reach by receiving gradual and repetitive explanations and practices by also referring to their common experiences through diverse means of learning. Divergence occurred because of the diverse nature of transmitting the new ideas to the learners and the variation in the learners' ability to interpret them by using their existing schemas of interpretations. The variation in individuals present, the participation and capability of learning the abstract ideas, as well as memorizing numbers and counting formulae, affected the diverse individual reception. The diverse results in the learners' knowledge were profound. First, there was an improvement in the learners' classification of insects by incorporating the idea of "predator" into their existing categories of insects. Moreover, there was a distinction made by the learners between insects that perform their function as predators and those that act as pests. A set of new schemas of interpretation, the prey-predator dynamics, became the basis of their recent understanding of the role of this new category of insect. Second, there was an effort on the learners' behalf to shift their paradigm in pest management as intended by the trainer, i.e., by taking up the meaning from another paradigm: "the killing of insects and the prey-predator dynamics." However, the old term in the earlier paradigm: "medicine" instead of "poison" persisted. Even the trainer himself used this paradigm in his effort to change the farmers' perspective. Third, the learners experienced an improvement in the skills of carrying out observation and analysis about their fields' conditions. Nevertheless, there was a modification or even a missed interpretation and incomplete understanding of alien concepts such as the economic threshold level and the ecosystem. Four, through learning about the white rice borer's life cycle and metamorphosis, their existing schema of animals' life cycles was extended. In addition to this, they learned to combine this schema of understanding with the strategies of controlling pests. If previously they had based their pest management on the presence of "whatever insects" in their fields and on regular spraying as a preventative measure, now they learned to look not only at the average population of both pests and predators, but also at the pest's life cycle. How the learners further interpreted these new understandings, validated and communicated them outside the "school" setting, will be presented in the following chapter.

5

"Now Our Way of Thinking Is Different"

> "Now, our way of thinking is different, isn't it? (*Sekarang itu jalan pikiran sudah lain ya, iya dong*)," said Iwan following his explanation of the difference IPM training made to him.

FOR IWAN and many other IPM farmers, training provided new frameworks or schemas of interpretations about pest management, including the consequences of the injudicious use of pesticides. By using these new frameworks, most of them were able to interpret and explain both their past experiences and previous phenomena for which they were unable to find solutions. The most frequent case referred to by the farmers was their ignorance about white rice borer and their mistakes in taking action to control them. Another example was the "explosion" of rats. Akim, in front of the other non-IPM farmers, explained that,

> rats can multiply out of control ... because those that prey upon rats have become extinct. Snakes, crows, ... now they have disappeared. Previously the pest and its predator were in a state of balance. Now, it is imbalance; that is why the rats multiply out of control.

The introduced knowledge was perceived as beneficial in advancing their knowledge rather than devaluing their previous knowledge. In the discussion about development and the role of scientific knowledge, some scholars argue, as Hobart (1993:10) says, that in development " ... local knowledges [are] being devalued or ignored in favour of western scientific, technical and managerial knowledge." For the farmers, awareness of the interdependence of their world of rice farming and modern science and technology makes plain the inadequacy of their knowledge to solve unforeseen problems and risks. The new inputs on the basis of the introduced scientific ideas fill the gap in their existing schema of interpretation. It is evidence that farmers are able to produce a new combination of ideas on the basis of their own and the introduced ones.

Despite appreciating the improvement in their knowledge, the IPM farmers perceived that the IPM ideas should be empirically proved in the course of daily farming activities. Local knowledge is embedded in practice, acquired from doing things, situated in time and place, adjusted and modified to particular circumstances and subjected to validation and modification (see chap. 3; also Bourdieu 1977, 1990; Dougherty and Keller 1985; Harper 1987; Richards 1989b, 1993; Lave 1988, 1996; van Beek 1993; van der Ploeg 1993). IPM knowledge, on the other hand, was introduced to the farmers as propositions and methods already established by scientific procedures outside the farmers' experiences. In the farmers' perspective, this knowledge still existed at the narrative level and had not yet been validated. The following discussion among IPM farmers reveals this concern:

> When I joined Adma's group in week VI of IPM training, Wira told me that "The PPL (extension worker) should cultivate rice by himself." "So that the other farmers can observe it," agreed Ardi. Adma imitated what the farmers would say if the PPL carried out his own rice cultivation: "Oh, the performance of PPL's cultivation is good, so he is right ...." For Adma, the PPL's activities " ... are only for experimentation .... He can be one of our rice-field neighbours. Thus, the PPL cultivates rice himself, together with us. He can cultivate one plot of rice-field." Akim said that, first, there should be evidence to be observed: "For example, there is a successful performance [of rice farming] in Binong. The farmers in Cabang are then invited to go there to take a look ... so that the farmers can have confidence, *bu*. The PPL should not just 'talk' like that. Hence, we can see [the results] ourselves."

This conversation illustrates how the farmers perceived the trainers as "expert-outsiders" who were only "talking" without "doing." So was the IPM school that, in the farmers' eyes, was not sufficient enough for a proof without real practices. In the course of training, the farmers were thus trying to prove and validate IPM ideas by their own methods. Through daily activities, the IPM ideas had undergone interpretation, verification, modification and elaboration. Each farmer interpreted the new ideas in light of previously acquired knowledge of various components of the rice environment and his own practical experiences, interests and beliefs. Each farmer had his own unique experience, a bundle of memory about past events and the ability to understand abstract concepts. To some degree, formal education assisted the IPM participants to understand the introduced abstract concepts. However, some of the participants who only had primary education were also able to gain a good understanding of the novel ideas. Diverse interpretations of IPM knowledge thus prevailed. Interpreting ideas and drawing inferences from new experiences also occurred as the farmers engaged in daily conversation and interaction with each other. In the first section of this chapter, I will describe how the IPM farmers interpreted these new ideas.

The second section of this chapter will examine the way they undertook such activities and referred to this knowledge in controlling pests and disease in the 1990 dry season. Reinterpretation, modification, or manipulation of knowledge can emerge, in particular under the condition of indeterminacy, inconsistency and ambiguity (see Moore 1975; also, see Rosaldo 1993; Bruner 1993). A complex set of contextual factors might also affect their decisions and behaviour. (See Jarvie 1969; Schelling 1978; Elster 1983; Vayda 1986 for factors affecting individual's actions.)[1] This section discusses the extent to which IPM knowledge—as a formula for analyzing and making decisions—functions in the farmers' complex situation. The third part deals with the efforts of IPM farmers to disseminate their recent understandings to those who did not internalize these alien terms and propositions through training.

Interpreting Novel Ideas

IPM came after a series of programs and problems in rice intensification. The farmers' assessment and interpretation of IPM should be seen as part of their ongoing experiences. Their recent problems and understandings were only parts of the consequences of the earlier rice programs.

Evaluating IPM: the benefits and weaknesses
The introduction of IPM knowledge not only provided the farmers with new categories to represent previously unknown phenomena,

but also functioned as a means of choosing alternative ways of gaining benefits while avoiding hazards from pest outbreaks. Variations, however, do prevail according to individual interpretations in relation to their needs, confidence, and understanding.

As presented in chapter 4, the farmers conceived the terms "natural enemy" and "predatorship" as beneficial in allowing them to differentiate insects and their roles in the rice environment. Previously, they did not know which insect eats which. They also thought that all insects found in the paddies were pests. The new understanding had further implications for the farmers' perceptions of their own practices: from the stage of being "satisfied with killing all animals" to being more careful in spraying pesticides. Asma reported that:

> I knew from SLPHT *[Sekolah Lapang Pengendalian Hama Terpadu]* that Thiodan is not allowed for use on rice because it can kill all [animals], all can die. Before, [I felt] satisfied that of them all were dead: frogs, spiders, dragonflies, parasites. Previously, I did not understand that some of these were the farmers' friends (*batur petani*) .... So, SLPHT is beneficial.

The other IPM farmers experienced an improvement in their state of mind, i.e., by being calm and not as concerned as before if they found pests in their *sawah*, since they knew that: "if there are pests, there will be natural enemies" (as told by Armin). In line with the introduced manner of observation, a different approach could be taken if they found pests in their *sawah*. "Now, we first observe the field to know the condition of pests and to follow its development," said Ayim and Ardi. They could now avoid unnecessary spraying of pesticides. As Arman and Haji Ali put it:

> "Before, while spraying, I did not see the development [of the pests]. If the time to spray came, I would just 'spray' it; whether there were pests or not," told Arman. "According to PHT, [we must] observe first," added Haji Ali. Arman continued: " ... this is the experience from PHT. [We must] observe whether there are pests, or whether the pests outnumber the natural enemies." "Yes, there are many benefits [from PHT]," agreed Haji Ali.

In this dialogue, Arman reinterpreted the concept of the economic threshold as the outnumbering of pests over natural enemies.

By understanding the need to conserve natural enemies, observe the insect populations and avoid the use of the most expensive and destructive insecticide, *Thiodan*, the major benefit seen by the farmers was cost reduction. Even for Adma, who was not confident about spraying "medicine" judiciously, reducing the frequency of spraying had reduced his expenses. Adma was a model farmer who was known by the other farmers as the most industrious person in "spraying medicines" (*yang paling getol nyemprot*). Another major benefit of IPM training was their understanding about the cause of the severe attack of WRB. Their new understanding of WRB reproduction helped them to take more appropriate action to avoid being careless, uselessly spraying medicines and killing natural enemies.

Not all farmers had the same perspectives about gaining benefits from understanding the other concepts, e.g., the economic threshold level, the manner of field observation, the life cycle, the food chain, or the way of enumerating pests and natural enemies. Some farmers were skeptical or unclear about the improvements they could gain by field observation and/or the enumeration method (e.g., Arman, Ucup and Win):

> Win told me that the only significant thing he gained from IPM training was the use of pesticide by referring to the economic threshold level. He did not think he learned anything new from training, since he already knew from his own observations that " ... spiders eat dragonflies and dragonflies eat *bobotolan* (*O. nigrofasciata, Carabidae*)," although he did not know what this particular insect preyed upon. He mentioned further that " ... it is not necessary to observe and count, because 'illnesses' can be controlled ... I also used to pull out the stems of the paddy. So, I do not understand the use of field observation and counting. Pests will die if we spray or apply *Indofuran*, that's all."

Win was known by the other farmers as a hard-working farmer and labourer, although he was not considered a model, expert farmer. Like Adma—the model, expert farmer—he felt confident of his own knowledge and strategies to secure the paddy from "illnesses." Onol, a nonfarmer (the head of a neighbourhood and a village officer), on the other hand, claimed that by following IPM training he gained knowledge of how to cultivate rice. His understanding was, however, limited. In training, he only listened and seldom participated in field observation and group discussions.

The extent to which IPM training provided benefits was also perceived in light of the individual's interests and needs. Diloh, Akim, and Asmid mentioned the advantages they gained from receiving information on fertilizers. Since there was no formal session on fertilizers in training, individual farmers acquired this information through conversations with the trainers or from the visitors from Jakarta. Iwan, on the other hand, complained about the lack of information on fertilizers, something he wished to know more about. Ayim and Idham also argued for the importance of having an adequate knowledge of soil fertility and the appropriate treatment of soils. Ardi, Iwan, and Idham complained about the incomplete information. They perceived the training as concentrating more on controlling pests than on rice farming in general (*budi daya tanaman padi*). Idham conceived the trainers' explanations of pests and diseases as not comprehensive enough compared to the entire complex of pests and diseases found in their overall environment.

The farmers had to respond to and solve all the problems occurring in their fields. In their eyes, rice farming is an integrated activity that cannot be fragmented as it is in agricultural bureaucracies and sciences. According to Shiva (1988:233), modern science, including agricultural, is " ... quintessentially reductionist." This science—as a dominant knowledge—is also fragmented, and the " ... fragmented linearity of the dominant knowledge disrupts the integrations between systems" (Shiva 1993:12). Although the competency objectives designed by the IPM experts covered other aspects of rice farming (see Appendix 4), the training focused more on shifting the paradigm in pest control. The training was also carried out in collaboration with the Directorate of Food Crop Protection with the pest observers as the primary trainers. Fertilizers and other aspects of rice farming were the responsibility of BIMAS and the extension services. Talking about these matters was beyond the pest observers' responsibilities (R. Dilts, personal communication 1991). Although training was supposed to have been based on "learning by experience," such experience contributed to the trainers' explanations only when problems emerged during field observation and training (van de Fliert and Winarto 1993:17). The trainers' explanation thus did not cover the entire range of pests/diseases in the rice environment.

Interpreting IPM: questions, arguments, and modifications

Farmers do not passively receive information. Rather, they interpret and transform information in a manner that is inflected by their pre-existing understandings and schemas of interpretations (see Sweetzer 1987; Rosaldo *et al.* 1993). The farmers interpreted recent ideas and events in a context not unconnected with past events, objectives and understandings (see Connerton 1989). In what follows I will show how the farmers as active subjects questioned, argued, evaluated or modified IPM ideas.

UNINTELLIGIBILITY AND DISAGREEMENT

The method by which trainers introduced new terms and propositions affected, to some extent, the farmers' understandings. Some farmers, for instance, questioned the missing link between several propositions explained separately by the trainers. Ardi could not connect several distinct propositions intelligibly:

> Ardi complained that he had always been in a whirl when thinking more about IPM. He told me that "the trainers said the development of pests was balanced by the natural enemies. But why, they made a problem out of it .... As Pak Idham said, '... the development of pests is balanced by the natural enemies, so there is no need to spray.' However, why is there an economic threshold level? As in the case of white rice borer yesterday (in the previous season), did the natural enemies prey on the pests? Why was there a severe outbreak? According to Pak Sardi, '... if there are many pests, there will be many natural enemies.' But, why do we have to apply *Furadan*? Why is there an economic threshold?" Then, answering himself, he said that: "Maybe that is just the theory, *ya*, in practice, in the field, it may not be like that."

While introducing the economic threshold concept, the trainers did not comprehensively explain its further consequences for pest populations, degree of damage or farmers' expenses following decisions to control pests. The population dynamics of pests and natural enemies were explained by the pest observer in a separate session without any linking to the concept of the economic threshold level. For Ardi, these two propositions, the economic threshold and the dynamics of pests and natural enemies, were contradictory. A similar confusion was also voiced by Idham and Usin who could not accept the pest observer's recommendations. They expressed their disagreement on two issues.

First, they could not understand the pest observer's explanation for avoiding the total eradication of pests, rats in particular, so as to allow future generations to have some knowledge about these animals. At the same time, the trainers trained them to count the rat population and reminded them to control this pest as soon as they found evidence of its existence. Idham and Usin not only questioned these contradictory statements, but also opposed this idea by referring to their own knowledge of damage to plants and difficulties in controlling this pest. Second, whereas the pest observer introduced the idea of the WRB reproductive cycle, he discounted the farmers' ideas on controlling the moths instead of the eggs. Idham expressed his doubts by referring to the fact that one moth could lay several eggs and from these eggs hatch hundreds of larvae. In Idham's reasoning, there would be no eggs if there were no hens, and he strongly argued that: " ... it would be better to eradicate the mother first and don't let her lay eggs." These examples show the confusion the farmers had in their efforts to understand the connection between several propositions that seemed contradictory.

Sometimes trainers made a statement about a particular phenomenon without providing a detailed explanation. This raised further questions. Idham, for instance, questioned the pest observer's statement about the increased resistance of insects as a result of the injudicious use of pesticides. This was a phenomenon beyond the farmers' ability to observe. He could understand people's resistance to "medicine"—a parable used by the trainers—due to their long life that enabled their bodies gradually to develop resistance. Insects, on the other hand, have a very short life that limits the development of resistance. In this analogy, their metaphoric understanding of pesticides could not help them explain the concept of pest's resistance due to the different characteristics of the two domains (the long life of humans and the short life of insects).

Throughout the season, the farmers were interpreting the new ideas through their reasoning and practical experience.

AGREEMENT, MODIFICATION AND CONTRADICTORY ASSUMPTIONS

The farmers' past experiences and prior knowledge are the common bases for interpreting, reinforcing, or reconsidering the value of recently acquired information or practices. Through this activity, they interpreted some IPM ideas as either correct, correct in certain conditions only, or completely incorrect. They were either reinforcing their own knowledge or modifying it to incorporate the novel ideas.

An example of a shared acceptance of information as "correct" was the trainers' explanation of the period when the paddy was susceptible to rice gall midge, i.e. planting the paddy by the end of December or early January (*akhir bulan duabelas* or *bulan satu*). They were then reinforcing the validity of their prior knowledge. This was also the case when some farmers related the recent information to what they had learned from older people. When Idham and Usin were discussing the trainers' explanation about the moths' habitat, i.e., the standing stalks, they referred to the story they heard from the "old people": " ... that from the decayed stalks emerged worms." They then inferred that the source of moths was the paddy.

> Idham said: " ... the decayed stalks or stems, according to the old people, could cause [the emergence of] worms (larvae) that became moths. Thus, in former times, when people planted the long-stem ones (*gagangan*), and the paddy could not become dry enough during the draining time, there would be moths inside." Usin: "So, the symptoms [of the moths] come from paddy." Idham: "Thus, the source of moths is paddy itself (*kupu-kupu itu dari padi-padi juga*). Because of the decaying smell, the paddy become worms, and the worms become moths ...."

In cases where several farmers argued against the pest observer's explanation, they proposed a modification by combining their experiences with the novel explanation. An argument, for example, was raised against the pest observer's identification of mole crickets (*gaang* or *belalangan*) as a natural enemy instead of as a pest. Some farmers confidently argued that the mole cricket was indeed a pest because of the damage it caused to the roots of the paddy when the field was dry. In this case, the farmers defended their own knowledge against the trainer's counter-suggestion. Haji Ali and Akim, on the other hand, tried to resolve the argument by admitting that the mole cricket was a pest in dry field conditions, or when the farmers themselves were "lazy" and let their *sawah* dry up. They accepted, however, that it could be a natural enemy if the plants were well covered by water:

"Now Our Way of Thinking Is Different" 171

[Akim:] " ... if the water dried up there were many mole crickets. If we say that the mole cricket is a natural enemy, it is in fact a pest. If we say that it is a pest, the PPL said that it was a natural enemy. So, it is a pest if there is no water in the fields and it is a natural enemy if the paddy is flooded ...."

Arguments about other IPM ideas emerged throughout the season, particularly on changing practices of spraying pesticide. Some farmers were still in doubt about the novel strategies and hence made some modifications. Ayim said that he could accept the idea of not spraying pesticides at the vegetative stage since there were only a few WRB moths found. He could kill them instantly with his bare hands. Drawing on past experience, however, he would still spray the plants at the reproductive stage. First, the plants would be tall enough to obstruct his observation of the moths. Second, there would be some indication of pests at that stage. Haji Ali argued against Ayim's ambivalence.

Haji Ali told Ayim: "Do not observe [the plants] only when they are young .... You have to pursue your observation until harvesting, [to see whether] there are rice seed bugs, or other pests. Thus, making observation in PHT is only [on the time] when the plants are still small and not paying attention when they grow older and then, continue spraying." Replying to Haji Ali's suggestion, Ayim agreed that from his observation, " ... it is true that only one-two paddy leaves are 'rolling' (*nglinting*), whereas natural enemies like spiders are numerous ...." Ayim then reconsidered his previous thoughts.

This conversation suggests that verbal communication, besides direct practices, can affect the individual's interpretations. Through conversations, the farmers mutually reinforced their acceptance of IPM strategies by evaluating their own and other farmers' activities. Adma's decision to pursue spraying pesticides in the absence of a pest attack was contested by the other IPM farmers in several conversations. They thereby reinforced their acceptance of the novel strategy.

Some IPM farmers drew inferences that contradicted the trainer's explanation, e.g., applying carbofuran after finding that the symptoms of pest attack had exceeded its ETL. Quite a number of IPM farmers thought that broadcasting carbofuran was a must, a requirement—indeed—a novel idea learned from training. The information received included the recommended amount to be broadcast. The assumption that applying carbofuran was a "requirement" and a "must" was closely related to the farmers' past experiences, i.e., the severe outbreak of WRB in relation to their actions of not broadcasting carbofuran or applying it inappropriately. Asma, for instance, understood that the application of carbofuran did not depend on observation. This contrasts with his understanding of spraying pesticides.

> Asma told me that "Previously I did not use *Indofuran*, so there were many *sundep* (deadhearts) and many *penggerek batang* (white rice borers). That was in in the 1989–1990 rainy season. Now, in this dry season I used *Indofuran*, and ... *ya, alhamdullilah* there are no *sundep* ...." Answering my question he further explained that " ... according to PHT, there is no need to know the condition of pests beforehand to apply carbofuran. This is only according to Pak Sardi. For carbofuran, it is a "must"; but for "spraying" [pesticide] we have to observe first ...."

Without a detailed explanation of how carbofuran worked, some farmers still maintained their understandings of the function of this insecticide as a preventative medicine.

MEMORIZING: VARIATIONS AND DISADVANTAGES

The introduction of abstract concepts into narrative form without direct practices and evidence affected the farmers' interpretations. In one conversation, Arman and Ucup related IPM lessons to thoughts occurring in the human brain, which contrasted with the farmers' practices using muscles. These occurred at opposite ends in a scale of refinement. Metaphorically, Ucup said that

> ... IPM practices are like "refined things" (*barang alus*), using the brain; whereas making bricks [referring to his work during the fallow period as similar to rice farming] is a "rough thing" (*barang kasar*). Our hands will be stiff if we do not use them for quite a long time, as indeed with the brain.

In relation to this metaphor, the farmers considered that abstract concepts were not easily understood. They perceived themselves as having "a slow brain." "*Otaknya lambat, enggak tertangkap* (My brain is slow, I cannot understand it)," said Arman, referring to the enumeration method imposed upon them in training. Both Arman and Ucup had a primary education. Arman had graduated from the primary school and was younger than Ucup.

In another conversation, Iwan, a migrant who had graduated from junior high school, told me that the IPM school commenced lessons immediately at grade three level of primary school instead of grade one. There was a jump in the degree of difficulty and hence, he found it difficult to follow the trainers' explanations. Since many concepts passed through the human brain, they perceived practice as a means of retaining those abstract concepts in their memories (see Connerton 1989). Arman and Ucup, however, consciously refused to memorize the ways of counting pests and natural enemies as Win did.

Arman and Ucup agreed that the most important thing for them was to know about natural enemies and pests and the balance of their populations as found in the field. Counting them in detail to know the economic threshold was not significant since:

> "Those are all flowers—the counting. It would be better to go straight to the fruits, rather than being dizzy (*Itu semua kan bunga, penghitungan. Langsung saja buahnya, dari pada pusing-pusing*)," said Arman.

For Arman and Ucup, gaining a best yield—the fruits—was more significant than counting the flowers. Since mastering this skill was difficult and time consuming, they did not want to be bothered with mastering it.[2] Many other IPM farmers, who did not consciously refuse to memorize it as did Arman, Ucup and Win, also had similar difficulties in remembering numbers. As Hunter (1977:40–41) says, there is " ... a limited amount of data which can be held in temporary memory" and this restricts the accomplishments of mental calculators (also see Restle 1975 on short-term memory). As a result, there is a diverse ability to recall the enumeration formula and the economic threshold level of pests and damage symptoms.

The mixing up of terms—as in the citation of numerical symbols and calculations—was also found in the farmers' understandings about insect reproduction.

FUSING TERMS

Insect reproduction and metamorphosis are subjects that the farmers did not know much about, whereas IPM trainers transmitted this knowledge without empirical evidence. The farmers had their own terms for symptoms of "illnesses" caused by insects. The novel terms that the trainers transmitted in a "foreign" language were not always interpreted by the farmers exactly as the trainers intended. The farmers fused old and new terms in an attempt to form a coherent synthesis. As a result, diverse reconstructions of insect reproduction emerged.

"Larva," for instance, was a new term for the farmers. The trainers used this term for the infant stage of both the seedling flies and white rice borer moths without a detailed explanation of insect reproduction. Idham and Usin interpreted larva as a particular animal, and hence got confused when the trainers used that term for both the flies and the moths.

> Idham told me that he asked the PPL whether the "larva moth" (*kupu larva*) would become "larva worm" (*ulat-larva*) again, or become "WRB worm" (*ulat penggerek*). He then expressed his confusions: "Now *bu*, the flies have different mothers from the "larva worms." The flies that look different from the moths, however, also become "larva worms." The mothers of these worms come from the flies. I got confused grasping the PPL words …."

The word *ganjur*—the symptoms of damage caused by rice gall midge—was also a foreign term to the farmers who used to say *kelèb* or *pèntil* for those symptoms. Since the trainers explained this damage symptom along with those of various other pests, e.g., seedling flies and WRB moths, the farmers mixed up their interpretations of the symptoms of damage to paddy by several pests.

> Armin knew that the conditional factor for the infestation of *ganjur* was the "west wind" (*angin barat*), because every time the "west wind" came the plants would be attacked by *ganjur*. After listening to the pest observer's explanation he raised a question about the source of this pest. "According to Sardi, there is a fly, a seedling fly that brings *ganjur* …."

Whereas Armin thought that the seedling fly—not the mosquito—was the "host" of *ganjur* (*pembawa ganjur*), Arman interpreted *sundep* as becoming *kelèb* because they had similar appearances of damage symptoms on the paddies. Since the trainer said that *ganjur* or *kelèb* was derived from a "red mosquito," *sundep* (which was the same as *kelèb*)—according to Arman—was also caused by the red mosquito. Arman's understanding of *sundep* was, however, fused with the "white pest" (*hama putih*, leaf folder) and the introduced term *penggerek* (for white rice borer). According to him,

> "... if the paddy is attacked by *sundep* when it is small, when the panicle comes up, it turns white .... But these white panicles are caused by the *penggerek* .... Thus, *sundep* is also caused by the *penggerek*. Yes, *sundep* is *penggerek* when the paddy is small. The paddy, however, becomes *kelèb*. *Sundep* and *kelèb* are the same. It is according to Pak Sardi."

The farmers had recently learned the term *penggerek*, and hence it was still confusing to them in its relation to *beluk* and *sundep*, the native terms. Iwan, for instance, thought that *beluk* and *penggerek batang* had the same origins, but were different in terms of the degree of damage to plants

> "... symptoms of *beluk* also come from the stems .... What is called *penggerek batang* is, however, the one that is abundant, whereas *beluk* is the one that is only found in one or two [paddies]," said Iwan.

On another occasion, the pest observer told the farmers about several types of moths. One of them was the cause of the recent severe attack of *penggerek batang* (WRB). According to the farmers, not all of these moths were pests nor had they the same reproductive behaviour:

> In defining which animals were pests and which were natural enemies, Ucup definitely said that from the five different moths identified by the pest observer, only one moth was a pest, i.e., the long white one: the *penggerek batang*. He continued that: "the other moths are natural enemies: the small one (*yang kecil*), the yellow one (*yang kuning*), the striped one (*yang belang*), the spotty one (*yang blirik*). All lay eggs, but they are not like the white one. The white one lays eggs and from the eggs hatch larvae which bore into the stems. The other moths lay eggs, but do not become *hama* (pest), they do not go down the stems, but fly again as moths ... become natural enemies."

Many other stories about insect reproduction imply a similar interpretation. Through such an interpretation, a great range of variation about insects' reproductive cycle and damage symptoms, including white rice borer, prevailed.

Implementing and Validating Knowledge: IPM in Practice

For the IPM farmers, the means of proving the truth of the abstract propositions lies in observation and practice. This section examines how the farmers implemented and validated the concepts and propositions concerning natural enemies, field observation, the use of "medicine" and knowledge of pests and diseases.

Natural enemies and predators

Observation was the main means to prove whether the propositions about the prey-predator dynamics and the negative impacts of "strong medicine" on natural enemies were true. The extent of the farmers' understanding and observation, however, affected their inferences. Ucup, for example, had never seen the larvae nor observed the metamorphoses of the other non-WRB moths, which—in his interpretation—were natural enemies. Besides, he found that in *sawah* "there are many moths, they fly if I move my hands up and down (*digebyag suka terbang*), but they do not disturb the paddy." His intentional observation of the WRB moth, on the other hand, strengthened his understanding that only the white moth was a pest because "it is true that the eggs become larvae." From IPM training he knew that the larval stage was the most dangerous for paddy.

The farmers' confidence about the truth of the proposition that natural enemies prey on other animals varied. This variation was related to the farmers' ability to see direct evidence. The evidence can, however, come from previous experiences. Before training, Armad had once seen a " ... spider eating a moth trapped in its web." After training, he did not find any other natural enemies preying on other animals. On the basis of prior observation and his recent understanding of predatorship (without further evidence), he believed that " ... natural enemies are my friends." Arman, on the other hand, had no idea about predators before training. His belief was gained through direct observation during training.

> In the period of training, Arman found that one *kukuyakan* (Coccinelidae) walked up and down the paddy, up again to the edge of the tallest stem and then moved to other places. He interpreted this as the Coccinelidae "... looking for food." In another event, he was chasing a WRB moth, which then landed on the edge of the field and "... a spider

chased the moth." Since then, he has believed that the notion of "… natural enemy is true. I thus believe it more than 100%, it is really true. I saw it with my own eyes." He continued that "it is true that we have to cherish natural enemies."

Some farmers found evidence through deliberate observations. Ardi told of his observation of the behaviour of natural enemies:

> Once, I observed a *kukuyakan* that was preying on a larva. It ate the larva's head. Since the trainers said that *kukuyakan* was a natural enemy, I wanted to know what its prey was. I was still wondering what preyed on *kungkang* (rice seed bug), since spiders did not like it. I even saw a *kungkang* trapped in a spider's web, but the spider did not prey on it. The spider that was usually found on the ground, however, was really savage. Once, I saw this spider when I went to the field to fill it with water. So, I put a WRB larva on the water. I wanted to know whether the spider would chase the larva. It did. According to the book, this spider is aggressive.

Not every farmer had the opportunity to observe the behaviour of natural enemies. The chance for observing the predatory activity affected the farmers' confidence. Diloh (a graduate from senior high school), for instance, was in doubt and was not convinced that natural enemies would prey on all the pests found in the field. Diloh told me that according to the trainers,

> … if natural enemies were plentiful, we do not need to control pests because the natural enemies would prey on the pests. I do not know, however, whether this is true, because I have never experienced it, I have never seen it. Thus, I am uncertain whether natural enemies prey on pests. For example, suppose there are ten natural enemies and five pests. Maybe the natural enemies will only eat one pest, so there are four pests left. Will these other pests be preyed upon by the natural enemies? I do not know since I have not experienced it. Maybe, the PPL has not yet made an experiment about it …. I am not quite convinced yet.

The degree of confidence in the proposition that natural enemies were killed by pesticides also varied. Win, for instance, was not convinced of the truth of this proposition through his own direct observation that "… not all natural enemies were killed while I was spraying." He explained further about his observation that some natural enemies flew away when he was spraying; the others hid behind the leaves; or were not caught by the pesticides sprayed from a different direction from the wind.

While some farmers started to feel "guilty" about "killing" natural enemies as Arman did, Win had the opposite perception. According to him, it did not matter if natural enemies such as *bobotolan* were killed. In his understanding, this natural enemy stayed outside the stems and could not prey on larvae that bored inside the stem and stayed there. Win did not gain comprehensive ideas about which predators preyed upon what pests. On the other hand, the other IPM farmers and some non-IPM farmers (e.g., Rustam, Haji Nafi) accepted the idea of predation without doubt. Ayim expanded the idea that "… by handpicking the pests (WRB moths and eggs), the natural enemies are not disturbed and hence, can multiply faster because no poison is there." Usman (Arpan's brother, another non-IPM farmer) who learned about the negative impact of pesticides found that natural enemies were not killed by the permitted pesticide, *Kiltop* (to control brown plant hopper). "*Kiltop* is good; it is appropriate to spray pests. The natural enemies are not disturbed, they are unaffected and are not killed," reported Usman. In a similar way, Amid found that natural enemies were not killed by a pesticide that was, in fact, "banned," i.e., *Sumibas*.

The majority of IPM farmers stated that learning about the behaviour of natural enemies in *sawah* and how to observe them were the most significant change to their cultivation practices.

Field observation: a novel way of controlling pests

In articulating the differences between new and old ways of observing, Ayim, Armad, Haji Ali, and many other IPM farmers opposed the word *meneliti* (to examine) to "looking around," "browsing" (*lihat-lihat saja*), or "at first glance only" (*sepintas lalu saja*). The word *meneliti* was adopted not only by IPM farmers, but also by non-IPM farmers. "To observe or to look at carefully" (*mengamati*) was also used by Ayim as a synonym for the word "to control" or "to manage" (*mengendalikan*). Observation was considered the significant feature of IPM practice and contrasted with the "spraying" (*menyemprot* or *disemprot*), which was the hallmark of previous practice. Explaining the meaning of IPM (PHT), Ayim suggested several steps to be carried out by the farmers.

⬥ First, the farmers had to carry out individual observation so as to reduce costs.
⬥ Second, they should carry out observation collectively on their own and neighbours' fields.
⬥ Third, the farmers should manage the plants from nursery to grain formation period.

Ayim's ability to reformulate the meaning of IPM in his own words shows his creativity and capacity for adopting novel ideas. With this understanding, Ayim explicitly stated that pesticides could be used judiciously (*pestisida boleh dipakai asal secara bijaksana*). In line with this novel method of controlling pests, a number of IPM farmers told me that they did not spray pests during the 1990 dry season, but carried out continuous "observation" up to harvesting and did handpicking if they found a few pests (WRB).

The significant change in the manner of observation was going into the *sawah* and opening up the rice hills (*nyibak-nyibak, nyuai*) to see what pests or natural enemies they found inside the hills, among the stems. The counting that had been taught in training was, however, not being practised by all the farmers, or was being practised only by some on particular occasions. Ardi, Amid, Diloh and Idham counted the number of *kungkang* (rice seed bugs) per rice hill when the population of this pest increased to know its economic threshold level. Four IPM farmers also reported that they observed particular rice hills but did not carry out the counting. Iwan put bamboo sticks (*ajiran*) in three different places in one field plot and examined five rice hills surrounding these sticks. Ayim and Wira observed five rice hills every three metres across their field plots, whereas Iyub did not maintain a particular distance between the five rice hills he looked at.

Besides adopting the method of examining pest populations, the farmers were becoming used to identifying insects, eggs, and larvae found in the fields. Individually they were collecting the "unknown" insects while working in the fields, raising questions and discussing them with other IPM farmers. On several occasions I found them arguing and correcting the other's identifications. Some farmers brought what they found to school. Plastic bags became the main means of collecting insects or eggs. For example, Ardi brought unknown larvae, which were then identified by the pest observer as the larvae of seedling flies. Iyub brought several egg clusters when he got confused in trying to distinguish spider eggs and WRB eggs. Arman, Ardi, and Iwan brought WRB larvae and parasites as a result of their observations of WRB eggs. Curiosity about the form of rice seed bugs' eggs, the number of eggs laid by the bugs, and the length of time until hatching led Haji Ali and Diloh to collect several specimens of rice seed bugs while mating. They put these bugs in plastic bags, placed some straw on top and blew air into the bags to keep the bugs alive. Observing through plastic bags was a novel way of learning.

By carrying out more detailed observation, the farmers became more alert to every symptom of pest or disease both in their own and in their neighbours' fields. Idham and Usin, for example, showed me the fields where the paddy was attacked by "red disease." Idham was anxious because—according to his observation—the disease spread quickly within two nights and days.

> On the way to Idham's *sawah* in another hamlet—Rajapolah—Idham, Usin and I stopped by the fields where the leaves of the paddy in several plots looked yellowish-red. Idham asked me whether the cause of the disease was the soil-pH or the weather. After questioning a labourer who was broadcasting fertilizer (KCl) as a way to "control" the disease, we went further. Idham then stopped and pulled out one rice hill affected by the disease. He then examined the leaves, "... this leaf dried up ... up to the second leaf. See, the second leaf was infected. It could not dry up like this if it were not a disease ...." Usin then counted how many stems had dried up and how many stems had stayed green. Usin: "There are 22 stems ... and only two of them have been 'saved' ...." "Within one stem the second leaf had been infected. So, where can the nutrition (food) be cooked?" asked Idham. After arguing about the ways to control this disease, Idham agreed to bring one rice hill infected by this disease to school on the following day.

During the training period, the trainers became the source of information. When the training was over and no one visited them, the farmers found difficulty in finding answers for their questions. The pest observer did not visit them again until the dry season in the following year (1991) due to further education, whereas the PPL seldom came.

The use of "medicine"

The most novel idea learned for the IPM farmers was the new strategy of using pesticides. Various practices to prove and validate the propositions about this new strategy were carried out by individual farmers.

THE "ECONOMIC THRESHOLD LEVEL": A NEW CRITERION FOR "SPRAYING"

In the absence of pest outbreak, the majority of IPM farmers tried to practise the proper measures for pesticide use by looking at the "economic threshold level" of a particular pest. By practising this strategy, they gradually gained greater confidence in not using "medicine" if there were only a few pests in their *sawah*. In this context, therefore, the ETL became the new criterion for "spraying or not spraying medicine." As Diloh said, "... the economic threshold is used to control pests with medicine (*ambang ekonomi itu untuk menanggulangi hama dengan cara pengobatan*)." With this understanding, some farmers picked off the WRB moths or eggs by hand, if only a few were found in their *sawah*; whereas others did nothing if they knew that some natural enemies were present that could control the pests.

Although looking at the condition of pests and using the term *"ambang ekonomi"* became a novel pest control strategy, it was not always the case that the farmers used the enumeration formula or each pest's ETL. Some farmers did mention, however, the use of ETL in controlling pests. For example, Iwan controlled WRB after finding egg clusters in as many as 0.3 eggs/m^2; and Diloh controlled rice seed bugs after finding five bugs/m^2. Only a few of them, however, cited the correct number and did the counting as taught in training. Asma, for example, decided to "spray medicine" when he found that his paddy—in his estimations—had been affected by leaf folder in almost 25% of the plants. He came to this conclusion by roughly calculating the average of how many stems were affected by leaf folder in each rice hill after counting the total stems found in several rice hills.

The majority of IPM farmers, on the other hand, did not do any counting. Ayim, made up his own formula without any numerical symbols as follows:

> When the pests are still below the economic threshold, leaves are intact. When there are only one or two pests it means that it is still below the economic threshold. "Below the economic threshold" means

that ... there are more natural enemies than pests. "Above the economic threshold" means that there are more pests than natural enemies ....

The other farmers based their decisions on their own estimations (*dikira-kira*) or "feeling": "... I saw that the pests had been a bit numerous (*hama sudah agak banyak*)," said Armad. Aming also decided to apply carbofuran when he found there "... had been many WRB eggs" in his *sawah*. After finding some egg clusters in several rice hills, he decided to apply carbofuran.

Knowing the economic threshold level of pests and damage symptoms did not mean that the farmers always used this as a criterion for decision making. Win expressed his doubts and anxiety about waiting until the pests reached the economic threshold level:

> While spraying I found *sundep*. At that time I remembered the economic threshold level of *sundep*. I did the counting, and it had not reached the economic threshold; but the pests were numerous. ... I only found one or two *sundep* in one rice hill, which was, in fact, still a few; but ... it was already "a lot." The best thing for the paddy is that there is no *sundep* at all. Hence, I was in doubt. I did not have a good spirit; I was daydreaming (*ngelamun*). So, I decided to spray so that the plants would look "nice" ....

Adma also had doubts about taking decisions on the basis of the economic threshold level in the period when paddy reached its reproductive stage. According to Adma, Ayim and several other farmers, this stage is the most susceptible period for pest/disease infestation. Although he kept spraying "medicine" at this stage of plant growth, he made adjustments according to rice variety. It was more difficult to spray *Cisadané* than *IR64* due to its taller stems. He also admitted that he had reduced the frequency of spraying. For other IPM farmers, decisions to keep spraying "medicine" were considered as showing noncohesive behaviour among the "schooled farmers."

The farmers' doubts about applying the economic threshold concept when the paddy had reached its reproductive stage were not the only constraining factor. The neighbour's spraying of "medicine," or the supply of "medicine" in the credit package could affect their decisions. Win convinced his neighbour not to spray the leaf folder since there were only one or two symptoms found. According to Win,

> My neighbour did not want to listen. I thought that if the leaf folders were sprayed, the number of larvae would be greater. He (the neighbour), however, sprayed again. As the larvae increased, I was afraid that the larvae would migrate into my field. Another farmer advised me to spray in case the leaf folder infected my plants. At first, I did not want to spray, but the other farmers sprayed. So, I was frightened ... I did not count any more. I sprayed with *Indofuran* ....

A combination of "anxiety"—from finding a number of pests in their *sawah*—and the fact that they had a stock of pesticides from a credit package could tempt the farmers to "spray medicine." Other farmers such as Haji Ali and Arman, on the other hand, decided not to use their stocks of medicine—from the credit package and own purchases—in the absence of pest outbreaks. Although there were some constraints in implementing the introduced ideas, the novel practice of "spraying medicine" without referring to a time-schedule proved a significant benefit.

"MEDICINE IS COSTLY": GAINING CONFIDENCE

Those who tried "not to spray medicine" in the period when they used to "spray by schedule" soon gained confidence from practicing this strategy. As a result, they accepted the trainers' explanation as true. They recognized that they did not need to incur additional expenses for spraying and could use the money for household needs instead of purchasing pesticide. Moreover—as Armin said—they became aware that "... using the 'spray' is wasting money. Those who profit are the 'medical companies' (*PT obat*) and the shops (*kiosk*)."

The reduction in costs for each farmer varied according to the price, types and amount of pesticides used. The cost also varied according to the number of sprayings for the whole season and the number and size of *sawah* being cultivated.

> Rustam, for instance, gave a detailed account of expenses for one plot of *sawah* (300 *bata* = 0.42 ha) in the 1990 dry season as follows: "In this dry season (1990) my total expenses reached Rp.150,000 for seeds, fertilizers, ground preparations, transplanting, weeding, and carbofuran. I did not count my own labour. If I do the spraying, I could spend up to more than Rp.175,000 (referring to the costs he incurred in the previous season), because I used to use the expensive medicine, *Thiodan*. The price of one can of *Thiodan* is Rp.9,000. I also used *Sevin*. The price of one package of *Sevin* is Rp.4,000. I used to apply 2.5 cans of *Thiodan*. Thus, the costs for spraying was up to Rp.26,500."

Wahyu used to apply three to four cans of *Thiodan* (two litres: up to Rp.36,000) for two *bahu* of *sawah* (1.42 ha). Now he did not need to spend as much money.

Those who employed wage labourers to do the spraying could save the costs of both purchasing pesticides and paying wages. Those who used to borrow money from moneylenders admitted that they no longer needed to do that and pay a "large amount of interest" to the moneylenders. Armad reported,

Before, if I borrowed Rp.100,000 sometimes I had to return as much as Rp.150,000 (50% interest), sometimes up to only Rp.125,000 (25% interest). Moreover, there were some moneylenders who asked for 100% interest. There were also some who set the interest rate according to the latest market price of paddy (*harga padi terakhir*). For example, if I borrowed Rp.30,000. I have to return it later on the basis of the latest price for grain. If the price reached Rp.35,000 it means that I have to pay the additional interest of Rp.5,000; but I do not need to pay it soon after harvesting. Now, the advantage of PHT is the reduction of spraying, so that I can reduce the amount of money I have to borrow.

Several other farmers who said they had "no capital" (*tidak punya modal*) and had to borrow money for production costs had a similar opinion to Armad. "At least we did not need to borrow money to buy medicine," said Akim. Although the costs of spraying pesticide declined due to the farmers' decisions to reduce the amount of spraying, the costs for broadcasting carbofuran could increase. For some farmers, expenses increased by applying the recommended amount of carbofuran. Sukim told me that in previous seasons he applied only 5 kg carbofuran/ha. "Now in this season I broadcast 20 kg/ha. I had to spend more money to purchase *Indofuran*. Hence, it is just the same. The costs for spraying reduced, the costs for *Indofuran* increased." Iyub—who did not apply carbofuran in the 1989–90 rainy season—also used one box (20 kg) of *Indofuran* at a price of up to Rp.40,000. The increase in expenses also derived from the increased price of carbofuran. In the farmers' perspectives, the costs could be higher if they kept spraying pesticides as before. Reducing the spraying, thus, still helped them save some money.

Akim, for instance, said that in the 1990 dry season he had to spend Rp.40,000 to purchase 20 kg of *Furadan* as compared to Rp.30,000 in the 1989–1990 rainy season. With the increased price of fertilizers, the total cost for the 1990 dry season was higher than the previous season (up to Rp.250,000). With such an increase Akim felt, however, that he could still save money by reducing the frequency of spraying from three times to once only. He said that "In the previous rainy season I sprayed three times and spent up to Rp.21,000; now I just spray once and spend Rp.3,500 only. Thus, the difference in saving my expenses is Rp.17,500."

By recognizing the negative impacts of *Thiodan* on natural enemies, they could also save their expenses by changing the type of pesticide they used from the most expensive one to the cheaper one (e.g., *Indobas* or *Kiltop*, both permitted pesticides).

Gaining confidence and realising that "medicine is costly" not only resulted from a comparison of recent expenses with previous ones, but also from a comparison of their own and other farmers' profits. Although they could obtain the same yields as their fellow farmers, they gained more profit by reducing production costs. Ayim reported that, "... *alhamdullilah*, my paddy is as good as those who sprayed twice and up to three times. This [decision to avoid the use of pesticides] reduced my expenses." Ucup also reported that he could obtain 6.6 tons for two *bahu* (1.42 ha) of *IR42*. "The grain was transparent, the 'illnesses' were absent, and I did not spray at all." The IPM farmers measured yields/outputs to assess their own and fellow farmers' practices, including the novel ways of controlling pests.

This new practice was thus beneficial for those who had a shortage of capital. However, Haji Ali, a "rich farmer," also claimed that he gained benefits from avoiding or reducing the frequency of spraying. Adma, who had "strong capital," was of the same opinion, even though he did not totally abandon the preventative use of pesticides. The farmers' ability to provide capital was thus a significant variable, but did not constitute the sole determinant factor in their readiness to follow IPM teaching.

"MEDICINE INDUCES PEST OUTBREAKS": VALIDATING KNOWLEDGE

"Medicine induces pest outbreaks" is an abstract proposition without any substance except by reference to previous pest outbreaks. The extent to which the farmers believe this proposition depends upon evidence from their daily farming practices—intentional or unintentional—and their own interpretation of that evidence. Not all farmers had the chance or the intention to validate this knowledge. Nevertheless, several IPM farmers did experience that "medicine really accelerates the growth of pests" and conceived it as valid. Win referred to this proposition while asking his neighbour not to spray the leaf folder. According to him, "if it is sprayed, the larvae will become more numerous." Since his neighbour kept spraying, Win observed the results of his neighbour's behaviour on the growth of leaf folder. "I saw that after spraying, the larvae increased. Thus, it would have been better to have left them intact," Win inferred.

Armad validated his knowledge about this proposition by comparing the results of his own activities in different *sawah* undergoing different treatments. After he found symptoms of *sundep* in his *sawah* (four plots of *sawah*), Armad sprayed the plants twice. He told me that at that time, the IPM trainers had not yet discussed ways of controlling WRB. In the other *sawah*, he did not do any spraying. After harvesting he found that the whiteheads were more numerous in the first *sawah* than in the other. By referring to the above proposition he admitted that "... those (the *sawah*) that were sprayed twice were more severely damaged, while those that were not sprayed were not damaged as severely as the first ones." On the basis of his understanding of WRB reproduction and predatorship as taught in training, he inferred that probably "... after the eggs hatched, the larvae went down, but the natural enemies were extinct because I sprayed twice. I knew this from SLPHT."

Whereas Win and Armad accidentally discovered this, Wira carried out an experiment by dividing his *sawah* into two plots: the PHT and the SUPRA INSUS. His treatment of the plots was the reverse of what they did in training: he sprayed the PHT plot and did not spray the SUPRA INSUS one. He wanted to know whether natural enemies were all killed by pesticide. From observation, he learned that in the PHT plot the pests increased. Because he first sprayed *Thiodan* in the PHT plot, he understood that it was true that *Thiodan* killed natural enemies and hence none preyed on the leaf folders. Then he sprayed this plot with *Azodrin* (a banned insecticide) and kerosene, waited ten days, and found that some larvae turned up again. Then he sprayed them with *Azodrin* again.

While showing me his experimental plots (the PHT and the SUPRA INSUS plots) he told me how he was convinced that medicine killed natural enemies and induced a pest outbreak. "It is true. When I opened up the hills I did not find any natural enemies ....Thus the natural enemies were gone, the pests came. After I joined the PHT school, I wanted to try it myself. Thus, I gained confidence because I knew it by myself. Not because 'it is said, it is said' so ... (*Bukan katanya, katanya gitu*)."

These were cases of how the farmers validated the information received through training. The farmers interpreted the results of their own practices and came to believe that such information was true.

"THE BANNED INSECTICIDES": CONTINUING PRACTICES AND FINDING ALTERNATIVES

From training, the IPM farmers learned that "medicines," especially a "strong" one like *Thiodan*—their favourite medicine—killed all animals in the *sawah* and hence were banned by the government. They did not know that there were another 56 insecticides banned for use on rice. The trainers did not inform them about these 56 banned insecticides. Although the majority of IPM farmers tried to avoid the use of *Thiodan*, one farmer, Adma, was still using it since he knew that this insecticide was effective in controlling "worms," but not brown plant hopper (BPH). According to him, *Thiodan* killed BPH slowly and for this reason, it was banned for use in controlling this particular pest.[3] Other farmers tried to find alternatives to *Thiodan*, including both banned and permitted insecticides.

Among those who sprayed banned insecticides, only one farmer (Wira, a graduate of junior high school) knew—from reading the label—that the insecticide he chose was allowed only for use on secondary crops. Wira decided to use the banned insecticide instead of various other "medicines" sold at the *kiosk*. He told me that,

> after joining PHT I began to think, what kind of "medicine" should I use? Before when I used *Thiodan* I asked somebody else to purchase it from the *kiosk*. Now, I went to the *kiosk* myself to get to know various kinds of "medicine." At that time I knew a "medicine" called *Azodrin*. It was like methylated spirits (*spiritus*), cold. I knew that this "medicine" was not allowed for paddy; it was allowed for use on groundnuts, but I tried it. It did not damage the paddy. I mixed it up with kerosene, because kerosene is hot, smelly, and irritates on the eyes of the pest.

From his observation of the impact of *Azodrin* and kerosene, he gained confidence that those "medicines" were good, killing pests but not damaging the paddy and natural enemies. Another farmer, Amid, chose *Sumibas* (a banned insecticide) to control WRB larvae. He explained that because of its unpleasant smell, the WRB larvae became dizzy and then died before boring into the stems. Like Wira, he gained confidence that this insecticide did not kill natural enemies. From observation right after spraying, he knew that "... spiders were still alive. Moreover dragonflies always moved around. Only worms were killed, fell over to the ground, or floated on the water surface." These are examples of how the farmers interpreted the trainers' advice about the need to avoid the use of the "strong medicines" by choosing the "medicines" that—in their interpretations—would not eradicate natural enemies. Without detailed information about the other banned insecticides, their choice—based on their ways of observation and interpretation—could, in fact, contradict the trainers' advice and the IPM planners' aim in leading them away from the use of banned insecticides.

Asma, on the other hand, realised that *Dursban* (another banned insecticide) killed both pests and natural enemies because it was a "strong medicine" and had a "strong smell." He chose this insecticide to control leaf folder at another farmer's suggestion. Besides, "... everybody used this 'medicine,' and it was true, all small and big worms were killed." In several other cases, the shop owner was the source of information. When Idham visited a kiosk in Sukamandi, the shop owner told him about an insecticide, *Matador* (for use on secondary crops) that was expensive. "Since it was expensive, it might be very effective (*ampuh*),' thought Idham. Idham compared it with other "medicines" in terms of price and size of can. The farmers did not consider written information as found on the label to be definitive information when choosing pesticides.

In this early stage of internalizing IPM knowledge, however, there was a significant difference emerging in the use of pesticides between the IPM farmers and non-IPM farmers. The use of pesticides was not reduced dramatically because of the infestations of some pests/diseases. A reduction in the average spraying in each location was, nevertheless, a marked change among the "schooled" farmers.

Whereas in the 1989–90 rainy season, the average spraying in each location (*sawah*) for all the farmers (IPM and non-IPM) was 3.44 times in one season (see chap. 3), and a similar figure of 3.4 was also found among the "lay" farmers in the 1990 dry season, this figure dropped to an average of 2.2 sprayings/location (from 56 sprayings in 25 locations) among the "schooled" farmers in this 1990 dry season. One factor that contributed to the persistent profile of pesticide use among the non-IPM farmers was the constraints in knowledge transmission in this early stage of introducing IPM.

CARBOFURAN: "A NOVEL IDEA AND A NECESSARY PRACTICE"
In IPM training, the use of the granular pesticide (carbofuran) was referred to by the trainers as the appropriate way of controlling WRB. They also mentioned the need to look at the WRB economic threshold level and the appropriate measurement when broadcasting carbofuran. In contrast to the use of a sprayed pesticide, not all farmers applied carbofuran, although the pesticide had been widely used mixed with fertilizer. It was also through training that the farmers knew for the first time the recommended measurement for broadcasting carbofuran.

Prior to IPM training, but shortly after the severe attack of WRB, the farmers learned about "false *Furadan* and *Thiodan*" from external sources and—for some farmers—their own mistakes in not applying the "basal medicine." Despite taking decisions based on the economic threshold level as taught in training, the majority of IPM farmers broadcast carbofuran mixed with fertilizer. In the 1989–90 rainy season, nine IPM farmers—from the total 18—did not apply carbofuran. In the 1990 dry season, as many as 17 IPM farmers—from 18 IPM farmers—applied this insecticide. The 1989–90 experience of WRB outbreak reduced the farmers' confidence in applying carbofuran according to the economic threshold level of pests. Nevertheless, diverse interpretations and practices prevailed.

For several farmers, the IPM school was the source of information about applying carbofuran with fertilizer to prevent the attack of WRB. Wira critically assessed the IPM field plots, particularly the IPM treated plot (*sawah* PHT). Without knowing that Arpan, the cultivator, was in fact applying carbofuran in both plots, Wira told me that the performance of the paddy in the PHT plot was not as good as in the

SUPRA INSUS one because no carbofuran was broadcast in that plot. Hence, there were no "poisons" on the ground or in the plants to kill pests, and therefore the plants could not grow well. A similar perception was held by several other IPM farmers, e.g., Arman, Haji Ali and Akim, although they knew from training about the need to look at the pest populations. The reason for applying carbofuran without first looking at the pest conditions was their worry about the possible attack of pests. According to them, the pests were more numerous in the dry season than in the rainy season. "I was very doubtful" (*Saya sangsi bener*), "worried" (*khawatir*) or "afraid" (*takut*), were their expressions while referring to previous experiences of WRB attacks.

The amount of carbofuran applied in the different stages of the paddy varied. There were also diverse interpretations about the correct amount of carbofuran. In practice, several farmers did not apply the amount of carbofuran suggested at training. Some applied more than the recommended dosage: 18 kg/*bahu* (0.7 ha) instead of 17 kg/ha. Others broadcast much less than the recommended amount (only 10 kg/*bahu* and 5 kg/*bahu* respectively) to save expense, yet protecting the plants from pest infestation. The frequency of broadcasting this insecticide also varied. While Asma applied carbofuran twice, Akim and Arman applied it once but in different stages of plant growth for different reasons. Akim broadcast *Furadan* in the first application of fertilizer since, according to him, there were more pests in the dry season than in the rainy season. He reasoned that

> according to PPL, apply carbofuran only if the pests reached the economic threshold level. If there are no pests, we do not need to apply it even at the first fertilizer stage. I am really afraid, however, that it would happen again as in the last rainy season. It is like meals where we have to put *vetsin* (flavour enhancer) in it ....If in the early stage the paddy does not grow well, I am afraid that it won't grow well again in the later stage. So, I had better use carbofuran so as to make the paddy fertile (*supaya subur*). In the second fertilizer application I do not need to apply carbofuran if there are no *sundep*. This is the advantage of knowing the symptoms of *sundep*, a really great advantage.

Akim's explanation suggests the farmers' confusion about the function of carbofuran, i.e., as basal medicine, as a protection against illnesses and as a substance to stimulate the growth of the paddy. The relationship between pest attacks and the stages of the paddy was emphasised by Arman in his decisions to apply carbofuran. His main consideration was the ability of the plant to compensate for the attack of *sundep*:

> In the first fertilizer application don't apply too much *Furadan*. Although the paddy is attacked by *sundep*, the paddy is still small so it is still able to grow more stems (*masih sempat beranak*). The most important thing is when the paddy grows big (*sudah gedê*). Apply *Furadan* at the second fertilizer application because the paddy is already mature. If the paddy is attacked by *sundep*, there will be no substitute for the stems.

Another farmer, Win, was just pursuing his own method of spraying boiled *Indofuran*. He also broadcast it in a mixture with fertilizer to kill all pests from the bottom to the upper part of the plant. According to Win, broadcasting carbofuran did not guarantee that the pests in the upper part of plants would die. Diloh, on the other hand, knew from the PPL that boiling carbofuran was forbidden because of its damage to the paddy leaves (not because of its toxicity). IPM trainers recommended that carbofuran, if required, be broadcast by mixing it with sand. This method was not appreciated by some farmers. Adma told me that carbofuran would be more equally spread in a mixture with fertilizer than with sand because of weight differences.

Thus each farmer's practice varied in relation to the individual's past experiences and interpretation of what he had learned from training.

Knowledge in practice: the farmers' responses to pest and disease

In the 1990 dry season, the farmers discovered WRB had appeared in much lower populations than in the 1989–90 rainy season. Red disease was the puzzling phenomenon in this season. A high population of rice seed bugs occurred at the ripening stage. This section discusses how the farmers responded to these pest/disease problems and acquired additional knowledge.

WHITE RICE BORER

From the previous outbreak of WRB, the farmers had learned that planting schedule, rice variety, and the "false medicines" were elements that contributed to harvest failure. During training, the IPM farmers gradually learned about the WRB life cycle and appropriate ways of controlling them. The farmers themselves—who were curious to know in detail about the pest's behaviour—raised the issue of WRB. At the same time, they found symptoms of *sundep* and moths in their *sawah*, although to a lesser degree than in the previous rainy season. The recent understanding that white moths were the "mothers" of the larvae that had damaged their paddy led them to be more alert to the presence of moths and eggs in their *sawah*. Although the majority of IPM farmers applied carbofuran as a preventative measure, their responses to the appearance of *sundep* were, again, diverse.

Understanding the possible dangers of moths, several farmers decided to spray the moths, besides having a stock of medicine as reported by Armad. "There are many moths in the *sawah*. From only one moth, how many eggs will be laid and how much larvae will hatch from those eggs?" asked Adma and Akim, rhetorically referring to their new knowledge. Like other farmers who had decided not to spray the moths, they also tried to control the moths physically by handpicking and squashing them. Several farmers, Arpan, Ayim, and Haji Ali decided to try mixing kerosene in fertilizer. Arpan explained his own theory of how the kerosene affected the moths.

> "When the fertilizer fell into the water, the kerosene went *pyaaaar* (expressing the way the kerosene dispersed in the water). The moths that were "swimming" in the water sucked the kerosene. Those flying above were affected by the odor, became dizzy, and fell down," said Arpan.

Knowing the potential danger of the egg clusters, Akim carried out a trial by spraying them with *Applaud* when his paddy reached 70 days of age. He referred to what the government said that *Applaud* prevented the hatching of BPH eggs (and not by retarding the growth of nymphs as it really does). He felt confident in his experiment because,

> "my paddy was saved, without anything 'white' (white ears, *beluk*) appearing. But how the medicine worked I do not know ....There were one/two eggs, but there was nothing 'white' [on my paddy], so it meant that the eggs died. I saw that there were no marks of the eggs. Thus, all eggs were killed by the *Applaud*," explained Akim.

Observing the egg clusters after putting them in a plastic bag filled with wet cotton was a novel practice for the farmers as taught by the trainers. Several farmers tried to observe the eggs found in their *sawah* in the middle of training. They brought the larvae and the parasites to school to ask the trainers for identification and explanation. This was the first time that they had recognized the forms and numbers of larvae and parasites that had hatched from the eggs. This knowledge increased their anxieties about the possible damage caused by such an amount of larvae. Whereas Ardi had previously applied carbofuran in a mixture of fertilizer in the second stage of application, Arman and Iwan applied carbofuran after seeing the results of their observations. Amid, on the other hand, did the spraying instead of applying carbofuran. On the basis of his recent understanding of the larvae's behaviour, Amid told me his reasons for spraying the larvae:

> I saw that the eggs had already hatched. After hatching, the larvae could bore into the stems within only two days. The next morning, before the larvae went into the stems, I sprayed them with *Sumibas* .... If the larvae had already bored into the stems, it would be difficult to spray them. They should be controlled by carbofuran.

Amid and Akim made their own interpretations and modified the trainers' recommendations with their own views.

Some IPM farmers were also assisting their parents/parents-in-law, or grandparents/grandparents-in-laws, who did not join IPM training. Transmitting knowledge to these older people was not an easy task. On the basis of his new knowledge about controlling the WRB, Ardi tried to correct his father's decision to spray moths in his *sawah*. His father, however, refused Ardi's proposal and asked his son to spray the moths, even though he needed to seek finance to purchase the "medicine." Although Ardi knew the ineffectiveness of this method, he obeyed his father's wishes and did the spraying.

From individual observation, interpretation and discussion with fellow farmers, the farmers acquired some new knowledge about WRB. To some extent, each farmer gained an understanding similar to or different from the others. Examples of this additional knowledge are:

◆ the presence of moths in paddy leaves in the mornings and not in the afternoons,
◆ the different forms of egg clusters before and after hatching,
◆ the difference in forms of WRB eggs and spider-eggs,
◆ the difference between larvae and parasites hatched from the eggs,
◆ the effective period of carbofuran,
◆ the place and form of larvae inside the stems that had white-head symptoms (*beluk*),
◆ the correlation between rain and the appearance of moths, particularly the "day-rain" (*hujan siang*) that was already known to "bring pests" (*membawa hama*), and
◆ varied degrees of susceptibility of rice varieties towards larvae infection.

By improving their knowledge, the farmers were able to explain previously puzzling phenomena, e.g., why the panicles suddenly turned white and stood upright (*jadi putih dan ngacung ke atas*), instead of bowing down. Through conversations, they also strengthened their own ideas about the need to control the moths, something that was not recommended by the pest observer. Several suggestions about how to control these moths were mooted by the farmers: on "handpicking the moths" or *ngarambèt kupu-kupu* (weeding moths); to pay wages to labourers to carry out this activity while weeding; the method of trapping moths; the rotation of rice varieties; and the burning of stalks left after harvesting to kill the pupae. In discussions, the farmers also acknowledged the constraints they felt in implementing some ideas particularly those that needed the assistance of those in power to put them into practice. The new knowledge also stimulated the farmers' ability to identify moths, larvae and eggs more accurately.

News of a pest outbreak in another village and district spread among them. Information about the mass mobilization control of WRB egg clusters to be held in three villages in the district of Ciasem stimulated the farmers to carry out such an activity in Marga Tani.[4] Several farmers—Ayim, Idham and Usin—had the idea of mobilizing the IPM farmers to handpick the moths by collecting money from the owner/cultivators as wages. Ayim had his reasons as follows:

Collecting money to pay wages for the IPM farmers is similar to purchasing medicine for spraying. The money could be divided equally among the IPM farmers. This movement could function as a way to provide an example to non-IPM farmers, so that they will be attracted to handpicking the eggs. Besides, the amount for paying wages is the same as purchasing medicines, but we could gain double advantages. First, the pests could be killed straight away. Second, the natural enemies would be intact and could reproduce faster.

A special meeting attended by twelve IPM farmers, including the hamlet's and the farmers' leaders, was held to discuss this idea. The meeting did not, however, reach agreement due to some reasons: the advanced age of the paddy; the collection of money from the owners/cultivators who would not be involved in the event; and the ineffectiveness of such a control if the number of eggs had exceeded the ETL. Faced with such disagreement, without any support from the local authorities (e.g., the BPP staffs and the village/district leaders), the innovative IPM farmers felt powerless to pursue any further action. As a result, knowledge of the WRB egg clusters was shared among the IPM farmers themselves and not widely spread among the other farmers and their household members as found in C. Tengah. In this latter village, mass-mobilization control provided an opportunity for the farmers and their families to learn about the form and impact of egg clusters on their plants. Since the farmers had applied the second stage of fertilizer, they had the opportunity to try mixing carbofuran with sand (also see Winarto 1993).

RICE SEED BUGS

Rice seed bug (*kungkang, lembing kungkang, walang sangit, Leptocorisa oratorius*) was a pest familiar to the farmers. The majority of them knew that this pest "urinated" on the grains (*mengencingi biji padi*) at the ripening stage, causing the grains to decay. Only a few farmers, such as Adma knew that this pest "sucked" on the grains (*mengisap biji padi*) instead of urinating on them. Later, Idham learned from the head of the BPP that this pest "stung" the grains (*menyengat biji padi*). The known term for grains that became discoloured was *pèstol*, an abbreviation for *"ya kempès ya trotol"* (it became empty and spotty).[5] The farmers began to notice the presence of this pest in their own and/or fellow's fields planted to a variety with a shorter-maturity age (*padi gènjah* e.g., IR64, Way Seputih, IR42) at the flowering stage. Pest numbers increased, exceeding its economic threshold (5 bugs/m^2), according to several IPM farmers. The numbers continuously accelerated at the late ripening stage (200–500 bugs/m^2 as reported by Idham), and migrated from one field to another according to the maturity of the paddy. The largest number of pests was found by the farmers in the fields planted with *Cisadané*, the variety with the longest maturing age.

The outbreak of the rice seed bugs was not anticipated. It was an unforeseen consequence of the farmers' strategy of planting a diversity of rice varieties to avoid the outbreak of WRB (see discussion on perverse effects in Boudon 1982:1–9; also see Jarvie 1969; on the consequences of human action). Kalshoven (1981:106) mentions that the damage caused by this pest in May-July occurs "... when several adjacent rice crops are planted soon after each other over a long period, allowing several generations of the *walang sangit* to develop."[6]

Since this outbreak occurred in the last week of training, the farmers were only able to ask the BPP staff about the most effective pesticide to eradicate this pest. The trainers did not give detailed explanations about this pest's behaviour except its economic threshold level. Several farmers reported that the eradication of this pest was difficult since the pests flew away during the spraying and kept returning to the field after two or three days of spraying. Faced with indeterminacy about the effective way of eradicating this pest, different farmers tried an array of pesticides, including fungicides, rhodenticides, and other chemical substances.

Several farmers perceived that spraying insecticides was ineffective and hence tried other methods. A method initiated by Ardi was to chase the pests away using a plastic string moved by him and his wife along the *sawah*. Iyub and Ardi learned from other farmers the way to control this pest as the old people used to do, i.e., by burning husks, debris and placing sulphur strategically at the edge of the field (*bikin kebulan welirang*).

They learned that smoke from this burning could lead the bugs away. They were not sufficiently convinced, however, to rely solely on this method since "... the number of the bugs was too 'dense' and the smoke could not reach the middle part of my *sawah*," reported Iyub. Iyub and Ardi thus kept spraying pesticides. Through the practice of burning sulphur, the farmers were reactivating their old local knowledge. An old farmer (Tarmi), however, criticised the reactivation of this old practice. He conceived it as ineffective in relation to the current rice environment:

> "Using sulphur was the 'old-people's method' when they planted *padi gèdèngan* (long-stem varieties). In this season, this method was used again by those whose paddy was attacked by *walang sangit* (*kungkang*). This method was not effective in chasing the pests away." Summarizing the situation during harvesting, Tarmi said that "only one field remained after the rest had been harvested, so all the pests moved to that field. Besides, the stems are now cut at the bottom. Before, burning sulphur (*dikebuli*) was still effective because the stems were still there. They were cut in the upper part by using *ani-ani* (traditional hand-knife). Hence, the pests were still there [in the field]. Now, if a harvest is late, that farmer will not get any, since all pests will move to his field. Nowadays there will be difficulties if the planting schedule is not uniform."

The negative impact of a nonuniform planting schedule (*tanam padi tidak serempak*) and the diverse maturing age of rice varieties were topics raised in many farmers' conversations as they evaluated this unexpected consequence. This was the most significant idea learned through the farmers' experience, observation and comparison of their own and/or other farmers' fields.

The farmers' ineffective responses to this pest outbreak led to an improvement in their understandings of this pest's behaviour and of the need to plant rice varieties with a similar maturity rate.

"PENYAKIT BEUREUM" (BACTERIAL LEAF STREAK) AND "KRÈSÈK" (BACTERIAL LEAF BLIGHT)

Krèsèk (bacterial leaf blight caused by *Xanthomonas oryzae*) is well known among the farmers as an illness that usually appears at or after the maximum tilling stage. The farmers know that this illness causes dryness in paddy leaves and reduces yields, particularly striking at the stage of early grain formation.[7] It was thus unexpected that at the vegetative stage (between 30–40 days after transplanting), a similar symptom spread quickly in several *sawah* planted mainly with *IR42*. The farmers named this symptom *penyakit beureum* (red disease), *merah daun* (red leaf), or just that the paddy "*kena merah*" (became red). They did not have any idea about the disease or its cause. In training, the pest observer identified the disease as bacterial leaf streak (*bakteri daun bergaris, BDB*). Only one IPM farmer, Arpan, used the right term. Idham mentioned it as BRS (*bacterial red stripe*, another disease mentioned by the pest observer). Whereas Idham and Sukim perceived either that this symptom caused *krèsèk* (referring to similar symptoms on leaves) or that *krèsèk* infected young paddies, several other farmers differentiated *krèsèk* from this "red leaf" disease. Rustam was definite that whereas *krèsèk* infected paddy at the flowering stage and caused emptiness of grain, the "red disease" appeared at the vegetative stage and did not lead to such damage.

In conversations, the farmers mentioned various factors as possible causes: the rice varieties that were susceptible to this disease (i.e., *IR42* and *IR64*); the condition of the roots; the need to manage the water; the weather that induced the spread of this disease (e.g., wind, hot and dry, and a sudden day rain); the soil-pH; late or excessive application of urea; and the ability of the plants to compensate and grow again. They also discussed how to control this disease as learned from other places and practiced by some non-IPM farmers (e.g., using herbicide). Since this symptom appeared in the middle of training, the IPM farmers had the opportunity to ask for and receive some information about this disease from the trainers. The pest observer mentioned several causes of this disease and the absence of any "medicine," but named several fungicides that could be used as a "preventative measure" (*untuk pencegahan*). In the absence of any "effective medicine," those whose plants were infected by this disease responded in different ways on their own initiative. Since the disease gradually disappeared and the plants grew again, all of them claimed that their practices were effective and the plants "got better" (*sembuh lagi*).

When training was over, the farmers experienced another disease outbreak identified as *krèsèk*. This outbreak was unexpected because of the serious degree of its attack in the dry season. The spread of infestation was fast, infecting various rice varieties with almost 80–90% damage (on the basis of the farmers' assessment). The farmers questioned the causes of this outbreak and wondered how to combat the disease, but had to find the answers on their own. At that stage, no IPM follow-up activities were undertaken by the trainers.

The farmers could not exert too much effort since the disease attacked their plants in the grain formation and ripening stage. Asma, for instance, reported that his paddy (*IR42*) had been attacked by this disease only a week before harvest, whereas the paddy of Arpan (*IR42*) had been attacked at an earlier stage of grain formation. They could expect only a poorer harvest. Several IPM farmers who had learned from the trainers the ways to control the "red disease" tried to manage the water by drying up the field as Ardi and Iwan did. However, Ardi's effort was useless and hence he let his *sawah* become wet again. Haji Ali, who had received one can of fungicide (*Dethane*) from a Bogor Agricultural Research Institute researcher, tried to spray the fungicide as recommended by the pest observer, but without a significant result.

The farmers' conversations thus focused on their evaluation and interpretation of their own and other farmers' practices. The farmers' main conclusion was that the excessive application of fertilizer, particularly urea, in such a dry season had led to the luxuriant growth of rice. This conclusion was, in fact, concomitant with the experts' findings. As mentioned by Ou (1973:14),

> high rates of nitrogen fertilizer increase the incidence of the disease, possibly because luxuriant growth of rice plants favours the spread of the organism. But levels of nitrogen do not seem related to the size of individual lesions.

Ou (1973:14) mentions too that "phosphorus and potassium deficiency and excess silica and magnesium also increase disease incidence." Farmers did mention the need to apply KCl (potassium chloride) in controlling "red disease." Several farmers also related the appearance of *krèsèk* to the lack of KCl, although some farmers did not agree with such an assumption on the basis of their own practice of not applying this type of fertilizer and having their plants remain healthy. The farmers had different viewpoints that led to diverse assumptions.

> Asma drew his conclusion in relation to excessive fertilizer use, but Ardi referred to the drainage system (by referring to the trainers' explanation as well). The latter possible cause was also assumed by Ardi's father on the basis of his comparison between his son's (*Cisanggarung* that was mistakenly identified by Ardi as *Way Seputih*) and Adma's plants (*Way Seputih*). His son's field was kept filled with water

(*direndam air*), whereas Adma's field was dried up. Adma, on the other hand, arrived at a different conclusion from Ardi's father because he had planted two different rice varieties (*Way Seputih*, uninfected, and *IR42*, infected). Since he had treated these two varieties with different fertilizer applications, i.e. urea and TSP twice in the *IR42* plot and without *urea* in the second application in the *Way Seputih* plot (only with ZA and KCl), he assumed that the use of urea in the second application was the cause of *krèsèk* in his *IR42* plot. Akim drew a similar conclusion from the different fertilizer applications he had made on his own and on his grandmother-in-law's *sawah*. In his sawah, Akim reduced the amount of urea in the second application (from one *kuintal* to 0.5 *kuintal* of urea), but in his grandmother-in-law's *sawah*, he had to accept her decision to double the amount of urea in the second application.

These are examples of how the farmers drew similar or differing conclusions by comparing the growing condition of the same or different paddy in their own and/or other farmers' *sawah*. They made these comparisons by using corresponding or dissimilar perspectives from their own and/or other fellow farmers' practices. Other variables mentioned by the farmers were the planting schedule, the growing conditions and the weather.

Through experiencing this disease outbreak and drawing inferences from their practices, the farmers again acquired additional knowledge.

Transmitting Knowledge: Farmer-to-Farmer Transmission

The introduction of IPM in a school run by the state made the farmers proud of their positions as students. Their emphasis on institution rather than the content of the course became dominant in their answers to non-IPM farmers. "*Sekolah Pertanian* (attending agricultural school)," replied the IPM farmers answering non-IPM farmers' questions about what was going on in their hamlets and *sawah*. This section describes how the IPM farmers answered their fellow farmers about the "school" and how they transmitted the new ideas to the lay farmers in daily conversations

Observing unusual events

The IPM farmers' activities such as insect collecting, going into plots of *sawah*, and their weekly gathering at Haji Ali's house were unusual events for the villagers. Because there was no formal notice or official ceremony to announce the IPM training publicly, only a few farmers learned that a school or training (*penataran* or *penyuluhan*) would be carried out. Both the farmers, who had heard of the training and those who did not know what was going on, had no idea of the school's aims and objectives. After several weeks of training, the notion of a school about pests/diseases and the 'medicines' to cure these was spread by farmer-to-farmer transmission. This did not mean, however, that all farmers took note of the school. Those whose residences were not near the riverbank and who did not have the IPM farmers as close neighbours did not know about the school.

The weekly training held in Haji Ali's residence attracted close neighbours, young villagers and children who deliberately watched and listened to the trainers' and the IPM farmers' activities. Through watching and listening, Apri—Haji Ali's motorcycle driver and close neighbour—learned that the school was about pests, illnesses, medicine, and that the farmers had to discuss, draw and write. He did not, however, receive any information from Haji Ali about the kind of knowledge learned, although other neighbours, Ayim and Idham did tell him about it. Several other farmers and nonfarmers, however, participated in the school on their own initiative or by substituting for IPM farmers who were absent on particular weeks. They mainly just watched and listened. On his own initiative, Rustam, a high school teacher, who always came to training if he was not teaching outside the village, participated in the farmers' activities.

Because of IPM training, the number of farmers carrying sprayers into the fields at the usual time of application was reduced. This was not, however, recognized quickly by the non-IPM farmers until the middle and towards the end of the season. They began to notice that something unusual had happened: that their neighbours had not sprayed their fields or that fewer farmers were spraying than in previous seasons. Win told me how his neighbour asked him why he did not spray his *sawah*:

> My neighbour from Karangsuwung asked me why I did not spray my field. Then I asked him back: "Ah, with what medicine should I spray? There are no pests." That person replied: "You did not spray

your plants enough. See, there are many pests." I told him: "There is no need to spray if there are only one or two leaf folders."

Win's notion was a strange one, so his neighbour continued to spray. Iman (a non-IPM farmer, Haji Ali's uncle-in-law, a neighbour of Idham, Ucup, Arman, Aming and Akim) also told me that he had observed and listened to the IPM ideas and so he was not spraying "medicine" this season, an unusual phenomenon in rice farming. Gradually, the farmers considered this nonspraying when evaluating and comparing plant performances.

IPM knowledge in conversations

How the farmers communicated IPM ideas in daily conversations affected their main interests in relation to the most significant problem during rice-farming activities. Power relations among the farmers themselves affected the extent to which other farmers gained trust in the IPM farmers' stories.

THE SIGNIFICANT ISSUES

IPM ideas were transmitted according to particular issues that were perceived to be most significant by both speakers and listeners. From the whole complex of novel ideas and propositions, the most frequent issues discussed by the farmers were the WRB life cycle and the ways of controlling both moths and eggs and how to identify larvae or parasites that would hatch from the eggs. The other issues were the ideas of "spraying medicine" after looking at the condition of pests, the banned use of *Thiodan* and the role of natural enemies. Idham, Usin and Ayim were known as the most vocal of the IPM farmers in disseminating such knowledge. These farmers looked on the 40 days of praying (*tahlilan*) before and during the pilgrimage of their relatives and neighbours (Haji Warma and wife) to Mecca as a good opportunity to communicate their knowledge of WRB to those in attendance.

The issues of spraying pests and the role of natural enemies were mainly related to the outbreak of WRB. The judicious use of pesticides so as to reduce production costs and conserve natural enemies was also mentioned separately, in relation to the presence or absence of pests in their fields. This issue was often raised in the

"Now Our Way of Thinking Is Different" 203

farmers' conversations in the fields when the IPM farmers found their neighbours spraying "medicine." Akim, Arman and Iwan told me how they raised a kind of rhetorical question to their neighbours as follows:

> "Why do you spray? What did you find in your field?," asked Akim of his neighbour from Sukamandi. Akim repeated to his neighbour's reply: "... there are some 'white leaves,' but there are only one or two." Akim replied: "Such an amount is okay. You do not need to spray." Then his neighbour asked Akim how he knew about that and Akim told him that he knew it "from school."

The speakers' emphasis in a particular conversation led to the transmission of only partial rather than the comprehensive ideas. The non-IPM farmers obtained ideas that were affected by the speakers' emphasis in a particular conversation. Different information could be gained by different farmers from the same source, or the same issues could be repeatedly mentioned by the same speakers in different conversations. What was understood by the listeners could also vary from farmer to farmer. The ideas were usually transmitted only partially. For example,

> Apri learned from Idham and Ayim to handpick the WRB eggs and brought them home to see what would hatch from the eggs. Anan (a non-IPM farmer, Usin's father-in-law, Haji Ali's uncle-in-law) learned from Ayim about the plan to pay the IPM farmers to handpick the WRB moths to prevent them laying eggs. From Idham and Ayim, another farmer, Tarma (an old non-IPM farmer) received information about the way to spray pesticide by looking at the degree of "illness" on paddy. From Ardi, his father (Romi) received an explanation about red disease and the need to handpick the WRB eggs; whereas Ardi's brother, Rustam, learned about the WRB life cycle. Rustam acquired information about various types of moths from Idham.

The non-IPM farmers also received the IPM farmers' own interpretations of information that was sometimes contrary to the trainers' explanations. One message that was frequently mentioned by the IPM farmers was the need to apply carbofuran. According to the IPM farmers, this carbofuran was not only a must in relation to the WRB outbreak, but also as a prerequisite in using "medicine." Askim (a non-IPM farmer, Haji Ali's wife's brother-in-law) learned from Eka that "... if we have applied *Furadan*, we scarcely have to spray at all.

The illnesses will be absent, because we have already applied fertilizer and basal medicine."

When the farmers found—according to their interpretations—that the alternate products they used as substitutes for *Thiodan* (including the other banned insecticides) were effective, they spread their findings to other farmers. These lay farmers perceived this information as something learned by the IPM farmers from school. Tarmi, for instance, learned from Wira that *Azodrin*, a banned insecticide in a mixture with kerosene was effective to control "red disease"; but not to control leaf folders as Wira actually did.

From the mass of novel terms taught in training, those that were mainly used in conversations were:

- *penggerek* (borer), *penggerek batang* (stem borer), *siklus hidup* (life cycle), and *parasit* (parasite) when talking about white rice borer;
- *populasi* (population) when referring to the rat population;
- *mengamati* and *meneliti* (to examine) or *mengendalikan* (to control) when talking about novel methods of pest control.

Iman told me what he had learned from Idham and Ayim, "... now the farmers are not allowed to spray but must examine (*sekarang itu petani tidak boleh menyemprot, tetapi meneliti*)." The IPM farmers used these terms in combination with their own words. The new term for natural enemy, i.e., *musuh alami*, however, did not crop up in the speech of non-IPM farmers. This term was either seldom used by the IPM farmers (except Ayim and a few other farmers) or was not easy to recall by the non-IPM farmers. Some non-IPM farmers told me that they had never heard this term from the IPM farmers. Others said that they did not remember the word. The IPM farmers only cited technical terms, such as the economic threshold level (*ambang ekonomi*) in their talks among themselves or in their conversations when I was present.

Since not every farmer was involved in conversations with IPM farmers—both in the hamlet and in rice field area—and not every IPM farmer dared to talk or was as vocal as Idham and Ayim, some farmers did not learn any new ideas from the school.

"Now Our Way of Thinking Is Different" 205

POWER RELATIONS AND THE NONEXISTENT DISCOURSE IN KNOWLEDGE EXCHANGE

IPM experts, government officials, and IPM farmers themselves expected that IPM knowledge would be disseminated to non-IPM farmers. When the IPM farmers began to talk to other farmers, they soon became aware of the constraints they had in communicating alien ideas. Not every farmer could comprehend what the IPM farmers said. The absence of the IPM's perspectives and paradigms, e.g., the prey-predator dynamics, constrained the non-IPM farmers to understand the novel ideas, propositions or pest control strategies introduced by the IPM farmers. The latter realised that some non-IPM farmers were hesitant and would not be convinced by what was said unless some evidence was provided. After experiencing difficulties in their efforts to introduce IPM knowledge, they drew their own assumptions of possible causes of these difficulties. First, people viewed as significant their own and the speakers' socio-economic status, whether rich or poor, labourer (landless) or owner. Second, people had confidence in their knowledge of rice farming (based on their expertise and experience in rice farming) as compared to the speakers' experiences. Finally, people were reluctant to adopt the novel ideas that would change their established ways of cultivating rice.

All the vocal farmers, such as Idham, Ayim, and Usin, belonged to the lower socioeconomic strata. Usin did not own *sawah*, Idham owned only small areas of *sawah* and worked as a wage labourer. Ayim's lands consisted of small plots of *sawah*. Some neither belonged to the group of expert/model farmers nor were they considered *tokoh masyarakat* (prominent figures in the community). In the first days of *tahlilan*, most of the responses they received from the farmers were complaints that the novel methods of controlling WRB were difficult and troublesome. For two decades, the farmers had been accustomed to practise the prophylactic use of pesticide without examining populations of pests and natural enemies. They also did not have any idea about the pests' reproductive cycle. The non-IPM farmers thus considered the new ideas transmitted by the IPM farmers, i.e., the need to examine, to think and to practise other methods, as causing more trouble. Without any ideas and concepts about the new strategy, understanding something alien was bothersome. This became a burden for the IPM farmers who did not receive any respect from the non-IPM farmers because of their low status, but were highly motivated to disseminate IPM knowledge.

Only through evidence of the WRB egg clusters and the larvae that hatched from the eggs presented by Aming and Idham, as well as the bombardment of information every night at the *tahlilan*, did some farmers (but not all) begin to listen to and believe in what they were saying. Itang (Idham-Ucup-Arman's neighbour) told me that at first he did not want to listen to Idham, but since he "kept talking, I finally heard what I had not wanted to listen to in the beginning." Iman (Itang's brother) also reported that at first he did not believe it but, then, he examined Idham's explanation until finally he said, "I believe what Idham said." Gradually, these vocal farmers—particularly Idham and Ayim—were recognized by other farmers as *petani-peneliti* (farmer-researchers), as "those who like to tell stories" (*yang suka cerita-cerita*). A new group of farmers emerged because of their curiosity and consistent attempts to look for reasons for unusual occurrences, and because of their willingness to talk about what they found and knew.

The other farmers' complaints were also related to the fact that in recent times, knowledge introduced to them by the agricultural officials had not significantly altered and improved their yields. "Up to now rice farming has been like that. Even without any 'lessons' those that were good, were good; and those that were bad, were bad," reported Arman, imitating the other farmers' skeptical replies. The non-IPM farmers conceived that the story about the need to look at the condition of pest-populations, and the decision to take control after the condition of "illness became serious" as something dangerous. A delay in spraying "medicines" could damage their paddy. They could not understand this idea: "Why should spraying be carried out after the damage symptoms have been serious?" reported Arpan, imitating his neighbour's reply.

The IPM farmers believed that the transfer of knowledge to rice-field neighbours, particularly those who came from different hamlets or villages, was ineffective and useless. They only met and talked occasionally, without a conversation at home. "I told him about the economic threshold of leaf folders and the need to spray pests only if necessary, but he kept spraying pesticide," reported Ardi. His neighbour, from Kebon Cau, was well known as a diligent farmer who sprayed his *sawah* quite often. The farmers perceived him as *petani tulèn* (a true farmer) who had the same reputation as Adma in their own hamlet (the model farmer). Since he had great confidence in his own strategy, it was not easy for the IPM farmers to convince him. Once their neighbours refused to accept their explanation, the IPM farmers preferred to keep quiet rather than to keep talking. Ayim was unusual in that he continued transmitting what he learned from IPM to his rice-field neighbours in the other hamlet, Rajapolah.

The young IPM farmers also faced constraints in transmitting knowledge to the older, knowledgeable farmers (*petani yang sudah pengalaman*), including their own parents or parents-in-law. Maturity in age and experience was a prominent factor in building up the farmers' confidence in rice farming strategies. They were adverse to receiving advice from young inexperienced farmers (*anak muda kurang pengalaman*). Ardi's father ignored his son's advice to control WRB by applying carbofuran instead of spraying "medicine." Asmin, another young IPM farmer, received an insult from an older non-IPM farmer in a talk about pest control: "What would you know? I have had years of experience of being a farmer." Because of their youth, they preferred to keep quiet unless questions were posed to them by the older farmers. "I am afraid that other farmers might say I am a 'know-all' (*Saya takut dibilang sok tahu*)," explained Akim. "My father might feel hurt (*merasa tersinggung*) for he has already had a lot of experience," said Ardi. The audience for the receipt of IPM knowledge from young IPM farmers was thus limited to themselves, the farmers of a similar age, and those who brought questions to them.

From the point of view of the older IPM farmers, transmitting knowledge to the young inexperienced farmers was also ineffective. Amid, for instance, did not feel comfortable about talking to his own son-in-law about IPM. His son-in-law was a beginner in rice farming and thus would not understand what he was talking about. However, he gave guidance about rice-farming practices to his son-in-law. As a permanent wage labourer who had the responsibility of taking action, Amid dared to talk to the owner, his master (*dunungan*), to allow him to make decisions regarding pest/disease control. Nevertheless, he did not transmit any novel ideas to his master who lived in another place, outside the village. The other IPM farmer who had a position as a master (Adma), did not transmit any knowledge of IPM to his labourers as well. As a result, none of Adma's three labourers ever received any ideas from him. Only one of them learned about WRB from his hamlet neighbours, the IPM farmers, but not about the idea of natural enemy or the judicious use of pesticides. The other labourers and relatives of the IPM farmers, who also lived close by never heard about IPM ideas. Proximity in neighbourhood did not mean that there was a close communication network among them, or that they had ever engaged in talk about IPM ideas.

The IPM farmers of similar age to Amid and even those who were known as knowledgeable and expert farmers, such as Adma and Wahyu, preferred to keep silent. For them, the lessons had not finished yet, and they had not had evidence about the effectiveness of this novel strategy. Both the IPM and non-IPM farmers required proof of the effectiveness of IPM strategies through plant and yield performances before they would accept the new knowledge and gain confidence in its implementation (see chap. 4). Some IPM farmers who had not been convinced yet about the result of this strategy on their plants' performances did not want to transmit any knowledge to non-IPM farmers.

On the basis of their experiences in communicating IPM knowledge and receiving unwelcome responses, the IPM farmers used several terms to indicate those who could not understand or refused to accept the new notions: "*orang awam* (the lay-men)," "*petani awam* (the lay-farmers)," "*orang-orang yang tidak sama pikirannya* (people who did not have similar thoughts)," or "*orang-orang yang membangkang* (the disobedient people)." In one conversation, the term "*orang sakit*" (the sick men) appeared to differentiate those who refused to consider the new ideas from those who decided to listen to and to try to understand what the IPM farmers were talking about (*orang sehat*, the healthy men). Haji Nafi whom some IPM farmers perceived as one of the healthy men, could interpret his own experience with what he learned from Idham. First, he related Idham's story about the WRB life cycle, adding his own observations and then he drew upon his own imagination:

> Idham came and told me about the white rice borer. "Oh yes, it is right. During transplanting when the seedlings were pulled, there were many white moths. The moths might lay eggs there. I saw the moths, but at that time, I did not understand that these were those who became *penggerek batang*. So, the last harvest failure could have originated from the moths in the nurseries. During transplanting, the eggs hatched and became moths again. In the flowering stage, the moths laid eggs again."

Second was the story about the food chain, as taught in IPM training. He learned from Idham that,

> those who prey on pests should not die. Snakes prey on frogs, frogs prey on ... what ... (?) This is similar to my experience. The rats did not damage the paddy. Snakes, civet cats and hawks preyed on rats. I saw it myself how the hawks hunted on rats ... but the birds have disappeared now. Hence, those that kill pests are also pests.

Haji Nafi was one among a few other farmers who was able to expand his understanding on the basis of what he learned from the IPM farmers. The responses of many other farmers, however, stimulated some IPM farmers to think over other strategies that might be more effective in transmitting IPM knowledge.[8]

IDEAS AND COMPLAINTS

On the basis of his own evidence that reduction in pesticide spraying did not decrease yields but did save expenses and his belief that the farmers needed proof of the introduced ideas, Ayim became confident that he would be capable of disseminating IPM knowledge at a formal meeting. Both Ayim and Idham perceived themselves as more appropriate sources of information than the extension worker who, in their perception, had never had practical experience in rice farming. The IPM farmers gradually realised that the trainers' knowledge was not much greater than theirs, since the trainers were only trained a step ahead of them. Ayim explained his reasons further:

> I want to present my words in the next agricultural extension in the beginning of the planting season ... I want to talk about ways of controlling WRB and other pests .... If only the PPL talks, the farmers won't believe them 100%. What does the PPL know? He only sits behind a desk. Behind a desk, so, if the farmers themselves present the words, the other farmers might believe what is said. Maybe not 100%,

but they might believe it because I have tried it myself. I did not spray at all throughout the whole season. Since transplanting, I only did the observing; I did not spray. I only applied carbofuran.

Although Idham agreed with Ayim's idea, he was aware that his position was subordinate to the extension worker. He was afraid that this action might embarrass the PPL and give no work to him. The IPM farmers were, in fact, aware of their ambivalent positions. They knew, on the one hand, that the non-IPM farmers would come to believe only by looking at the speakers' experiences and evidence. After gaining confidence about IPM strategies through their practices, some IPM farmers were prepared to disseminate IPM knowledge. On the other hand, they recognized their own limitations as farmers who did not have any authority to influence the other farmers' behaviour. In such a situation, they looked up to those in power as the appropriate source of influence to modify people's actions. Metaphorically, they perceived the government as their "shepherd" (see Foucault on his statements about the state as a new form of pastoral power in Foucault 1982/83:215–16). Idham explained this term as follows:

> People are like buffaloes. If the shepherd is inattentive, the buffaloes can only take a bath in the water, without having something to eat. A leader is like a "shepherd." The shepherd should lead his flocks. The government should lead us, the people. If they do not lead us seriously, nothing will be improved. (See chap. 2.)

Understanding their own positions as ordinary people without authority, they realised the constraints in disseminating IPM knowledge. They had no official support to authorize their actions. They thus complained about the absence of any official IPM ceremonies held in their hamlet. These ceremonies were perceived as significant institutions to recognize publicly their identity as the schooled farmers: those who had acquired special scientific knowledge about rice farming. Another complaint was the cancellation of the order for IPM shirts. An IPM shirt was perceived as a very appropriate way of letting other farmers know that they were IPM graduates. The IPM farmers, particularly the young, inexperienced, landless farmers, felt constrained when talking to lay farmers without any formal identification. They also grumbled about the late arrival of IPM certificates.

When they received the certificates, some were not in their names due to participant substitution and alteration.

While complaining about such a frustrating situation, they still proposed new methods of disseminating IPM knowledge. Ayim, again, suggested the use of written boards put everywhere, to let everybody read and raise questions about IPM. When proposing this idea, he referred to other government programs using similar boards. Another suggestion was to include model farmers instead of young farmers in IPM training. Diloh also proposed to have two schools sequentially, each with participants of a similar age (i.e., old farmers and young farmers in separate schools). These participants consisted of pairs of parents and sons or sons-in-law—the common working unit instead of farmer-labourer—to avoid conflicts between these two generations. These were all ideas that they did not know how to put into action because they were not in positions of authority. Trainers did not return to their hamlet to carry out follow-up activities as was promised by the pest observer. So, they did not know where to direct these ideas and complaints.

As LAVE (1988), KEESING (1987), and other scholars say, the everyday activities provide a wide room for individual choices, alternatives, constructions, and creativity. This was what I found in following the farmer's daily practices where they interpreted and validated IPM ideas. The theories were interpreted subjectively on the basis of individual empirical observation, understandings, needs, interests, confidence, prior experiences and existing knowledge. The individual subjective interpretation occurred in a situation where the farmers could not objectively prove their assumptions within the constraints of empirical observation in an uncontrolled environment. As a result, despite the internalization of the common new schemas of interpretation, a diverse range of interpretations and practices was apparent. Reinterpretation, modification, disagreement, confusion, misinterpretation and, in some cases, contradictory assumption to the original IPM principles and objectives were evident in daily farmers' conversations and practices. Not only was the degree of individual reception different, but also the degree to which the various concepts and propositions were incorporated into the IPM farmers' own body of knowledge. The IPM farmers did not favour the skills and concepts they perceived as impractical in relation to their time, energy and resources.

In this early stage of learning IPM strategies, the farmers incorporated the new ideas that were outside their ordinary reasons and concerns in pest management, into their decision making. (See H. Gladwin and Murtaugh 1980:117 on the preattentive process in agricultural decision making; also see Nazaria-Sandoval 1995:16–17.) Through trial-and-error, the majority of IPM farmers who were convinced of the advantages of the new strategies gradually adopted the ideas of carrying out an observation before making a decision; looking at the population of pests and natural enemies, the degree of damage on plants; and making a judgment whether "spraying medicines" was necessary. In this stage, however, the IPM farmers were still consciously practicing the new strategies and evaluating the results. These had not become part of what Gladwin and Murtaugh (1980:117) call the "unconscious processing which underlies the routine decision of everyone." This unconscious processing constitutes the stage of eliminating aspects in decision making.

It was also the time when only among themselves could the IPM farmers subjectively share the meanings of the IPM ideas and the new schemas for interpreting the phenomena about pest/disease outbreaks. D'Andrade (1987:113) explains that a

> "schema is *intersubjectively shared* when everybody in the group knows the schema, and everybody knows that everyone else knows the schema, and everybody knows that everyone knows that everyone knows the schema."

The IPM farmers soon realised that this was not the case when they engaged in conversation with the "lay farmers." The non-IPM farmers could not easily understand or accept the IPM farmers' explanation. These new ideas had not been part of the non-IPM farmers' interpretation schema, and thus had not been inter-subjectively shared by everybody in the farmers' community. Moreover, the speakers' expertise and status in rice farming did not always conform to how the farmers usually trust the sources of valid and reliable information. Only by encountering evidence, such as the

WRB egg clusters and larvae, and the IPM farmers' detailed observation and nonspraying, could the lay farmers begin to notice what the new ideas meant to their daily farming activities. So how did the IPM and non-IPM farmers make these novel understandings part of subjectively shared knowledge? The following chapter will examine how the IPM knowledge was transformed into the farmers' own body of knowledge and practices in the 1990–1991 rainy season following the IPM training.

6

Voicing for Freedom, Striving for Harvests

> "Now, I have the time to rethink, to comprehend fully and to analyze what the trainers said," reflected Idham on his learning experience in the 1990–1991 rainy season.

IN THIS SEASON, the farmers had the opportunity to validate, evaluate, modify or criticise IPM knowledge in encountering an unforeseen repeated outbreak of white rice borer. At an earlier stage, when the farmers planned how to find and use resources efficiently, they found they were powerless to command government-subsidized input. The farmers' responses to these unexpected events provide good examples of how they came to know things accidentally. Previous studies reveal farmers' abilities to adjust sequentially to unpredictable conditions and make decisions in the course of action (e.g., Ortiz 1973, 1979; Richards 1986, 1993). As responses develop, their knowledge improves. Action, experience and knowledge are always in a dynamic and continuous interaction "… [K]nowledge is continually being refined, enriched, or completely revised by experience," argue Keller and Keller (1993:127). This revised knowledge becomes the basis for further actions from which people interpret new experience. Understanding how knowledge is created over time through human action and experience is the main objective of this chapter. I will examine this process of knowledge construction as "… some sequences of intelligibly connected actions and events" (Vayda *et al.* 1991:318; see chap. 1).

With this objective, I first describe how the farmers selected rice varieties in the season following their decisions to plant diverse rice strands. The choice of rice variety and planting schedule can contribute significantly to the nature of WRB infestation and the farmers' interpretations of this outbreak. Part one examines how the farmers arrived at their decisions and what knowledge was gained from the previous dry season. By the end of the 1990 dry season, IPM farmers enthusiastically drew up their plans to implement the new idea of the judicious use of pesticides. They proposed a request for a partial credit package without having the liquid pesticides in advance. However, ideals are not always congruent with reality (see Moore 1975). This occurred in the situation when the farmers had to interact with an authority that specified the rules of their entitlements in government-subsidized schemes. In section two I discuss how the farmers struggled in this interface and its effects on their understanding on policy and the provision of input. With additional knowledge about the WRB's reproductive behaviour and its control strategies, the IPM farmers generated practices and gained knowledge in their daily responses to WRB outbreaks. In part three I examine how these activities occurred and the extent to which they contributed to knowledge formation and transmission.

Consensus and Diversity: Choice of Rice Variety

"Choose a resistant variety and rotate varieties season to season," were messages the farmers learned from the IPM trainers. Choosing a resistant variety has been part of the farmers' learning process. Rotating varieties is indeed a context-dependent decision. Chapter 3 describes how the farmers made decisions following the harvest failure of the 1989–1990 rainy season. A set of intelligible variables—which could vary seasonally—affected their decisions to select and/or rotate varieties. The selected rice strands—produced in the absence of a severe harvest failure—illustrates what Barth (1981:36) says about the social form as "... the cumulative result of a number of separate choices and decisions made by people acting vis-a-vis another." The farmers may have their reasons for choosing a particular variety but they still need to consider other farmers' choices (see Schelling 1978; Watts 1983). A gradual decision was made throughout the 1990 fallow period.

Revalidating and improving knowledge: assessing plant performance

Assessing plant performance not only revalidated the farmers' experiences of growing rice in dry weather, but also improved their knowledge of that particular season's weather and the complexity of the diversifying varieties.

A yield reduction in the dry season was not unexpected. The farmers had shared knowledge that yields in the dry season were always less than those in the rainy season. Grain could not form fully under hot and dry conditions. However, they discovered an unexpected reduction in the 1990 harvests. Chapter 5 describes the unforeseen attack of *krésék*. Several farmers inferred that the very hot and dry weather in this season was conducive to the emergence of diseases. The dryness could reduce yields even further in a late harvesting schedule. The lodging of stems that was not caused by heavy rain and wind as in the rainy season was a new phenomenon for the farmers. They interpreted this lodging as the result of disease infestation, or their own fertilizing or water management. The farmers also perceived the unforeseen outbreak of rice seed bugs as reducing yields (see chap. 5). The diverse yields gained from the same varieties complicated their assessments. Not all farmers perceived their outcomes as unintended. Those who planted particular varieties to avoid risk could, in fact, attain their purposes; although in some cases, the yields declined. Other farmers, on the other hand, experienced unexpected outcomes. Thus, the farmers could not easily refer to a single variable as the possible cause. Nevertheless, these unintended consequences improved their understanding of different varieties and of cultivating rice in very dry weather.

Learning from these consequences, they drew inferences about the promising varieties and their market price and their resistances toward pests and disease. The farmers reached a consensus about the surviving varieties against certain pests and diseases, but had an ambiguous evaluation of several other varieties, which, in their eyes, were susceptible to pests and diseases in the rainy season. One of them was *IR64*. The farmers contested *IR42* because of the diverse range of performance this variety produced. The following is an example of how the farmers assessed various aspects of the different varieties:

Adma reasoned that: "*Ciliwung* is not quite good enough; the number of stems is not plenty, the same as *Way Seputih*. I still do not know what to plant in the next rainy season. I am not quite sure with all the varieties: which one is resistant and provides a high yield. *IR64* provides good yields, has a high number of stems and panicles and the panicles' stems are long; but I am afraid it is not resistant enough. *Cisadané* has already been infested by brown plant hopper in the rainy season. *IR42* is good; it was not infested by white rice borer in the last rainy season .... *Dèlis* was also not infested by white rice borer in the last rainy season."

Adma then mentioned *IR99* as a promising variety. Yet he had not been able to firmly define his choice. In the early fallow period (September 1990), many other farmers were still confused. "I do not know what to plant; it's confusing, there are so many different paddy," said Arman, even though his favourite was *IR42*. Other farmers could not make a decision yet because they had no idea what their neighbours' choice was. Several farmers, however, had been able to make up their minds. Ayim, for example, chose *IR41* for consumption and *ketan* for its high market price. Individual farmers made their decisions gradually throughout the fallow period (up to November 1990), and eventually, many farmers preferred to replant *IR64*.

Producing a recurrent strategy

Besides assessing plant performance, a set of other variables affected the farmers' decisions: projections of varieties that would be promising in future weather conditions and in the face of possible hazards; recurrent concerns of a likely "famine" season; neighbour's choices; and the authority's advice on what to plant in the following season.

The farmers' projection of the future conditions of the weather, pests and disease was based significantly on their past experiences (see Ortiz 1979 for the farmers' expectations on the basis of past experience). Moving towards the forthcoming rainy season, the farmers had some expectations of the possibility of rain and wind at the ripening stage. Hence they looked for varieties that would survive and perform well in such weather. Among other varieties, *IR64* was still promising. In the absence of pest attacks (e.g., rats or WRB), this variety had a high number of stems and panicles and good weight and quality of grains. Some farmers regained their confidence and were not anxious about a recurrence of pests. In their views, the long drought could eradicate "illnesses in the ground." Last year's pest outbreak was just "bad luck" or "misfortune" (*nasib*) and a "calamity" (*musibah*). By gaining new understanding, reevaluating their past experiences and validating them with information from other places, some farmers now assumed that there was no direct relation between the outbreaks and the susceptibility of *IR64*.

> Sukim told me that "if I plant *IR64*, the traders would not hesitate to buy it. The only anxiety is the attack of the 'white' (*kena putih*). But, this was only a 'calamity' (*musibah*). The hazard was not because of the susceptibility of the paddy, since other varieties at the same age as *IR64* were also infested. If we harvest *IR64* earlier, it won't be attacked. I had an experience of planting *IR64* in one *bahu* of *sawah* in the rainy season. The paddy escaped from pest attack because I did the planting seven days earlier than the others. Another example was that, in the last dry season, the paddy in Karawang was attacked by the 'white' whereas here the paddy was attacked by *krèsèk*. It means that this hazard was not because of the paddy, but because of nature (*karena alam itulah*)."

The farmers knew, however, that their choices of particular varieties still entailed risks and hence made plans to prevent or reduce these risks.

Economic reasons and capital play an important part in the farmers' decisions. Every year, the dry season's harvest marks the beginning of a long "famine" season (*masa paceklik*). The farmers have to survive until the next rainy season harvest, waiting up to seven months. Longhurst et al. (1986:1) state that the "… period before harvest—the 'hungry season'—is one of considerable stress for rural people, exacerbating their poverty" (also, see Chambers et al. 1981). Many farmers thus chose to plant short maturity-age varieties (*padi yang gènjah*), "… so that the famine would not last too long," said Ucup, Romi and many other farmers.

The famine season of 1990 was severe for those who had experienced a poor harvest or a harvest failure in the rainy season of 1989/90 and had not been able to pay their previous debts. They had to pay them at compounded interest rates in the future. To pay debts sooner became one of their main reasons for choosing *IR64*. Economic reasons also underlay the farmers' motives for choosing other varieties, e.g., *ketan*, so as to enable them to gain higher profits for celebrating *Lebaran* (the Moslems' celebration at the end of *Ramadhan*, the fasting month).

Apart from individual preferences and reasons, the farmers' decisions are inseparable from their neighbours' choices. In the early fallow period, "... what the 'community' would like to plant (*masyarakat mau tanam apa*)," had not become a widespread issue. The farmers decided to wait to know the other farmers' choice. The main reason for suspending their decisions was their anxiety about pest outbreaks. Learning from the recurrent rat attacks and the emergence of rice seed bugs in an environment of heterogeneous rice varieties, many farmers agreed that "... ideally there should be a collective decision to plant a uniform variety," as Ardi said.

As the end of October 1990 approached, the news about the choice of varieties began to spread. Gradually, every farmer learned about his/her neighbours' choices. Some made up their minds firmly, some evaluated their previous choices, changed their decisions or made adjustments in their strategies to reduce possible risks. Some pursued their strategies to diversify varieties in several plots of *sawah*, even though they made a reference to what the "community" said. The authority's recommendation to replant *IR64* came later (in November 1990). The farmers thus perceived this recommendation as confirmation of their own decisions. For some, this recommendation became their main reason for planting this variety.

Reaching a consensus and maintaining diversity: rice varieties of 1990 and 1991

The common perceptions the farmers had of the promising varieties under the economic and ecological constraints, the role of their neighbours' choices and government recommendations all contributed to the consensus reached to plant a particular variety. Yet, the choice of rice variety was an individual decision. Desire to try new promising varieties or to pursue planting a particular variety also varied. As a result, 89.4% of farmers replanted *IR64* in 88 of 121 *sawah* (72.7%), whereas the number of *sawah* planted with *Cisadané* and *IR42* dropped to 3.3% (close to the percentage of *sawah* planted with these varieties in the 1989/90 rainy season, see chap. 3). Diversity persisted, however, as can be seen from the farmers' choice of a number of other varieties such as *Ketan, Way Seputih, IR41, IR99, Semeru* and *Dèlis*.

In this season, some farmers diversified varieties by planting *IR64* in one or several locations while planting other varieties in other *sawah*. As a result, there were patches of *sawah* planted with diverse varieties, even though *sawah* planted with *IR64* increased. There were always patches of heterogeneous varieties from season to season. As Ardi said, "… it is difficult to ask the farmers to make a collective decision in planting one variety," whatever varieties are suggested by the authority.

Knowledge and Power: IPM and Credit Package

The choice of a rice variety reveals a situation in which the farmers are left to make their own decisions. The farmers encountered an entirely different situation in their efforts to have command of government-subsidized input. Those in power and authority determined the farmers' entitlement to government commodity bundles.

From the early 1970s up to recent times, various subsidized inputs have come to form part of the resources and constraints of the farmers' rice production strategies. The introduced high-level inputs of technology forced the farmers to rely on these subsidies, which then constituted part of their entitlement sets. In the recent rice intensification program, the need to use certified seeds, fertilizers and pesticides became crucial to improving production (Sekretariat Badan Pengendali BIMAS 1990). In 1987, the government introduced a credit package known as *Kredit Usaha Tani* (KUT). Even though the farmers had the freedom to choose whether to apply for the credit, the government defined how the farmers could command these resources and the terms that the farmers had to meet (see the provision of credits, Sekretariat Badan Pengendali BIMAS 1990:62). The credit was provided in a "total complete package" without any room for the farmers to have them in a partial form. Thus, although any improvement in the individual knowledge base on the use of production resources could alter the farmers' perceptions and choices, in reality the farmers could not affect the rules specifying their entitlements to subsidized inputs.

The "forced-selling" scheme

The farmers had incorporated the objectives of rice intensification by aiming to obtain high yields and profits. To achieve this, they learned that a relatively high level of inputs was necessary, particularly fertilizers. On the other hand, out of their seasonal income the farmers had to meet not only debts, but also make payments for the *ulu-ulu*, the government tax, donations for village expenses, social and religious obligations and household expenditures. In some cases, the sharecroppers had to share the owners' obligations to pay taxes and donations and to pay their own additional costs, e.g., for extra applications of granular and liquid pesticides. Hence, reliance on other sources of capital—landowners, relatives, moneylenders, shop owners—was a common occurrence, even though the farmers had to pay high rates of interest to moneylenders (25–50% per season) (Winarto 1995). The following are the farmers' complaints about serious debt with multiplying rates of interest:

> Iman (a landless non-IPM farmer) told me that "the farmers now have problems, because they are not able to pay debts after the 1990 harvest failure (*bapuk*). Aduh, ... *payah* (Oh, it is so hard). My debt from the previous rainy season and dry season, up to now, amounted to Rp.3,000,000. I borrowed money from H. Ari and others for planting and other expenses. I hope I can now pay this debt. From this dry season's harvest I can earn Rp.2,500,000 to pay my debt. For my own household consumption, I have to borrow again. I only have about 100 kg rice left. So, I need to borrow money again to cultivate rice ... and I have a debt to pay to the shop owner, so my debt accumulates."
>
> H. Ali complained that, "I get dizzy if I cannot pay my debt, because the debt is not a 'cold-debt' (*hutang dingin,* debt with low interest). The debt is a 'hot-debt' (*hutang panas,* debt with high interest). If I have a debt of Rp.100,000 I have to pay up to Rp.140,000. If I borrow money up to Rp.1,000,000 I have to pay Rp.1,400,000." Iman said that such an amount of interest was still low (*masih ringan*). "There are cases where we have to return debt with interest up to Rp.1,500,000, one and a half times. Sometimes there are some moneylenders who ask for interest of 100 kg of rice (*satu kuintal*). Thus from Rp.100,000 we have to pay up to Rp.125,000."

In such an economic environment, having the input of credit through the government-subsidized scheme was beneficial. However, the farmers had numerous complaints about the handling of this scheme, such as: 1) the inclusion of nonfarmer applicants (e.g., the local authorities) who made improper use of the credits; 2) the use of the money for other purposes by the *Koperasi Unit Desa* (KUD) officials instead of delivering them straight to the farmers; 3) the late delivery of input, particularly fertilizers; and 4) the loss of the farmers' savings accounts for the past four seasons due to bad debt in their KUD. The major complaint was the forced-selling scheme (*jual paksa*) of the input so that they did not have freedom to choose the types of inputs on their own. The farmers grumbled that,

> "The KUT has already been allotted. There were various instructions. Thus, it did not depend on the farmers' will. We would like to protest, but we could not do it," Akim said. Arman supported Akim's complaint: "Thus, there was no room for the farmers' own choices, there could not be any room; there has never been any deliberation (*Jadi keinginan petani enggak ada, enggak bisa, enggak pernah ada musyawarah*)."

The farmers could not refuse the unwanted components and had to accept the complete package. They thus assumed that there was a play behind the screen between the chemical companies, the KUD and the BPP officials. Comparing this forced selling scheme with borrowing money from moneylenders (*rentenir*), the farmers conceived the latter option as more beneficial, providing them with the freedom to choose.

> "If I borrow as much as Rp.100,000 from other people I have to pay my debt of Rp.125,000—not much difference from the KUT. The price of fertilizer in the shop is Rp.175/kg. From KUT the price is up to Rp.182/kg and we still have to pay the transportation costs. Our own savings are also gone. Each farmer had to spend Rp.3,000/season from his savings account. Four seasons meant Rp.12,000. From all farmers in the Cabang, the savings were up to Rp.500,000. It was all gone. If I borrow money by myself, I am free. I do not need to use ZA (S fertilizer), 'medicines,' and I know ... what I need," explained Akim.

The farmers' complaints indicate their position as the recipients of the program handed down by the authorities who also took advantage of and exercised their power in handling the allocation of resources. Once the farmers decided to have the subsidized inputs, they lost their freedom to exercise choice and command on commodities they preferred. Under this condition and the problem of a bad debt in their KUD in the 1989–1990 rainy season, some farmers preferred to be free by managing their own capital or looking at other possible avenues that provided freedom to choose by borrowing money from relatives, landowners or moneylenders. Several farmers applied credit packages from the KUD in other places where the components suited their needs.

The "partial credit package": voice, action and failure

Officially, the SUPRA INSUS program incorporated the IPM strategy. The farmers, however, only became aware of this recent policy on pesticide use through training. By receiving this policy in a formal setting, the "school," they perceived that the government was serious about getting them to change their previous practices. In the 1990 dry season, some IPM farmers already validated the truth that using pesticides judiciously indeed reduced their expenses. By associating their recent identity as schooled-farmers with legitimate knowledge received from the state, the IPM farmers had the courage to voice their understandings to the state's agents.

To voice, according to Hirschman (1970), is a response expressed by a firm's customers or an organization's members due to the deterioration of the quality of a firm's products or an organization's performance. Hirschman (1970) describes three kinds of behaviour: voice, exit, and loyalty. This behaviour can further compel the firm or the organization's managers to evaluate performance. He says that the voice option is the expression of the customer or members "… directly to management or to some other authority to which management is sub-ordinate or through general protest addressed to anyone who cares to listen …" (Hirschman 1970:3). In this case of the forced-selling scheme, the farmers decided firmly to voice against taking the component of liquid pesticides from the package scheme.

UNWANTED COMPONENTS: THE FARMERS' REFUSAL

Throughout the fallow period, a shared decision to voice their protest against the provision of a complete credit package was gradually reached among the farmers. They perceived this protest as the best way to empower themselves. In mid September 1990, the farmers' leader proposed this idea to the extension worker who came to process the credit-request-form (RDKK, *Rencana Definitif Kebutuhan Kelompoktani* or the Definitive Plans of the Farmers'

Group Requirements) for the 1990/91 planting season. The extension worker handed in the already determined components written in the form without the farmers' consent. He left his message that all the columns in that form had to be filled in. The farmers then understood that there was no chance to oppose it. Disappointment soon spread among the farmers. They came to question the conflicting policies among the government agencies.

By referring to IPM lessons, according to which they were not allowed to spray if the pest population was low, the farmers questioned the policy of compulsory purchased pesticide. It meant they had to buy pesticide in advance and to prepare the "medicines" before any outbreaks of pests or diseases. In other words, they had to spray. If they decided not to use the pesticide later, they still had to pay debts with interest. Furthermore, if they received an inappropriate type of pesticide to control particular pests/diseases, they had to spend extra later to buy the appropriate one. Again, they had to carry the burden of the expense (Winarto 1995).

The farmers gained the understanding that there was no collaboration between the central and the regional or the middle-level government agencies in implementing IPM policy. The KUD officials might also be ignorant of IPM strategy. The farmers perceived that there was a conflict of interest for KUD officials between helping the farmers and gaining profits. The farmers knew that gaining profits became the basis for the collaboration between the chemical companies, the KUD and BPP officials. Haji Ali assumed that,

> "*Darmabas* is in fact not very much in demand. This medicine was included in the package because ... as usual ... the KUD received an amount of money. Thus, the companies approached the KUD, whereas the KUD did not know that there were IPM schools." Haji Ali also understood that the chemical companies approached the BPP as well. "The chemical companies and the BPP determined the type of medicines: they compromised. If the 'medicines' go through BPP they will be sold, if the 'medicines' go through the shops, they might not be sold .... Thus the BPP could earn profits ... if only from salaries, it won't be enough for the BPP."

Even though the farmers realised that they had to carry social burdens (*ini jadi beban masyarakat*), those who badly needed the fertilizers but could not afford to pay cash, decided to accept the complete credit package. "I need the fertilizers, although I do not need the pesticides," said Haji Ali. Some preferred to "exit" as had other farmers. The "exit" option, according to Hirschman (1970:3), refers to the action of "some customers who stop buying the firm's products or some members leave the organization."

> Arpan decided to exit from the scheme: "I feel more comfortable being free to choose whatever I want rather than being forced to buy something." Arpan preferred to manage whatever he had.

Other farmers looked for cash or credit from other sources. In the end, only 13 farmers (17.7%) were named as applicants.

On his own initiative, Haji Ali asked Ardi about the appropriate steps to take. To express their refusal of the unwanted components Ardi suggested not filling in the column for liquid pesticides and herbicides (including foliar fertilizers that were in the same column as herbicides) in the credit package request form. Haji Ali agreed to leave the two columns blank. Receiving the incomplete form, the extension worker asked him to explain. In his reply, Haji Ali raised the question:

> "Why was there an IPM school? According to IPM, spraying has to be carried out on the basis of the pest's condition. So, why do we have to take the 'medicine' now?" Replying to him the extension worker answered that " the 'medicines' have to be taken." Haji Ali said: "I still have many 'medicines,' so there is no use for IPM (*enggak ada hasilnya itu* PHT)."

In that dialogue, the extension worker finally accepted Haji Ali's explanation and agreed to process the form. Later on, however, he made modifications by completing the columns himself. According to the rules, the farmers must approve the type of components in a farmers' meeting. Officially, the farmers could determine the types of components in coordination with the KUD and the chemical companies appointed as the supervisory companies (*perusahaan pembimbing*) (Sekretariat Badan Pengendali BIMAS 1991). In reality, there was no flexibility in choosing the inputs as also found by Kern (1986:114):

> The central government's BIMAS program also did not respond well to borrower needs, even though the thrust of policy making was borrower related and not lender related. Borrowers did not want fixed packages of loan inputs, but wanted the flexibility to choose the inputs needed for their particular circumstances.

Officially, the form must be co-signed by the individual applicant. Nevertheless, there was room for modification in the follow-up stage, since many parties (the extension worker, the head of BPP, the village and district leaders) had to sign the form as a requirement for the bank to clear the input.[1] In this distribution scheme, the extension worker served as the link between the farmers and the KUD officials (see Leonard 1977 for his study of extension service in Kenya).

THE STRUGGLE: THE FARMERS' VOICE AND THE EXTENSION'S REPLY

In their position as a messenger, the extension agents felt responsible for ensuring the implementation of their superiors' policy and did not dare to take divergent steps from their superiors' decisions. Under this condition, the head of BPP firmly said that there was no room for a partial credit package, even though, officially, the farmers were allowed to make a request according to their needs, except for foliar fertilizer. This component was determined directly by the head of the *Pos Komando I* (POSKO I). By pointing to the hierarchy of policy making, the head of BPP explained the sources of the rule he had to follow, i.e., the decree of the governor of West Java province, which was further clarified in the decree of the *Bupati* of Subang (Sekretariat Badan Pengendali BIMAS 1990, 1991).

This rigid rule of providing inputs occurred in a context in which the achievement and maintenance of high productivity in rice became the major goals of the rice intensification program. With this objective, the main function of extension services was to

> ... optimise agricultural extension to achieve the improvement of production through intensification (*mengoptimasikan penyuluhan pertanian untuk pencapaian pengingkatan produksi melalui intensifikasi*) (Sekretariat Badan Pengendali BIMAS 1990:63).

Gradually, the extension workers had become the agents who introduced and encouraged the farmers to adopt new technologies. As found by Sawit and Manwan (1991:92), the role of extension workers changed from

> one of helping, encouraging and influencing farmers to one in which they are first forced (*dipaksa*), then feel compelled (*terpaksa*) and finally become used to (*biasa*) the new technology.[2]

In such a situation, the extension staff felt free to exercise their power in handling the farmers' requests. The reply of the head of BPP to their requests reveals this situation.

Some IPM farmers asked the most vocal IPM farmer to "voice" their requests for a partial credit package in an extension meeting held in November 1990. What the farmers did was in line with what Hirschman (1970:30) states about "voice" as being

> any attempt at all to change, rather than to escape from, an objectionable state of affairs, whether through individual or collective petition to the management directly in charge, through appeal to a higher authority with the intention of forcing a change in management, or through various types of actions and protests, including those that are meant to mobilize public opinion.

The head of BPP, however, refused the farmers' requests. He reasoned that the farmers had to receive all components of the credit package since it was too late to ask for a partial credit package. The pesticide was provided so as to let the farmers be ready for the occurrence of pest/disease in the future (i.e., as "stock"). The farmers' voice failed. Great disappointment was felt among them. The explanations of the head of BPP were, in their eyes, not logical. In their complaints, they imitated the answers of the head of BPP as follows:

> "*Eh*, he said it is as if it is a car; a car needs to have a spare tire. If there is no spare tire, it might be difficult if the car gets damaged. 'Medicines' should also be prepared, for reserve. For me, I do not have money; I cannot pay. But he said it was for 'stock,'" grumbled Akim.
>
> Answering the head of BPP about the farmers' need to have "medicines" as "stock," Idham raised a question about the expiration date of the "medicines" if they had to keep them as "stock." Idham was disappointed again when he received the answer of the head of BPP that the "medicines" had no expiration date so that they could keep them for quite a long time. He did not believe what the head of BPP said and kept grumbling about this reply.

Given their powerless position in this interaction, the farmers' voice was ineffective in bringing about any changes in the government's policy of subsidized inputs. Providing knowledge to empower the farmers as intended by the IPM experts was not a reality when the external power constrained the opportunity the farmers had in their entitlement sets. From this case, the farmers not only learned about the conflicting policies of different government agencies and their position as the victims of this conflict, but they also had an opportunity to validate their previous assumptions about the "shadow-play" between the chemical companies and government officials (Winarto 1995).

THE SMALL PACKAGE AND CASH WITHDRAWAL: AN UNINTENDED CONSEQUENCE

The farmers were again powerless in their position as the recipients of inputs in the delivery process. Until January 1991, from all components listed in the package,[3] the farmers only received fertilizers (for 20 ha *sawah*) and 40 kg of carbofuran, far less than the total amount of carbofuran requested by the farmer applicants. The reason advanced by the KUD officials was the limited carbofuran they had. The farmers' leader decided to provide this small amount of carbofuran to three farmers only. The other applicants, therefore, only received fertilizers. Since many farmers perceived carbofuran as *obat dasar* or a preventative "medicine" against WRB, they complained about the absence of this component in the package. Moreover, they did not receive any cash. The KUD officials made a special visit to Haji Ali to make their offer to withdraw the cash because of the farmers' refusal to accept the complete package. Haji Ali accepted the proposal, but: only "... as long as we do not need to pay the administration costs and saving accounts." However, he did not spread this offer widely.

This event demonstrates, again, the exercise of power by these government officials. By offering the cash withdrawal, the KUD officials manipulated the farmers' resentment for their own benefit. This withdrawal was not intended by the farmer applicants. Their "voice" action had an unintended impact on their opportunities (see Elster 1989:92 for action and unintended impact on opportunities).

The majority of farmers thus began their planting season without pesticide inputs from the government. In this situation, the farmers had to respond to the recurrent outbreak of WRB. The question was whether they would abandon the preventative measures in advance because of the unavailability of pesticides. The farmers' decisions, however, were based on a set of other factors, e.g., objectives, confidence and belief built up from past experiences, the individuals' ability to provide resources, other farmers' actions, the nature of the pest outbreaks and their ongoing adjustments to and interpretations of unintended and unpredictable events (Ortiz 1973, 1979; Johnson 1976; Elster 1989; Richards 1993).

Striving against White Rice Borer: Accumulating Knowledge

The recurring WRB outbreak provided an opportunity for the farmers to exercise the theory received from training by responding directly to the outbreak. The nature of WRB infestation is specific, i.e., larvae boring inside the stems and not infesting plants from outside as brown plant hoppers (BPH) do. The IPM strategy, on the other hand, was initially aimed at preventing the recurrent outbreak of BPH. The 1989/90 WRB outbreak was also an unexpected phenomenon for the experts, even though some WRB had been found in 1969/70 (Suhardjan 1971 in Suharto 1989:285), and again in 1988 in the agricultural research stations of Pusakanegara and BALITTAN Sukamandi (Suharto 1989). On the basis of the 1989–1990 experience, these experts attempted to disseminate information about the possible outbreak and its control strategies to the farmers throughout JALUR PANTURA. The bureaucratic channel through agricultural and administrative agencies was the only means of transmitting knowledge to the farmers. The extension workers in collaboration with the local village officials became the linking mechanism in this trickle-down message transmission. This mechanism was, however, ineffective in providing an appropriate explanation in time. Hence, the farmers had to struggle on their own.

The stories in the following sections present the farmers' gradual responses to the outbreaks, the accumulation of knowledge, and the spread of this knowledge and control practices to a larger number of farmers in Marga Tani. Throughout the season, I found how knowledge and action were interlinked in a complex way. Keller and Keller (1993:125) say that "knowledge and action are each open to alteration by the others as behaviour proceeds." The farmers' behaviours proceeded sequentially within the local social and ecological context day-by-day, week-by-week.

Nurseries: unforeseen pest outbreak

The fallow period in 1990 was a long one. There was insignificant rain until the end of November 1990.[4] The farmers' prediction of the late planting schedule became a reality. With deep cracks and very dry soil, they could not begin preparing their ground without sufficient water. Only a few farmers were able to make nurseries in the first week of November, relying on the available water from irrigation canals. At the same time, the government (the ministry of civil engineering) decided to renovate irrigation canals which also delayed the supply of water into the farmers' fields. Until the end of November 1990, the water was still inadequate to prepare the ground for many *sawah* in the eastern and northern parts of Blok Cadas. Hence, there was a long schedule for ground preparation, making nurseries and transplanting from the first week of November in the western part up to the third week of December 1990 in the eastern part of Blok Cadas. Under such ecological conditions, the farmers began their planting and grumbled about the government's decision to renovate canals when they badly needed water.

The farmers felt confident that the long drought had killed insects in the ground and hence there would not be a significant pest attack. This confidence improved when they found that their seedlings were healthy. This experience strengthened some farmers' belief that the bad year in the Javanese calendar (eight years in a cycle, *satu windu*) had brought hazard in 1989/90. According to the Javanese belief, one year in eight (*satu windu*) is a bad year. The eight years in one cycle consists of: *alip, éhé, jimawal, jé, dal, bé, wawu* and *jimakhir* (Hull 1976). Sosromarsono (n.d.:2), referring to van der Goot (1925) also discusses the relationship between the Javanese calendar and rice stem borer attacks:

> According to the Javanese calendar being divided into a cycle of eight years (*windu*), the second year is the year of *éhé*, when there are rice borer outbreaks in the rice production areas (my own translation).

The farmers, however, mentioned the year of *alip* instead of the year of *éhé* as the bad year in the cycle. In the conversion table presented by Hull (1976), *alip* fell as the year of 1990/91 and *éhé* as 1991 and 1992.

With such a perspective, the recurrence of WRB as predicted by the experts was something unforeseen by many farmers. The head of the Centre for Pest/Disease Surveillance in Jatisari had predicted another outbreak of this pest based on the findings of the enclaves of WRB larvae (*kantong-kantong larva*) in several places in the fallow period (see figure 6.1). He predicted that the moth flights in the forthcoming season would take quite a long time and that there would be overlapping generations of WRB.[5] His message to the farmers delivered in November 1990—to collect WRB eggs in nurseries and to pay greater attention to sanitation—through the officials at the *kabupaten* and *kecamatan* levels, reached the farmers in Ciasem Baru only in mid-December 1990. At this time, the farmers were ready to transplant their plants.

EARLY MOTH FLIGHT: SYSTEMATIC OBSERVATION AND MECHANICAL CONTROL

The first IPM farmer to find moths in nurseries was Ayim when his seedlings were one week old. He was the only one who had an advance plan and a particular intention to control WRB moths and egg clusters with his bare hands through detailed and systematic

Figure 6.1 *Location of larvae during the dry season*

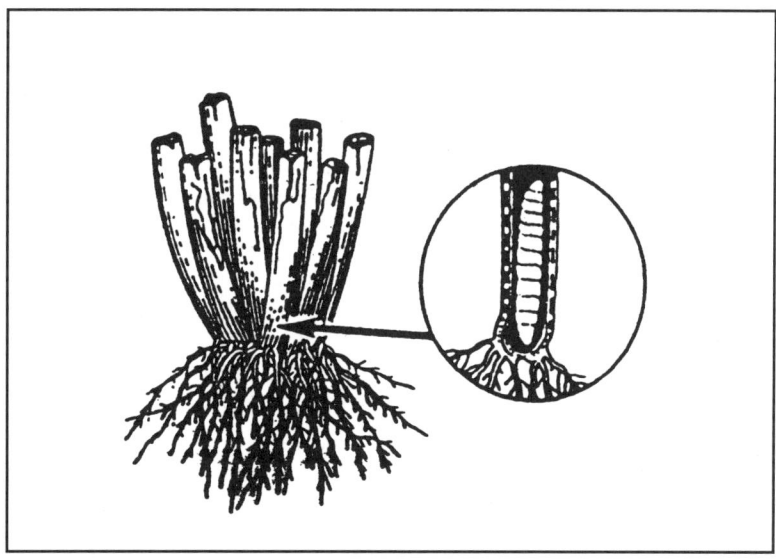

Source: Reissig *et al.* (1986:137).

observation. For this purpose, he made smaller seedbeds to allow him to move easily to the other part of the seedbed while carrying out observation. Regularly, he observed his nurseries twice a day (in the morning and afternoon).

Ayim counted the number of moths and told me that,

> Every day, from my observation, I found five, six, three, ten moths. I did the counting from the time when my seedlings were one week old. Now my seedlings are 15 days old. I have already picked 60 moths, including leaf folder moths.

On December 3, 1990, Ayim found two egg clusters in one of his nurseries. What he did was a modification of IPM teaching for observing a sample of egg clusters. He did the collection of egg clusters as a control measure rather than as a way to determine whether chemical or biological control was necessary. He was also the first farmer who spread his findings that controlling moths in this way was effective and did not need extra expenditure.

Whereas Ayim had discovered moths and eggs and had gained confidence from this control strategy, other farmers still contested the emergence of WRB moths:

> On December 17, 1990, Ayim reported his findings to other farmers who attended the extension meeting at Haji Ali's residence: "From 145 *areal* of *sawah*, I got 40 moths. In the area of 40 *bata* (572 m²), I found 150 moths. In the nurseries, I did the observation every day." These 150 moths consisted of 90 WRB moths and 60 leaf folder moths. Ayim mentioned this while arguing against other farmers' findings that their seedlings looked green, how could there be larvae inside? Iwan and Aming also argued against Ayim by defending the results of their observations that there were no moths in their fields. Idham commented that of course the moths were absent, because "after laying eggs, [the moths] flew away. If [they] finished their work, they went away." Ayim argued against Iwan and Aming about the absence of moths by emphasizing the need to carry out examination. "It is not because the moths were absent, but because [you] did not examine the paddy," criticised Ayim.

These arguments indicate the variations in observing nurseries. Although Ayim and Idham already recognized the importance of detailed observation as a means to control pests, other farmers still carried out their observations while taking care of their nurseries. They did not observe their nurseries as regularly and intentionally as Ayim.

Carrying out detailed observations for these innovative farmers became a significant means to improving knowledge. Ayim, for example, was able to differentiate WRB moths from leaf folders and relate the emergence of moths to the pupae stage.

> "The leaf folder moths had some spots on their wings. The WRB moths were white all over (*putih mulus*)," explained Ayim about his findings from daily observation. He also found that WRB moths were not as nimble as leaf folders and hence interpreted that: "maybe the moths just emerged from the pupae. According to PPL or the researchers, the pupae could stay alive for three to four months in the stalks, although the weather was dry. I believe that because after the seedlings were only one week old, the moths had already come to the nurseries. Before they were not there. Since I did the observation, walking around the nurseries, I knew that the moths were a bit weak. Their flight was also not strong and fast. Maybe they were still young, just emerged from the pupae."

Ayim is an example of those who improved their knowledge by making their own interpretation of the observed phenomenon based on the theory received in training.

At this early stage, Ayim emerged as a prominent innovative IPM farmer in controlling the WRB. With Idham, he was anxious to understand every new phenomenon. Neither of them was considered a rich farmer, but Ayim was known as a "real farmer" (*petani tulèn*) from his industriousness.

PESTICIDE USE IN NURSERIES

Having a shared knowledge of the insignificance of the pest/disease threats did not automatically lead the farmers to abandon preventative measures. Belief in the need to prevent seedlings from "illnesses" was still predominant, even though there was a shortage of capital. Some IPM farmers (Akim, Arman, Ucup and Idham) decided to apply carbofuran as a preventative measure since "... seedlings were the basis for future plants (*Bibit itu pokoknya*)," as Akim said. Other farmers made adjustments and modifications in the use of pesticides to meet the limited resources they had rather than abandoning them.

Under the same economic constraints, there were some IPM and non-IPM farmers who decided not to protect their plants because of good seedling performance or because of their habits of not broadcasting carbofuran in nurseries. Following the emergence of pests, i.e., armyworms and deadhearts, some of these, as well as other farmers, took control action by using pesticides. They changed their minds because of the unexpected outbreak of armyworms in nurseries that they believed had not been treated with carbofuran. This strengthened their beliefs about the preventative efficacy of carbofuran, which, according to IPM teaching, was unnecessary if there were no pests infested plants.

Early vegetative stage

In several fields two weeks after transplanting, the farmers found sporadic symptoms of deadhearts. This was the period when the farmers broadcast fertilizers. The newly appointed extension worker came to deliver news about the potential outbreak of WRB (the second generation) at an extension meeting on the December 17, 1990. As usual, two distinct means of communication occurred when the farmers attended a formal meeting, i.e., farmer-to-farmer and provider-to-farmer transmissions. What was evident was the varied nature of the communication and the farmers' reception in these different settings.

"OBSERVE AND HANDPICK MOTHS": FARMER-TO-FARMER TRANSMISSION

The farmer-to-farmer knowledge transmission is conducive to the reception of new ideas, but arguments and disagreements always constitute part of their discussions. Borofsky (1994c:338) says that:

> People share certain knowledge *because* they have learned how to interact with one another. What people share culturally is the *experience* of getting along with one another, of participating in meaningful activities together.

In the era of the Green Revolution, the high costs in rice farming have always been a constraint for the farmers. Once several farmers met, this problem became their main topic of discussion, especially if they faced risks of damage or harvest failure. When about 25 farmers got together before the extension meeting, Ayim and Idham spread the idea of hand-collecting WRB by relating it to their economic constraints and the most effective way to avoid pest infestation.

On the basis of his assessment of the possible damage to plants and the absence of any "medicine to rot the egg clusters," Idham confidently argued that there was no other way except to observe and handpick moths and eggs (... *Pokokna mah kudu diamati. Diamati jeung diala*). Another possible strategy raised was to look for a substitute for carbofuran, e.g., the use of kerosene.

By analyzing the cost-benefit of the hand-collection strategy, Ayim convinced other farmers about its advantages, not only to control WRB at a reduced cost, but also to create job opportunities for the younger generation. Ayim was an example of an innovative farmer who was able to provide reasons for his idea and to modify the original one to suit the farmers' economic condition.

> "If [we] would like to save our capital ... get five people to enter the field .... The cost [of having five people] would be the same as purchasing one can of *Thiodan*. The advantages of doing this are threefold: First, the white rice borers together with the egg clusters, will be reduced. The moths would be killed, slapped by hands. Second, the natural enemies will not be disturbed. Third, our neighbour's kids who used to be unemployed, would be employed, receiving wages." He convinced the other farmers again that "using spray will cost you double. First, the price of 'medicines' is expensive. Second, the natural enemies die. By handpicking them, the advantages are double."

The idea of not spraying pesticides and using, instead, a mechanical control such as handpicking moths and eggs, was a new one. Many non-IPM and even some IPM farmers disagreed with Ayim's idea. Through conversations, Ayim was gradually able to convince his colleagues to understand the costs and ineffective results of spraying, as well as their ignorance of the use of pesticides.

> First, Idham himself argued that paying wages already amounted to Rp.6,000. for three teenagers. Wahyu argued against this idea because of the work he had to do. "Collecting moths and eggs complicate my job and made me dizzy (*Ngala gitu hoream eta teh*)." Another farmer complained about the large area of *sawah* that made the work difficult. Ayim agreed that it does make one "dizzy." By referring to a smaller area, e.g., 100 *bata* (0.14 ha) Ayim continued his story, saying that pursuing this strategy should be repeated: "Do the handpicking when the plants reach 20 days. The second time, if the plants reach 30 or 35 days .... *Alhamdullilah paréna mah*." Another farmer still preferred to spray: "It would be better to spray ("*Mending disemprot*"). Answering this argument, Ayim reminded them about the price of *Thiodan* and its results. Wahyu agreed that there were no effective results in spraying

Thiodan. By comparing the costs for purchasing insecticides and for paying wages, Ayim emphasised again the benefits of collecting moths and egg clusters. Understanding Ayim's explanation, a farmer referred to their mistakes from spraying pesticides: "The farmers are careless (*Petanina ceroboh nyak*)." Another farmer disagreed with this statement and corrected it by saying that "The farmers are not careless, but [we] do not understand (*Teu ceroboh petani mah, enteu ngarti*)."

The last statement reveals the growing understanding the farmers gained of their own situation. For several non-IPM farmers, this was the first time to learn about the WRB's life cycle and a strategy for controlling it, as well as the function of natural enemies. Ayim, again, transmitted the idea of natural enemies by introducing the book/leaflets he received from training. By incorporating the idea of natural enemies into their own experience, several old non-IPM farmers were able to explain why there were many outbreaks of pests nowadays. "If we control [the pests] using the old practices, we will have fish again (*Kudu dikendali cara baheula, lauk bisa aya deui*)," argued Ayim.

MESSAGE TRANSMISSION AND THE FARMERS' REACTIONS

In contrast to the farmer-to-farmer's transmission, the extension worker delivered his messages about WRB and its control measures in a conventional way of a "training and visit" system as a more knowledgeable person than the farmers. The IPM farmers did not receive any significant new explanation, except some additional information they had not learned from the IPM trainers. Some information was, according to the farmers, contradictory to both the IPM trainers' explanations and their own observations, such as the number of larvae hatched from one egg cluster which reached up to 600. Many IPM farmers disagreed with this explanation. They admitted that this number could be the total of larvae hatched from all egg clusters laid by one moth, but not of larvae hatched from one egg cluster. (Kalshoven [1981:244] does mention that "Between 150–250 larvae emerge from an egg cluster in the early hours of the morning ..."). Without a detailed explanation of why and how the current outbreak of WRB was possible, one non-IPM farmer (Rustam, the school teacher) questioned the warning, given the fact that there were few moths or deadhearts at this stage. The farmers did not have basic information and ways to forecast a possible outbreak. "So, why is the government already anxious?" asked Rustam.

Gaining confidence in the ideas transmitted in such a forum was also determined by the provider's way of communicating ideas. After the extension meeting, Ayim, Haji Ali, Idham and Ardi criticised the ways the extension worker had presented his explanation.

> "He [the extension worker] has not been upgraded yet, *nyak*, his talk was not quite clear (*Enteu ditatar manèhna nyak, ngomongna mah ripuh*)," commented Ayim. "*Nyak*, Pak Ayim is better at explaining [things] (*Nyak, mendingan Pak Ayim nyak ... anu nerangin*), said Haji Ali. Idham: "He only has the obligation [to provide the information], he does not know that the people here have already been trained." Haji Ali also said that: "He should talk first with the BPP, with Pak K. (the previous extension worker, the IPM co-trainer) that the people here already knew, so he should say so-and-so." Idham was also dissatisfied with the extension worker's inability to provide detailed answers. "There were three forms of egg clusters. *Nah*, which is which? Which one is the egg cluster from the leaf folder, which one is from the white rice borer? *Kan* he could not explain it in detail," complained Idham. All of them agreed that they had more confidence in the pest observer (IPM trainer) than this extension worker.

This conversation demonstrates how the farmers resented the inconsistent information they received, the unreliable source of the knowledge and the way the provider disregarded their own knowledge.

EARLY MOTH FLIGHT AND DEADHEART SYMPTOMS

After finding deadheart in mid December 1990, some IPM farmers perceived that the degree of intensity of deadhearts was low. They referred to the ETL of deadheart by looking at the infested paddy within the whole area of their *sawah*, not by using samples and the calculation method as taught in training. No moths or deadhearts were found by the farmers in the eastern fields of Blok Cadas where the paddy were still in an early stage (one week after transplanting). Aming, on the other hand, found that deadhearts in the field of Anin (Akim's and Arman's father) were already numerous.

Since there were still only a few moths, the farmers handpicked them while carrying out other activities. Asma, for example, caught moths while fertilizing. He had other work to do and could not do exactly as Ayim had. Instead, he disseminated this idea to the weeding labourers. Ayim, on the other hand, had an idea of conducting a "competition" (*mau bikin sayembara*) with a reward of Rp.500/moth and Rp.250/egg cluster.[6] He mentioned this to Haji Ali who decided to follow Ayim's idea of paying wages or rewards for collecting moths.

The farmers' questions in this situation and in the absence of carbofuran were whether to apply this pesticide now, what amount, when and where. The farmers' decisions again varied. Five IPM farmers (Idham, Eka, Armad, Armin and Diloh) decided to avoid the use of carbofuran. The majority of farmers repeated their previous practices of making some modifications to the recommended

Table 6.1 *Diverse strategies in carbofuran application*

Name	IPM/Non IPM farmers	Strategies in carbofuran application
Haji Nafi	non-IPM	applied carbofuran in the first fertilizer application only
Anan	non-IPM	applied carbofuran in a mixture with KCl 10 days after the first fertilizer application
Iman	non-IPM	did not apply carbofuran in all fields (five *sawah*) in the first fertilizer application, applied this pesticide in only one place in the second application.
Adri	non-IPM	applied carbofuran in the first and second applications
Anin	non-IPM	reduced the amount of carbofuran in both fertilizer applications
Haji Ali	IPM farmer	applied carbofuran only in one *sawah* in a mixture with fertilizer
Ayim	IPM farmer	applied carbofuran only in two *sawah* planted with glutinous rice in a mixture with fertilizer
Aming	IPM farmer	mixed kerosene with fertilizer as a substitute for carbofuran, applied carbofuran at the second fertilizer application
Wahyu	IPM farmer	applied carbofuran both at the first and second application, but reduced the amount up to half of the recommended amount.
Adma	IPM farmer	reduced the amount of carbofuran at the first fertilizer application to save costs, increased it at the second fertilizer application to prolong its "power" in protecting plants; spread insecticides in between.

use of pesticide while protecting plants. Some diversified their strategies (see table 6.1). Even with the insignificant pest attacks, the farmers still perceived carbofuran as a necessary substance in plant protection.

Vegetative stage: the first moth flight

The farmers first recognized the appearance of the "first moth flight" (*penerbangan kupu-kupu yang pertama*) on December 25, 1990. In the experts' view, the first moth flight occurred earlier, at the nurseries' stage. The farmers related this outbreak to the weather conditions. On the basis of the understanding of moth's migration, some IPM farmers interpreted this flight by referring to the idea of light attraction and migration.

> "The moths became numerous after we had rains for several days followed by three nights of full moon," described Ayim about the weather conditions when the first moth flight appeared. In his perspective, the numerous moths appeared not only from the pupae left in the stalks, but also as migrants from other places attracted by moonlight. "Thus, the moths were immigrants (*imigran*), or as Idham said, the moths were in the urbanization process (*kupu-kupunya berurbanisasi*)," explained Ayim further.

These farmers were able to relate several ideas received in training into one explanation about the flight. They did not, however, wait until they found egg clusters as they had been taught in training and extension meeting. Instead, they looked upon the new way of handpicking pests initiated by Ayim while pursuing their habits of spraying insecticides.

MOTH FLIGHT: INNOVATIVE PRACTICES

Gradually, handpicking moths and egg clusters was adopted as a method of pest control. This was the initial period when a number of farmers began to adopt this strategy on the basis of their judgments and assessments of its advantages. This was how the farmers modified the theory about the WRB control strategy. Despite this innovation, the farmers' habit in spraying pesticides persisted.

Mechanical control: hand-collecting moths. Ayim was, again, the IPM farmer who initiated picking moths with his bare hands; he was followed by Idham. These two farmers warned others of the large moth population by pointing to the total number of moths caught in the fields. They also assisted other farmers (e.g., Haji Ali, Iman and Haji Nafi) who decided to utilise this strategy and were willing to pay wages. I counted seven IPM farmers and four non-IPM farmers who followed Ayim and Idham at this stage. From this moment on, the farmers adopted a way of paying wages to collect moths by also inventing new practices and devices:

- several people walked in one line, one or two metres apart and moved together along the fields;
- they splashed water with their feet while walking across the fields to make the moths fly, and then caught them straight away;
- they counted their findings by referring to the size of *sawah* in which they carried out the practice; and
- invented tools to avoid itchiness in their hands, e.g., Haji Ali invented small nets wet with kerosene and Haji Nafi invented bamboo sticks to kill moths.

The farmers began to report to one another the number of moths collected from a certain size of *sawah*. At this stage, not many egg clusters were found. Not all farmers in Marga Tani, however, decided to adopt this strategy and instead they chose to spray.

Chemical control: spraying pesticides. Unconvinced by the effectiveness and advantages of the new strategy in reducing their burdens in pest control, many farmers still looked at pesticide use as the main means of controlling pests. Wira perceived the hand-collecting activity as ineffective in preventing the appearance of deadhearts. Iyub referred to the migration of moths from field to field that made this strategy ineffective. The difficulties of collecting moths in a large area of *sawah* and the costs of paying wages did not induce other farmers to adopt this practice. Since they did not apply carbofuran, some farmers considered spraying as an option to save costs.

A significant difference between IPM and non-IPM farmers in spraying pesticides was apparent. The IPM farmers sprayed pesticides as a control measure for moths and other pests, i.e., leaf folders, brown plant hoppers and white-back plant hoppers. Most of the non-IPM farmers, on the other hand, sprayed pesticides regularly, according to the schedule. At the same time, the moths appeared. Several banned insecticides were still used by the farmers in a mixture with or without permitted insecticides. The majority of farmers still had confidence in *Thiodan* as the most powerful substance, including IPM farmers (Adma, Asma, Eka and Diloh). Several farmers boiled carbofuran to reduce costs and mixed it with other insecticides.

Detailed observation, experimentation and queries. Understanding pest behaviour and ways of infestation on plants gradually became of interest to the farmers while carrying out control measures. A detailed observation and interpretation by referring to some ideas of pest behaviour could enrich the farmers' knowledge of WRB. Ardi recognized that the moth flight always occurred in the afternoon and that moths migrated from other places. At this time (afternoon), no natural enemies were found in the fields and hence, nothing preyed on moths. Idham noticed the differences between the small and the big white moths, their number and places on plants. He deduced that:

> The big one is the female; the small one is the male. This is my own thought. The female one is pregnant. She placed herself on top of plants or on the edge of leaves so that she could get warm, to hasten the process of laying eggs. The small one is always found at the lower part of the plants.

This is an example of how the farmers expanded the knowledge received in the "school" with their own observations.

Experimentation was another means to improve knowledge and an integral part of the farmers' ways of learning. Rustam decided to spray moths and stems with a mosquito repellant (*Baygon*) to see whether this substance was effective in killing moths and to discover its effects on plants. Whenever he returned to his field he observed the rice hill where he had sprayed the stems to see what changes occurred. From this experiment Rustam concluded that mosquito repellant was effective in killing moths and had no detrimental effect on plants.

Ardi carried out a systematic experiment by using comparative plots to test the impact of hand collecting moths on deadheart. His *sawah* in Blok Cadas was divided into three plots. He collected moths with his bare hands within two-and-a-half plots of *sawah* and left the half plot of *sawah* without any control. Ardi's activity was the first systematic experimentation by the farmers. Other farmers, e.g., Haji Ali, Iman, Haji Nafi also decided not to handpick moths in all of their *sawah*. Later on, their decisions contributed to their evaluations of the diverse effects of their practices on the degree of deadheart attacks in different *sawah*.

Because of the appearance of puzzling phenomena that they could not explain, Idham and Ayim decided to visit the BPP office—for the first time—in early January 1991. This was the period when deadhearts appeared in their fields. They wanted to present knowledge of their invention to enable the farmers in other places to prevent the outbreak of WRB. They also had questions to ask the extension workers:

✧ What did the moths feed upon?
✧ Why were there two different moths (big and small ones) and why were there differences in the population?
✧ Why were there differences in deadheart attacks between paddy at age 30, 20, 15 and 10 days after transplanting?
✧ What were the appropriate ways to control moths?

The farmers did not receive satisfactory answers and appropriate advice, nor was the extension worker appreciative of their inventions. This was, again, another event when they lost their trust in the extension workers' knowledge and credibility.

DEADHEARTS: EVALUATION AND CONTROL

Even though the farmers had mechanically or chemically tried to control moths, in the first week of January 1991, they found the emergence of more numerous and widespread deadhearts than in December 1990. This was an unforeseen phenomenon that provided, again, an opportunity for the farmers to learn. The main question they raised was "why are deadhearts still appearing?"

Evaluation: "why are deadhearts still appearing?" In their inferences, several farmers linked this event with the weather conditions, i.e., the "red rain." From observing the occurrence of the same phenomena in the last two years, Armin and Haji Nafi felt confident about their assumptions. Armin even challenged the experts to test this hypothesis in the laboratory:

> If there is a "mid-day rain" there will always be many pests. Before the plants got infested by *sundep*, the rain had a "red" colour. The water was red like *tayeng* (rot). When there was a harvest failure (*bapuk*) in 1990, the rain was red, quite often, up to three times. Please, examine it in the laboratory, if it can be proved. Up to now, nobody has examined its relationship. If it were not because of rain, the attack would be sporadic. Now, all fields were attacked by *sundep* evenly.

In seeking answers as to why deadhearts were still appearing, the farmers made references to their own practices and to the different strategies carried out by other farmers and what they knew of WRB reproductive behaviour. By doing this, they also learned from their mistakes as Ayim did:

> The period of moth flight lasted up to mid-January, at which time the moths died after laying eggs. We did not catch all of them, so there are many *sundep* now.

Both Ayim and Haji Ali agreed that when they caught a large number of moths, some moths had already laid eggs that they did not find. Hence, "the *sundep* now came from those egg clusters that were not collected," or "there might be some egg clusters already hatched when we caught the moths," assumed Ayim, Ardi and Haji Ali. Ayim also referred to the theory that larvae bored into the stems a very short time after incubation. Haji Ali and Haji Nafi came to the same conclusion about late collection by hand. Hence, Haji Ali found more *sundep* in one of his fields that was treated later than his other fields, as did Haji Nafi when comparing his fields with his neighbours." Ayim argued that the ineffectiveness of this strategy was not merely due to late implementation, but also because of migrants from other places.

Several farmers referred to the absence of, or inappropriate practices, in carbofuran application. Haji Ali found more *sundep* in his *sawah* that was not treated with carbofuran than in those *sawah* that had been treated with carbofuran. Haji Nafi realised his mistake in broadcasting carbofuran in the first and not the second fertilizer application when attacks had become numerous. Wahyu learned from his mistake of not applying carbofuran in the recommended amount. Ardi blamed himself for not applying fertilizers twice.

When *sundep* appeared he could not broadcast carbofuran without fertilizer. To carry sand to his distant field was too heavy. While appreciating Adma's preventative strategy (see Table 6.1), Armin and Diloh came to the same conclusion: if they had capital, it was best to broadcast carbofuran in both fertilizer applications.

From this evaluation, the farmers again gained greater confidence in the function of carbofuran to protect plants as well as to control deadhearts. On the other hand, Idham and Ayim found that carbofuran application would be effective only if the time the eggs take to hatch was taken into account. By referring to the WRB's life cycle in which after day eleven (11) the larvae would not feed anymore, it would be useless to apply carbofuran after this stage. After seeing this, both recognized their mistake in not bringing the egg clusters home as recommended by the trainers because they did not then know exactly when the eggs hatched in the field. From these findings they advised other farmers to apply carbofuran and, at the same time, transmitted knowledge of the WRB's life cycle and the need to collect a sample of egg clusters. This was the first time I noticed the farmers' knowledge advancement about the need to timely broadcast the granule insecticide after being able to relate the theory to their empirical discovery. The IPM trainers did not mention in detail the relation between the larval stage and the efficacy of carbofuran in their recommendation.

Referring to their fellows' practices, Ardi, Idham, Ayim and Rustam complained about the lack of collective and uniform activities (e.g., the transplanting schedule, carbofuran application and moth collection). Many farmers were still spraying pesticides injudiciously.

Chemical control and no remedial action. As a response to the appearance of deadhearts, each farmer found ways to control this symptom on the basis of his understanding, confidence and capital. Diverse practices again emerged. Broadcasting carbofuran as a control measure following the IPM trainers and extension worker's recommendation was a new practice. The farmers did not, however, broadcast the recommended dosage and made decisions according to their capital. Those whose plants were aged over 40 days after transplanting (at the generative stage) decided to mix carbofuran with sand instead of fertilizers, a recommended practice learned in the IPM "school." A number of IPM and non-IPM farmers persistently sprayed diverse mixtures of insecticides, including boiled carbofuran; whereas others did not carry out any control mesures. Outside Marga Tani, I found a female farmer who had reactivated the old practice in controlling deadhearts by walking around the field while splashing water to wash rice from a bucket containing *dringo* and *benglé* leaves, perfume and seven flowers. No farmers in Marga Tani reactivated this old practice.

In mid-January 1991, on learning that carbofuran would be effective for only 15–20 days, Idham assumed that applying carbofuran at this period, when the larvae had possibly already become pupae, would be useless. This substance would neither kill the recent pupae nor the forthcoming larvae. Idham raised this argument in every conversation with his fellows and advised them to neither broadcast carbofuran nor spray pesticides. Other farmers, however, did not automatically adopt his suggestion. Iyub, who received Idham's advice to pull the infested stems instead of broadcasting carbofuran, decided to broadcast carbofuran in a mixture with sand. He had the idea that,

> larvae or pupae will go down to the bottom of the stem. I will flood the field so that the infested stems will also be covered with water and hence the larvae will be struck by carbofuran.

How carbofuran worked and how larvae/pupae in the stems were affected by insecticides were beyond the farmers' ability to observe. They then used their imagination to infer how larvae inside the stems could die from insecticides.

Apri (non-IPM) had a similar idea. He insisted on spraying although Haji Ali had suggested that he should not spray and had refused to lend Apri money to buy insecticides. In Apri's imagination,

> "The water in the ground will be mixed with 'medicine.' At night, the larvae will go out of the stems and down to the ground to drink. If the larvae drink the water mixed with 'medicine,' they could die," explained Apri as his reasons for spraying.

This kind of imagination strengthened the farmers' confidence in controlling deadhearts through spraying.

Spraying was also used to control other pests. As usual, a number of IPM farmers (Akim, Arman, Ucup and Amid) and non-IPM farmers (Iman, Anin, Asim and Askim) boiled carbofuran and kerosene and mixed them with other insecticides (both banned and permitted ones) to reduce costs and yet still have a powerful impact on pests. Several farmers tried to use new insecticides (*Delcis* and *Padan*, used to control stem borers in other crops, banned insecticides; and *Karpos*, the new insecticide to control WRB). Some modified the use of an insecticide to retard the growth of BPH nymph, *Applaud* (buprofezin), to prevent WRB egg clusters from hatching (see table 6.2). In the event of a pest outbreak, the farmers quickly adopted newly introduced insecticides while testing them to see whether the information they received was true. Aming and Diloh, for example, perceived that *Karpos* was ineffective. Hence, the use of this substance was not widespread.

Those who decided not to take any remedial action (Haji Ali and Haji Nafi) had confidence that new stems would compensate for the infested ones. Haji Nafi had a plan to broadcast carbofuran at a later stage after listening to Idham and Ayim's suggestion not to broadcast carbofuran at this period. Later on, several farmers found that new stems did grow.

From their consistent efforts in observing and interpreting the nature of WRB outbreaks and disseminating their assumptions and discoveries, two IPM farmers, Idham and Ayim, had gradually been

Table 6.2 *Diverse mixtures of pesticides*

Farmer	IPM/non IPM farmer	Mixture used
Itang	non-IPM	*Delcis* (to control stem borer in other crops)
Iman	non-IPM	boiled carbofuran (*Indofuran*), *Darmabas* (permitted insecticide), *Delcis* and *Sevin* (banned insecticides), and kerosene
Romi	non-IPM	*Thiodan* and *Elsan* (banned insecticides) with *Indobas*, *Baycarb* and *Mepcin* (permitted insecticides)
Anin	non-IPM	boiled carbofuran (*Darmabas* and *Indofuran*), *Sevin* (a banned insecticide), *Kiltop* (a permitted insecticide), and kerosene
Arpan	IPM farmer	*Indobas*, *Darmabas* and *Mepcin* (permitted insecticides)

widely known as "diligent farmers" (*petani yang rajin*) or "farmer-examiners" (*petani teliti, petani yang suka meneliti*). They then became advisers to other farmers. A small group of IPM and non-IPM farmers, such as Haji Ali, Ardi and Rustam, also consistently carried out observation and evaluation of their own and other farmers' strategies. Again, these farmers found puzzling phenomena: a diverse degree of deadheart attacks and varied size of larvae inside the stems.

"Why is there diversity in deadheart attacks and size of larvae?" Encountering these puzzling phenomena, the farmers improved their learning by looking at several possible significant variables and drew a correlation between these variables. Individual farmers began to discover a pattern of deadheart infestation. They drew the same conclusion about the relationship between deadheart infestation and age of plants. Since the more severe attack of deadhearts were found in young plants, the farmers looked further at differences in their transplanting schedule. They assumed that paddy planted at a later transplanting date were more vulnerable than paddy transplanted earlier. From detailed observations, Idham differentiated further the degree of infestation between paddy at different ages, i.e., the 30th–20th–15th and 10th days after transplanting.

The farmers mentioned rice variety as another possible factor, although their assumptions of what varieties were more susceptible than others were still contested. Armin, Adma and Diloh agreed that IR64 was more susceptible than other varieties. "IR64 was already weak (*IR64 sudah cèngèng*). It should not be replanted," said Diloh. Comparing the performance of his own paddy, *Way Seputih*, with IR64, Armin felt confident that *Way Seputih* was more resistant than IR64. Rustam, Armin's rice field neighbour in Blok Rawa, argued against this assumption since he found many deadhearts in Armin's field. Ardi found that *ketan* was also infested with deadhearts.

From finding a severe attack of deadhearts in older plants, Ardi drew his conclusion by relating this attack to the cultivators' control strategies. This conclusion was supported by his experience of diversifying moth collection strategies, i.e., he found that the more severe deadhearts attack in the half plot of *sawah* without control than in the two and a half plots with control. Following this finding,

Ardi undertook a further experiment to follow the extent of deadheart infestation:

> I put bamboo sticks on rice hills with severe attacks. In the half plot of *sawah* I put 10 bamboo sticks. I want to know whether the deadheart infestation will develop in other places. If new symptoms appear, they will be easily identified.

From their observations, Ardi and Rustam also recognized the differences in the degree of deadheart attacks and the population of moths between fields close to canals and those further away. Although they understood the moths' migration, they did not know why there was such a difference. Ayim explained his understanding of the direction of moth flight toward light,

> It is because of the water [in the canal]. The moths sought light. During their flight, there was moonlight for three nights consecutively. So, the water became bright and the moths came toward brightness. The same condition applied to young plants because the water could still be seen; thus the moths came.

Ayim supported his inference by referring to the extension worker's finding from collecting moths in different fields (in another hamlet) planted with paddy of different ages. On the basis of this inference, he answered the question of why deadhearts were more severe in the younger plants.

In another case, the farmers discovered that there was a variation in deadheart attacks on one rice hill: some stems were already dried out, some had recently dried, while others looked green. This discovery—which was not mentioned by the trainers—improved their knowledge. By referring to the theory of the WRB's life cycle, Idham critically questioned the notion of reproductive stages. In his interpretation the egg's incubation should have happened at the same period. They discovered, however, that the laying of eggs did not happen at the same time nor did the hatching. This, they realised, could have been the cause of the variation in deadheart infestation.

Pulling out infested stems to see what was inside or to know the form, size and number of larvae became a habit with the farmers when they found deadhearts. By doing this, Haji Ali and Rustam found larvae of different sizes inside different stems at the same period. From detailed observation about the place of holes, what was inside the infested stems and whether larvae were still boring them, Ayim discovered that larvae migrated from one stem to another. From this he assumed that the larvae that had migrated were larger.

These cases demonstrate how individual findings, interpretations and experiments contributed to their knowledge of pest behaviour. Besides an initial common knowledge of the relation between planting schedule and degree of pest infestation, the farmers' knowledge varied according to individual experience and interpretation, the people with whom they exchanged ideas and the ideas they received in such exchanges.

Evaluation of carbofuran application. Diverse carbofuran applications and their impacts on plants provided another significant opportunity to learn, from which the farmers' knowledge improved (see Johnson 1972 on the importance of variation and experimentation in adaptation and evolutionary change). Several practices became points of reference in evaluation and discussion, although viewpoints varied. Wira, Armin and Diloh interpreted Adma's practice as effective because his plants were not infested severely by deadhearts (see Adma's strategy in table 6.1). They drew attention to his practice as an example of a preventative measure the farmers should adopt at the sensitive period in the growth of plants. On the basis of their recent understanding about the timely application of carbofuran, when the eggs have recently hatched, Idham, Ayim, and Haji Ali interpreted Adma and also Anan's practices as appropriate. Arpan's practice by broadcasting a total of 56 kg of carbofuran in his parents' *sawah* since the beginning of the season became a point of reference as an ineffective and inefficient strategy since deadhearts still attacked the plants. Many farmers agreed that this strategy was too costly. This evaluation strengthened the farmers' views about the need to broadcast carbofuran appropriately. "Pull out the infested stems, see if there are larvae inside, broadcast carbofuran," said Anan. "When the eggs have hatched, half a day later broadcast carbofuran—that is the best strategy," Idham convinced the other farmers. These interpretations of various farmers' practices improved the earlier understanding of the need for timely carbofuran application as raised by Idham and Ayim.

Their findings about the diverse size of larvae, moth migration and the different time of the eggs' incubation proved the complexity of this outbreak and complicated their inferences. Their main question was when to broadcast carbofuran and how much.

> "But, there are big and small larvae inside the stems, so when and how should I apply carbofuran?" asked Haji Ali. "When you find the deadheart symptoms on your plants, then broadcast it. But, broadcast it selectively, only on the infested rice hills," answered Idham. "How much carbofuran should I broadcast in one rice hill?" asked Haji Ali again. Based on the recommended amount of 17 kg/ha, Idham then asked Haji Ali to count the rice hills in one hectare of *sawah* and divide the total amount of carbofuran with the total of rice hills.

With reference to the continuous outbreak and future moth flights, these farmer-innovators agreed that a repeated carbofuran application was necessary, but that would be too costly. Hence, what should they do to control the forthcoming outbreak? They raised ideas and arguments about the costs and effectiveness of particular strategies.

> Rustam argued against the idea of spraying the moths and egg clusters with *Applaud* as mentioned by Ayim. He said that this insecticide only functioned to rot the brown plant hopper's eggs and not all insect eggs. Idham was confident that broadcasting carbofuran was the most appropriate strategy although it would be too costly for him. Haji Ali argued against this since the moths would come continuously, so he expected that there would be resistant varieties for rice stem borers.

Armin criticised the IPM strategy for carrying out observation first and taking control measures later. By referring to the widespread deadheart attacks, he and Adma firmly preferred preventative measures. Idham repeatedly criticised the incomplete explanation of WRB and other pests/diseases in training and the incongruence of the theory with reality.

Even though the farmers had already acquired new understanding, they still became confused when they faced reality. Rustam did not know what to do when he found three-centimetre long larvae inside the stems. The question was whether at this stage the larvae had already became pupae and hence, whether carbofuran would still be effective. The larval stages and the length of larva at each stage were not part of the farmers' knowledge.[7] Rustam then decided to carry out an experiment, i.e., to broadcast carbofuran in one plot only where deadhearts were mostly found. He aimed to know whether three-centimetre-long larvae would still survive, also whether moths would be found in larger numbers in this plot than in the other ones.

By using the theory of WRB as a reference point and by questioning it, some IPM farmers were able critically to evaluate both their practices and the nature of pest outbreaks. From evaluating their fellows' practices and referring to the reproductive behaviour and length of the WRB life cycle, Idham, Ayim and Ardi were able to forecast the second forthcoming moth flight. Their forecast, in fact, corresponded to the experts' finding about the possible third and fourth moth flights (see Kalshoven 1981:247).

Generative stage: the second moth flight

The accumulated experience the farmers had during the first moth flight became the basis for their interpretations during the forthcoming moth flight. Through these sequences of interaction between action, consequences, reinterpretation and further action, knowledge improved. As mentioned by Keller and Keller (1993:125), "not only ideas about the world affect action in the world, but ongoing perceptions of that action in the world affect the organization and content of ideas." As the farmers' experience grew, their interpretations of the relationship between variables about pest outbreaks had also become more complex. However, the improvement and dissemination of this understanding did not occur evenly among all the farmers in Marga Tani and those who cultivated *sawah* in this area. Although the IPM farmers already based their interpretation of the moth flight on the WRB's reproductive cycle, many non-IPM farmers did not have such an idea. Some of them still looked only at natural conditions, e.g., rain and moonlight in their explanations about the origin of white moths. This was the significant difference between the two groups of farmers. Idham, for example, was even able to question the shorter length of the reproductive cycle than the one mentioned by the trainers.

Besides critically evaluating the recent flight, several farmers were also able to verify or confirm their interpretations or expand their understanding. From observing the result of his experiment, i.e., the larger number of moths found in the plot treated with carbofuran than in the untreated plots, Rustam validated his assumption that larvae from three centimetres long had already stopped taking food (see Sosromarsono n.d.:5 on the length of larva, 25 mm, that already reached the end of its moulting stage [*pada akhir instar*]). Ayim drew his conclusion from correlating several variables, i.e., number of moths, degree of previous deadhearts infestation in particular areas in relation to the age of the plants, the fertility period of female moths, extent to which moths could fly, and height of plants that might or might not attract moths. He then assumed that the flight condition related particularly to areas (*hamparan*) that were previously attacked by deadhearts.

By referring to the age of plants and the WRB's life cycle, IPM and some lay farmers assumed that this flight was the last outbreak for plants already reaching the generative stage and hence, was more dangerous than the previous one. Careful observation and control and immediate collective action were thus urgent. Idham understood that many farmers were still controlling this pest inappropriately and were not receptive to his advice. He then drew his conclusion that the most effective way of controlling WRB was mobilizing the farmers by government command. Again, he felt disappointed when he learned that the extension worker visited the farmers' leader for a few minutes only. The farmers felt that they had been left to take control by themselves and that those in authority had ignored them.

Many farmers noticed two distinct features of this outbreak: the prolonged flight and the larger moth population. Those who consistently followed this outbreak repeatedly evaluated their predictions of the flight. Ayim, for example, revised his prediction from a two-weeks flight to a one-month flight. Finally he found out that between the two outbreaks there was only a decrease in the number of its population, not a complete disappearance. The flight was continuous.[8] After day 22, he criticised the absence of any BPP staffs to inform the farmers about the length of the flight, a factor that would significantly affect the farmers' control practices. The news of a severe outbreak in Karawang caused Rustam and Ardi to infer that there would be a possibility of migrants coming from that area. Idham raised the question of how far the moths could migrate.

CONTROLLING WHITE RICE BORERS: ADOPTION AND VARIATION

In this period, the wider adoption of the farmers' innovative practices, i.e., the hand collection of moths and egg clusters along with the broader dissemination of knowledge of the WRB's reproductive cycle were prominent. A larger number of farmers adopted this control strategy than in the first outbreak (63.2% of IPM farmers and 48.0% of non-IPM farmers compared to 42.1% of IPM farmers and 16.0% of non-IPM farmers). The use of chemicals, however persisted, with fewer farmers carrying out this practice than before (21.0% compared to 52.6% of IPM farmers, 28.0% compared to 68.0% of non-IPM farmers in the first outbreak; see Table 6.3).

Handpicking moths and eggs: continuation and distribution. The farmer-innovators continued the handpicking of moths and later the egg clusters. Catching moths at the top of taller plants rather than younger plants was easier since they did not need to move stems or to splash water with their feet to chase the moths, although the height of plants constrained their movements. They used bamboo sticks or bare hands instead. The egg clusters found a week later

Table 6.3 *Control strategies in the first and second moth flight*

Control strategy	First moth flight		Second moth flight	
	IPM[a] % of total	Non-IPM[a] % of total	IPM[a] % of total	Non-IPM[a] % of total
Mechanical control[b]	42.1	16.0	63.2	48.0
Chemical control[c]	52.6	68.0	21.0	28.0
Cultural control[d]	5.3	16.0	5.3	0.0
No activities	0.0	0.0	10.5	24.0
Totals	100.0	100.0	100.0	100.0

Source: My survey, conducted in 1990 and 1991.

[a]The total cases of IPM farmers are 19 and non-IPM farmers are 25.

[b]Mechanical control: handpicking moths and egg clusters. The percentage refers to the cases adopting this control action only or in combination with other control strategies (chemical control and/or biological control).

[c]Chemical control: broadcasting carbofuran and/or spraying. The percentage refers to the cases carrying out this strategy without adopting mechanical control.

[d]Cultural control: drying up fields.

were much more numerous than in the first flight. Now, they could easily find egg clusters on top of the plants. "The top or 'flag' leaf is an excellent place for the moths to lay eggs' (Kalshoven 1981:246). The farmers cut the edge of leaves where the eggs were placed, put them in plastic bags, brought them home and burnt or submitted them to Haji Ali, or destroyed the eggs directly in the fields.

Learning from previous activities, the farmers perceived this practice as the most effective and efficient way of preventing the boring of larvae into stems and reducing costs. Ayim came to a firm decision to pursue his hand-collecting activity by drawing up a cost-benefit analysis to predict whitehead infestation:

> "I will not broadcast carbofuran any more, because first, it will be more appropriate to collect the eggs, so that at least 85% of all the egg clusters will be controlled. Second, if the application of carbofuran is inappropriate, it will be useless. If, for example, our grain production will be up to 100%, the remaining egg clusters will amount to 15% [from the egg population]. Will the grains be finished by those 15% egg clusters? If there will be up to 15% [yield reduction], it will still save the costs without 'medicines,' because the other 85% egg clusters would be controlled. Yes, maybe some eggs are hidden, more or less 15% being left." "If the farmers do not diligently control moths/eggs, there will be 25–30% whitehead infestation. If they control it, the infestation will only be around 10%."

Other IPM farmers had similar reasons, but with less detail than that presented by Ayim.

Handpicking gradually became one alternative among various available strategies. The major factor contributing to its adoption was the nature of the outbreak itself, i.e., the high population of egg clusters and the continuous nature of moth flight. Hence, the farmers concluded that it would be too costly to broadcast carbofuran repeatedly. An understanding of the ineffectiveness of spraying pesticide in eradicating egg clusters or larvae also increased.

For the majority of non-IPM farmers, the presence and form of egg clusters, how dangerous these were for plants at this stage, and how ineffective their old practices of spraying insecticide were, represented entirely new ideas. Knowledge about these ideas and the need to hand collect egg clusters were gradually transmitted throughout the period of moth flights in various ways. Occasions for the transmission of this knowledge occurred daily in conversations,

conversations on particular occasions, e.g., while renovating the mosque, watching television or playing badminton, watching other farmers' activities in collecting moths and eggs and finding out what the reasons were, participation as labourers in other farmers' handpicking activities, and specific dissemination about the subject with other farmers or relatives.

Asmudi (a young non-IPM farmer) learned for the first time about the need to control eggs from Idham during their work at the mosque. Idham also advised him to collect egg clusters repeatedly. Another young non-IPM farmer (Nadi) told me that Akim had said to

> collect the eggs. After that, spray them with *Applaud* so that they would not hatch. Spray them with a mixture with *Dursban* to kill the moths. Bring 10 eggs home; keep them at home. If at home the eggs hatch, it means the eggs in the fields will also hatch, so spray them straight away.

This case indicates the role of other farmers besides Idham and Ayim as the source of information. Akim transmitted his own modification of the WRB control, i.e., collecting egg clusters as a sample to know when the eggs hatch and then to spray instead of broadcasting carbofuran. Nadi followed Akim's advice in collecting egg clusters, but adopted the ways of other farmers, i.e., collecting all of the eggs in his field (of 300 *bata* or 0.43 ha) alone, within three consecutive days.

Haji Ari (an owner-nonoperator who seldom went to his fields) accepted his parents' (Haji Nafi and wife's) suggestion and advice to control eggs. He, his wife and his permanent wage labourer (an old non-IPM farmer) felt more confident in spraying pesticides. However, "other farmers are talking about collecting eggs and *emak* (mother) kept telling to us to collect the eggs because many other people do that," said Haji Ari's wife. This is a case where the farmers' wives played a role in transmitting and receiving knowledge, where older people had the power to persuade the younger generation and where an individual's decision was affected by the activity carried out by a larger number of people (see Schelling 1978).

Other non-IPM farmers learned through watching and participating in other farmers' activity:

> When Haji Ali was collecting egg clusters in his *sawah* behind his house, Parman walked along the edge of the field and asked Haji Ali what he was doing. Haji Ali then showed Parman the egg clusters that

would later on become stem borers (*penggerek batang*). Parman told Haji Ali that he already applied carbofuran after receiving Idham's advice to control deadhearts. From Idham, however, he did not receive any information about the need to collect egg clusters. By pointing to an egg cluster, Haji Ali advised him: "This is the most dangerous one. If this becomes larvae, it will bore the stems, become stem borer pest (*hama penggerek*). If the eggs hatch, there will be hundreds of larvae Man, up to 150 Man." "... Oh, it's hard (*Aduh, payah*), so we have to be diligent," replied Parman. "Come to my place and see, there has been thousands of eggs, submitted by the farmers," told Haji Ali. Parman mentioned that he had met Asmudi the day before, taking plastic bags from his fields accompanied by some teenagers. Asmudi, however, had not told him anything about his activity. Parman then asked Haji Ali and me to follow him to his field. Haji Ali went straight into the field and found numerous egg clusters. He also found a spider's egg. By showing the two kinds of eggs, Haji Ali told Parman again: "Man, tell your other friends, please collect the eggs. But don't collect the white one, that is spider." Haji Ali also advised him to pay wages to young teenagers to collect the eggs. The day after, Parman reported to Haji Ali that he and some teenagers collected 500 egg clusters.

In Parman's case, Haji Ali—the other source of information—had the opportunity to show the differences between WRB egg clusters and spiders' eggs. Awi (an old non-IPM farmer) who received some, but not all, of the same information from Haji Ali as Parman had, did not receive the information about the form of spiders' eggs. He then collected both eggs in the following days. Awi's wife learned about the form of spiders' eggs and the function of the spider as a natural enemy from Adma who found spiders' eggs in Awi's collection. Awong (Haji Ali's neighbour, a non-IPM farmer) learned from Haji Ali in a different way, i.e., by participating as his wage labourer in collecting moths and eggs. These cases demonstrate the diverse forms of knowledge transmission and through a common message— the spread of diverse information.

The content of the farmers' discussions focused on the results of collecting eggs: how many eggs were collected, when and from what size of *sawah*. The large number of egg clusters was a very striking phenomenon. Gradually, Haji Ali's residence became a place for reporting activities, submitting the collected egg clusters and for discussing their findings.[9] Idham suggested other farmers submit their findings to Haji Ali with the intention of getting an acknowledgement from the authority. Haji Ali kept all the plastic bags submitted to him with an expectation that the hamlet leader would take them to the village office, or the extension worker/village official would come and collect them.

Learning from the radio about the government's reward to the farmers in Karawang for submitting egg clusters, Haji Ali expected a similar appreciation and recognition from the government for all the efforts he and other farmers had made. By referring to the commercial promotion, Ayim developed an idea for the most effective way to transmit knowledge as well as stimulate the farmers to collect egg clusters, i.e., through advertisement and prices. "The success of the farmers' actions is important not only nationally, but also internationally," argued Ayim by referring to the involvement of FAO in IPM training. Nobody, however, came to visit. Again, this caused great disappointment. After consulting the hamlet leader and receiving his suggestion, Haji Ali and Ayim decided to burn the egg clusters at the end of February 1991.

Again, not all farmers had the same foresight and confidence in collecting moths/eggs. Their reasons were that moths would not lay eggs in mature plants, the height of plants would constrain the hand collection without damaging plant roots, or the previous pesticide control would prevent the outbreak of whiteheads. Other farmers burnt moths by fire at home, put a kerosene-light (*petromax*) on the floor or on a tray with kerosene poured around the light or filled the tray.[10]

Chemical control: reproduction and modification After the fertilizing period, only a few farmers could afford to purchase carbofuran. Only four farmers utilised the government's support, and only Arpan broadcast carbofuran as his main strategy in controlling WRB. With this action, he had already applied carbofuran four times with the total of 80 kg/2.1 ha, a far too costly practice for most farmers. Six other farmers took this action as a complement to mechanical control. Iwan, for example, took this decision after receiving Haji Ali's advice to broadcast carbofuran immediately after finding out that the egg clusters had hatched the same day he had collected them.

Several IPM farmers (Idham, Ayim, Haji Ali) already spread the idea that spraying was ineffective in eradicating larvae inside the stems. Nevertheless, more farmers still carried out spraying as their main strategy than those who broadcast carbofuran. Broadcasting carbofuran was too costly. Other farmers sprayed to complement their mechanical control. They had doubts about the effectiveness of handpicking only. Spraying was easier than being made dizzy by the search for moths and eggs. For the majority of non-IPM farmers, spraying pesticides was still part of their preventative measures against pests and disease. They had not comprehended the WRB's reproductive cycle and the ineffectiveness of spraying to control this pest. The appearance of other pests at this stage, rice seed bugs, constituted part of the farmers' reason to spray.

Some IPM farmers modified the teaching by spraying instead of broadcasting carbofuran following the hatching of egg clusters. Adma did the spraying following the hand collection of eggs. He and Akim had their reasons for eradicating moths or larvae before they bored into the stems:

> When Akim noticed the appearance of moths, he decided not to spray because: "… first, I did not have the money and second, it was useless. Three days later I went to the field and found out that the moths had already laid eggs, so I went to find money to purchase 'medicines.' Three days later I went to the field again to collect eggs. There were plenty of eggs in the fields but I only brought home 15, as a sample for observing the hatching of the eggs. I left the others in the fields because I would spray them later. "Because," as the PPL said, "if the eggs at home hatch, those in the fields also hatch." Thus, I was ready with 'spraying-medicines': *Matador* and *Indobas*. After day seven, I asked somebody to spray …. The larvae that were recently hatched would bore into the stems within around 24 hours. Thus, the larvae were still outside the plants; the larvae were still small. The larvae bored into the stems after two days."

Akim's explanation indicates the farmers' ability to adjust the theory to the economic resources they had. To be able to spray at the appropriate time in different fields, Akim differentiated the egg clusters from each field in separate plastic bags to monitor the hatching of the egg clusters in each bag. Based on the condition of moths and egg populations and the age of plants, he sprayed different types of insecticides or used different strategies in different fields. At this period, the effectiveness of *Matador* (a banned insecticide) had been spread by labourers or cultivators in PERUM to the farmers in Marga Tani.

Biological and cultural control and no remedial action. Among IPM farmers, only Iwan found that among some collected egg clusters, parasites instead of larvae hatched from the eggs. After referring to IPM teaching, he returned the parasites to the field. No other farmers did this. Drying the field, as the old people advised, was also practised by several farmers. Although Armad, Haji Ali and Arpan did this in conjunction with carrying out other strategies, Iyub chose to do this solely because he had already broadcast carbofuran and did not favour the collection of moths and eggs. Those whose plants had already reached maturity (after the period of "booting" or *meteng*) felt calm. Wahyu, Ucup, Anin and Romi, for example, said that their plants would not be severely attacked by whiteheads (*beluk*). These farmers thus took no action.

ACCUMULATING KNOWLEDGE:
OBSERVATION, EXPERIMENTATION AND INTERPRETATION

The nature of the outbreak with the continuous flight, the high population of moths and egg clusters and the critical stage of plant growth provided a very productive climate for intensive generation of ideas and hypotheses. Other factors contributing to this favourable condition were the farmers' innovative practices; the diverse age of plants, rice varieties and activities that provide opportunities to make comparisons; the farmers' socio-religious activities that brought them to meet and chat; and the emerging role of several farmers as consultants or sources of information. In line with the inability of the extensionists to assist the farmers *in situ*, the farmers became even more disenchanted with the bureaucracy. Through their own discoveries, they became more confident in their own conclusions.

White rice borer population and reproductive behaviour: new understanding and knowledge increase. The finding of moths, egg clusters and larvae and the knowledge transmission by the IPM farmers improved the non-IPM farmers' understanding of the WRB's reproductive behaviour. Knowledge of this behaviour became increasingly significant as a basis for appropriate control measures. The farmers now understood that white moths (*kupu-kupu putih*) were the most dangerous insects and that they caused *penggerek batang*. Nevertheless, the complete cycle of the WRB's reproductive and metamorphic behaviour was not always directly visible or easily observed. The farmers had to construct this notion with their own imagination. Bentley (1992:11) also found from his work in Honduras that the Honduran *campesino*'s knowledge about caterpillar reproduction was that it was "important but difficult to observe." Despite the difficulties to observe the complete reproductive cycle, the nature of WRB attack in two different stages of plant growth (deadhearts and whiteheads) complicated the farmers' inferences. As a result, diverse interpretation still existed.

> Idham, Ayim, Rustam and Armad understood that the same moths and larvae caused both deadhearts and whiteheads, but other farmers such as Haji Ali and Ardi were in doubt whether deadhearts were caused by larvae hatched from WRB egg clusters. Their theoretical understanding had not been proved by empirically finding eggs at the place where larvae were found. Armin confidently said that whiteheads were caused by larvae hatched from WRB eggs laid by "white moths"" but deadhearts were caused by "illnesses coming from the ground." This interpretation was shared by some non-IPM farmers. Wahyu and Haji Nafi, on the other hand, perceived that the larvae causing the appearance of whiteheads derived from those causing deadhearts that persistently stayed in stems. Eka was not able to identify which stage comes before that of the moth. Another non-IPM farmer, who had never been in contact with any IPM farmers, told me that "white-moths will become larvae and plant hopper, whereas *beluk* (whiteheads) come from moonlight."

Learning the action necessary to control pests did not always entail verbal communications about the behaviour of the pests. The following is a case where close neighbours from different socio-economic strata engaged in handpicking moths and eggs with no knowledge transfer about WRB reproductive behaviour.

> Awong who participated as Haji Ali's wage labourer in collecting eggs told me that "white moths will become larvae, but I do not know what the larvae will be. They are not larvae that will become *beluk* because *beluk* are caused by larvae on the leaves." Answering my question about what information he received from Haji Ali, Awong said that he did not receive any explanation from Haji Ali, whereas he himself did not dare to ask since "Haji Ali is a rich man, I am a poor man. I feel ashamed to come to talk to or to ask questions of him."

Another case demonstrates how verbal explanation by the extension worker did not guarantee that the receiver would acquire a comprehensive understanding about the pest's reproductive behaviour (also see chap. 5).

> Asmin lived not far from Haji Ali's residence, but he had never been in close contact with him and other IPM farmers. He came to the extension meeting held in mid-December 1990. He knew that "*sundep* and *beluk* come from white moths. *Sundep* attacked plants from the transplanting age until 40 days." However, in his perception, "If I fertilize again, the *sundep* will become *kelèb*, *pèntil* (rice gall midge), because the larvae of *sundep* won't die."

Haji Ari, who seldom went to the fields but had a higher education (junior high school) than the non-IPM farmers in the above cases, was able to explain the metamorphosis of this pest.

> "*Penggerek batang* experience periods of metamorphosis (*mengalami masa metamorfose*): moths lay eggs, which become larvae and then pupae, then become moths again. The white moths are those that cause damage." He also knew the period when larvae attacked plants at the vegetative and generative stage.

Handpicking moths in the field provided an opportunity to improve knowledge, for example, by introducing ideas of reproduction. After discovering some yellow fluids in the big moths' stomach, the farmers decided that these were the egg fetuses (*bakal telur*) and that the big ones were females. Umid and Haji Ali interpreted, "If the big moths rest on the leaves without any movements this means that they will lay eggs soon and then die." The farmers' interpretation of the difference between the big and the small moths varied. Adma, Armin and Amid interpreted the small moths as the young females that were not yet pregnant; this was different from Idham's interpretation that they were males. Other farmers, who did not pay careful attention to the differences, particularly if they did not handpick moths in the fields, could not differentiate them.

From general observation and accidental discoveries, some farmers found further puzzling phenomena. In their responses, some farmers raised questions but were unable to get answers, or drew their own interpretations:

> Ardi and Rustam questioned the fact of the overlapping generations of WRB. Idham raised the questions of why larvae of both of more and less than 11 days could be found together in one rice hill, and why larvae of more than 11 days could still absorb food. He also found that egg clusters on leaves always faced the sun. He concluded that

"maybe moths laid eggs in the afternoon or in the evening." Ayim found some differences in the form of two emptied egg clusters: one was dry and the other had holes in it. He concluded "the first one was an egg cluster that had been emptied from hatching and the latter was emptied because of parasites."

Through these means of knowing, different farmers came up with different findings, interpretations and questions. In other cases, the farmers tried to find answers from the "expert of the *penggerek batang*."

> Asmudi found a moth that had died before laying eggs and brought the dead moth and its eggs home. In the evening when he came to Haji Ali's house he asked how a dead moth could still lay eggs. Haji Ali and his wife did not believe his story: "It is impossible that the moth died first and then laid eggs. It should lay eggs first and then die." The next morning Asmudi brought the specimen to Haji Ali's residence when Ayim was there. Answering, Ayim concluded that "the moth was attacked by a natural enemy when laying eggs, maybe by a parasite or another natural enemy." Asmudi asked again why the moth could be glued to the leaf. Ayim continued his interpretation. "Maybe when the moth was sucked by a natural enemy, it produced liquid. At that time, the weather was hot so that the liquid dried up and the moth was glued to the leaf." Ayim then told Asmudi that natural enemies would always be in the fields and could become plenty if the farmers used insecticides judiciously. Asmudi then told Ayim that he also found parasites like *rembetug* (a kind of mosquito) that were walking on top of the egg cluster. Ayim continued to imagine that "Although white moths die soon after laying eggs, the parasites' mother will accompany her children until they are able to prey on the eggs by themselves."

In Asmudi's example, Haji Ali and Ayim became sources whom one could ask puzzling questions. From their persistent detailed observations, Ayim and Idham had become the two well-known expert farmers of *penggerek batang*, whereas Haji Ali's place had become the centre for the farmers' activities and communications. The following is another example of how a non-IPM farmer intended to seek Ayim's explanation about a puzzling phenomenon he found in his field:

> Anan asked Ayim: "Why are there more egg clusters in two plots in the west than in the other three other plots in the eastern part of my *sawah*?" Ayim answered by referring to wind direction and rice varieties. "The field in the west of your *sawah* is planted with *IR64* which is smaller than *ketan* (planted by Anan in his field), whereas the wind came from the west. Hence, moths that were brought by the winds

perched straight on the tall leaves of *ketan*. Since they already found a comfortable place to lay eggs, not many moths flew to the other plots in the east."

Anan was an example of a farmer who trusted Ayim. In Ayim's view, he gained greater trust from other farmers than Idham because of his frequent visits to his widespread *sawah*. Idham, who was known as a poor farmer only had a small piece of *sawah* in the middle of another hamlet. Other farmers could not witness his activity. Idham, however, was prominent for his persistent activity in discovering puzzling phenomena. He was curious about the form and place of pupae, when pupae came out from stems and when larvae stopped feeding.

The use of transparent plastic bags, as practised in training, had been adopted by the farmers as a means of collecting moths and eggs. Bringing specimens home was a new method of knowledge acquisition adopted by some IPM farmers in the previous dry season (see chap. 5). In this intensive period of pest control, this means contributed significantly to the farmers' and their household members' knowledge, for example, of the different period for hatching and the way larvae bored into the stems.

> Adma found from his observation that "threads came out from the egg clusters, surrounded the plastic bags, then the larvae crawled down. I glued again the bag with the cigarette fire, but the larvae made holes again. Thus, it was like a spider. Hence, the larvae did not fall down directly, but used the threads (see Figure 6.2). So, it is true that the larvae bore into the stems in only four or five minutes." Again, his finding proved that the narrative explanation he received from the IPM trainer/extension worker was true. This finding was validated again the next day when he found another four threads coming out from the bags. Since he found this evidence in the morning, he assumed that "the eggs hatch in the morning and the larvae bore into the stems in the morning too. So, broadcasting carbofuran should be carried out in the morning." When he put some larvae on his hand, he was surprised to see how fast the larvae walked. Again, he said that "it is true as the PPL said that larvae bore into the stems in a very short time." Since Adma did his observation at home, his wife, children and other neighbours had the opportunity to watch and listen to him.

Following up their control practices, the farmers unintentionally learned novel ideas or proved their abstract ideas empirically. The farmers also used plastic bags as a means to carry out observation

Figure 6.2 *Newly hatched larvae*

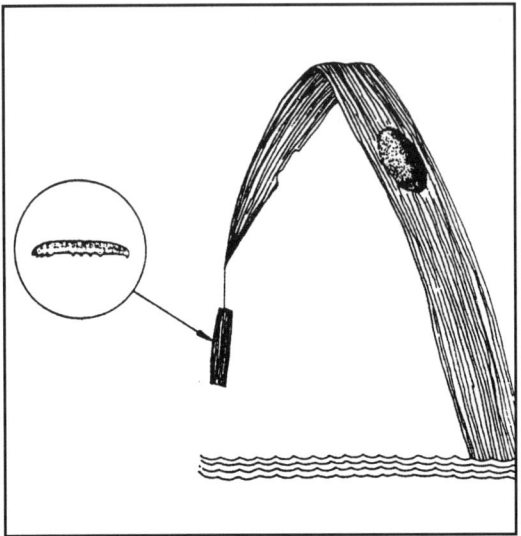
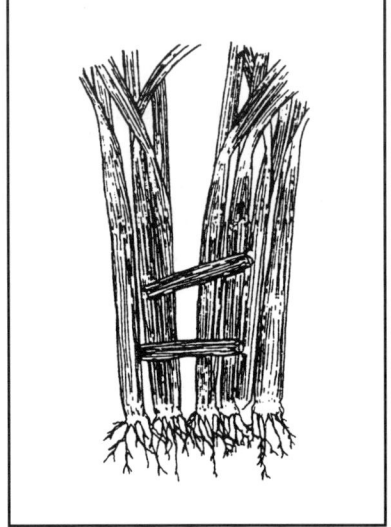

Source: Reissig *et al.* (1986:131).

and experimentation with the intention of discovering the unknown. The farmers, according to Rhoades and Bebbington (1988:328), "… like most human beings, are curious. It is not uncommon for the farmers to set up an experiment just to test an idea that comes to mind." Richards (1989a, 20) also says that "the so-called 'traditional' cultivators … are quite capable of experimenting for intellectual as well as practical reasons." Akim had a practical reason when conducting a systematic observation on a diverse set of samples of egg clusters so as to enable him to take timely control measures. The farmers were also motivated to experiment for intellectual reasons: for their own understanding. Both intellectual and practical reasons also stimulated them to experiment. After finding moths, egg clusters and different sizes of larvae during handcollecting, Haji Ali intended to find out the exact egg laying and its incubation period and whether larvae of particular sizes still absorbed carbofuran.

> After collecting a sample of moths, egg clusters and stems with different larval size, Haji Ali put them in separate plastic bags at home.

He put straws to blow oxygen into the bag filled with moths. Umid, his permanent wage labourer, got a box of *furadan* to pour into the bag filled with stems. Haji Ali asked me: "How could we have similar conditions like those in the field?" Then he asked Umid to get some soil from the fields. After pouring in the soils, some granulars and stems inside the bag, he hung the bag on the wall. Seven hours later in the afternoon, both Haji Ali and I found that larva outside the stems were already killed but not those inside the stems. He doubted that the pesticide was a false one. Early in the next morning we found that all larvae inside the stems already died. Haji Ali then concluded that "the working period of carbofuran took more than 12 hours. Exactly when the larvae were killed, I do not know since we did not look last night before going to bed. We should have looked at them again last night. Now I really believe that carbofuran works and it works after more than 12 hours and larvae at that size, 1–3 cm long, still absorb carbofuran." That morning we also found that the moths we put in the other bag had died. Haji Ali found that the moths had already laid eggs. "So, only in one day and one night moths are already laying eggs." The egg clusters in the other bag had not yet hatched.

Since Haji Ali did this experiment at home, his wife, children and labourers had a chance to follow his activities.

Systematic observation was also carried out by Haji Ali directly in the field—like Ardi earlier—when he accidentally found an emptied egg cluster on top of a leaf. He also found small larvae already bored inside several stems from the same rice hill. He did not, however, find larvae in the adjacent rice hills. From this discovery he gained some new understanding and proved the theory that:

- larvae truly came from egg clusters;
- larvae had already infested green stems that still looked healthy;
- in plants at the generative stage, larvae bored the stems in the third internode (from below);
- the size of larvae was the same as those recently hatched from egg clusters brought home, and hence the larvae had probably just recently bored into the stems;
- the larvae went straight down with threads and bored into the stems in a very short time as the trainers said;
- larvae that bored into one rice hill came from one egg cluster; and
- at this stage of hatching, larvae had not migrated to the adjacent rice hills.

Since he was curious to know the extent to which larvae migrated to other stems, he made a knot in the leaf where he found the emptied egg to enable him to follow through subsequent observations. Making a knot or putting a bamboo stick to identify the place for further observation was also carried out by several other farmers. In the first visit around a week later, Haji Ali found that the infested stems had already reached another rice hill and up to the fourth rice hill toward the east on his second visit a week later. He also counted how many whiteheads were found in one rice hill. From this finding, he discovered and validated the idea that larvae from one egg cluster could migrate to other rice hills.

In such an intensive pest outbreak, the IPM teaching provided initial understanding and stimulation for the farmers to discover things in their own innovative ways. The farmers' experimentation was strengthened rather than undermined by adversity (see Richards 1989a). Through knowledge exchange, their discoveries and assumptions spread. These findings improved other farmers' understandings, raised critical arguments, or ended with no answers or solutions. Again, they criticised the absence of any assistance from government officials.

Prey-predator relationships: transmission, validation and critique. Some farmers had the intention of testing the prey-predator relationship by avoiding injudicious use of pesticides. Only a few farmers (Iwan, Haji Ali and Asmudi), however, reported that they found parasites hatching from the egg clusters. These findings validated the ideas they received from training or increased their consciousness of the correct way to collect egg clusters as Iwan, Ardi, Idham and Armad did.

> "If the parasites hatch from the eggs, they could benefit us. We could return them to the field. Our mistake was piling the eggs altogether," said Iwan. Ardi agreed that they made mistakes in not separating the egg clusters while collecting them so it would be impossible for them to return the parasites if these were mixed up with larvae.

Armad came to the same conclusion from a different experience. He found ants swarming in the bags of egg clusters brought home. This finding validated his discovery while drying the field that ants were attracted to swarming larvae on the ground or even in the plants.

From his continual observation, Idham questioned the validity of the prey-predator relations theory from his finding that even though he already avoided spraying insecticides, the population of spiders did not grow faster. Nevertheless, he recognized that his knowledge was not comprehensive enough to explain the recent outbreak. He did not know how fast the life cycle of natural enemies was and whether it was slower than WRB. At a later stage when whiteheads did emerge, he was able to formulate his discovery that in the early stage of the planting season, the population of natural enemies was low. Moreoever, it was evident that natural enemies could not control the remaining eggs because whiteheads still emerged. Hence, biological control as taught in training was inappropriate to control WRB. A non-IPM farmer (Anin) raised a question whether there was an uneven distribution of natural enemies after finding that there were no significant differences in the degree of whitehead infestation between the treated (those egg clusters collected mechanically) and untreated *sawah*.

Without empirical evidence about the effective results of predation in controlling pests, the farmers became critical of the theory. Hence, some farmers began to lose confidence in the truth of prey-predator relations. Diloh, for example, was not convinced that natural enemies were able to control pests. "If it is true that all natural enemies can control pests, there would not be any damage like this," said Diloh. Diloh, Iwan, and Idham criticised IPM training for not providing detailed explanations on the life cycle of natural enemies and which natural enemies preyed upon which pests.[11] After gaining an initial understanding of prey-predator relationship, they needed to know more to enable them to explain puzzling phenomena, yet they recognized the limitations of their own discoveries.

Assessing the economic threshold level (ETL). The farmers' questions and arguments of the ETL of egg clusters demonstrate again their critical assessments of the IPM teachings. From hand-collection activities, the farmers accumulated and exchanged knowledge of the total egg clusters collected by themselves and other farmers from a certain size of *sawah*. For example, Iwan collected 872 egg clusters from 300 *bata* (0.41 ha) and Idham collected 3,780 egg clusters from one hectare of *sawah* cultivated by another non-IPM farmer. By using total counting as representative of the population of egg clusters instead of samples as taught in training, the farmers questioned whether these numbers already exceeded the economic threshold of egg clusters. They made a reference to the ETL of WRB egg clusters as learned from training, i.e., $0.3/m^2$. Although some farmers (Iwan, Ardi, Rustam and Idham) reached a consensus that the population already exceeded its ETL, they were arguing how the experts could come to $0.3/m^2$ as the criteria for taking control action. They also questioned how the farmers could find that number while collecting egg clusters in the field and whether this criterion was an appropriate indicator in such an intensive pest outbreak in terms of damage and the farmers' losses and gains.

With the same purpose to assess precisely the loss or profit from carrying out mechanical control strategies, Ayim decided to collect all the empty whitehead stems emerging in one of his fields throughout the grain formation stage. He did his assessment by finding the percentage of damage through counting:

$$\frac{\text{total collection of white head stems } (beluk)}{\text{total stems from a particular area of } sawah} \times 100\%$$

This assessment was similar to what the other farmers did in counting the ETL of egg clusters, i.e., from total collection and not from taking a sample. This was the modification the farmers made within the context of their own ways of controlling pests.

Control strategies: evaluation, experimentation and argument. The farmers kept attempting to evaluate their new practices in controlling WRB in terms of its effectiveness and efficiency. Such evaluations improved their understandings while they learned from mistakes in their trial and error activities. From experiences in spraying moths, Akim confessed that his strategy of spraying a "cocktail of insecticides" including boiled carbofuran, was ineffective in eradicating moths. Moreover, he got "dizzy" (*mabok*) and was almost unable to return home. From observing the continuous moth flights, the farmers drew their conclusions for the need to carry out repeated control practices, both by mechanical and chemical controls. From discovering further egg clusters on a day on which he had already collected egg clusters, Adma inferred that "there is no other way except to collect eggs repeatedly." On the basis of his observation of the length of moth flights and his reference to WRB's reproductive behaviour, Ayim was able to formulate his recipe that in such a prolonged flight,

> the farmers had to repeat collecting egg clusters every five days. Carbofuran broadcasting should be repeated out every seven or eight days.

Following this formula, Ayim reevaluated the cost of repeated applications of carbofuran. Anan, on the other hand, argued that a timely carbofuran application in addition to hand-collecting eggs would still advantage the farmers, because

> "if we broadcast carbofuran at the right time, we can still reap profit from the unreduced yields although we have increased costs by purchasing carbofuran." Ayim still disagreed with Anan. "It is much cheaper to collect egg clusters by hand as long as we practise it continuously. For example, in such a long flight we need to collect egg clusters four times by paying wages to four labourers @ Rp.1,500/labour. It means we need to spend Rp.24,000. If we use carbofuran, we have to apply it twice @ 12 kg = 24 kg @ Rp.1,700. This amounts to Rp.40,800. Hence, the difference is Rp.40,800 minus Rp.24,000 = Rp.16,800."

Even though these two farmers argued against one another, their conversations reveal their ability to calculate the cost-benefit of their inventive strategies.

In their search for effective control strategies, the farmers in Marga Tani kept experimenting as discovered by Rhoades and Bebbington (1988:328) in Peru that the Peruvian farmers were keen to seek solutions to problems such as insect damage through experimentation. Two IPM farmers tried to spray egg clusters with the intention of discovering whether eggs would "freeze" (a metaphor they used to mean "would not hatch"). Akim sprayed egg clusters wih *Applaud* whereas Diloh used *Thiodan* and *Azodrin*. Both of them brought several egg clusters home to follow the hatching of those samples. Diloh intended to make a comparison of this sample with the previously unhatched sample of egg clusters. Akim felt confident with the result of his experiment that the eggs did not hatch, whereas Diloh concluded that his experiment had a "sufficient result (*hasilnya lumayanlah*)," after finding that only some of the egg clusters hatched. Although Akim and Diloh followed the results of their experiments through observation, several other non-IPM farmers only believed that their sprayings would prevent the hatching of the egg clusters (*membungkeri telur*) without bringing any samples home.

The farmers had, in fact, the ability to criticise the experiments carried out by their fellow farmers. Among their conclusions were

⋄ insufficient samples (number of egg clusters should be larger);
⋄ insufficient observation period (the length of observation should be longer);
⋄ invalidity of their experiments (the egg clusters comprised a strong substance and were covered by hairs that made the penetration of insecticide impossible, or the possibility that the egg clusters escaped from the sprayings); or
⋄ incorrect conclusion.[12]

Since the ripening stage took 30 days, the infestation of whiteheads went on gradually without the possibility for the farmers to forecast the result. The farmers' diverse control practices stimulated them to follow up the results of their strategies. A non-IPM farmer decided to spray his paddy (*ketan*)—where numerous egg clusters were found—continuously, without carrying out any mechanical control or carbofuran application. Ardi, Iwan and Haji Ali became curious to know as Iwan said, " If I found later that his plants were not attacked by whiteheads whereas mine were, what would be the answer to this?"

Whitehead infestation: control, comparison and evaluation. "I surrender (*Saya pasrah*). I do not know what else I have to do," said Iwan hopelessly when whiteheads gradually emerged in his field. Many farmers shared his feelings and believed that no control action could change the outcome. Only Haji Ali and Ayim began to collect the infested stems, but not with the aim of controlling whiteheads. "I felt uncomfortable (*risi*) looking at the whiteheads," said Haji Ali when he found that many *beluk* had appeared in his plants where he had already frequently undertaken hand-collection activities. Unintentionally, by carrying out this activity he discovered some new phenomena. For example,

- the size of larvae in the white stems were as small as those found in the green stems at the earlier ripening stage;
- not all stems were found with larvae inside;
- all larvae were found in the upper part of the stems;
- collecting stems at this stage was still beneficial in preventing the migration of larvae to other stems.

As usual, the farmers were eager to find the explanation for the new puzzling phenomena. At this stage, a new idea used in interpreting Haji Ali's finding was plant structure. Ayim referred to the small radius of the upper part of the stem that hastened its rotting process although the larvae were still small. Haji Ali referred to the hard tissue of the stem that constrained the boring of small larvae to the lower part.

Ayim did a more systematic stem collection than Haji Ali by repeating this activity until grain formation was completed, to know the total percentage of damage. After gaining some expertise in controlling WRB from discovering the profit and loss from his control strategies since the early planting season, he would then think of how to improve production. As the most consistent farmer in implementing an IPM strategy, he was greatly motivated to know to what extent the IPM strategies succeeded. In his version, the criteria for a successful IPM strategy in the context of WRB outbreak were

> cost saving; a low degree of *beluk* infestation, even though the yields are only small. These criteria reveal the success of IPM.
>
> *biaya menghemat, terkena serangan beluk sedikit saja, walaupun padi "tipis." Kriteria inilah yang menunjukkan "keberhasilan* PHT.*"*

Ayim's statement is a particular case of the farmers' ability to reinterpret IPM objectives in the context of their economic and ecological conditions.

The existing variations in the degree of whitehead infestation provided a good chance for the farmers to make comparisons and evaluations. Similar to what they had done in assessing deadhearts, the farmers compared the diverse degree of attacks in different plots of one *sawah* or between different *sawah* by looking at control strategies and other variables (e.g., transplanting schedule, rice field areas and varieties). Several cases of the prominent appearance of whiteheads infestation (e.g., more than 50% damage in the farmers' estimation) or to the contrary, the best plant performance, became points of reference in the farmers' discussions. By doing this, each individual farmer either came to a firm conclusion that reinforced their previous inference, became more confused about the phenomena that contradicted his expectations and previous inferences, or gained further understanding.

Through such evaluation, the farmers validated their previous inferences about the function of carbofuran or the need to time the broadcasting of carbofuran to the critical reproductive stage of WRB. Another validation the farmers gained was the need to collect egg clusters repeatedly at appropriate times. Ayim learned from his own mistakes of not controlling egg clusters in one of his *sawah* in the middle of flight because of illness. He used this validation to explain the whitehead infestation in the other farmers' fields. He was also able to classify different degrees of whitehead infestation in relation to hand-collection practices:

> Those that belong to category number 1 were fields with 50% whitehead infestation where the egg clusters were not collected. Number 2 were fields with 25% infestation, similar to the 50%, i.e., without egg-collection. Number 3 were fields with 10% infestation, i.e., those that were managed [with egg-collection]. My field at the back of my house (300 *bata*) belonged to this third category.

Other farmers had the same confidence as Ayim but referred to a bundle of diverse control strategies instead of one activity only.

Individual farmers gained increasing confirmation of their conclusions as they gained consistent evidence from what had previously been inferences (see Goodenough 1994:269). The farmers' interpretations became more complicated, however, when they found that their practices yielded unexpected consequences. Moreover, they found that the same results emerged from different strategies, or different results came from undertaking the same activities. "Inconsistent experiences are critical .... They call one's conclusions into question and lead to revised understandings of how things work," says Goodenough (1994:269). Nevertheless, understanding how things work in pest infestation was not a simple matter. The farmers did not have any tools to discover, measure or control the effects of other intervening variables in the correlation between control practices and the degree of damage (see Bentley and Andrew 1991:116 for the limitation of the farmers' knowledge bases). They became confused in formulating their inferences about the relation between these two variables:

> Arpan got confused when he found that both, his fields—which had been treated with carbofuran applications four times—and his neighbour's fields—which were not treated with carbofuran—had the same results: both had a similar degree of whitehead infestation.
>
> Both Ardi and Haji Ali wondered why *beluk* were not plenty in his neighbour's field, whereas Haji Ali's paddy (with hand-collection and carbofuran application) were still infested with whiteheads. Their neighbour did only frequent spraying without broadcasting carbofuran or collecting eggs. Since he planted *ketan*, they questioned whether *ketan* was resistant to WRB.

After spending time and effort thinking, evaluating, interpreting and finding answers for taking what seemed to be effective and efficient control measures, and without any place to ask questions, such a puzzling result was very discouraging for them. It was particularly discouraging for those who tried to implement and spread the IPM notion of avoiding hazards by reducing costs and conserving natural enemies. Idham could not say anything when Asmudi—in great disappointment—blamed him for his advice to avoid carbofuran application. By only collecting egg clusters, Asmudi's paddy was still badly infested by whiteheads.[13]

Feeling desperate and hopeless, Arpan said that it was difficult to predict anything and "what will be, will be." Diloh surrendered to God's will and Iwan referred to the Javanese belief about good and bad years. Their knowledge—on the basis of experience, logic, and to some extent, IPM knowledge—was insufficient to explain these puzzling phenomena. In such a situation when they could not find answers for their actions, they referred to supernatural powers. The farmers were Moslems, but they also had a mixture of Javanese and Sundanese traditional beliefs. From his discoveries in Central Java, Vayda (1993:63–64) found that as pest infestation became more severe and the measures taken proved unavailing, some Central Javanese farmers had recourse to Javanese ideas that pests in outbreaks were brought forth by Nyai Loro Kidul, the goddess of the

Southern Ocean.[14] Grumbling about the absence of any direct assistance from the government officials again became their outlet.

"If we have another harvest failure, who will be blamed? People, the farmers again, whereas there was no guidance from the government," complained Ardi.

Although they had no simple answers for the connection between pest infestation and control practices, the farmers were able to draw a correlation between the transplanting schedule and degree of damage to plants. With the absence of whitehead infestation in plants that had already reached the grain formation stage (*sudah mratag*) after being transplanted in November 1990, they believed that an early transplanting schedule was effective in preventing plants from pest hazards. Anin (a non-IPM farmer) strongly emphasised this as a solution to the farmers' arguments about the relationship between whitehead infestation and control practices. Anin cited the previous year's harvest failure which was found to be severe in *sawah* that was transplanted in December 1989 in order to support this conclusion. Several farmers (Anin, Sukim and Haji Nafi, all were non-IPM farmers) also came to the same conclusion with Ayim's previous inference about the different degree of pest attacks according to rice field areas (blocks) with different ages of paddy. Idham, on the other hand, assumed that the areas of infestation correlated with light attraction when he found that rice fields close to the main road and settlements had more severe damage than those away from the road.

At the early ripening stage, the farmers also recognized that some varieties performed better than the others. With a slight variation, they agreed that *IR42* and *ketan Sumatera* were more susceptible than *IR64*; whereas *IR64* was more susceptible than *Cisadané* or *Way Seputih*. Ayim disagreed with this assumption and confidently said that there was no single variety that was resistant to WRB. Anin related the variety to the transplanting schedule.

Harvesting: the voice of women and the farmers' theory. The majority of farmers' wives or female farmers were not directly involved in pest management decisions and activities. Harvesting was the time to share the joy or sorrow of cultivating rice after following their husbands'/relatives' efforts in managing the growth of their paddy. This was also the time to know the exact yields they received.

> "The yield is good, there are not many *beluk* found in the paddy because my husband did carbofuran application," said Rustam's wife when I approached her and her sister at Haji Nafi's residence. Her sister, Haji Nafi's daughter, was disappointed with the yields she got from her *sawah* managed by his father. "My yield is bad since *Abah* (father) did not apply carbofuran when there was a second moth flight and did not collect eggs either," she complained. On another occasion, Haji Ari's wife complained that even though her labourers had collected eggs, she had very disappointing yields. She and her husband referred to the variety and the late transplanting schedule of their *sawah* as possible contributing factors.

These are examples of how the wives/female farmers adopted their husbands'/relatives' way of assessing plant performance. They evaluated and drew inferences by referring to the yields, the degree of whitehead infestation and their husbands'/relatives' control practices that probably contributed to such a result. Wives/female farmers validated their husbands'/relatives' control practices or otherwise got confused about what they had learned throughout the whole planting season. They learned these from observation, listening to the farmers' conversations and following their relatives' practices.

The exact yields the farmers gained from a particular size of *sawah* became the key criterion for assessing their control strategies. Their inferences had a more valid foundation than their earlier estimations. Individual farmers either validated or questioned their previous assumptions, or improved their understandings. They had their own conclusions. Hence, there was a great diversity in the individual's assessment of the pest control strategies. The assessment of other farmers about somebody else's plant performance could, however, contradict the cultivator's own evaluation. Although Idham, Ayim and Haji Ali gained some degree of confidence in their practices, their yields and plant performance were not considered by many farmers to be good. Good plant performance and high yields were the two main criteria used in evaluating their strategies. Both were easy to assess. The criteria Ayim used, i.e., gaining profits by reducing costs, were not easy for other farmers to assess without an explanation of the costs spent throughout the planting season. As a result, he and Haji Ali received other farmers' taunts that even though they diligently collected eggs, their plants were still infested by whiteheads.

The other farmers praised the yields Akim gained from one of his fields as the best (up to 4 ton/*bahu*). Whereas some IPM farmers perceived Akim as having relied more on spraying than on nonchemical practices, both his father and father-in-law praised his strategies for controlling pests at the appropriate time. Adri, his father-in-law, recognized this while admitting that he had quarreled with Akim over the matter. In his perspective, Akim's suggestion was too complicated and had too many regulations based on IPM teaching. The farmers' perspectives in assessing individual strategies varied, even within the discourse of implementing IPM knowledge. Johnson (1976:266, also see Johnson 1972) identified one kind of difference in agricultural practice, i.e., "differences which result from disagreement among individuals over the facts of the case or their meanings." Variation also follows from ecological differences (Johnson 1976:266). In the case of WRB, the complex nature of the outbreak, the rice environment and the farmers' practices complicated their assumptions of the correlation between yields, whitehead infestation and pest control strategies. Hence, the farmers' conclusions remained contested.

On the other hand, there was a more solid and widespread consensus among many farmers about the correlation between the transplanting schedule and whitehead infestation than there had been earlier. Previously, they were only able to differentiate the earlier from the later transplanting schedule. Now, they could differentiate three kinds of yields and transplanting schedules. The worst yields came from *sawah* transplanted in mid-December 1990; while those transplanted earlier (in November 1990) or later (late December 1990) escaped from whitehead infestation. This discovery increased the farmers' confidence that these two outbreaks had, in fact, a similar nature, i.e., "the first [harvest] was good, the second [one] was bad and the third was good again (*yang pertama bagus, yang kedua jelek, yang ketiga bagus lagi*)." By taking detailed notes and observations, several farmers were able to provide a precise date for the worst period in transplanting or grain formation stage with some variations.[15]

In relation to rice varieties, more farmers now had a perspective similar to Anin's, i.e., there was a connection between the varieties and the transplanting schedule. *IR64*, for example, performed worse if transplanted in mid December 1990, but performed well if transplanted in November 1990. Since the stage of grain formation was already completed and they knew exactly how severe the infestation of whiteheads was, they could formulate precisely what varieties were more vulnerable than the others in relation to the transplanting schedule. There was a change in their assumptions compared to previous inferences drawn at an earlier stage. Three varieties were now considered as having the worst performance, i.e., *IR64, IR42* and *Way Seputih*. Many farmers raised varied questions and interpretations as to why particular varieties performed worse than others. Despite varied arguments about each variety's performance, the farmers were able to correlate the transplanting schedules and rice varieties, as well as the age of plants and WRB infestation.

The farmers now had a fuller picture of the nature of WRB infestation throughout the season. They looked again at both deadhearts and whiteheads infestation at particular stages of plant growth and reconstructed the appearance of these two events together. The ability of the farmers to specify this relation varied. Arpan, for example, could not specify it in detail though he knew that,

> paddy that were attacked by *sundep* escaped from *beluk*, those that previously escaped from *sundep* were now attacked by *beluk*, but paddy with the latest schedule of flowering—even if they were previously infested by *sundep*—were now saved from *beluk*.

Other farmers could identify matters further by pointing to the most susceptible stage in plant growth, i.e., when the paddy was just starting to form ears (the booting stage, or *meteng* [*bunting*, pregnant]). Armad said that paddy attacked by *sundep* at the vegetative stage before *meteng* could recompensate by further tillering, but it would not happen when larvae attacked paddy at the booting stage. The farmers formulated this relation as follows:

- ✧ *sundep* attacked paddy before *meteng*, but without any significant damage in yields;

⋄ larvae that attacked paddy from the booting stage until flowering would cause *beluk*;
⋄ paddy would be saved from *beluk* if there was no moth flight when the panicles had already come out; or if there was a moth flight at the completed stage of grain formation.

Armin's conclusion about the critical date of whitehead infestation was also based on such an interpretation. He explained that

> larvae bored into the stems in month two (*bulan dua*), around day five (5th of February 1991), when the paddy was just about to form ears. Paddy where panicles came out on the 28th of February escaped from *beluk* because the paddy was not pregnant when the eggs hatched. Hence, paddy that escaped from *beluk* were those in which panicles had recently appeared and also *ketan*.

Haji Ari was able to formulate further why the booting stage was critical. He explained that "at this stage the stems were soft and sweet because plenty of materials were produced to support the pregnancy, for example glucose (*zat gula*)."

This inference (the relationship between the age of the plants and WRB infestation) was merely based on their inductive generalizations without any theoretical reference. IPM farmers said that they did not receive any explanation about this relationship from the IPM trainers. This was their most important discovery from experiencing, evaluating and thinking about the puzzling phenomena of the WRB outbreak and this discovery was, in fact, concomitant with the expert's findings (see Kalshoven 1981:247). At the end of the season, another moth flight emerged.

Post harvesting stage: the third moth flight

When another moth flight appeared on March 13, 1991, some farmers had already finished harvesting, some had not, due to a late transplanting schedule or late maturing varieties. The farmers again used their experience and theory about the WRB's reproductive cycle to interpret this flight:

> "These moths might come from pupae left in the stubble, at the bottom of the stems," interpreted Haji Ali, referring to his experience that he had found no larvae in some empty whitehead stems. Hence, "the larvae should have already bored into the bottom of the plants and become moths again."

Using the same reference, that recent moths might come from pupae left uncontrolled from earlier outbreaks, different farmers had different interpretations:

> Ayim referred to the larvae boring to the stems of the plants that were now at the ripening stage, not of those already harvested. The larvae had reached the pupa stage before the plants were harvested. In his interpretation, the recent moths came from these pupae.

"What should we do? Nothing," said Idham hopelessly. The majority of farmers had the same opinion since the critical period had already passed.

Foreseeing the future, Ayim realised the difficulties in implementing what he thought of as ideal ways to prevent future outbreaks, i.e., to burn the stalks or carry out ground preparation as soon as possible. This view is similar to the experts' opinion about the difficulties in recommending that the farmers carry out sanitation activities (see Oka 1991 and the Head of the Centre for Pest/Disease Surveillance's opinion; also see Kalshoven 1981). Ayim referred to the existing rains and the farmers' decisions to delay planting, so as to avoid plants having an attack of "May illnesses" and to fast in *Ramadhan*. He also foresaw the impossibility of eradicating moths totally, since there would be a moving habitat for the reproduction of WRB during ground preparation. The growth of *turiang* (or *singgang*, the regrowth of plants in the stubble) provided a habitat for moths to reproduce. This habitat would persist because of the staggered nature of the rice environment (fields with *turiang*, seedlings or just open fields) since the operation of tractors continued until ground preparation was completely finished. His story indicates the farmers' ability to explain their own circumstances by referring to theories received in training and their own experiences. In such circumstances, Ayim perceived that the only possible way of preventing a future outbreak was to carry out detailed observations in nurseries as he already did. With the same prediction of a possible future outbreak, other farmers came up with different solutions. Armin, for example, mentioned the need to apply carbofuran in nurseries.

The farmers remained critical in interpreting recent phenomenon. Again, Idham raised the question that "if ground preparation could kill pupae, why is there still a large population of WRB?" He then referred to the continuous planting season by PERUM that created a continuous habitat for WRB reproduction. The farmers realised that whatever measures they took in controlling WRB, the condition of the rice environment itself made a favourable habitat for pest reproduction.

THE FARMERS' RICE environment is only a part of the larger world. The wider socio-political and ecological world constitutes parts of their circumstances in striving for freedom and harvests. This chapter presents how in such a world, the farmers' learning process occurred through their everyday struggle. Central to the meaning of learning according to Lave (1996; Keller and Keller 1993) are changes in knowledge and actions. Gradual changes and improvement in the individual's knowledge and action were evident. Through sequential responses in encountering everyday problems, hazards and constraints, individual farmers reinterpreted, evaluated, modified and validated the theories received in the "school." Their continuous and diverse actions that produced intended and unintended consequences and unforeseen phenomena provided rich opportunities for the farmers to learn. The informal and unstructured experience became the sources of new information for their existing ones, which further produced an enriched combination of the old and the new ones, or a set of diverse combination of inputs. As Bourdieu (1977) and Strauss and Quinn (1997) say, the major part of people's knowledge does not originate from learning the formal instruction, but through daily observation, practices, and experience.

The learning process is also part of what Lave (1996) calls a "situated activity" where diverse practices of other farmers enrich individual interpretations through comparison. Considering other farmers' decisions was significant because the farmers learned that in selecting rice varieties, pursuing their own decisions without looking at others' choices would not yield a promising harvest. The farmers also learned that their social world was only a part of the wider bureaucracy of the rice intensification program. Being subordinate to the larger structure and being subjects for bureaucrats' policies, the farmers faced the fact that freedom to decide, as they had learned in the IPM school, was not their right in dealing with the government's programs. Contradictory policies between the government's own agencies, and economic interests between all parties involved in the scheme, were what the farmers learned from their voice to refuse the "total, complete-credit package." Failure to make a change was thus a part of the farmers' learning process.

The government's "trickle-down-messages" in dealing with pest outbreaks, on the other hand, proved ineffective. In such a situation, the case of the farmers' responses to continuous outbreaks of WRB reveals that the learning process was very rich where the local ecological hazards and economic constraints forced the farmers to continuously think and be innovative with pest control strategies. The farmers were indeed capable of modifying the teachings learned in the "school" into their own reasoning, interpretations, labour and economic scarcities. By putting their knowledge into action, the inventive farmers made their knowledge available to other lay farmers. At the beginning, the farmers' inventive handpicking strategy was a strange practice for the lay farmers who did not understand its meaning and purpose, as were the other ideas of the timely use of insecticides. Only gradually, by encountering evidences complemented by farmer-to-farmer knowledge exchange, the lay farmers came to understand the novel ideas of the pest's reproductive cycles and their control strategies. This was the time when a larger number of farmers began to share the meanings of these ideas (see D"Andrade 1987; also see Holy and Stuchlik 1981).

However, diverse interpretations and receptions prevailed. Both the old and the new paradigms of controlling pests were still part of the farmers' decisions. Being persistent with the old practices was still prevalent without a total change in the farmers' paradigm of using "medicines," the persisting metaphor about pesticides. The uneven spread of information and diverse experiences contributed to the different receptions and understandings. Unobservable phenomena, such as the complete cycle of the pest's reproduction led to varied interpretations of the damage symptoms. The complexity, inconsistency and uncertainty of their rice environment constrained the farmers' agreement and confidence about the most effective control strategies. The farmers' observation of a similar pattern of phenomena, on the other hand, contributed to their agreement about the relationship between several variables, e.g., planting schedules, age of plants, and the nature of the pest's infestation. In the following chapter I will examine the extent to which this process of knowledge formation and dissemination recurred and/or changed in different times and circumstances.

7

Recreating Knowledge and Persisting Paradigm

> "This is the politics of people. God will not change people's destiny. People themselves have to use their brains and change their own destiny," expressed Armin, the Marga Tani's hamlet leader about how the farmers had to react to their everyday problems in rice farming. This was the confidence the farmers had gained from their own efforts in encountering various problems in the last two years.

IN THE ABSENCE of any assistance from those in authority, the farmers had to go through the hardships by themselves. They raised many questions and problems to which they could not find the answers. Even though they kept grumbling of being left to their own efforts, the farmers gained improvement in their knowledge through daily responses and reinterpretations. Chapter 6 has examined how, in their responses and learning, the farmers were curious, creative and inventive. The most innovative and persistently inquisitive farmers played a significant role in stimulating creativity. The farmers' inventiveness flourished because of the necessity to survive under conditions of a high-risk environment, the unpredictability of hazards, economic and power constraints, lack of access to sources of knowledge or encouragement from the higher-level bureaucracy. They also experienced incongruence between knowledge and reality and between different notions and perspectives. In response to the complex nature of hazards, new ideas as provided by the IPM training proved useful in stimulating their inventions and discoveries (see Bentley et al. 1994:179).

Throughout, the ongoing knowledge in the making among the community of practitioners who interacted daily in response to common problems, diversity, contestation and convergence was produced through individual learning and decision making. Inconsistent experiences in a complex environment and the absence of any means to examine phenomena beyond unaided empirical observation contributed to levels of contestation. The same individuals could have different ideas and perspectives at different times and in different circumstances (see Barth 1989, 1993; see chap. 1). The acquisition of a particular piece of knowledge did not mean that an actor would generate further practice automatically. Factors affecting individual decisions at different times and in different contexts varied as well (Vayda 1994).

In some cases, however, shared knowledge was gradually achieved. The farmers were encountering common experiences, problems, risks and hazards. They drew similar conclusions from comparing a diverse range of practices and outcomes with consistent experiences over time. Individual's decisions to imitate or adopt their fellows' practices led to the spread of common practices and understandings. Chapter 6 reveals that to some extent, IPM teaching provided initial knowledge of pest behaviour for the schooled farmers that enabled them to communicate and share their experiences. On the other hand, the farmers' own knowledge, metaphors and discourse in the old paradigm of pesticides use, as well as the farmers' own ways of assessing expertise in rice farming, persisted.

This chapter examines how such mechanisms of knowledge formation persisted in the longer term. In the first section I discuss the extent to which past experiences and the ecological and economic conditions of the 1991–1992 seasons affected the farmers' choices of rice variety. As they continued their experimentations, what rice varieties were selected, abandoned or readopted? How the farmers responded to persistent economic constraints and to the policy of providing subsidies and what the consequences were in the use of resources will be described in part two. In the 1991–1992 rainy season, another outbreak of WRB occurred. However, the nature of this infestation was different from the 1990–1991. It is significant, therefore, to examine in the last section, the farmers' reactions to this outbreak after gaining some knowledge from previous experiences. Through all these actions, to what extent were IPM ideas again expanded and modified?

Continuing Practices and Reinventing Tradition: Choice of Rice Variety

Throughout the 1991–1992 planting seasons, the farmers' activities in selecting rice variety revealed the continuation of previous practices. Yet, these practices were accompanied by the adoption and/or rejection of new and old varieties. Part of these was the re-adoption of their tradition of planting a long-stemmed variety in the contemporary rice environment.

Individual decisions and coping strategies

The farmers learned from their mistakes that planting diverse maturing rice varieties in different schedules proved unsustainable in the current rice environment. The recurring pest outbreak in the 1990–1991 rainy season reinforced their learning. The same phenomenon, a diverse degree of WRB infestation on paddy planted in different schedules, occurred in two consecutive years (1989–1990 and 1990–1991 rainy seasons). This phenomenon improved their understanding that the transplanting schedule was a critical variable in preventing harvest failures. These experiences contributed to the formation of a shared knowledge for developing better coping strategies, for example,

- having a uniform harvesting schedule;
- transplanting paddy at an appropriate schedule; and
- planting varieties with the same or similar maturity period.

This shared understanding was made possible in the situation where the farmers were able to formulate a correlation between two variables (i.e., transplanting schedule and degree of pest infestation). A significant result of this discovery was a gain in their own knowledge-acquisition powers, which in turn became a powerful force in changing beliefs and ideas. Understanding the particular ecological conditions in different seasons, the farmers adjusted their coping strategies seasonally.

As the 1991 dry season approached, the farmers maintained their strategy of an appropriate dry season planting schedule. The farmers held to their preference of avoiding "May illnesses" as traditionally practised by the "old people." By referring to this, they did not favour the idea of a "crash soybean planting program" introduced by the BPP staffs, who would enforce them to reschedule the dry season's planting. Toward the 1991–1992 rainy season, the farmers reinforced the need to have a uniform harvesting schedule. Learning from the previous year's experience, the farmers also tried to prepare the fields as early as possible to prevent their plants from suffering the WRB infestation at the reproductive stage. The early rains made this possible. The entire transplanting schedule for Blok Cadas was thus accomplished within two weeks. This accomplishment was supported by the farmers' own efforts to provide a greater number of tractors to prepare the fields in a much shorter time. This is an example of how the farmers learned from past experiences. If a planting schedule had gradually become part of the farmers' pest/disease management strategy, to what extent were the experts' recommendations to rotate rice strains and choose resistant varieties being implemented?

The majority of farmers chose the most preferred variety, based on individual rather than on collective decisions for a uniform variety, by contrast with the neighbouring village, C. Tengah. Collective rotation of rice variety was not the preferred choice, even though some farmers had already confirmed the need to rotate varieties and indeed changed varieties every season. When approaching the 1991–1992 rainy season, the farmers also considered choosing varieties resistant to BPH, although in some cases, their choice turned out to be misguided. Adma and Romi decided to adopt *PN19*, a new seed variety from an agricultural research station (*Pusakanegara*). They did not know that the seed was still in the experimental stage.

The factors underlying the farmers' choices had not altered significantly. High productivity of yields, palatability and good market value were still the primary reasons for selecting varieties. After experiencing recurrent pest/diseases outbreaks, yield sustainability had gradually become important. "What the community wants to plant" had become more significant as part of individual concerns to avoid future hazard.[1] The farmers' strategy thus reveals what Ortiz (1979:231) found among the Colombian farmers.

> If a small farmer wants to survive and succeed, he must not only learn to combine resources to obtain high inputs, but he must take into account possible disastrous results.

In conjunction with the diverse seeds available within and outside their administrative boundaries and the farmers' curiosity and creativity in adopting new varieties, what kind of rice varieties were then selected by the farmers in the 1991 dry season and the 1991–1992 rainy season?

Selecting rice varieties: the flow of seeds and knowledge

On the basis of their objectives of productivity, sustainability and palatability, the farmers' choice centred on the preferred high yielding variety, *IR64*. A range of other varieties persisted as well. The number of plots planted with a recently adopted variety increased. The previously selected rice strains declined. A relatively "new" variety was adopted. But, the kinds of varieties selected by the farmers varied seasonally. The continuous trial and error, imitation, adoption and plant assessment by individual farmers led to this dynamic and continuous process in seed selection.

MAINTAINING THE "PRIME" VARIETY

IR64 was again the dominant high yielding variety (HYV) planted by the farmers in the 1991 dry season and the 1991–1992 rainy season. From the total of *sawah* cultivated by both the IPM and non-IPM farmers, as many as 73.5% of *sawah* were planted with *IR64* in the 1991 dry season and in the 1991–1992 rainy season (see table 7.1 for the percentage of each variety planted in *sawah*).

From the farmers' comparison with the performance of other varieties either in yields, number of stems and panicles, weight of grains, or palatability, the majority still perceived this variety to be the best ("*IR64 masih paling unggul*"). Those who did not suffer from WRB attack in the 1990–1991 rainy season referred to the yields they could earn from one *bahu* compared to the other varieties. As the 1991 dry season approached, the farmers gained confidence about the absence of WRB attack. By referring to the Javanese belief, a few farmers confidently mentioned that 1991 was a "good year" in the Javanese calendar. "*Masih penasaran*" ("I am still anxious"), said some farmers who were still enthusiastic about *IR64*'s good performance even though it had already suffered a pest attack. *IR64* was, again, preferred because of its short maturity period. Many other farmers referred to others' decision to replant this variety. "*Harus tahu lingkungan* ("We have to know the environment")," said Suta. Even though they noted the unsatisfactory performance of *IR64* in the 1991 dry season because of its reduced weight and yield and the reappearance of the "red phenomenon" (*gejala merah*) or "*krèsèk*," this variety was again predominant in the 1991–1992 rainy season. The farmers selected *IR64* on the basis of the cooler weather in the rainy season, a factor conducive to the growth of this variety. Their confidence grew along with their affirmation of the need to have an early planting schedule. In the farmers' eyes, no other varieties could replace this variety in its performance throughout different seasons.

It is through this mechanism of assessment and decision making that a promising variety is maintained rather than rotated. The farmers understood, however, that good quality seeds were significant in sustaining the best yields. The seed history was thus important, including the number of seasons the seeds had already been replanted and the quality of their latest performance. Observation and collecting information about the seeds preceded the farmers' decisions on where, from whom and how they could get good quality *IR64* seeds. Through this mechanism, the farmers abandoned the seeds of lesser quality in favour of the better ones (see Winarto 1997a).

ABANDONING UNSATISFACTORY VARIETIES, ADOPTING THE NEW AND OLD VARIETIES

Through the same mechanism of selection and rational calculation after two seasons of trial and error, in the 1991 dry season, the majority of farmers abandoned the varieties that had been planted in the 1990 dry season as a substitute for *IR64*. Those that were not preferred by the majority of the farmers were *Cisadané* and glutinuous varieties due to their long maturity period and the sharp decline of the glutinous variety's price earlier. The others were *Way Seputih*, *Dèlis* and *IR42* for not producing a high enough yield and resistance toward pests and disease. The decision of the farmers could, however, vary in different seasons. Individual concerns and selection also varied among individuals. Each farmer's particular situation affected his/her concerns and selection. As a result, less favoured varieties were replanted, whereas the others were not reconsidered in the 1991–1992 rainy season.

Table 7.1 *Rice varieties in the 1990–1992 planting seasons*

Variety	Percentage (%) of variety planted in *sawah*		
	1990–1991[a]	1991[b]	1991–1992[c]
IR64	72.7	73.5	73.5
Cisadané	3.3	1.7	0.0
IR42	3.3	0.0	1.8
Way Seputih	5.8	0.9	0.0
Muncul	1.7	0.0	0.0
IR99	0.8	12.8	2.6
PN19	0.0	0.9	1.8
Paddy *merah* (red variety)	0.0	5.9	0.0
Gènjah Melati (Paddy *Clingkrik*)	0.0	0.0	5.3
Others[d]	2.5	1.7	2.6
Glutinous variety	9.9	0.0	4.4
Combination[e]	0.0	2.6	8.0
Total	100.0	100.0	100.0

Source: My survey, conducted between 1990 and 1992.
[a]Percentage of each variety from a total of 121 *sawah* cultivated by 44 farmers in the 1990/91 rainy season.
[b]Percentage of each variety from a total of 117 *sawah* cultivated by 44 farmers in the 1991 dry season.
[c]Percentage of each variety from a total of 113 *sawah* cultivated by 44 farmers in the 1991/92 rainy season.
[d]Others: 1990–1991 rainy season: IR41, Semeru; 1991 dry season: IR36, Semeru; 1991/92 rainy season: Sidomuncul, Walanai.
[e]Combination: a number of plots were planted with a combination of varieties. 1990 dry season: PN19-Cisadané, IR99-IR64, paddy merah-IR64, IR64-Semeru. 1991/92 rainy season: Way Seputih-IR64-IR99, IR64-IR99-Sidomuncul, IR64-IR36, IR64-PN19, Walanai-Paddy Clingkrik.

All the farmers' efforts in selecting varieties were indications of their inventiveness. "The farmers are always looking for the best, those that have a high productivity," said Akim firmly. Curiosity led them to always experiment with novel varieties. Through this mechanism, in the last three seasons (following the 1990 dry season), some innovative farmers adopted some new varieties (or old varieties that were relatively recently introduced to their area). Their decisions to try a novel variety were crucial factors from which other farmers could learn through observation and then make a decision about whether to adopt it in the next season. If these varieties performed well, dissemination through seed exchanges followed. Again, the extent of this dissemination fluctuated in different seasons due to the farmers' adoption or rejection of the novel varieties.

The source of seeds varied between different varieties and depended on the social network each farmer had. Not all varieties adopted by the farmers in the 1991 dry season and the 1991–1992 rainy season belonged to the officially released HYVs, and not all seeds were obtained through official channels. Examples of the officially released certified seeds that were obtained through farmer-to-farmer seed exchanges were *Walanai, IR36* and *Bahbutong*. Seeds originating from agricultural research stations but not yet released were *IR99* and *PN19*. The others were locally named varieties, such as *Sido Muncul* and *IR-merah/IR64-merah* or *beras merah* (red-rice variety).[2] In the farmers' understandings, some of these varieties were not entirely new and had already been planted elsewhere. The farmers acquired the seeds from diverse sources as revealed in the following example:

> Anin, who planted *IR99* in the 1990–1991 rainy season, obtained the seeds through exchange with a harvest labourer who earned the *bawon* (harvest share) from harvesting the fields of a farmer from another village. After observing the good performance of this variety, six farmers decided to purchase or exchange *IR99* seeds with Anin. Five other farmers obtained seeds from different sources: purchasing seeds from a harvest labourer (also from the *bawon*) and another farmer in the neighbouring villages, and collecting seeds from their neighbour's plot without the owner's knowledge. Even though, in the farmers' evaluation, the performance of this variety in the 1991 dry season was the best in yields, price and resistance to "red-illness," the number of farmers planting this variety in the 1991–1992 rainy season dropped because of their anxiety about BPH and rat infestation.

Another example is how the farmers obtained a locally named variety that originated from further away, namely the hinterland of West Java.

> One of the farmers who came from Majalaya in Central West Java brought *beras merah* seeds (awnless) from there. He tried to plant the seeds in one part of his plot (in 100 *bata* of the total of 1200 *bata*) in the 1990–1991 rainy season. Even though this variety was infested by WRB

in that season and was mixed with another type of *beras merah* variety (awned), other farmers noticed that the yields were still promising. They also knew that the price of *beras merah* was always high. When the owner brought the seeds to the huller factory, the information soon spread among the farmers. Several farmers quickly decided to purchase the seeds and shared them with their relatives. Many more farmers had the same intention but missed out. Rustam who had already purchased these seeds also decided to purchase the awned *beras merah* (*Bahbutong*) that he knew had developed from *Cisadané* instead of *IR64* and was planted in PERUM in the 1990–1991 rainy season. He acquired the seeds from a wage labourer who did the collecting of the left over seeds (*nyasak* or *ngarak*) in another farmer's plot in PERUM. None of these farmers, however, replanted this variety in the 1991–1992 rainy season. One of the reasons was their anxiety about brown plant hopper attack on this variety.

These cases reveal how seeds were distributed and disseminated from distant and adjacent places from whomever and through whatever channels and opportunities were available. Through this flow of seeds, the information and knowledge about the origins and performance of the seeds spread and further generated a wider distribution of the seeds.

READOPTING THE "TRADITIONAL" VARIETY

"That is *Padi Clingkrik*, the *Gènjah Melati* variety," explained the farmers while pointing to the tall plants growing at the edge of a number of *sawah* in Block Cadas in the 1991–1992 rainy season.

There was also the striking phenomenon of the return of old long-stemmed varieties (*padi gagangan*) recognized by the farmers as having a short maturing period. *Gènjah* refers to a short age. The farmers classified this variety as an awned paddy. In daily conversation, they named it *Padi Clingkrik*, a term referring to the way people plant this traditional variety in the new rice environment, a reinvention of the old tradition of planting long-stemmed varieties.

The term *Padi Clingkrik* originated from the way the first cultivators, i.e., the local government officials from southern villages, planted the seeds in other farmers' *sawah*, relying on their generosity to surrender some space along the edge of their fields (*numpang tanem, di pinggir-pinggir galeng*). In my research area, there were no common lands provided to local government officials to carry out cultivation as a source of income. By planting this variety on other farmers' lands, they could obtain rice for their own consumption. Some farmers told stories of how these government officials planted the seeds by squatting on the dikes. They did not go into the fields and transplanted the seeds wearing their shoes.

Initially there were four farmers who planted this *Padi Clingkrik*, i.e., Idham, Anin, Iman and H. Ammad. Idham's seeds, however, failed to grow. The farmers used to broadcast the HYV seeds in the seedbeds. They had to think of how to grow a small amount of these long stem's seeds in their current environment. Arman told me the story of Idham's failure:

> Idham's wife said that Idham did not scatter the seeds, but just put the stems with the panicles on top of the ground. So, the stems were pulled up by rats.

The other farmers prepared a special seed bed to grow the seeds. The transplanting was, however, peculiar: by the farmers themselves along the edge of their fields after the transplanting of the main HYVs in the plots. The farmers used again their *ani-ani* to harvest this long-stemmed paddy by themselves and their families. They then brought the harvests home in the old way by tying up the bundle of stems. One farmer threshed the panicles with a modified thresher.

Although Iman purchased seeds from a farmer who had planted this variety in the last four seasons in Talang Sari, the adjacent village, Anin acquired seeds from Akim, his son. Akim confessed that he stole one handful of grain from the paddy planted in Talang Sari by pulling out the stems during harvesting time. From observing the performance of this plant and wanting this palatable rice for their own consumption, a number of farmers expressed their intentions to purchase seeds from these farmers. "People have already put their names on my list to buy *Clingkrik*," said Iman who already had a plan to sell it at a higher price.

By planting this old long-stemmed variety, the farmers not only readopted their traditional cultivation practices, but also conserved the seeds and improved their knowledge about cultivating long-stemmed varieties in a recent rice ecosystem of the Green Revolution era. Together with the farmers' adoption of other varieties, their decisions led to the conservation of traditional as well as high yielding varieties. This was a promising indicator of the return of rich genetic resources (see Winarto 1997), in the midst of a severe decline of the biodiversity in the Green Revolution era (see Fox 1991; Shiva 1993).

Continuing Struggle and Inventions: Coping With Power and Economic Constraints

In the following years (1991–92), the provision of the credit package scheme to the farmers formed an arena for the "interface" between the two parties: the local farmers and the bureaucrats. The "interface," according to Arce and Long (1992:214), "... conveys the idea of some kind of face-to-face encounter between individuals with differing interests, resources and power." Differences in the interests between the two parties and the play of power of the local bureaucrats in allocating resources through the subsidized scheme persisted. No changes of policy had happened. The farmers in Marga Tani were still not able to voice their freedom to choose. The farmers' responses to this policy over time again varied, and so did the consequences for their knowledge and practices.[3]

The 1991 dry season: loyalty and its consequences

In contrast to the situation at the beginning of the 1990–1991 rainy season, at the end of the season, the farmers did not argue against receiving the complete credit package. Early that year (1991), the government announced an increase in the price of fertilizer. The farmers complained that over time, the price of fertilizers had become higher than the market price of grains (per 100 kg). Purchasing fertilizer with cash was a burden for them. As they approached the 1991 dry season, some farmers expressed their beliefs that pests and "illnesses" in the dry season would be more severe than in the rainy season. Pesticides were thus still necessary. For them, having the granular insecticides and fertilizer in advance were beneficial. Yet, learning from past experiences they recognized that any voice against the government's policy was useless. Idham felt helpless: "How could we make a fuss over the package, it has already been allotted, so how ...." Hence, being loyal to the scheme was one alternative for them to cope with increasing economic constraints. The farmers' leader then decided to accept the subsidy. It was now open for individual farmers to make up their minds whether to apply for the credit. Although some farmers decided to take the subsidy, other farmers decided to purchase resources on their own. One significant consequence of accepting the complete package was the incentive to still use insecticides.

"PHT KURANG JALAN" ("IPM DOES NOT WORK WELL")
"When discrepancies exist between ideology and social reality, what do people do?" Moore (1987:210) raises this question in her article on *Epilogue: Uncertainties in Situations, Indeterminacies in Culture*. Besides congruities and regularities, she strongly argues that there are paradoxes, conflicts, inconsistencies, contradictions, multiplicities, and manipulabilities in social life (Moore 1987:217). In chapter 6 I described how the farmers reacted when they found discrepancies between their recent understandings of IPM and the existing policy of subsidized inputs. In the 1991 dry season, the farmers' official reaction to be loyal to the scheme reveals that—in specific situations and at different times—they could respond in different ways. In the previous season they received an incomplete package. In this season, the farmer-acceptors received the complete form of the scheme. How did the IPM farmers deal with the package?

"If we take it, what should we do with the 'medicine'? Shall we sell it at a lower price?" asked Wahyu rhetorically. That was not the solution they took. What the farmers did with the package is an example of the incongruence between what the farmers knew and what they had to do. Since many farmers still perceived pesticides as "medicines" for protecting plants and they already had them, mixing these "medicines" with fertilizers was the answer.

> Haji Ali sprayed the foliar fertilizer in a mixture with insecticide twice. "I used *Darmabas* (the liquid insecticide) for protection. Well, the KUT (credit package) had to be purchased, so I used it." Wahyu also gave me a similar answer by elaborating on the conflict he had: "According to IPM, *Darmabas* is permitted; it is okay. *Thiodan* was banned because it damaged the environment; everything was killed. So, I sprayed *Gemari* (the foliar fertilizer) by mixing it with *Darmabas*. According to the label, it is okay to mix *Gemari* with insecticide. I used the insecticide for protection. According to IPM, however, 'do not spray even with *Darmabas*.' But, since KUT gave it to us, *ya* I used it." He explained further that: "According to IPM, in cultivating rice, we have to save capital. According to KUT, however, fertilizers and

medicines have to be taken. Hence, they are contradictory. So, no observation. IPM cannot be implemented. The KUT tends to make IPM not working well because everything provided should be taken."

Wahyu's explanation reveals the paradoxes they encountered, not only between knowledge and reality, but also between the various messages they received from different sources. Such a conflicting situation constrained the IPM farmers to implement IPM strategy. Not all IPM farmers, however, felt it was a pity not to use the liquid insecticides they already had. Armin, the hamlet leader, received four cans of *Darmabas* for 1 ha of *sawah*, but he left them untouched.

In this first dry season after training, the farmers' belief in the power of carbofuran to protect plants was still strong. Only two IPM farmers decided not to use carbofuran in both nurseries and transplanting. Ayim, who had already gained an understanding about the timely application of carbofuran and had in fact, delayed its use after observation, still had a plan to use this insecticide in transplanting. "If there will be no moths, I will use it so as to enable the paddy to grow well," explained Ayim. While they strongly felt compelled to use the liquid insecticides, they did not have such feelings in the use of carbofuran. Their knowledge and metaphors of "illnesses" and "medicines" still underpinned their decisions as explained by Wahyu.

> According to IPM, if we would like to use carbofuran we have to examine first the economic threshold level. If the natural enemies outgrow the pests, we do not need to use it. What is common here, however, in the dry season, almost all farmers use carbofuran for protection. As if a person gets sick, that person has to drink medicine first for protection so as to make him more resistant.

Again, the function of pesticides as preventative "medicines" still underlay the farmers' reason.

By accepting the package, the farmers-acceptors also learned to use the introduced technology: the foliar fertilizer in both liquid and granular forms.

The 1991 Dry Season: Individual Exit and Ongoing Experimentation

From the time the farmers recognized problems in handling the scheme, in particular when they lost their savings because of the bad debt problem in their previous KUD (in the 1989–1990 rainy season), many farmers chose to "exit" from the scheme. In this 1991 dry season, the increased economic constraints motivated these farmers to experiment with a reduced amount of inputs rather than taking credit.

CONTROL OR PREVENTATIVE MEASURE: A DIVERSE USE OF CARBOFURAN

Mixed beliefs about the function of carbofuran, either as a control or as a preventative measure, and a diverse strategy in the use of this insecticide persisted. Only a few farmers gained confidence in the control function of this insecticide. For these farmers (e.g., Anin, Anin's brother and Rustam, all of them non-IPM farmers), broadcasting this insecticide only if they found damage symptoms or pests was definitely the answer. Anin used the same metaphor of "illness" as Wahyu, but rephrased it within the context of the new strategy (see "PHT *Kurang Jalan*": ("IPM Does Not Work Well").

> If there are no pests, we should not use it. Just like a sick person; that person only needs to go to the doctor if he gets sick.

Anin's explanation is an example of how the farmers reinterpreted their recent understanding by using their own metaphors. This farmer's understanding reveals the enduring acceptance of the early metaphoric transmission of pesticides as "medicines" (see Mayer 1993; Petrie and Oshlag 1993 for the role of metaphor in transmitting scientific concepts). The farmers, however, reinterpreted their recent experiences differently followed by different implications. Wahyu's interpretation constrained him to implement the IPM strategy. Anin's interpretation, on the other hand, stimulated him to use pesticides judiciously.

CHEAP BUT USEFUL: THE USE OF KEROSENE

Memory of past experiences has a significant role in the formation of recent knowledge (see Connerton 1989; Shore 1991). The farmers still had a vivid memory of how kerosene had helped them in solving the problem of a severe brown plant hopper outbreak in 1976. This memory became their main reference in looking for solutions when they faced an increase in costs and pest attacks. Nevertheless, it was only through the action of some inventive farmers that the use of kerosene in the recent rice cultivation began to spread. Gradually over time, this practice was adopted by a larger number of farmers. This kerosene adoption is a case of Shore's (1991:13) formulation of learning as "a transformative activity of the mind upon the world that employs external experience to continually resurrect and recreate previously incorporated forms of knowledge."

Contrary to the enforced introduction of foliar fertilizers through the credit package scheme, the adoption of kerosene is the result of the farmers' own initiative and reasoning by using their memories. Although the introduction of foliar fertilizer was official, the farmers recognized their own experimentation as "unofficial," "illegal," or "secret" (*tidak resmi, tidak boleh, rahasia*). With this perspective, at the beginning of their experiments, some farmers did not dare to talk about using kerosene. Isman (a non-IPM farmer) told me about the first time he saw Usin (IPM farmer) carrying kerosene out to his field in the 1990 dry season. He gained the information about using kerosene from his questions to Usin, and observing that the pests "... were floating, fell down quickly to the ground." He then decided to try it, but still did not dare talk about it. Through the same mechanism as Isman, some farmers imitated this experiment in the following 1990–1991 rainy season and again in the 1991 dry season.

There was a shared opinion among these farmers in their assessments of the impact of kerosene: to prevent the melting of urea (N) in the farmers' hands during broadcasting;[4] the direct evidence of the "instant death of pests," and the lower costs they would incur compared to the costs of carbofuran (Rp.250.00 [US$.12 for 1 litre of kerosene as compared to Rp.35,000–40,000 [$17.50–20.00]/20 kg of carbofuran). Ease of observation and direct evidence proved to be effective in promoting the farmers' confidence. The farmers' arguments focused on the different impact kerosene had on pests compared to carbofuran:

> A non-IPM farmer told me that, "*Indofuran* (carbofuran) is not as good as kerosene, because kerosene hastens the death of pests." Another farmer argued that, since he could not see it straight away, he could not be certain whether pests were killed by carbofuran, not as certainly as kerosene.

Those who already understood about the presence of natural enemies were able to interpret the impact of kerosene. In their understanding, kerosene did not kill natural enemies, not in the way that carbofuran did. "All worms, frogs, fishes were killed by carbofuran," said Wahyu. Even though at this stage the use of carbofuran was still widespread, the findings of kerosene and the farmers' confidence of its advantage became a basis for wider adoption of this substance in the following season (the 1991–1992 rainy season).

CHEAP BUT EFFECTIVE: TRIAL AND ERROR WITH FERTILIZERS

The increased price of fertilizers and the recurrent outbreak of the "red-phenomenon" in this 1991 dry season stimulated the farmers to continue their experiments with fertilizers. In their perceptions, the extension worker's recommendation about fertilizer was good, but too costly. One of the main questions raised by many farmers was how to save costs but be effective. Diverse experiments were again prominent.

Frequently the farmers reduced or increased the amount of a particular component, either urea, TSP, or KCl in nursery or transplanting. However, some farmers did their experiments in a different way. Learning from Haji Nafi's successful experiments in the early years of the Green Revolution—i.e., increasing yields by pouring fertilizers onto the rice hills (*mupuk diprolok, dienclok*)— Idham decided to imitate this practice. His other reasons for performing this experiment were to reduce the amount of fertilizers because of the large debt he had and to investigate the effect of this practice on plants with 25 cm planting distance. By pouring fertilizers he perceived that, "all roots can 'eat' them." In broadcasting, not all of the roots can absorb the nutrition. He had no idea about the volatility of urea in broadcasting. This experiment, again, is an example of the recreation of "old" knowledge that still constituted part of the farmer's memory. The other farmers kept evaluating this experiment, particularly when they found that many of Idham's rice hills were "burnt" (*kering, terbakar*) afterwards. Even though Idham was the only one who did this experiment, the other farmers learned it. This also happened when the farmers observed Haji Nafi's experiment in broadcasting organic fertilizers.

Three farmers (Haji Nafi, Rustam and Adma) carried out their experiments by broadcasting animal dung in one of their plots. They reintroduced and modified their traditional (pre-Green Revolution) practice of broadcasting organic fertilizers. Haji Nafi broadcast a mixture of burnt domestic wastes with the dung of goats, chicken and ducks after transplanting in a wet field. Rustam broadcast goat dung before transplanting. From comparison with his other plots treated with the inorganic fertilizers, Haji Nafi felt dissatisfied with the slow growth and bad performance of the paddy treated with the organic fertilizers. Together with Adma he learned that using organic fertilizers in the recent environment was ineffective. Compared with his past experience, Haji Nafi assumed that the current soil saturated with nutrients from inorganic fertilizers could not absorb the organic nutrition as well as in earlier days. He then decided to refertilize his plot with inorganic fertilizers.

These experiments are examples of the farmers' inventiveness that led to the resurrection of the old, traditional practices in new forms. However, the results taught them that returning to traditional practice under current conditions for rice cultivation was ineffective and inappropriate.

The 1991–1992 rainy season: collective exit, enforced loyalty and continuing inventions

The growing certainty of the need to save expenses by avoiding the unnecessary use of pesticides motivated some farmers to voice again their reluctance to accept the complete credit package. Learning from the failure to negotiate requests with the BPP staffs, in the early rainy season of 1991–1992, a non-IPM farmer took action to request a partial package (without pesticides and foliar fertilizers) directly from the KUD officials, bypassing the BPP staffs. The answer he received was, again, the alternative of either taking or not taking the package in full. Learning of this persisting policy, the farmers' leader, supported by the other farmers, decided to "exit" from the scheme. In constrained economic circumstances, exiting and reducing unnecessary expenses became a better option than receiving a forced-sale package with interest from the state. By doing this, the farmers excluded the credit package from their endowment as a way of avoiding the responsibilities underlying the entitlements to that property. The exit option, according to Hirschman (1970:21), is widely held to be uniquely powerful: by inflicting revenue losses on delinquent management, exit is expected to induce that 'wonderful concentration of the mind.'

In this case, no effective results occurred. No changes in the policy at the regional and local level had happened up to 1992. There were, however, implications for the lower authority level, the BPP. In the face of a possible vacuum, which would reflect on the BPP's achievements and to some extent their profits (see van de Fliert and Winarto 1993; van de Fliert 1993), the BPP staff persuaded the farmers' leader to accept the package, even though the package would cover only a few hectares of rice fields. In a difficult position, the farmers' leader accepted this offer without informing others and distributed the limited credits among his close kin. Hence, his loyalty to keep taking the scheme was the result of enforcement by those in power rather than by his own will (Winarto 1995).[5] Experiments to reduce unnecessary costs persisted.

LEARNING FROM EXPERIENCE AND REPRODUCING INVENTIONS

In this 1991–1992 rainy season, the farmers developed a greater certainty about the function of carbofuran in controlling rather than preventing "illnesses." Questions of its effectiveness were, however, raised by some farmers. Ayat (non-IPM farmer) who still believed in luck argued that "whatever I used, during the period of harvest failure (*jaman bapuk*), it would fail (*bapuk waé*). Hence, it depends on luck."

Other growing arguments among the farmers were not only about the costs of carbofuran, but also about its eradication of all other animals, including natural enemies. The concept of "natural enemy" had already been integrated with the farmers' knowledge and vocabularies. This concept had become a point of reference in assessing the results of their own practices as Wira showed in his comments after broadcasting carbofuran:

> In Wira's eyes, "although the natural enemies were first killed, the 'origins' (*bibitnya*) were killed, after 15 days (referring to the working period of carbofuran) the natural enemies reemerged. I don't know, from where they came." Nur who listened to Wira agreed: "Yes, as long as there is water, there are fishes."

Hence, Wira and Nur did not feel guilty about broadcasting carbofuran.

Under the continuing of economic constraints and the insignificant number of farmers who received the compulsory package, the farmers had greater flexibility to decide whether to use carbofuran. The number increased of those who decided not to use carbofuran at all, as did those who broadcast it in the nursery only. Those who used carbofuran in transplanting practised this in response to the outbreak of WRB. Anin and some IPM farmers were examples of those who persistently used carbofuran as a control measure. The farmers also kept experimenting by reducing its amount, by boiling or selectively pouring (*dipruluki*) instead of broadcasting the recommended package. Haji Nafi carried out, again, an experiment by dividing his fields into those that were treated with carbofuran, those that were not, and those that were treated with both carbofuran and kerosene.

The reduction in the use of carbofuran was concomitant with the increased use of kerosene. When the farmers talked about carbofuran, they also mentioned kerosene as its substitute. In my calculation, among 20 farmers, there were—in total—around 250 litres of kerosene that were "poured" into 35 ha of rice fields (van de Fliert and Winarto 1993). As many more farmers adopted this practice, the "fear" of using or discussing kerosene publicly disappeared. The arguments about kerosene became widely and openly raised in the farmers' daily conversations. They exchanged ideas about how many litres were used in how many hectares/*bata* of rice fields. The farmers also argued about the advantages in broadcasting fertilizers and in reducing costs, as well as its impact on plants, pests and natural enemies.

At this stage, the farmers began questioning the truth that kerosene killed pests and not natural enemies. Without additional tools to examine these issues, the farmers could only subjectively interpret what they observed. The farmers' arguments about the impact of kerosene on natural enemies, as raised by the IPM farmers, were again an example of how they interpreted this invention according to their recent understanding of IPM principles. Aming, who believed that kerosene did not kill natural enemies, felt confident that this practice was not contrary to IPM principles that "natural enemies still live. Hence, using kerosene is not wrong according to IPM, because it does not kill natural enemies," said Aming firmly.

Not all farmers, however, were convinced about this practice. "I did not use it, it is only wasting money," said Amid, an IPM farmer.

ABANDONING THE INTRODUCED COMPONENTS AND EXPERIMENTING WITH A NEW IDEA

Without a given package of inputs, using foliar fertilizer was an additional burden for those who had a shortage of capital. Only Haji Ali and a few farmers continued their trials in using this component. Under conditions of economic difficulty, without any significant evidence of promising differences in yields, the farmers preferred not to continue with it. On the other hand, the farmers' experiments with fertilizers went on. Again, several IPM farmers adopted a novel practice, i.e., using cooking salt in a mixture with fertilizers, adopted from a farmer's practice in a distant place. Similar to the other experiments, the other farmers—who learned about this trial through farmer-to-farmer transmission—looked forward to learning the results by, again, assessing the plant performance and yields. Imitation and adoption would follow if—in their perceptions—the trial were successful and yet efficient. Rejection and abandonment would be the case if they did not perceive it as significantly useful in terms of cost and yields. By doing these, their knowledge again, improved.

Recreating and Improving Knowledge: Response to Recurrent Pest Outbreaks

For the farmers in Marga Tani, their understanding about the pest outbreaks and the nature of infestation in the 1991 dry season was still in process. Some farmers had gained more extensive understanding than others. Some parts of the pests' behaviour were known quite well by some farmers, but the other parts related to the pests' metamorphosis or the work/function of insecticides were not well comprehended by them and other farmers. If knowledge, as Borofsky (1994:335) says, is the understanding that is definite and delineated, then for the whole group of farmers in Marga Tani, knowledge about WRB's behaviour and its control strategies have not been definitely and delineately formed. On the basis of Borofsky's criterion, I argue that individual farmers had gained some "knowing" about these phenomena. Knowing, according to Borofsky (1994:335),

> is not only diverse because it changes in different contexts but because there are parts of what is known which can be precisely delineated and parts which cannot. And finally, at the other end of the continuum, is knowing that generally tends to be fluid, that tends to be rather hard to pin down with precise parameters, with formal, set descriptions.

Borofsky (1994:338) mentions further that one important step to do in our analyses is examining "... the conditions that *structure knowing into knowledge.*" The experiences of everyday life are the most prominent factor structuring knowing as also presented in earlier chapters. Besides sharing the ways of learning and communicating with one another, the farmers in Marga Tani structured knowing of the pests' behaviour through several means. These consisted of

- activities in modifying control strategies;
- learning from mistakes, unintended consequences, unforeseen phenomena and diverse outcomes of the farmers' practices;
- learning from individual observation and experimentation; and
- drawing up comparisons.

The latter was a significant means to validate, reformulate, or even falsify earlier propositions. Through these means, the recent discoveries were incorporated into their schemes of interpretations, which, in combination with prior assumptions, became the basis for further reinterpretation, evaluation and action.

From the sharing of knowing in responding to common experiences, some ideas were commonly gained by both the schooled and the lay farmers. The use of plastic bags, which had not been practised prior to IPM school, had become a significant means to learn. The use of plastic bags was disseminated through farmers' knowledge exchange, were used not only for collecting specimens, but also for carrying out observation and experimentation. Some common ideas achieved by both groups of farmers were the need to understand the behaviour of pests, the nature of their infestation of plants, and the impact of control practices on pest populations and their plants as points of reference in pest management.

Nevertheless, the "lay" farmers only gained pieces of information from the comprehensive IPM premises, sometimes in modified form through transformation and reinterpretation. These "lay" farmers also received diverse information from different farmers or from the same farmers at different times. These pieces of information received in combination with existing knowledge became, again, the basis of individual reinterpretation of current phenomena. As Sperber (1984) has pointed out, the construction of different individual thoughts—as a result of knowledge dissemination—is only more or less closely related, never in precise replication. Facts that many farmers had no way of knowing, such as those pertaining to WRB metamorphoses, left a space for subjective imagination to play a part. The varied understandings were about the details of WRB reproductive cycle, such as the stage of what the larvae would be; what kinds of moths laid WRB egg clusters; the kinds of moths emerged from larvae (only a few understood about the pupal stage); and the cause of *sundep*.[6]

In such diverse and common understandings of WRB, how the farmers formed and recreated knowledge at different times and in different circumstances will be examined further.

The 1991 dry season: improving knowledge and continuing practices

Even in the absence of a severe WRB outbreak in the 1991 dry season, the farmers' knowledge of this pest improved. Yet, the farmers' preventative measures in pest control also recurred with some modifications.

PRIOR KNOWLEDGE AND NEW DISCOVERIES

The farmers in Marga Tani learned about the changes of WRB outbreaks in the preceding three years. They came to recognize that WRB outbreaks had been more severe in the rainy than in the dry season. Approaching the 1991 dry season, the majority of the farmers were thus mentally disposed toward avoiding problems related to the dry-season planting rather than the emergence of WRB. Only a few farmers, such as Ayim and Idham, foresaw a continuous WRB reproduction as a consequence of a delayed ground preparation. The delay was related to the farmers' aim to have an appropriate dry planting schedule. Other farmers, such as Haji Nafi, foresaw the outbreak by referring to the ecological conditions of the larger rice environment, the JALUR PANTURA region. He argued that a WRB outbreak would only be possible if WRB infested paddy in the eastern regions of JALUR PANTURA, which had a late harvesting schedule. The eastern winds would thus bring the moths to their region. These are examples of how the farmers were able to construct some image of what is likely to happen (see Ortiz 1980:178), by incorporating their recent understandings into their existing s of interpretations.

An unexpected phenomenon again enriched the farmers' understanding. This time, the phenomenon improved the farmers' awareness about the possible continuous reproduction of WRB. The delay of ground preparations in a humid climate is conducive to the regrowth of stalks with shorter panicles (*turiang* or *singgang*). Labourers used to harvest these panicles with a traditional knife, *ani-ani*. The condition of *turiang* in this season was unexpected: fertile growth of panicles in the plots where, in the farmers' views, the original paddy had been severely damaged by WRB. Individual farmers came to this conclusion by correlating the degree of damage and the transplanting schedule, as they had done before. A common inference was again drawn through individual observation, reference to their knowledge of the degree of damage, comparison and communication with other farmers. What caused that fertility was, however, beyond their knowledge. Individual farmers also found moths and larvae inside the panicles. For Ayim and Idham, the presence of moths and larvae in the *turiang* validated their prior assumption. For many other farmers, this improved their knowledge of the continuous reproduction of WRB. They gained this understanding not only through the formation of *turiang*, but also from the creation of a patchy environment due to different schedules in harvesting, ground preparations and nurseries.

This understanding became the basis for the farmers' interpretation when they found moths and egg clusters in the nurseries and transplanting stage. Individual farmers—including the lay farmers—were then able to formulate a proposition about the ideal way of preventing the outbreak of WRB: carrying out the ground preparation immediately after harvesting. A new idea in pest control was created by encountering the unintended result of their own practices and by combining this with their earlier knowledge. However, this ideal thought could not be implemented due to the other concerns the farmers had (e.g., avoiding May illnesses, or labour scarcity during *Ramadhan*, the Moslem fasting month).

Even though the farmers knew that moths were still present in their environment, not all farmers found moths or egg clusters in their own nurseries. Those who had the chance to find egg clusters, for example Iman, Idham and Ardi, gained new knowledge about the appearance and location of egg clusters in the seedlings. The size was smaller than those found in grown plants. The location of egg clusters was not the top leaves, but in the middle or the bottom leaves of the seedlings. As usual when making discoveries, Ardi related his finding to the puzzling phenomenon in the last rainy season. Now, he was able to explain why *sundep* appeared without the farmers' consents: their ignorance about the location of egg clusters in the nurseries. A more careful observation of the seedlings was thus necessary. Since only a few farmers experienced this, not all farmers came to such a conclusion.

Many farmers agreed, however, that the population of moths in this season was low compared to the last rainy season. Nevertheless, arguments about the possible damage to their plants persisted on the basis of different concerns. These concerns were also based on the novel understandings. Idham referred to his discovery that natural enemies were absent in the early planting stage and their growth was much slower than the WRB. He thus felt anxious about the possible outbreak. Ayim felt confidence that there would not be a severe outbreak after finding moths at the time when his plants reached 25 days. As usual, Ayim expanded his interpretations by referring to the stage of plant at the time the next generation would come, i.e., the grown panicles. Plants with panicles would not be preferred by the moths to lay their eggs on.

On the basis of these recent understandings and diverse concerns, what would be their decisions on pest control measurement?

KNOWLEDGE AND ACTION: PEST CONTROL STRATEGIES
Throughout the 1990–1991 rainy season, "spraying medicines" on WRB moths and egg clusters was gradually being eliminated by a

larger number of farmers in their decision making process. Instead, "slapping moths and handpicking egg clusters" introduced by the inventive IPM farmers began to replace the pesticide spraying as one alternative for controlling WRB. As their understandings grew, a gradual change occurred in the farmers' process of decision making (see Gladwin and Murtaugh 1980:117). The inventive farmers' creativity also led to a dissemination of the meanings behind the novel strategy. Even though—at the end of the 1990–1991 rainy season—the farmers still contested the effective outcomes of this mechanical control in securing yields, slapping moths and handpicking egg clusters whenever they found them in the fields had become embodied knowledge (see Bourdieu 1976; also see Dougherty 1985; Gatewood 1985 for actions that embody meanings and knowledge). What had first been considered a strange action was gradually acknowledged by the other farmers as meaningful. The inventive farmers' actions became "observable," i.e., nonproblematically available to the observers (see Holy and Stuchlik 1981:3).

Throughout the 1991 dry season, this was the strategy the farmers used in finding moths and egg clusters in *sawah*. Their reports to each other on how many moths or egg clusters they found in their fields became a way of monitoring the pest's population growth and estimating the possible damage. The adoption of this idea, which originated from individual learning, further affected the distribution of knowledge through imitation and adoption (see Boyd and Richerson 1993). Boyd and Richerson (1985:9) have argued that such individual learning—through trial-and-error and rational calculation in what they describe as guided variation—are very important forces in human cultural evolution.

Nevertheless, the farmers' discourse on insecticides as "medicines," which underlay their reasons for protecting plants from "illnesses," was not altered significantly. Their anxiety about the more susceptible dry season planting increased after finding moths and egg clusters in the nurseries. Another major constraint was the provision of the complete credit package. I found, however, that some farmers carried out some modification in their use of pesticides. Some lay farmers reduced the frequency of spraying when they found that the "illnesses" in this season were in fact not severe (*penyakitnya ringan*). Several IPM farmers (Adma, Wira, Diloh, Eka and Akim) also modified their strategy. Diloh who explicitly said that he was still not quite convinced of IPM, worked out his own strategy by using *Thiodan* for a control measure and using the less powerful insecticides preventatively. Akim proudly told me that he was practicing IPM principles by "… carrying out the observation first and then control" for his strategy of spraying a banned insecticide—*Matador*—before the coming of moths. His reasoning was that the smell of that insecticide would drive moths from his plants. Akim explained this old reason for spraying in his new understanding about IPM principles. In his reinterpretation,

> the IPM objectives were: "reducing costs, obtaining good yields and killing pests."

The use of banned insecticides, including *Thiodan* was also still common among the non-IPM farmers. The only source of information for the banned insecticides was the IPM farmers, who consistently tried to avoid their use. The agricultural officials were absent, and the shop owners did not tell their clients about the ban. However, some of the "lay" farmers told me that they seldom communicated with the farmers like Idham and Ayim. In other cases, even though they communicated with IPM farmers, they did not receive information about the banned insecticides.

SEEKING SCIENTIFIC EXPLANATION: VISITING EXPERTS

The introduced IPM ideas stimulated the farmers' own discoveries, but their main means of knowing constrained the scope of their search. The farmers raised questions about things unable to be discovered by their own methods of learning:

- the transparent impact of carbofuran on leaf folders;
- detail of the stages of WRB larval development;
- the place of pupae in the stalks;
- the process and period of the moth's generation from the pupa stage; and
- the inconsistencies of degree of damage on plants at different stages (between *sundep* and *beluk*) or between different varieties.

When the farmers had the chance to communicate directly with the extension worker and pest observer, several IPM farmers (Idham and Ayim) raised these questions. The extension worker acknowledged that he was not a researcher and directed the farmers to address their questions to the pest observer. Because Idham replied that the pest observer seldom visited the farmers again, the extension worker asked the farmers to address their problems to the village officials who would then forward them to the extension service officials. The farmers were very dissatisfied with the extension worker's reply. They complained that the village officials were not the right people to address questions about agriculture. The pest observer who once visited the farmers' leader unofficially answered their questions. However, besides suggesting that the farmers conduct their own experiments and observations, he asked them to communicate with the extension worker. The pest observer argued that it was the main job of the extension worker to assist the farmers.[7] The farmers were puzzled by such conflicting answers. Understanding the inability of those officials to assist them, Idham asked my assistance to arrange a meeting with the experts at Jatisari (at the Centre for Pest/Disease Surveillance and the location of the IPM field training facilities).

In the dialogue between the three farmers (Idham, Ayim and Rustam) and the experts (from the division of Pest Management), the farmers gained answers for their questions. The most significant idea matched to their experience was the shorter length of the reproductive cycle (32–35 days) compared to the information received in training (43 days). Since they had relied mostly on the latter account in the last rainy season while also informing other farmers, they were puzzled again by the conflicting information they had received from the experts.

These three farmers were also dissatisfied with the experts' inability to answer their questions about fertilizer and excuses for not answering. Back home, this dissatisfaction became one of the issues in conversation with the other farmers. "They only know about insects, pests and disease. About fertilizers, they cannot explain it," grumbled Idham. This information validated their earlier assumption about the experts' specialization (also see Shiva 1988 for the reductionist science). That was why IPM training dealt with pests and disease only, not with the overall problems of rice cultivation. At a later stage (in the 1991–1992 rainy season), they realised the constraints in seeking knowledge from the experts. It would be impossible for them to gain an explanation for all their problems in rice farming by communicating with particular experts only. The narrow perspectives of the scientists stood in contrast to their general problems in rice cultivation.

The 1991–1992 rainy season: recreating and inventing practices and modes of knowing

The experts had, again, predicted another outbreak of WRB in the 1991–1992 rainy season. From the data on rainfall in October and early November 1991, the experts forecasted the first moth flight around two weeks after the first rain (from the middle to the end of November 1991). On the basis of the uniform pattern of rainfall throughout JALUR PANTURA and the similar ages of larvae at several places in this region, the experts came to the conclusions that

- there would be no overlapping generations as occurred in the 1990–1991 rainy season. There would be only one generation at one period of moth flight;
- if there were no effective control activities after the first moth flight; there would be two other subsequent flights at the end of December 1991 (for the second flight) and in mid-February 1992 (for the third flight), each time with a larger population and a longer outbreak.

From these findings, the experts worked out a crash program for WRB control in JALUR PANTURA until January 1992, namely: 1) controlling WRB in the nurseries (handpicking egg clusters or broadcasting carbofuran) from the middle to the end of November 1991; 2) eradicating larvae in the transplanting stage by using carbofuran before the middle of December 1991; and if the first two were ineffective, 3) eradicating moths by using light traps; handpicking egg clusters in the nurseries (not in the transplanted fields); releasing parasites into the fields; and broadcasting carbofuran. Again, the experts used bureaucratic channels to transmit the warnings and the recommended control strategies. How did this bundle of recommendations reach the farmers? In this section I will examine how and to what extent the farmers improved their knowledge in response to the forthcoming hazard.

PERSISTING TRICKLE-DOWN MESSAGES

Up to the 1991–1992 rainy season, there had been no changes in the way information from government officials was provided. As usual, through trickle-down messages from intermediaries (the extension service, regional/local agricultural and administrative officials), the farmers received warnings and recommendations to control WRB. The meeting was held in the village office. The recommendation was that the farmers should collect egg clusters in the nurseries and report their findings. The farmers again complained about the handling of this event. They criticised the use of the village office as the place for the meeting. They objected that village officials, hamlet and local religious leaders had all been invited, but only a few farmers were called as representatives. They pointed out that the meeting was held at an inappropriate time. They were soon going to transplant their seedlings. They argued that the information was provided in the form of instructions without pictures and examples. Finally, the farmers were left to carry out the instruction without direct involvement and guidance from the extension worker *in situ*. Although the hamlet leader did announce the instruction to collect egg clusters in the nurseries to the farmers in the mosque before the Friday-prayer, the farmers' leader did nothing. Only those who attended the meeting followed the recommendation.

After gaining experience in finding answers and explanations for their problems, several IPM farmers not only criticised the extension workers, but extended their critique to fellow farmers (e.g., Idham). They felt that the extension workers and their fellows provided inadequate explanations and addressed their peers in "instructional tones." In summary Akim and Ardi told me that their wish was as follows:

> "Don't preach to the farmers on what they have to do" (*jangan menggurui petani*); don't provide instructions to us" (*jangan merintah*), but give us adequate explanations (*berikan penjelasan yang tepat*)."

Ardi confidently expressed his belief that if the farmers were provided with books on pests and disease and extension skills, by combining these theories and their own experiences, they would have knowledge at the same level as the extension officials who graduated from the university (*Petunjuk Penyuluh Spesialis*, the specialist extension officials).

Until the end of December 1991, the farmers did not receive any information about the possible outbreak. The extension worker decided to take no remedial action to the experts' recommendation, since in his perspective, there had been no serious indication of damage (*sundep*) yet. This was his and the pest observer's reply to the head of the Jatisari's Centre for Pest and Disease Surveillance. He visited the BPP office to examine directly the extent to which the experts' recommendations were put into action. Hence, only by encountering the presence of moths on 20 December 1991, did the farmers themselves recognize that a moth flight had occurred.

The farmers then received a message to trap moths from the hamlet leader who was informed by the extension worker, again, at the village office. What was new for the farmers was the instruction to put the light trap (kerosene light or *petromax*) at the edge of the fields. This instruction was followed by the distribution of kerosene (supported by the Jatisari's office) by the leader of their neighbourhoods in cooperation with the BPP and village officials. This support was allocated for one night only (26 December 1991) and only for that night did 18 farmers follow the instruction. However, only a few farmers received an explanation from the agricultural officials of the correct way to use the light. Hence, diverse practices of trapping the moths also occurred. Haji Ali, who was not well informed about the instruction, kept complaining about the absence of any explanation on how to use the light trap appropriately.

For the first time, the village and extension service officials distributed printed announcements to all village and hamlet officials to disseminate their messages for controlling WRB. I found, however, that because of the heavy and continuous rains, only those that were put on the wall of the mosque survived. The farmers did not pay much attention to these printed warnings, nor did they mention them in their daily conversations. At the time of the third moth flight (mid-February 1992), there were again a warning from the district agricultural official and a message of the possible carbofuran delivery on credit. This message did not have any further effect since the hamlet leader decided not to accept the pesticide's delivery. He felt confident that the plants would escape from severe damage. He made a reference to the mature age of paddy at the time the larvae would bore into the panicles. The trickle-down messages were thus ineffective and, in some cases, followed by inaction by the intermediaries.

REPRODUCING AND INVENTING CONTROL PRACTICES

One significant feature of this 1991–1992 planting season was the earlier and more uniform schedule of ground preparation, nurseries and transplanting compared with the 1990–1991 rainy season. This early planting schedule affected the timing of the WRB outbreak in relation to the age of the plants. In such ecological conditions, the farmers repeated their previous responses while persisting with their critical questions and observations. The different nature of pest infestation, the newly introduced method and insecticides, as well as the farmers' own accumulated experience and interpretation led to some changes in their knowledge and action. The same mechanisms of individual learning and decisions contributed not only to the variation and contestation of pest control, but also to the persistence of the old paradigm. The combination and modification of the old and new paradigms of pesticide use were still in practice. Through the mechanism of encountering the same phenomena, some degree of convergence in their understanding recurred.

Selective eradication and insecticide use. At the early stage of transplanting (early to mid-December 1991) when the experts predicted that larvae would have already bored into the stems, the farmers did find symptoms of *sundep*. They discovered an unusual sign of sporadic damage: in patchy spots with symptoms in the neighbouring four or five rice hills only (*segerombol-segerombol* or *setemplok-setemplok*). Still, the farmers received no warning about the possibility of future moth flights or recommendations of any control practice. The farmers' evaluation of symptoms and their responses to such symptoms again varied. As in the previous outbreaks, the farmers interpreted the current phenomenon in terms of their prior activities in pest control and fertilizer use, or according to their preceding discoveries of moths or egg clusters. In response to the sporadic nature of damage and the economic constraints they had, the question was what would be the most effective and efficient strategy to prevent the migration of larvae to the healthy stems?

For the first time, Ardi and Arman proposed a new strategy to eradicate the infested stems selectively. Ardi argued for eradicating the larvae by cutting the bottom part of the infested stems with scissors. Arman preferred to pull the infested rice hills out and replace them with healthy ones. Askim, a non-IPM farmer, did the same and buried the infested stems in the dikes. Other farmers decided to broadcast carbofuran selectively, only surrounding the infested rice hills. Following the farmers' early initiatives, some farmers, such as Adma and Aming, used kerosene instead of carbofuran. In these instances, the farmers' intention was the eradication of the source of damage, i.e., the larvae. In other instances, the farmers' intention was to make their plants healthy again by using "medicines." I even found that the same farmer had these two reasons in carrying out control measures.

> Anin (a non-IPM farmer) understood that broadcasting carbofuran selectively and, ideally, whole plot was the most effective option. However, he realised that this strategy was too costly. So, he developed his ideas to use this granular insecticide later (during the second fertilizer applications) and purchased liquid insecticide (or "medicines") to make the plants look healthy again. The "unhealthiness" of his plants was the underlying reason. He mixed *Thiodan* with *Applaud* on the basis of his interpretation of how these insecticides worked. If he sprayed *Thiodan* on the leaves, the "medicines" would go down to the ground and become mixed up with water. Since the water covered part of the stems, larvae inside the stems would die because of its strong smells. *Applaud* was used as a prevention if there were some egg clusters left, since from his experiment, this insecticide could "freeze" the egg clusters.
>
> Arman (an IPM farmer) who had replaced the infested stems with the healthy ones also expressed his intention to spray his field with strong insecticides (*pestisida kelas berat*) because his paddy looked unhealthy.

Handpicking moths and egg clusters: establishment and contestation. When the farmers began to discover moths, the population of moths, in their view, was lower than in the 1990–1991 rainy season. The moths also arrived at a later period in the planting season. Several farmers related these conditions to their earlier and recent control practices: from handpicking and broadcasting carbofuran as well as using kerosene and spraying *Thiodan*. As usual, the farmers had different conceptions when arguing about the possible damages. Ayim, once again, was not anxious. He referred to the low population of moths, age of plants and his recent findings about pupae. His experimentation with pupae in the last dry season provided additional knowledge:

> If a pupa is moved from its place, it won't stay alive. I tried to move a pupa from the stalk into a bottle. Then I put a wet cotton ball in it. I observed that the pupa died. Hence, I was relieved, because at the time when the pupae would hatch, the tractors would come and crush them. That was why the population of WRB in the last dry season was low. Now it is similar. However, the paddy that was transplanted later will be infested. Now, the paddy have already been fertilized and weeded, so they will be safe.

Arman, on the other hand, was anxious because of his understanding of the robust growth of this pest. He also referred to the increased use of *Thiodan*, which eradicated natural enemies:

> "Now there will be *bapuk* (harvest failure) again, because many farmers used *Thiodan* so that the natural enemies were killed. If the moths come, the natural enemies have already gone." By referring to his discoveries in both his own and Eka's field, he further mentioned that "the natural enemy is more powerful than *Thiodan*."

The farmers soon found, however, that the number of moths increased daily. The first farmer who discovered the presence of a large number of moths in *sawah* was a "lay" farmer, Romi (Ardi's father). In the 1991 rainy season, he refused his son's advice for not spraying the moths. A change in his decision was evident. He initiated handpicking by asking Ardi to supervise some hired teenagers as previously carried out by Ayim. Again, the farmers reported to each other on how many moths were caught in the fields. Even though the farmers still contested the effectiveness and efficiency of the hand-collecting method, a larger number of farmers repeated this strategy or adopted it for the first time. Since the 1990–1991 rainy season, hiring wage labourers—including teenagers—had been a common practice. To avoid itchiness from slapping moths with bare hands as had been experienced the previous year, Arman invented tools. He placed bamboo into a pair of half-cut rubber slippers. These were examples of the farmers' inventiveness by learning from prior experience. Several other farmers followed this idea. Anin, Arman's father, improved this tool by using a flat tire so as to avoid having the slipper's curve. Other farmers kept slapping moths and handpicking egg clusters with their bare hands.

Despite the adoption by those who had not implemented this strategy in the last year, some who had originally done it abandoned this activity for several reasons. For example, there was no effective result without the involvement of all farmers or troublesome to carry out the handpicking in all landholdings. Understanding the introduced ideas of handpicking this pest did not automatically mean that the farmers would adopt it in their control strategies.

Insecticides use: the persisting "old paradigm." The use of pesticides persisted for reasons similar to the 1990–1991 outbreaks: the existing belief in "medicines" to eradicate pests, the skeptical reactions toward the hand-collecting strategy and the emergence of other pests. To control leaf folders at his parents' fields, Arpan, for example, hired five labourers—including four IPM farmers—to spray pesticides so as to save time.

The farmers' use of *Thiodan* in this season not only persisted but was also readopted by those who had already abandoned it in the last two or three seasons. One of the reasons was the expense of carbofuran. Some schooled farmers carried out a modification in the use of this powerful insecticide. Akim, for example, developed his strategy on the basis of his knowledge that the population of natural enemies was low when the paddy were still young (20–25 days old). Hence, the use of *Thiodan* at this age would not eradicate many natural enemies. He further proposed that: "Later, after the second weeding, don't spray with *Thiodan*." Besides the use of *Thiodan*, the farmers kept mixing several insecticides, including the banned insecticides and nonrecommended substances such as kerosene and/or boiled carbofuran. The idea was to have a powerful impact and yet be cost efficient by mixing the expensive (the more powerful) with the cheap ones (the less powerful), or by combining different objectives. The other persisting phenomena were the adoption of the banned insecticides (*Padan*) and the use of the recently introduced insecticide to eradicate moths (*Bancol*). A shop owner who received the substances from, in her perception, an "agriculture official," introduced the new insecticide.

> One day when I joined a group of farmers in their conversations, those who already tried this newly introduced insecticide and read the labels raised questions about two things. First, why was this insecticide sold in the market whereas they discovered that it should not be sold? Second, why did the bottle not have sealed protection as the other insecticides had so that they could easily open it? The latter question raised their anxiety about the probable falsity of this insecticide and the possible danger if innocent persons like children found the bottle. In my search I discovered that this insecticide was, in fact, still in the process of trial and was provided to the agricultural officials to try it in collaboration with the farmers. The shop owner said that she had received the insecticide not from the company's dealers, but from an "agriculture official." She reached this interpretation by noticing the uniform the person used. The farmers were, in fact, aware that if the insecticides had not been released in the market yet, it meant that, again, they always became the first "victim" (*Petani itu selalu jadi wadal, jadi korban, duluan*). The farmers were quite aware of their positions as the subjects of whatever opportunities possible to gain economic profits by various parties.

Despite the arguments about the insecticide's falsity, once the farmer initiated to try a new branch of insecticide, other farmers would follow.

These cases reveal not only the persistence of the farmers' knowledge and belief about insecticides, but also the discrepancies between knowledge of WRB and the control actions they pursued. I also discovered the expressions of their persisting metaphors and discourse on insecticides in daily conversations, sometimes in the modified form. Iyub, for example, reformulated the old phrase of using insecticides as introduced by the agricultural officials:

> Carbofuran could kill larvae. But, the paddy were already attacked by *sundep*. Thus, 'having an umbrella ready after the rain comes' (*sedia payung sesudah hujan*), after our clothes get wet.[8]

A flow of information about various products and strategies in controlling this pest also came from elsewhere. This information might not have been in accord with the IPM principles. The IPM leader said that the farmers were receiving "polluted information" from diverse sources, one of the major constraints in the implementation of IPM (R. Dilts, personal communication 1992). An example was the dissemination of information about the effectiveness of *Matador* (another banned insecticide) in killing larvae inside the stems. Arman, who learned about this insecticide from the farmers working in PERUM, told Haji Ali who then decided to try it. Trial and error were—according to him—the only means to prove its effectiveness. Several other non-IPM farmers adopted this insecticide in a similar manner. At the later stage, several non-IPM farmers, who also learned from those working in PERUM, readopted the banned substance (*Portas*) that was previously used by the farmers to catch fish. The IPM farmers who later participated in the visit to the nearby agricultural research station and received information about an insecticide that was, in fact, banned for use on rice (*Padan*), did indeed try it out. These examples reveal farmers' desire to try whatever substance is available or whatever new products are introduced to them.

Two methods were dominant in how the farmers assessed the effectiveness of insecticide use.

- ✧ The first method was to assess the direct effect of insecticides either on moths or egg clusters. In the case of egg clusters, the farmers made their interpretations by looking to see whether the eggs would hatch.
- ✧ The second method involved assessing the appearance of damage symptoms.

Akim found *Bancol* to be effective from observing the instant death of moths, but Iyub and Eka did their assessments by observing the damage symptoms. Hence, these two farmers questioned the effectiveness of *Bancol* after observing that their paddy was still infested by *beluk* (whitehead). Adma raised the same question; he used *Thiodan* and found that damage symptoms kept appearing.

Light traps: an ineffective method. Although the injudicious use of insecticides persisted and the mechanical control as developed by the farmers began to be established, the newly introduced idea of using light traps was not favoured by many farmers. In the absence of detailed explanations on how to carry out this practice appropriately, the actions of the farmers who followed the agricultural officials' instruction varied. Examples of these practices are as follows:

Some farmers placed a tray with water and kerosene under the *petromax*. Other farmers only brought the lamps into the fields, without any trays. One farmer (Ucup) placed the *petromax* on a chair that was brought to the field and sprayed the moths with mosquito repellant. Iyub had the initiative to build a small hut with a roof and a place to put a kerosene light and a tray below it. He then mounted the hut at the edge of his rice field. Other farmers did not favour placing light traps because of their observation and concern that many moths attracted to the lights did not fall into the trays and more severe damage might occur in their own fields.

Since most of them perceived that this way of trapping moths was not quite effective in the absence of a widespread collective action, this practice ceased, especially without the continuing support of free kerosene and assistance. Later on, Iyub confessed that although he had built a hut, he ceased to light the kerosene-lamp because of the absence of collective action by his neighbours.

Biological control: no action, new discoveries. As discovered in the previous two seasons, biological control was insignificant. None carried out this practice. Only a non-IPM farmer told me that he found "black ants" hatched from the egg clusters he collected in a plastic bag. However, since he never received information about parasites from the IPM farmers, he did not have any idea that those "black ants" could function as a biological agent in controlling WRB. Although some IPM farmers mentioned the low population of natural enemies in the early planting season, they (Idham, Ayim and Haji Ali) later found a large number of dragonflies. Occasionally and by chance, they saw that dragonflies caught moths. This discovery improved their previous knowledge that only spiders preyed on moths. Another farmer discovered that birds (*burung pinis*) also preyed on white moths. On the basis of a more detailed observation, Idham found that dragonflies only preyed on moths while these moths were flying. Hence, he still doubted that natural enemies could constrain the population of WRB moths. These farmers' discoveries reveal that once the farmers had the understanding about the prey-predator dynamics, they were able to use it for interpreting new findings. This was not the case with the "lay" farmer who did not have any idea about the WRB's predators.

On the basis of his understanding about the prey-predator dynamics, Arman, who found that natural enemies in Eka's field were abundant, asked Eka not to spray his fields to conserve them. Arman himself initially planned to spray some "heavy class medicines" on his paddy. At a later stage, after gaining some more understanding through observation, he advised other farmers to protect natural enemies. This is an example of how the farmers changed ideas at different times (see Vayda 1993; Barth 1994), and improved knowledge over time. By comparing the condition of natural enemies in Eka's and his own field, Arman later gained an understanding that a higher population of natural enemies was found in the older than in the younger plants.

Carbofuran and pulling out panicles: controlling larvae. At the time of the last moth flight (February 1992), the paddy had already reached grain formation stage. Many farmers felt sure that this flight would not seriously damage their paddy. Several farmers also held the view that any chemical application, such as carbofuran, would not kill the larvae inside the panicles. However, several farmers believed that carbofuran would be the only way to protect their plants at this stage. Akim, for example, modified his previous year's decision. Instead of spraying insecticides after observing the incubation of egg clusters as he had done in the 1990–1991 rainy season, he decided to apply carbofuran after observing the hatching of the sample of egg clusters.

Some farmers questioned whether the larvae could still feed on the stems and migrate to other stems. Several farmers decided to collect the infested panicles after finding that several larvae bored inside one panicle as Ayim and Haji Ali did in the 1991 rainy season. Askim, for example, took this action because of his anxiety that these larvae could migrate to the other panicles at the stage when his paddy had not completed grain formation. On the other hand, he thought that carbofuran would not kill larvae on top of the plants. In his understanding, carbofuran would only work on the ground or at the bottom of the stems through its smell. However, he also raised the question whether carbofuran did work. In the absence of any provision of an adequate and comprehensive knowledge about the work, use and impact of insecticides on plants, the farmers used their own imagination about how these chemical substances actually worked. Without any additional equipment and ideas, the work of chemical substance was beyond the farmers' ability to know. This was part of the farmers' ignorance (see Bentley and Andrews' discoveries among the Honduran farmers, 1991).

NEW AND RECURRENT WAYS OF KNOWLEDGE ACQUISITION
The Marga Tani responses to the subsequent WRB outbreaks in the three planting seasons reveal the linkages among events of pest outbreaks, the farmers' responses, expected and unexpected results, and the farmers' ongoing reinterpretations. Throughout these events, the individual farmers pursued their learning activities under the conditions where they were free to behave. As Vayda et al. (1991:328) remind us, in explaining sequential relation of one event to another, the conditions under which the linkages of events do or do not obtain, have to be revealed. My discoveries show that individual learning and knowledge exchange among the farmers became prominent under the condition of a particular nature of pest outbreak. Since I had a chance to observe the farmers' responses to different pest outbreaks, I found that the puzzling phenomena and the complex nature of WRB infestations were significant. However, the recurrent outbreaks and the existence of two stages of damage symptoms (at the vegetative and generative stages) provided an opportunity to evaluate their prior assumptions and practices within a single planting season. These were apparent in a relatively shorter time scale.

In contrast, the impact of insecticides on brown plant hopper resurgence was unobservable. The experts discovered this impact at a later period but not the farmers. What the farmers found was the direct or indirect "killing" of BPH as a result of the pesticides spray. Comparing the BPH and WRB, there was thus a different time scale in the feedback loops for the farmers' strategies for different pests. Despite that, I found the farmers' own confession that controlling BPH was easier than controlling WRB, i.e., by spraying "medicines" straight toward the pests. Ironically, at the end of my fieldwork in 1992, some IPM farmers raised questions about why they were still ignorant about the detailed stages of the BPH life cycle after learning about WRB life cycle. Referring to Bentley's (1989, 1992) arguments about farmers' ignorance, I found that the development of BPH nymphs and the effects of insecticides on the nymphs were not always observable to the farmers without using additional equipment or carrying out systematic observations.

As individual learning took place, their queries, questions and discoveries varied. Besides differences between the schooled and the lay farmers, there was a consistent variation among those (from both groups) who maintained their curiosity and always found ways to investigate further, and those who did not question or bother too much with puzzling questions. For the latter, the most important issues were how to produce high yields, kill pests and reduce costs. Therefore, it is not easy to pinpoint that differences between the farmers' responsiveness and inquisitiveness to new and puzzling phenomena were related to the criteria such as socioeconomic ranks (the rich, middle, or poor as formulated by Cancian 1980 in relation to risk and uncertainty); access to land (the landowner and landless); or age classes (the old and young farmers).

In relation to inquisitive behaviour, I heard for the first time that several farmers had used the word "professor" as a term of address for two farmers (Idham and Ayim). The two farmers were prominent for their observations, examinations and activities in disseminating their findings. Arman, for example, told me that, "Professor (*profesor*) Ayim said that he already found a pupa in the dry season, whereas I have never found one." Sometimes they also used the term *pakar petani* (farmer-experts) to refer to these farmers. Some other farmers (Ardi, Haji Ali, Rustam, Iwan, Arman, Armad) also had similar intentions and attitudes, but they were not as talkative as the two "professors." In using these terms, the farmers associated these expert farmers with the leading scientists from the universities. Gaining a thorough understanding of puzzling phenomena in rice cultivation was similar to gaining expertise in scientific agricultural knowledge. In other places in my later studies between 1996 and 1998 (in Indramayu, east of Subang and in Central Lampung, one of the regencies in the most southern province of Sumatera), I also found the same term: "*profesor*" addressed to those who possessed behaviours and attitudes similar to Idham and Ayim. What did these farmers and others find from their questions and discoveries?

Discoveries, propositions and questions. The issues the farmers raised in their conversations derived not only from recent discoveries, but also from the previous seasons' experiences. A wide range of issues became their main concerns with the same purpose, namely how to better cope with this pest. Some farmers validated their earlier assumptions, others were able to formulate more developed propositions.

Learning from the difficulties of coping with WRB, Ardi—for example—proposed taking detailed notes of the dates of moth flights, egg laying, incubation and larval development, because greater understanding of these details would assist him in taking more effective action. On the basis of accumulated knowledge of the stages of larval development (*instar*) and the difficulties of appropriately controlling this pest, Idham argued for the need to understand the relation between degree of damage and larval development. Akim validated his assumption on the need to diversify rice varieties on the basis of his evaluation about the damage to his brother's (Asim) plants. Asim's fields were all planted with the same variety, *Semeru*, and were all infested by WRB. These were examples of how different farmers drew varied conclusions from different assumptions about the same object.

In other cases the farmers were able to formulate propositions on the basis of knowledge they gained sequentially. At every stage of the moth flights, the farmers made new findings. By combining these findings, they revised their propositions at a later stage of the outbreak. Ayim's evaluation and proposition at different stages of the outbreak reveal this ability. Before the last moth flight, he was able to forecast a future outbreak by adding his recent discoveries to his existing understanding. Hence, he combined his earlier knowledge about the larger population of natural enemies at later stages of plant growth with his knowledge of the stages of larvae (*instar* three and four).

From daily observation, the farmers made new discoveries, which could vary individually. Idham, for example, discovered moths at the bottom of the plants after the sun had just risen (at 7 am). The higher the sun, the higher the moths were perching on plants. From observing moths at different periods, the farmers found different behaviour in the moths. Ayim made his observations at night. When the female moths appeared from the stalks, they would fly high up in the sky to attract the males. At a later stage, they would fly horizontally according to wind direction. At the reproductive stage, some farmers found—for the first time—the location of holes in panicles and the number of larvae within one panicle. Although many farmers had recognized the forms of moths, egg clusters and larvae, they were still ignorant about the form of pupae. Only Ayim and another non-IPM farmer (Ayèn) had found pupae accidentally. Ayèn was able to describe the place, form and colour of pupae, but he did not have an idea that what he had found were known as pupae or in the farmers' word: *kepompong*. Ayèn was a non-IPM farmer (a brother of Anin, Iman and Haji Nafi) who cultivated one piece of land in Blok Cadas, but lived in another hamlet. He had never heard about this term from the IPM farmers in Marga Tani.

Idham was the farmer who most wanted to find pupae. In line with the farmers' questions of the relation of rice varieties to degree of damage, Idham later decided to establish an experimental plot. The farmers questioned again the correlation between rice varieties and degree of damage due to the reappearance of this phenomenon in this season. Another question was how to identify male and female moths, which had been raised by Idham in the previous year. The lack of understanding of the reproductive cycle of the moth to be found among the non-IPM farmers affected their interpretations. Idham interpreted the male as the smaller one, but Ayèn referred to the brown moth, which was in fact a leaf folder moth, as the male and the white moth as the female. He supported his argument by claiming its validity from observing directly that these two moths did copulate.

Other lay farmers who did not have a comprehensive knowledge of the WRB life cycle also made up their own interpretations. Ayat (a permanent wage labourer) said that

> The source of *sundep* is moths that lay eggs. From eggs hatched larvae that bore into the stems to become *sundep*. When they come out of the damaged stems (*kelèb*), they become flies because flies are dangerous. The flies lay eggs, which then become larvae, go inside the stems again. When they come out of the stems, they become moths and flies—spiders *anggang-anggang* etc.—diverse sorts.

As Ayèn did, Ayat believed that his interpretation was valid because he performed an experiment by bringing the egg clusters home and putting them in a plastic bag. From direct observation, he saw that from those egg clusters emerged various sorts of insects. Similar to many other non-IPM farmers, Ayat did not have a detailed understanding about the different kinds of egg clusters. He also confused the damage symptoms of WRB (*sundep*) and rice gall midge (*kelèb*) as many other farmers did. This is an example of how the farmers drew up their assumptions by relating the observable things that emerged at the same time. Such an assumption was complemented by their imagination about the unobservable facts, or a mixture between the observable and the unobservable ones.

Sometimes, the IPM farmers criticised the piecemeal knowledge they acquired from IPM training. In their words: "IPM training has many limitations" (SLPHT *itu banyak kekurangannya*). In some cases, the explanation they received was incompatible with their own knowledge and discourse. Idham, for example, complained that he did not understand why moths—which had a very short life span and kept changing—could develop resistance. By referring to their metaphor of pesticide as "medicine," Idham argued that he could understand if people became immune from taking too much "medicines," but not WRB moths. He got confused in incorporating the new concept of "resistance" within his metaphoric perspective of "medicines" because it applied to insects, not to the human body or plants as the farmers usually did. He expressed his question as follows.

> Thinking about resistance, I could not easily understand it. I think about people as an example, but the stem borer moths keep changing. People consist of only one person. A person takes *Bodrex* (medicine for a cold), one or two [tablets], but does not die. Whereas the moths keep changing, how can they become resistant? Like a baby, could a baby quickly become resistant?

These curious farmers then decided to initiate their own experiments and to communicate directly with the scientists.

Learning to become experts. The desire to know the behaviour of pests motivated the farmers to carry out more systematic observations and experimentation. The terms "to observe," or *mengamati,* and "to examine," or *meneliti,* had become more established as part of their vocabularies than in the 1990s. These new categories of behaviour had also been internalized as meaningful behaviour before taking up decisions to control pests for both the "schooled" and some "lay" farmers. The carrying out of these activities was the marked difference between the farmer-researchers and those who recognized themselves as cultivating rice only as an enterprise or business activity. This recent phenomenon was also acknowledged by a farmer from the neighbouring hamlet in his explanation of why the farmers in his hamlet did not gain an understanding about pest behaviour as the farmers in Marga Tani had. As an outsider, he could differentiate what the farmers in his own hamlet and the Marga Tani farmers did throughout the last two-year period.

Individual farmers also kept experimenting in the hope of discovering more about the nature of WRB infestation and the impact of their control strategies on plants. For instance, they marked the site of an egg cluster left in the field and observed later the extent of damage (see Haji Ali's and Ardi's activities in the 1990–1991 rainy season). Other farmers did a comparison between plots with carbofuran and without carbofuran, or plots with different treatments of insecticide in terms of the degree of damage. Several farmers sprayed the egg clusters to find out whether egg clusters could be prevented from hatching. Individual observation through investigating larvae inside the stems or panicles and through bringing egg clusters home was also pursued. Learning from the previous year's experience in observing egg clusters, Haji Ali decided to take notes on when the sample of egg clusters—submitted by other farmers—was collected from the fields and when they hatched. He aimed to learn precisely the length of incubation. He also paid more careful attention to whether larvae or parasites hatched from the egg clusters. The previous year he had simply piled together all the egg clusters submitted by the farmers without taking detailed notes.

To some extent, the farmers' activities resembled those of the scientists. Comparison in a trial-and-error activity and comparison of various practices and outcomes were perceived as particularly important in order to test or validate empirically their own hypotheses. Comparison was also a means to objectify their subjective interpretations and to generalize propositions. Evaluation, modification or confirmation of prior hypotheses was an ongoing phenomenon. As argued by Agrawal (1995:4–5), scientific and "indigenous" knowledge share similarities and thus, it is not useful to dichotomize these two kinds of knowledge (also see M. Brookfield 1996). However, the farmers often remain in a trial-and-error stage of discovering not only the content of knowledge, but also the most effective means by which one comes to know. In many cases, the farmers told me that they should have carried out their experiments in a better way, in a more controlled comparison, or in a more regular observation. One significant understanding expressed by Ardi was the need to have a shorter time scale in knowledge acquisition as the scientists did. In Ardi's view, the scientists had tools to gain knowledge more quickly. Relying only on experiences over time would not assist them with quick effective responses to hazards. This was the main drawback the farmers learned about their knowledge in contrast to the scientists.

Understanding the constraints of knowing based on accidental findings and with the expectation of gaining answers under conditions where they could not rely on the experts' assistance, several farmers initiated experimental plots in the form of an "insect zoo." By following this activity I was able to discover how the farmers developed their ideas sequentially through experiments and observations.

At the time when the farmers found sporadic symptoms of *sundep*, Idham—motivated by his curiosity to examine the place and form of pupae and the emergence of moths—decided to bring home one infested rice hill. He chose the variety, *Gènjah Melati*, the long-stemmed variety planted by several farmers, which, according to Idham, had the same characteristic as a glutinuous variety. The reason underlying this choice was his curiosity in the 1990–1991 outbreak. In that season, the glutinuous rice plants were not severely damaged even though many egg clusters were found in the fields planted with this variety. His further question was "if the larvae do not like the stems, would they move out of the stems and if so, when?"

When Arman knew Idham's intention, he advised Idham to use mosquito nets so as to prevent the moths flying away. Even though the practice of making "insect zoos" was left out in IPM training in this area, Arman arrived at this idea by adopting what he had observed at the local agricultural research station (BALITTAN Sukamandi), where his brother-in-law worked. Idham, after purchasing the net with my financial assistance, prepared the "insect zoo" at Haji Ali's residence so as to enable Haji Ali and me to observe the pot. Since Idham himself had to collect fodder for his cattle daily, he was afraid that he would miss observing the critical things.

Following Idham's explanation about his intention, Haji Ali asked about the date when they could observe the formation of the pupae. By calculating the period between the laying of eggs and the development of the pupae, Idham was able to predict when the pupae would be formed. As in many other conversations, the word "life cycle" that they used referred not only to reproductive stages, but also to the length of each stage and the complete life span of the WRB. The farmers did not have special terms to refer to these particular things and thus used the new term "life cycle" for several related aspects. The following was an example of such a conversation:

> "How many days is the life cycle (refers to the complete life cycle, *Siklus hidup berapa hari*)?" asked Haji Ali. Idham replied: "According to the life cycle (refers to the length of each stage, *Miturut siklus hidup*): [after] day nine the larvae hatch from the egg clusters, [after] day eleven they bore inside the stems and on day twelve the larvae become pupae." Haji Ali asked again: "When do the larvae become pupae?" Idham answered: "It is expected to be in the first month (*bulan satu*), more or less: now is the 18th of month twelve (*bulan duabelas*), plus 12 days more equals the 30th of month twelve. So, after month twelve, it should become pupae already, in the first month, on the first or second date."

Idham's prediction was generally accurate: on the 31st of December 1991 I found one moth in one of the "zoos" (IR64). Idham and Haji Ali then decided to find whether there were still some pupae left inside the stems. Together with Romi (Ardi's father), they discovered one pupa at the bottom of one stem. At last, feeling happy and relieved, they found what they had been longing to know for months.

After examining the form of the pupa, which in Idham's imagination had a hard, brown colour, Idham doubted that it was a WRB pupa. Romi convinced Idham that the pupa they found was a WRB one. From this finding, Idham not only realised that his imagination was incorrect, but also discovered the special form of a WRB pupa.

> It is not covered by the pupa's skin as the dragonfly's pupa and others. The larva keeps quiet, fasting, and then out come the wings.

Questions, evaluations and critiques followed this finding. Examples of these are:

- whether pupae inside the plants had the same form as those inside the dried stalks after harvesting;
- whether pupae inside the plants in the fields covered with water were also located at the bottom part of the stems;
- how it could be possible that moths come out from the very tiny holes in the stems when the first stage of larvae bored inside the stems;
- for how long did the wings become longer and the body become shorter; and
- whether the term *"kepompong"* used by the trainers to identify pupa was correct.

Following Idham's curiosity about the emergence of moths, Haji Ali and Idham decided to place the stem with a pupa inside it and the pupa that had been placed outside the stem in a plastic bag. Later on, Haji Ali did indeed discover the moth that just emerged from the stem. These discoveries improved their knowledge and stimulated further questions and discussions. Through farmer-to-farmer transmission, other farmers could gain information from those discoveries. Haji Ali and Idham soon corrected the word *"kepompong"* in daily conversations with other farmers. Ayim, who was not present during that particular event but learned from Idham and Haji Ali, validated his earlier finding about the pupae. For them, such an experiment proved useful in gaining knowledge they were unable to discover from daily field observations (see figure 7.1).

Besides examining pupae, Idham made "insect zoos" with the intention of discovering if WRB infestation varied with rice variety. Hence, he subsequently made two other plots with different varieties: *IR64* and *Sido Muncul* (see cover for the insect zoos made by the inquisitive farmers). Because of his curiosity about the source of rice gall midge, he made another plot after finding a rice hill infested by

Figure 7.1 *Location of pupae and the emergence of a moth*

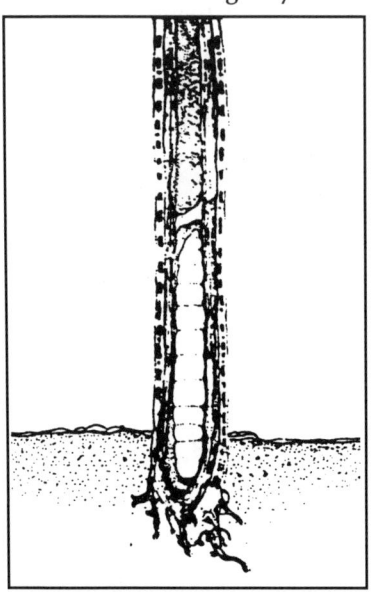
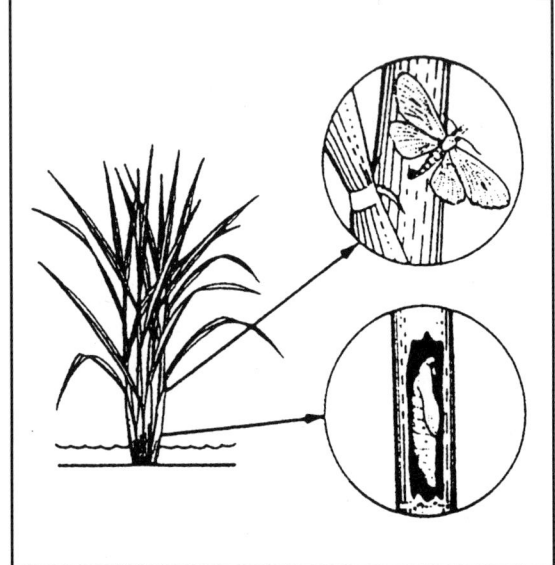

Source: Reissig et al. (1986:132).

rice gall midge. At last, Idham found what he had suspected since the previous year, namely the "red mosquito," as mentioned by the pest observer and the expert at Jatisari, as the source of rice gall midge. However, his project to examine the variation of WRB infestation by variety was unsuccessful because two rice hills dried up. Idham acknowledged that the "zoos" did not have the same water treatment (i.e., water management) as rice planted in the field. Haji Ali referred to his action of pouring all larvae hatched from the egg clusters into one plastic bag into the *Sido Muncul*'s "insect zoo." By referring to the notion of predation, he explained that the failure of this experiment was caused by the absence of any natural enemies. He also learned from his mistake of pouring too many larvae into one rice hill only. Using a comparative perspective, he learned that they should put some natural enemies in one "zoo" but leave the other one without natural enemies. A comparative perspective was again dominant in the farmers' learning activity. From this activity, Haji Ali had the chance to improve his knowledge by observing how long it took larvae to bore inside the stems. Apparently he discovered that not all larvae bored at the same time.

From their experiments, the farmers had the chance to match reality with the trainers' narrative explanations and their own imaginations. They also learned from mistakes and formulated further propositions and critical questions. Nevertheless, in many cases they complained about their inability to examine further without additional tools. At this point, they did not have any ideas of how to compensate the limitations they had. Thus, the scientists' assistance was considered necessary. Several farmers (the same inquisitive farmers such as Arman, Idham, Rustam and Haji Ali) had the initiative to seek knowledge again directly from the scientists.

Seeking scientific knowledge: communication between the farmers and the scientists. Seeking knowledge directly from the experts was a new experience for the farmers. They soon realised that building up links with the scientists was not easy. Bureaucratic problems were beyond their expectation. The farmers' first idea was to visit the nearby agricultural research station, BALITTAN Sukamandi, where Arman's brother-in-law was an employee. Arman was the one who proposed that idea when Idham and Rustam insisted on seeking knowledge straight from "the experts at the top level, from the centre, not from those at the bottom level, the extension worker." This was the most reasonable plan given the closeness of their hamlet to that centre.

When Arman visited the centre to seek permission, he had difficulty in obtaining it because of a visit from the Minister of Agriculture. He told the police who asked him to leave: "Oh, what good fortune, because I am also a farmer," and he insisted on going inside. He felt disappointed when the people at the research centre refused to process his request because there was no local extension worker's signature on the letter he brought. The extension worker should also accompany them on the visit. The first idea was to bypass the extension worker. Now, they would have to involve him in the visit. Even though Arman and Idham complained about this requirement, they pursued their aims with my assistance, and contacted the extension worker and obtained the permission. The main complaint the farmers had was that the visit was delayed to suit the staffs' availability. Their immediate need was to have answers for their urgent problems. A delay meant postponing the decisions they must take in the face of the pest outbreak. The bureaucratic requirement was also a burden for them in terms of time and cost.

When the arrangements were settled, the extension worker accompanied the farmers (both from Marga Tani and the neighbouring village, C. Tengah) on their visit on January 30, 1992. The scientists became the source of information, and the farmers were the recipients throughout the whole session that combined a question-and-answer segment, a slide presentation and observations of the scientists' field experiments of rice varieties, the cultivation of algae for nitrogen fixation, and the mixed cultivation practices. The farmers' questions focused on the issues that had become their concerns throughout the recurrent WRB outbreak. Examples of these questions were:

- the form of each larval stage from the first to the fifth stage (*instar satu sampai lima*) and how to identify the stages from the damage symptoms;
- whether carbofuran application in a wet soil (but uncovered by water) and a selective broadcasting on the infested rice hills or only on one side of the rice hill could be effective;
- the source of the moths;
- the emergence of moths and damage symptoms after carbofuran application;
- the appropriate way to use the light trap;
- whether larvae inside the panicles (*beluk*) could migrate and whether carbofuran could still control the larvae at this stage; and
- the preventative measures under conditions of pest outbreak.[9]

In addition, the scientists informed the farmers about problems in broadcasting urea fertilizer due to volatility (up to 25–40%). The farmers also received information about how different types of chemicals worked. The scientists suggested that the farmers try a banned insecticide for rice (*Padan*, a semi-systemic substance) rather than broadcasting carbofuran inadequately.[10]

This event not only contributed to a wider horizon for planting rice, but also made them aware that they were in fact allowed to come to the centre. While arranging this visit, the farmers had already asked my assistance to invite an expert on WRB. The farmers, however, realised that they should invite the extension staff to avoid any unhappy feeling among the local agricultural officials. The extension workers indeed felt that by becoming more knowledgeable, the farmers were now seeking knowledge directly from the scientists and no longer needed their assistance.

Examples of the most significant new ideas they gained from their conversation with the WRB expert—held on the 7 February 1992—were, among others:

- the appropriate control strategies for reducing the number of larvae entering the diapause period, and controlling the pests as early as possible so as to avoid an abundant population at later stages;
- the appropriate way to use light traps in combination with handpicking egg clusters surrounding the light and the need to undertake collective action;
- the unreliability of using the degree of damage in relation to larval development as an indicator for pest control due to variability of plants;
- understanding about the genealogy of varieties to differentiate which varieties were more resistant (e.g., *Céréh Beureum* and *Cisadané*, which had 45% native Indonesian origin) and were more vulnerable to WRB (e.g., *IR46* which had only 10% Indonesian origin);
- a more detailed knowledge of WRB life cycle; the period of each stage and its relation to the most effective time for carbofuran application in the nurseries;
- larval development; pupa formation and its place in the stems; and the process of becoming moths;
- the difference between male and female moths; the time of mating and laying eggs; the female's behaviour before laying eggs;
- how the larvae flew away like Tarzan by using strings and the extent to which larvae were brought by winds in the absence or presence of natural enemies;

⟡ the idea of predation and intracompetition that could reduce the number of larvae boring inside the stems; and
⟡ the negative impact from boiling granular insecticides and the ineffective results of inappropriate mixtures of different kinds of chemicals.

The scientist—a lecturer at the Department of Entomology, Bogor Agricultural Institute and the team leader of the FAO-IPB Field Laboratorium on WRB—also invited the farmers to observe directly the moths in the fields and examine the degree of damage. In the farmers' perception, the scientist's explanation was much more significant than the instructions without explanation from the agricultural officials, or mastering the calculation skills as learned in IPM training. The farmers not only gained a more comprehensive knowledge of WRB, but also learned about the scientist's attitude in providing his explanation and addressing their problems. The scientist perceived the farmers as equals, invited them to share their experiences and problems and vice versa. The farmers felt happy with this attitude and appropriate ways of explanation. This was the kind of communication they had expected to have with the agricultural officials. In the farmers' words:

> "His talking is good, because he is a field-person (*orang lapangan*), without emotion"; "his answer is quick and appropriate"; "his explanation is clear, reasonable and in line with our own experience"; and "he does not blame us, he does not accuse us of doing something wrong."

Several farmers found the information valid because the expert had gained knowledge in a way that was similar to theirs. They could now better explain their own questions (e.g., the correlation between number of larvae and the extent of damage) and gained confidence in the more advanced knowledge they had compared to the extension worker's or village officials'. Without feeling insulted because of their actions in the use of insecticides, they gained a greater understanding of the need to know more about the work and impact of chemicals.

The scientist suggested that the farmers get more information about how to mix chemicals appropriately from the faculty and staff at the Bogor Agricultural Institute. Several farmers from Marga Tani and C. Tengah joined me on my visit to this university. In this event, these farmers gained some knowledge of the diseases of rice, the need for collectively controlling WRB, the ways to avoid the inappropriate mixture of insecticides and to prevent disease outbreak on plants. For the first time in their lives, the farmers tried to examine seeds through microscopes and realised the importance of preparing healthy seeds.

These events reveal that through such a communication, the scientists can fill the gaps in the farmers' knowledge based on everyday practices and the learning process (see Bentley 1992; Bentley et al. 1994).

INSULTS AND PRAISE: PERSISTING CRITERIA FOR EVALUATION
In conjunction with the growing knowledge of pest behaviour and the need to master this knowledge as a basis for an effective pest control strategy, I noticed a gradual change in the farmers' beliefs. At the end of the 1989–1990 rainy season when they were not able to explain the unforeseen severe attack of WRB, a belief in "God's will," "bad-year," "bad luck and misfortune" was widely expressed by the farmers, in addition to the strong rumours about the counterfeit insecticides. The recurrent WRB outbreak provided an opportunity to develop and improve their rational control of this pest. Throughout the 1991–1992 rainy season, through continuous experience, the farmers became more confident in their own efforts in pest management. By the end of the 1991–1992 rainy season, Armin, the hamlet leader, could say that, "It does not depend on how God [wills]. It is true that God determines [everything]. But, this is the politics of people (*politik manusia*)." Then he further mentioned the efforts the people themselves had to do. Many other farmers shared Armin's confidence.

With this growing confidence, IPM principles, with some modifications, had been gradually incorporated into the farmers' own knowledge repertoire. Ayim, for example, stated that even though his yield was not satisfactory, reducing costs, applying chemicals wisely and conserving natural enemies were what the IPM principles meant. Nevertheless, throughout all their efforts in overcoming the problems of pests and disease outbreaks, the farmers persistently claimed expertise in rice farming on the basis of "good plant performance and yields." In many cases, these criteria were not always in keeping with the implementation of IPM strategies, namely avoiding unnecessary costs and using pesticides judiciously. Even though some farmers tried to use pesticides wisely, the complexity of the pest outbreak constrained the achievement of high yields. Damage to their plants complicated their assessments. Many other factors such as fertilizer use, water management, planting schedule in relation to pest/disease outbreak, type of varieties and weather condition also affected plant performance and yields. In such a situation, it was not easy for the farmers to assess the effectiveness of IPM strategies.

Ayim and Idham who avoided the unnecessary use of pesticides and kept telling the farmers what they had to do in response to pest outbreaks, received insults from other farmers for not achieving good plant performance and yields. At the end of the 1991–1992 season, Ayim had the intention of cultivating rice in PERUM instead of pursuing his cultivation in this area. The underlying reasons were his embarrassment at the insults and his difficulties in convincing and motivating other farmers to implement IPM strategy collectively. He understood that in the situation where individual variability was prominent and in the absence of any assistance from those in the authority, it was difficult to change the farmers' attitudes and practices through farmer-to-farmer transmisson only. By cultivating rice in PERUM, he could use the mechanism of providing instructions from the employers to persuade them to implement and disseminate IPM principles to the workers.

The farmers who held positions as leaders, such as Armin (the hamlet leader) and Haji Ali (the farmers' leader), were also criticised by the farmers for their lack of success in producing good plant performance and yields. In the farmers' views, a leader should be able to perform well as a diligent farmer. He should be an example, a guide for other farmers to follow.

The persisting belief in pesticide use and the lack of understanding of pest behaviour (in particular among the lay farmers) also affected the IPM farmers' self-esteem. Haji Ali complained about the farmers' insults when they observed him collecting moths or egg clusters. He felt humiliated when the farmers said:

"Why are you collecting egg clusters? Are you going to cook them for your meal?" asked a non-IPM farmer while laughing. Haji Ali said further that "they should follow what I am doing. Instead, they laughed at me."

Arman also complained that the farmers insulted him as if he did not have money to purchase insecticides so that he had to slap moths with the tools he made or collect egg clusters with his bare hands. In these cases, the lay farmers had not shared the meanings of these control strategies.

On the other hand, Akim, who still used banned insecticides despite his timely carbofuran application, was praised by many farmers for his successful strategy in producing high yields. Adma, who had not abandoned regular spraying and kept using *Thiodan*, was also praised for his effective strategy in controlling pests and maintaining good plant performance and high yields.

These examples indicate that the criteria by which alternative actions in rice farming are evaluated, persisted over time. The persistence of such evaluations in the absence of any follow-up activity, recognition or reward from the authorities and experts for their efforts in controlling pests judiciously, constrained the farmers' confidence in the IPM strategy. Bentley et al. (1994) have pointed out that recognizing and rewarding farmers' efforts in stimulating creativity were important.

KNOWLEDGE IS ALWAYS in the making. This chapter proves that in different times and circumstances, the farmers continuously reinterpreted and reevaluated their prior assumptions on the basis of their responses to new and persisting phenomena. In the subsequent year, there had been a variation in the ecological condition of pest outbreaks and the kinds of seeds flowing through the farmers' knowledge exchange. Through the latter, there was a return of an old traditional variety. The farmers faced, however, no alteration in their relationship with the government in the context of pursuing rice intensification programs. There were no changes in the government's policy of subsidized scheme, trickle-down messages, and the ways of assisting the farmers' needs, whereas economic constraints increased their burdens. The farmers continued to be subjects as the major customers of agricultural products. They were also left to their own devices in the midst of continuous pest outbreaks, in which they felt incapable of explaining the unobservable and puzzling phenomena (see Bentley and Andrews 1991; Bentley 1989, 1992). However, in such circumstances the farmers were indeed creative and inventive in order to survive, both in selecting varieties, managing their resources, and responding to pest outbreaks.

Looking into the details of their responses in such constraining circumstances, it was evident that the basic meaning and ideas received in the IPM "school" proved useful as a basis to interpret the ongoing problems, both the foreseen and unforeseen phenomena. Making experimental plots, carrying out detailed and systematic observation, and seeking the experts' explanation reveal the practices they learned through their interaction with the "experts." Once those ideas filled the gaps in their previous knowledge, they were able to activate them in their responses to the current situation. In addition to the new understanding, basic ideas and concepts, such as pests' reproductive cycles and integrated pest management strategies were improved and advanced. The same mechanisms of knowledge formation that had occurred in the previous year prevailed. The repeating of old as well as the new practices not only strengthened and enriched the newly formed interpretation schemas in pest control, but also improved the farmers' self-reliance. By putting knowledge into action, accompanied by the continuous spread of ideas and meanings, the new schemas of controlling pests in line with the ideas of pests' reproductive cycles, were gradually adopted by a larger number of farmers, even though they were adopted in diverse forms of practices and understandings. A novel criterion of rice cultivation by examining the details of the phenomena in *sawah* as a basis for farming efficacy was gradually established as well. These occurred through experiences over time and thus, the time dimension was significant.

The ongoing process reveals what Shore (1991:10) calls "meaning construction," or "learning-as-construction metaphor" in Ortony's words (Ortony 1993). Yet, in such a process, the interaction between the intrapersonal aspects of cognition and the extra-personal ones is significant (see Strauss and Quinn 1997). The farmers' responses to the existing circumstances reveal this interaction. Throughout the construction process, the distinction between "local practical" and "scientific" knowledge becomes insignificant. All relevant inputs are combined into one schema or a set of diverse schemas of interpretation, which are strengthened, advanced, or modified through experience. These phenomena reveal the significant and fruitful consequences of a particular event when a dialogue is opened between the farmers and the experts. Even though the intensive dialogue occurred in only one planting season when information and experience between the two groups was shared and valued through the sequential events of knowledge formation afterwards, changes in farmers' knowledge and strategies could significantly occur in a relatively short period of time.

It is important to note, however, that the role of a few inquisitive farmers in the ongoing process of knowledge formation and transmission was prominent. Nevertheless, these farmers also experienced disappointment and insults because they encountered unyielding perspectives in the use of pesticides and assessing plant performance and expertise without evaluating the efficacy of the novel strategy. The creation and establishment of social institution, in particular the social evaluation of reward and punishment from the farming community, as well as from those in authority, were absent. Without the provision of consistent policies, assistance, and rewards from fellow farmers and government officials, these farmers had great difficulty maintaining their spirits and the efforts to learn. Motivation and emotion are two significant aspects in the construction and sustenance of new knowledge and practices, which, in this case, were overlooked by the agents of change. The following chapter will discuss further the prominent features of this process of knowledge formation and dissemination, including the issues of diversity and consensus, changes and continuity.

8

Seeds of Knowledge

"Seeds that falls on good ground will yield a fruitful harvest."

THE STORIES of the "seeds," the farmers, presented in this book reveal how knowledge is constructed, transformed and transmitted through the everyday struggle of the "seeds" to stay alive. As experienced by many local people throughout the world, the "seeds" have to grow within a changing environment. The environment has been considerably altered for the sake of development. My study reveals a strong need to move away from the earlier cognitive analyses that saw knowledge as something static and ideal, held in the minds, expressed in the form of language and other verbal actions, and reproduced repetitively from generation to generation. The introduction of IPM among a group of farmers is a good case to examine this dynamic aspect of knowledge. In this case, the "folk" or cultural model of farmers (see D'Andrade 1987)—which was formed in the past 30 years of the Green Revolution—is now being challenged by the new paradigm and schema of managing the crops. This is also the case among a group of farmers who are trying to regain their power in decision making. By doing so, their creativity flourished.

The implementation of the Green Revolution in many parts of the world has shown how local farmers have lost their autonomy in the use of production inputs and resources. In such a situation, the beginning of integrated pest management in Java and other provinces in Indonesia has provided hope for millions of farmers to reclaim their freedom and tradition in crop farming.

"IPM wants to bring us back to the old condition of growing rice without medicines," reflected Ayim and Haji Nafi about the IPM strategies. These are farmers who began cultivating rice in the period before the beginning of the Green Revolution in Java, more than 20 years ago.

This is only one example of the farmers' reflections concerning how IPM is able to resurrect positive memories of their tradition of growing rice. IPM also enables them to explain puzzling phenomena and correct their failed practices and perspectives in pest management. The IPM "seeds of knowledge" grow with confidence to produce more sustainable harvests at a reduced cost compared with previous years. The most significant advantage is the return of the farmers' dignity in the task of cultivating rice on the basis of their own discoveries. Like the "seeds of crops" that grow healthily in a good environment, the IPM farmers were able to improve, enrich and expand their knowledge. The stories of their efforts reveal how, to what extent, and under what conditions their practices produced new understandings and affected the existing schemas of growing crops; in particular, growing crops with pesticides.

The IPM provides a good opportunity for a close examination on how the formation of the new "paradigm" and the intended practices in pest management took place. The process during and after the intervention reveals that it is not as simple as transferring new ideas and strategies to a group of people and reproducing them through the people's practices in its initial form and meaning. Throughout the sequential events of a continual modification of knowledge and practice, the people were actively interpreting and reinterpreting. They modified, evaluated, criticised, reformulated, agreed, or rejected and abandoned the new ideas. Some of the new ideas might be understood, partially understood or reinterpreted subjectively, misinterpreted in a different way, combined with different sets of interpretations to yield an entirely different understanding, or expanded into new propositions and ideas.

Such a complex process cannot be examined in the same way the old cognitive analyses were. Wassmann (1995:174) argued that cognition is "no longer an expression of a culture as a whole and abstracted from linguistic material." Instead, he formulates the cognition as

> "*mental activity of individuals who actively apply knowledge in different contexts*, in that they think, generalize, draw inferences, perceive,

recognize and categorize; analyze, combine, assess possibilities, solve problems and make decisions; classify, differentiate and choose; remember and master new situations."

In their everyday struggles, the individual farmers in my study did what Wassman says. Wassman's study does not clearly define and examine how, through such activities, individuals or group of individuals arrive at and form new knowledge. Keller and Keller (1993)'s work on blacksmithing is able to show how knowledge is created through practice and vice versa. Knowledge is not only being reproduced through action, but "... being refined, enriched, or completely revised by experience ..." (Keller and Keller 1993:127). Underlying this argument is their assumption that knowledge can never be sufficiently detailed or precise enough to anticipate exactly the conditions or results of actions. Experience then enriches knowledge. In line with this, Strauss and Quinn (1997) argue that some particular combinations of units of information will only be activated by certain stimulants. The more frequent the stimulants are experienced and received by individuals, the more established the combinations are. The stimulants do, of course, originate from individuals' experience and interaction with their environment in particular situations. The schemas, as a result of the strong interconnection of units, will assist individuals in solving a problem in a particular situation. The actions carried out by individuals on the basis of these schemas might act as stimulants in the future and to other individuals, so that they produce a structure of new extrapersonals, or strengthen the existing ones, again, to be the sources for further schemas. What happened in the aftermath of IPM training reveals such a process.

As described in chapter 4, the IPM planners and facilitators only introduced basic premises, concepts, and ways of carrying out a more detailed observation. It was up to the individual farmers to make a decision on the basis of their own monitoring and observation, and to learn from their experience and discoveries. It was expected that from the initial teachings and farmers' own learning activities, a new combination of knowledge elements, or a new schema of interpretation on the basis of IPM strategy would emerge in the minds of individual IPM farmers. Individual farmers were free to exercise their individual choice and decisions, as well as to find alternatives in pests/diseases control. When they were able to form the new interpretation on the basis of IPM strategy, they became aware of the alternatives to their existing "cultural model" of pest control and that they were allowed to search for the more judicious alternatives.

This kind of discovery learning process, which was based on initial knowledge transmission rather the transfer of technology, has significant consequences in fostering farmers' own creativity. It provides great opportunities for the construction and emergence of knowledge that is not necessarily a reproduction of what the trainers initially taught the farmers in the "school" setting. Such a phenomenon does not reflect what Bourdieu means with the reproduction of disposition, of *habitus* and structure (Bourdieu 1977; also see Harker *et al.* 1990). Not only is the exact reproduction absent, but also the *habitus* or the disposition within the context of the new IPM paradigm itself is still in the making. My study is thus well suited to the emergence and growth of knowledge rather than merely a reproduction of disposition.

My study also reveals the need to take the stand for individual agency seriously. I believe that individual agents are the "core" of changes, transformations, and growth of knowledge. They are the "seeds of knowledge." The farmers in my study were indeed able to take the introduced knowledge and extend it in terms of a novel situation. By taking this stand, individual diversity appears as a common phenomenon. The discrepancies or variations from the initially introduced ideas formed by the individuals cannot be perceived as deviating from the ideal schemas of IPM. My study reveals that knowledge is differentially distributed among different actors and in different contexts, between different actors in the same contexts, or among the same actors in different contexts. From her study in the Philippines, Nazarea-Sandoval (1995) found that the social distribution of indigenous knowledge is uneven but patterned, with different socioeconomic and gender categories possessing significantly different ways of understanding phenomena in their environment. Although I agree with Nazarea-Sandoval that variations according to socioeconomic and gender categories do affect the social distribution of knowledge as described in chapter 2 (see the labourer's knowledge acquisition strategy which may differ from the owners' or the cultivators' ways of learning), it is apparent that variations at the individual level and through different contexts and times are enormous.

By referring to the debates about the "omniscient informant" and the "just plain folks" categories in studying knowledge, it is true from my discoveries that farmers acknowledge who the "model" farmers are. However, my study proves that using any categories to frame and explain the differences in the farmers' acceptance of IPM premises is not worthy. Both the "commoners" and the "healthy" farmers emerged as innovative and inquisitive, and the opposite was also true. Among them, I also found those who did not care much about the new "teaching" and kept pursuing their own strategies. We need to go beyond the "social categories" or the simple dichotomy between the "omniscient informant" and the "just plain folks" to look at variations in other aspects. The individual motivations and interests, curiosities, beliefs and confidence, as well as the resources they are able to provide, the kind of risks they have to overcome, the unexpected discoveries they have to encounter, the individual history of learning experience each person has, and the sociality they are used to engage in their everyday struggle play a significant role in knowledge formation. Since the IPM planners selected only a number of farmers to be "trained" in a "school without walls," how the IPM ideas were adopted, interpreted, reproduced or modified, and transmitted to the rests of the community would depend very much on the individual IPM participants. This explains the difference in the outcomes in the IPM "schools" in two hamlets in Ciasem Baru facilitated by the same IPM trainers. The farmers' performances and activities after participating in the "school" might also differ from the stories presented in this book if very inquisitive and attentive farmers had not been selected to be the IPM participants.

The actions of the farmers may also be significant in the way knowledge is conventionalized into culture. As suggested by D'Andrade (1995:xiv), this is one of the ideas to which cognitive anthropology should pay attention. How can we examine that? Even though I take the agency approach seriously and pay attention to whatever behaviours and practices seem relevant to my research questions (see Vayda and Setyawati 1995; 1998), it would not be easy to examine D'Andrade's suggestion without following the mechanisms and processes by which the individual agents pursued their everyday struggle over time. By allowing myself to follow the responses of individual farmers at each stage of their cultivation practices and the subsequent events, I gained a greater confidence that the processual approach I used would answer Barth's (1994: 359–360) question of how we can enhance the power of our analyses. Sillitoe (1998:230) also considers that a theoretical shift from a structural to a processual perspective is significant, even though he admits that moving towards this direction in ethnographic research is not easy. I realised, however, that by being consistent in my examination of the ongoing phenomena, I could follow the sequential events over time. In following those events I kept focusing my attention on how variations and consensus occurred and to what extent these would or would not contribute to the conventionalization or the formation of IPM knowledge. I focused on the extent to which the new interpretation schemas became the schemas of not only some inquisitive IPM farmers, but also a larger number of farmers.

I do not, however, turn away entirely from the focus of cognitive anthropology in examining how the meanings are stored in the form of words and stories besides artefacts and behaviours. As Barth (2002) recently points out, one of the three mutually related aspects of knowledge is the communication of the knowledge in one or several media as a series of partial representations in the form of words, concrete symbols, pointing gestures, and actions. The other aspect is the distribution, communication, employment and transmission of knowledge within a series of instituted social relations. My focus was also more on the transfer, reception and transmission of these novel meanings rather than the abstraction of how people conceive of and think about the objects and events that make up their world. By also taking into account how the individual farmers continually interpreted and reinterpreted the introduced meanings expressed in words, propositions, or assumptions, my study reveals the variety of ways in which knowledge is produced and transmitted. In many events, the individual farmers learned through unsupervised, unguided, unintended, and unexpected discoveries and outcomes of their strategies. Such learning is very important in farmers' lives, and is often being overlooked in other studies of knowledge transfer.

My study also reveals that some other aspects have to be taken into account. It is not only how the trainers introduced the new meanings and schemas that has to be analyzed, but also the extent to which the connotative aspect and metaphor of the new schemas were used by both the trainers and learners. The learners' attitudes, motivation, interests, confidence, experience, and, to some extent, their emotions, as well as the external circumstances they had to encounter are also important. For example, the bureaucrats' attitudes and decisions, the policies and economic circumstances, the continual offer of pesticides and pest/disease outbreaks, and the ongoing practices of the injudicious use of pesticides among their fellows and neighbours must be considered. These intelligible factors affected the farmers' reception. According to Strauss and Quinn (1997), both the extrapersonals and the individual motivation and emotion are significant factors that affect the formation and strengthening of schemas. "Schemas are highly context specific," claim Strauss and Quinn (1997:52). The contextual analysis of the ongoing phenomena of introducing and accepting IPM ideas contributes significantly to a richer and deeper understanding of how and why such phenomena occur. This enables me to consider other contextual factors that have not been analyzed in detail in previous studies.

The IPM is, thus, a significant case to learn not only the interface between the facilitators and the farmers, or between the "scientific" and the "local" knowledge, but also how the interface and the interaction took place within the real world of rice farming. In this case, the interface within the real world of farming reveals that the knowledge farmers gained and created relates to direct and concrete needs and problems *in situ*. This gives a strong "local" characteristic to their knowledge. Methodologically, their ways of learning, e.g., carrying out studies and formulating assumptions, hypotheses and propositions, or even falsifying them, were affected by the practices taught in the IPM "school," which was based on the "scientific" domain (also see Choesin 2002). The result was a mixture of ideas and methods in a dynamic way. Nevertheless, in the farmers' real world, the wider context of national policies, economic and ecological conditions, and the actions of various actors to still gain benefits and advantages come into play. This wider environment affects the growth of the "seeds": the potential and how talented the "seeds" are. Since various kinds of "development programs" will still be implemented in third world countries in the future, including in the agricultural sector, the IPM experience provides a good lesson for dealing with such a circumstance while also assisting and facilitating the local people to reach prosperity. Breaking down the dichotomies between "scientific" and "local" knowledge, while also reevaluating the development paradigm to affect or alter the existing circumstances should be seriously considered. In the following sections I will summarize briefly the findings of my study about each aspect of how the "seeds of knowledge" grow and struggle in their reception of the new ideas.

From "Spraying 'Medicines'" to "Understanding the Pest's Behaviour"

The change from "spraying 'medicines' (*menyemprot obat*)" to "understanding the pest's behaviour" as the basis for pest control is an example of change in the IPM farmers' knowledge and practice of pest management. In the case of Marga Tani's IPM farmers, this happened in a two-year period after three decades of controlling pests with "medicines." Returning to my questions in the introductory chapter, it is evident that without the introduction of the new metaphor of pesticides as "poison" rather than "medicine" and the related schemas of prey-predator dynamics, pest's life cycle, economic advantages, etc., it would be hard to understand how the change could take place in such a relatively short period of time. In this case, the role of scientific knowledge transmitted in the form of "metaphors" (e.g., pesticides as "poison," predators as "farmers' friends and helpers") eased the learners' understanding (see Kuhn 1970). The transfer of those metaphors and models of interpretations through the IPM "school without walls" proves to be significant as the source where further changes occurred.

Whether changes really take place depends on some other factors. The failure of the IPM School in Kebon Cau and the performance of the IPM farmers in Marga Tani strengthen my argument that the individual farmers selected to be the IPM participants played an important role in the "constructive" mode of knowledge transmission afterwards (see Ortony 1993; Mayer 1993). This is not to overlook the other significant factors, such as the way the IPM trainers entered the "scene" without first building up a good rapport and collaboration with the local community, appropriately selecting the participants, or understanding their existing knowledge and how people learn. The story of Kebon Cau and the doubt of some IPM farmers of the efficacy of IPM strategies might be different if the IPM trainers considered carefully what Bentley et al. (1994:179) say: "Find out what people know and explain what they don't know in a way that is compatible with what they do know." How the people learned in the "school" was not quite compatible with how they learned from their fields everyday through real practices. The stories in chapter 4 illustrate how the farmers did the observation in "the experimental plots" but without pursuing the group's decision in actual practice. The facilitators also did not quite successfully avoid the "chalk and talk" method of teaching. Some IPM farmers also criticised how the trainers only "talk" without carrying out the cultivation practices together with the farmers. By considering these drawbacks, the explanation for the changes should also be attributed to the farmers' own activities in their responses to both economic and ecological constraints and hazards.

Under these constraints, the novel meanings and interpretation schemas have been proved, validated, verified, or falsified by the individual IPM farmers through practice. The IPM is thus an appropriate case to show how the relations between cognition and action and between cognition and ecological change take place, in particular, the agroecological change. The stories in the two neighbouring villages of how knowledge of white stem borer grew among the IPM farmers again illustrate that under the same economic constraints, but with a different kind of pest outbreaks, the results in knowledge formation and transmission could diverge. The ecological change as exemplified in the unprecedented pest outbreak is another significant variable to be taken into account in examining the changes in farmers' knowledge.

The outbreak of white rice stem borer in the 1989–1990 planting season and continued outbreaks until the 1991–1992 season provided a rich opportunity for the farmers to learn. The nature of infestation of this pest that is entirely different from the brown plant hopper stimulated farmers' curiosity to know more about the pest's behaviour. On the basis of the farmers' own perception that this pest is more difficult to control than the brown plant hopper and of my observation in the four planting seasons, it seems likely that the brown plant hopper is easily controlled within the existing schema of "spraying 'medicines.'" In the farmers' view, only by spraying "appropriate 'medicines' or "strong 'medicines'" could the brown plant hopper be controlled. This is the way that was initially planned by the IPM experts to be altered through the IPM "school" referring to the unintended consequences of the BPH's outbreaks. Such a conventional way of controlling BPH, of course, did not work well with the white rice stem borer. The IPM teachings about the WRB life cycle, its nature of infestation, and the control strategies, which were developed by the IPM planners in the course of the pest's outbreaks, provided a basis for understanding that "spraying 'medicines'" would not work. These basic understandings also stimulated the IPM farmers to develop some alternative ways as presented in the earlier chapters. The continuous outbreaks with the overlapping generations of WRB in the 1990–1991 rainy season, and the two stages of infestation in only one season enabled the farmers to learn continually about the efficacy of their strategies, as well as the pest's behaviour and its nature of infestation.

The existence of both the newly introduced knowledge and the farmers' novel practices in response to the ecological hazards is the major contributing factor in expanding the alternative strategies for controlling pests. In addition to knowledge, action, and hazards, however, individual innovation and curiosity play significant roles. By also looking closely at how knowledge relates to action and vice versa, and how new ideas are internalized into a person's knowledge repertoire and strategies, the IPM case reveals the importance of the formation of confidence and belief in changing farmers' perspectives.

From Knowing to Believing

By transmitting a bundle of IPM principles and ideas, the experts were not only bridging the gap from what farmers did not know to what they did know, but they were also providing the meanings of events and objects that previously had been unimportant and were now culturally important in growing healthy paddy (see Bentley 1992; Bentley and Rodriquez 2001). The expression of an IPM farmer that his "way of thinking is now different" reflects the changes he had experienced, i.e., by being able to give meanings to the unknown or to change the meanings of the known phenomena. Because observation is a basic means of learning, direct observation of the phenomena related to the new meanings was the main requirement for assessing the truth of the new ideas. For the farmers, "without seeing the evidence, it is hard to believe (*tanpa melihat buktinya, sulit untuk percaya*)." Only by believing the new ideas received from various sources or generated from their own thoughts on the basis of observation and experimentation could these ideas be integrated into their memories of "true knowledge."

Knowing from the IPM "school" only is not enough to make the farmers believe in what they had learned. Through practices in their own ways of learning and seeing that the results conformed to the "theories," the farmers gained confidence in what the trainers said. However, their arguments and critiques, as revealed in the stories presented in the earlier chapters reflect their doubt when they discovered that the "theories" were not true, or only partially true. The significant contributions of the IPM "school" in improving the farmers' confidence and belief of the truth were the carrying out of a more systematic and detailed observation and the use of the additional means such as plastic bags. The use of plastic bags made the "seeing" possible outside their own *sawah*. Observing specimens outside their natural habitat was something novel. By bringing the specimens home, the farmers' families and neighbours had the opportunity to also "see" what they were not able to "see" by themselves. This additional means also improved how the farmers carried out experimentation and comparison, for example, by observing their findings in the field and in the plastic bags at home, or between different specimens and treatments in different bags. Greater confidence and stronger beliefs could be built in a shorter time outside the farmers' *in situ* experience. This was one significant contribution to the formation of farmers' knowledge provided by the IPM "school." The idea behind the use of these additional means, including the "insect zoo," which was, unfortunately, left out in Marga Tani and the neighbouring village, was the farmers' own ability to gain knowledge, confidence and belief. The establishment and advancement of "farmers' own studies" (*studi-studi petani*) were hallmarks of this program throughout the country.

Once the farmers had gained confidence that the theories were true, they would keep them in their memories. Once the new understandings were kept in their memories, they would use these as references to interpret new discoveries. However, by examining closely the cycle of individuals' interpretations of their discoveries and how these interpretations accumulate, it is apparent that subjective interpretations about the basis of past experience and imagination play a great role in drawing up inferences. Variability is great here due to diverse individual imaginations, in particular, if they were not able to observe directly some hidden phenomena or those beyond their empirical observation. By being within the community of practitioners, the farmers, this great variability becomes one of the major sources for conversation and comparison. Daily conversation and comparison are the other means through which farmers share what they hear and see. These are also the means to prove whether their interpretations and inferences are true, and if so, confidence and belief are gained.

In this circulation of interpretations, the actors, who convincingly back up their inferences by the means the farmers consider valid and appropriate, gain greater agreement and support from their fellows. The social positions or categories of the farmers have become less significant than the reliable and valid information they could provide. Thus, the IPM farmers who were later known as the "experts of white rice stem borer" and the "farmer professors" became the "consultants" of other farmers. Both the lay farmers and the schooled farmers agreed that the knowledge the "experts" gained was true by observing how those "experts" acquired new discoveries. This was also the way they judged the expertise of outsiders, i.e., the agricultural extension workers, the pest observers, and the scientists.

On the other hand, within the constraints and limitations the farmers had in their ways of learning, many queries and questions still remain unanswered. Ambiguity and doubt about the truth that pesticides were really harmful is an example of how the newly introduced propositions about pesticides have not been validated and proven in the ways so that farmers gain their confidence and belief. The *ex situ* experimentation of the killing of natural enemies carried out in the school had not been convincingly supported by the teachings in the midst of the ongoing outbreaks of pests and disease. How the chemical substances work and the objective results of the mixture of various chemical substances on pests, plants, and their habitat have been part of the farmers' ignorance. The IPM school did not incorporate any lesson to fill in that gap and ignorance in the farmers' knowledge. The rest of the community, the non-IPM farmers, continued to spray "medicines." The chemical companies, shop owners, and even the local bureaucrats and agricultural officers still provided the "medicines." Ironically, by interpreting the results of the farmers' use of "medicines"—the instant killing of all pests—many farmers still gained their confidence and belief in the efficacy of those chemical substances. "Spraying 'medicines' still constituted part of the farmers' true knowledge, even though this true knowledge was gained through farmers' ignorance.

The paths from knowing to believing, which further enhance the knowledge an individual has, as shown by the IPM program, are not simple ones. Without a supporting climate for the "seeds" to grow well, with great confidence and belief, there is still a question as to what extent the "seedlings" can consistently produce "healthy crops" without "medicines." Despite this complex process of gaining belief, it is apparent that gradually the individual actions by individual actors produce collective practices in some respects. Following up farmers' practices over time provided a rich opportunity to see how the aggregate's action was formed through individual behaviour.

From Individual Behaviour to Collective Performance

Individual farmers are managers in their own fields. How the crops grow and what the paddy looks like are the result of individual strategies, which, in Richards's (1989) term, constitute "performance" rather than the defined plan and intention. The condition of entire fields of rice crops in one area is thus an outcome of the collective performance of how the aggregates are formed from the individual strategies in growing crops. The example of the farmers' choice of rice varieties presented in chapters 3, 6, and 7 is a good case for understanding how the aggregate of selected and/or rejected rice varieties came about. This is also true of the plants' performance toward harvesting time, after a series of sequential events of individual strategies to control pests and diseases throughout the season. The extent to which the IPM premises and strategies constituted part of not only the individual farmers' knowledge and practices, but also the community's was also formed through the actions of individual IPM farmers and the interactions among them and between them and the rest of their community.

The mechanisms and processes of how the collective performance or the aggregate behaviour has been formed through individual actions and interactions should be examined thoroughly. In relation to IPM, it becomes important to examine them by referring to how the IPM planners designed the intervention. The IPM program is distinguished from the earlier Green Revolution technological transfer because it involves transmitting scientific knowledge to only a small number of farmers. It is expected that this small number of farmers would transmit their knowledge and practices to other farmers. Another alternative is to undertake again an IPM school for different farmers in the following season, or in some other seasons, or not at all. It is thus a great challenge for the selected IPM participants to take actions on the basis of the new strategies in the midst of the ongoing "old" practices of controlling pests by the rest of the community. It is also interesting to analyze how the novel ideas and practices, whether these were carried out properly or not by the individual IPM participants, affected the others' understandings and behaviours and led to some changes in the aggregate behaviours.

Curios, doubt, disbelief, discouragement or otherwise, support and encouragement from their fellows and neighbours fluctuated in different time and contexts. These would affect significantly the efforts of individual IPM participants, including the most inventive and inquisitive IPM farmers, either in pursuing their own strategies or in convincing other farmers.

The cases of the farmers' responses to the total complete credit package scheme were examples of how the interaction among and support from the peers produced great motivation to react against the persistent policy. Despite a comprehensive understanding of IPM principles, the accumulated problems and burdens underlie their common feelings toward the bureaucrats' policies and actions. The case of the farmers' responses to white rice stem borer outbreaks reveals that in the absence of the penetration of IPM discourses, concepts and interpretation schemas among the lay-farmers, it was not easy for the individual IPM actors to pursue their strategies in collaboration with their peers. What farmers do not know cannot help them to assure an alert and conscious stance in regard to the "new important pest control strategies." Hence, discouragement and disbelief were the reactions that the few IPM farmers received from their peers, in particular at the early stage of introducing these novel ideas. The conventional perspectives in appreciating the peers' actions in terms of expertise, age and experience, or properties still underlie their fellows' appreciation of the speakers' efforts to disseminate knowledge. It was thus understandable if the IPM farmers felt that a legal identity of their new position as the schooled farmers was necessary.

Only through experiencing the burdens and hardships together in their own ways of sharing and communication over time, and through gaining confidence and belief in what the "experts in white rice stem borer" said would wider acceptance of novel understandings begin to emerge. The practices of various alternatives in pest/disease control in the aftermath of the IPM school that moved away from the sole strategy of chemical control were thus the aggregate behaviours created from daily interactions among individual actors. The stories presented in chapters 6 and 7 reveal how the changes emerged from the initial practices by only a small number of farmers, how the dynamics of the changes occurred, and how the understandings of the pest's behaviour expanded gradually.

The approach I have used in my study has enabled me to discover not only how these aggregate behaviours were formed over time, but also how these behaviours changed through time and under what conditions. The aggregate behaviours that were formed at the same period of time also varied among different groups of farmers or among the same group of farmers in different contexts. The extent to which these behaviours occurred among farmers were fluid, without definite similar boundaries over time. Examples are the farmers' "voice," "exit" and "loyalty" responses to the policy of the subsidized scheme, or diverse pest control strategies that were found at the same period of time among diverse group of farmers. Examining how and why these behaviours were formed through time by taking into account the contributing factors enabled me to understand the occurrence of these phenomena contextually. Another advantage is the understanding of how diversity, contestation and consensus of people's knowledge and practices were formed.

Diversity, Contestation and Consensus

The great range of diversity in the farmers' understandings and practices in every phase of crop farming has shown that diversity is the reality, not the exception. By looking at how diversity occurred, individual variation in agriculture consists of more than the three kinds of variation pointed out by Johnson (1972, see chap. 1). The variation that has not been mentioned by Johnson relates to individual histories of experiences and learning in cultivating crops; the diverse networks of communication each individual has with diverse kinds of information exchanged through these networks; the diverse degree of observation of every aspect in crop farming (e.g., plants, insects, fungi, microbial, etc.); and the varied degree of individual confidence in particular crop farming strategies, or of individual inventiveness, readiness to accept new ideas, and curiosity in advancing knowledge and/or strategies. The range of variation related to these aspects cuts across the boundaries of the established social categories among the farmers on the basis of age, gender, landownership, or the particular kind of job in rice farming.

The introduction of IPM knowledge to only one group of farmers (25 farmers in each school) created a further difference among the farmers. Only the selected farmers received a bundle of new ideas and paradigms of IPM, whereas the rest of the community members did not have the chance to receive the comprehensive set of ideas directly from the experts. In this particular context, variation thus relates also to individual difference in gaining access to an outsider's knowledge. This access was created by the outsiders through the selection process of who were nominated to be the IPM participants. This condition applies also to other communities receiving the same treatment from the National Indonesian IPM program.[1] In cases of the school initiated by the local people as found in some other places, the access was created by the local IPM farmers. New categories of farmers thus developed as the consequence of such a treatment by the IPM planners (see for example how the IPM farmers distinguished themselves as the schooled farmers as opposed to the unschooled or the lay farmers).

Even though knowledge transmission to the lay farmers did occur throughout the course of pest outbreaks, the received ideas were not always in the same form or were not comprehensively disseminated. Many cases also reveal that the transmitted ideas were those that had been reinterpreted and modified according to individual reception and understanding by diverse sources. The reinterpreted notion might also have been transmitted in its modified form. Disagreements among farmers also occurred when there was a "missing link" of ideas in the whole set of ideas necessary for understanding the unobservable or the puzzling phenomena. There was also great variability in the situations in which the conventional strategies for protecting crops could not be used effectively to overcome the new nature of pest infestation. There was an anomalous situation where the majority of farmers did not know the efficacious strategies. The newly transmitted basic ideas were also at the stage of being validated and modified to suit the reality. The cultural rules about the appropriate pest control strategies for a pest, such as the white rice stem borer were still in the making. The farmers were still looking for effective and yet less costly strategies. In such a situation, the small group of IPM participants gained advantages by acquiring some basic ideas from the school. Consensus among the IPM farmers was thus more common than among the lay farmers because the transmitted schemas and concepts allowed them, but not the lay farmers, to better cope with such phenomena.

However, the process of the making of IPM-culture became more complicated when the farmers faced inconsistent experiences in an open, uncontrolled environment. They did not have the tools to control the intervening variables, nor could they explain the unexpected results without additional concepts or categories. Questions, such as why different strategies produced similar results, or why the same strategies produced different results, or why the nonspraying strategy failed to produce as good a harvest as the spraying one were raised without knowing what the appropriate answers were. Without any objective reasoning on which all the farmers could agree, e.g., the basis of a valid explanation, individual farmers became confused. Confusion was also caused by the inconsistency between the introduced ideas and reality, which was again, interpreted subjectively. Hence, confusion and contestation of arguments were ever present in daily conversations. Despite having contested arguments, the diverse results provided a basis for comparison and evaluation for individual strategies and thus, improved individual learning.

If diversity and contestation are enormous, on what basis do the farmers reach consensus? As the stories in chapter 3 have shown, common ideas formed on the basis of common understandings, observations and interpretations gained through similar experience, comparison and conversation are the ordinary phenomena. But, a consensus or an agreement about the efficacy of particular strategies or propositions could also be formed on the basis of diversity. Because of the farmers' detailed observations and vivid memories, individual farmers could reach a consensus about diverse strategies and crop performances when they could observe consistent experiences over some time. An example of this is the relationship between the transplanting schedule and the degree of damage to the plants. Diversity and consistent experiences over time can thus produce not only a shared common assumption, but also confidence in their own discoveries, which could further lead to the formulation of new knowledge or strategies. The early and appropriate transplanting schedule and the uniform harvesting schedule were the examples of what the farmers regarded as control strategies that they themselves discovered. Once individual farmers had confidence in the efficacy of the new findings, they would use it as a point of reference for other considerations, such as selecting rice varieties, preparing ground efficiently at an appropriate time, etc. Changes could thus follow. This reality supports the arguments by other scholars who perceive the significant role of diversity for human life. Marglin (1996) argues that diversity is indeed the key to the survival of the human species. He further says that "diversity is as necessary to our development as human beings as it is to ecological balance (Marglin 1996:241)."

Diversity and consensus could thus lead to changes in an open, dynamic, and sometimes, unpredictable environment where farmers were not able to control the intervening variables. It is interesting to examine further whether similar mechanisms will occur in a different kind of context, including different abilities of the people to understand and control their environment. After all, within such a circumstance, how continuity persists despite the changes is another significant factor to be taken into account.

Change and Continuity

The stories presented in the earlier sections and chapters have shown how changes occurred through various means and processes. One significant perspective the farmers gained from learning about IPM was their comparison of the new teaching with their "old condition" of growing rice: without "medicines," when pests and diseases were not as abundant as today; even though they realised that the return to that condition would not be possible in their current habitat. Analogy and metaphoric perspectives were prominent in the farmers' learning processes. Significant also to the changes they experienced were the enrichment of their preexisting categories about predators, the use of previously nonexisting discourses and interpretation schemas in decision making and the paradigmatic shift of the pesticides use. Changes in actual practices were evident in the establishment of the alternatives in pest control strategies, not solely on the basis of chemical control. These marked the beginning of IPM in Java in the early 1990s, after almost three decades of cultivating rice with "medicines," and have always been under the government's regulation and recommendation.

The gradual changes the farmers experienced reveal how important the time dimension is in the farmers' learning process. Having indirect experiences outside the time dimension as the scientists or the agricultural bureaucrats do is not part of the farmers' conventional way of learning. This nature of learning provides both advantages and limitations. Despite the rich and detailed knowledge the farmers could gain sequentially over time, they were only able to carry out trial-and-error practice, by also adopting the novel ways of observation without being able to firmly know in advance what the results of their actions would be. During intensive pest outbreaks, they badly needed to know the appropriate and effective responses. This was the reason for their great motivation to seek knowledge from those who could gain knowledge more quickly than they do. However, access to the sources of appropriate knowledge was not easy to obtain, not as easy as the access to the sources of agricultural production inputs, including the pesticides. They also soon realised that the specialized knowledge that a particular expert had would not always be compatible with their general knowledge, needs and problems.

In general, the ways of learning pursued by all the community members had not altered much, except the carrying out of some studies; nor had the conventional ways of using insecticides and the paradigm of protecting plants from "illnesses" by using these substances: the "medicines." The persistent use of this term is an example of the very powerful use of metaphors in transferring scientific knowledge (see Kuhn 1993). Introducing pesticides as "medicines" in the early stages of the Green Revolution proved to be very effective in affecting farmers' pests/diseases control strategies. Unless they were confident—supported by evidence that was interpreted subjectively—that using this substance would not work, the farmers would still refer to the "medicines" as the main solution. It is evident that the new scientific metaphor of pesticides as "poison" could not replace the old metaphor immediately. This was supported by the farmers' own paradigm of growing plants like growing a "healthy" body, and preventing their own bodies from "illnesses" by having preventative medicines. "Having an umbrella ready before it rains" still constituted part of the farmers' perspective. They also still held the schema of "curing" the plants' "sicknesses" by using curative medicines, the "antibiotics." Introducing new brands of pesticides went on through all means by all parties, including the manipulation of the trial stage of a new insecticide for WRB to gain profits.

Within an inconsistent and complex environment where it was not easy to have firm and consistent indicators to evaluate the new ideas and strategies, it was really constraining for the farmers to prove the efficacies of those practices. Cost-benefit analysis of carrying out IPM strategies was not directly observable without explanation. This evaluation was not as tangible as measuring yields and plant performances. The latter was the persistent criterion to evaluate individual's expertise. This was the most significant value in rice farming even though "spraying medicines" was practiced. These were all evidence that without the creation of a new kind of social evaluation, of a new system of rewards and punishment supporting the novel idea of IPM strategies, it would be difficult to paradigmatically shift the farmers' social evaluation of their fellow farmers' farming practices. The best yields, rather than producing healthy crops and environment and reducing unnecessary costs, would still constitute the very basic evaluation. Changing the notion of "medicines" to something "poisonous" would also be difficult to achieve. The farmers had to use a new symbol from a domain other than "medicines," which in some respects worked, but was not consistently used in the major paradigm of growing crops.

Detailed ethnographic analyses of how the processes and mechanisms of knowledge formation proceed sequentially enabled me to discover change and continuity, as well as variability and convergence in the events of knowledge formation and transmission. Processual and contextual approaches focusing on the actors' behaviours and understanding in their everyday struggles revealed the strength and advantages of these approaches by looking at the linkages of events over time, and the contextual factor affecting those interlinking events. This is a promising aspect for future studies of knowledge in the making, one possible way to examine "the cultural in motion." The question is whether these approaches will provide similar advantages and results in a different context of the relationship between cognition and action, and in particular, between cognition and agro-ecological change. Further examination in different situations is necessary.

Seeds of Knowledge

"Today's seed brings tomorrow's harvest" is a proverb that hopefully suits the portrayal of what the IPM experts intended to achieve in these early years of 1990. In this stage of the beginning of IPM in Java, we noticed the growth of the "seeds": the IPM farmers who were struggling to survive in their current fields, full of weeds, pests, diseases and poisonous chemical substances. Yet, they managed to grow. Full of confidence with their new "legitimate knowledge," they moved forward to struggle against the conflicting policies and they failed. Without any *in situ* assistance from those in authority, with the new ideas they had, they moved forward to survive by inventing strategies and discovering more understandings about the nature of pest/disease outbreaks. The constraints and hardships the farmers suffered do not reflect a supporting environment for the "seeds" to grow well. However, as another proverb states, "The seed that falls on good ground will yield a fruitful harvest." Once the "seeds" are sown in "good potential and talented individuals," "fruitful harvests" would indeed be the promising outcomes. This was the case with the sowing of the "seeds" among some inventive and inquisitive IPM farmers in my study.

A larger number of farmers, who at first felt strange with the new ideas and strategies of those farmers, began to imitate them. The novel ideas gradually became embodied knowledge, established as a fact through practices, and became a new structure of extra-personals and stimulation for other farmers. Individual knowledge or knowledge owned by only 25 among hundreds of farmers cultivating paddies in Marga Tani began to spread, unevenly in varied forms and understandings to wider members of their community. The IPM "seeds of knowledge" were, to some extent, able to generate the growth of "new seeds."

On the other hand, IPM was only a part of the long relationship between the farmers and the government in which the farmers have always been the targets of all government programs. The latter has always had the power to give instructions and recommendations to the first. Such a relationship has not changed much yet. The rice intensification programs continued, and so did the supporting subsidized scheme in both the normal and the critical situation of pest/disease outbreaks. The IPM program had not been able to do much to change the entire world of rice farming in Java. Yet, a window of opportunity had been created for the "seeds to grow" in their own niche, in a healthier and promising way to produce good harvests. A resurrection and recreation of old memories and practices, together with a creation of entirely new ideas and strategies or a modification of the introduced ideas were what the "seeds" produced in the two-year period. Even though the old freedom of growing rice had not yet fully returned, a feeling that they could overtake the extension agents' role began to blossom. "Give us books, and in combination with our rich experiences, we will be able to be the specialist extension agents," a young educated IPM farmer proudly said. "I will use the opportunity of talking in front of my fellow farmers during the extension meeting," confirmed a diligent older IPM farmer. "I will also prove that the IPM strategies were effective and benefit us," was his promise.

Such a story is the most promising one originating from a serious effort to build up a dialogue and bridge the gap between the two worlds of practitioners, the scientists and the people. Farmers can be as scientific as the scientists are in their research and knowledge formation. Knowledge is constructed on the basis of whatever information and stimulation are received by individuals, which are considered useful in particular situations regardless of their origin or sources. The farmers' self-reliance of their own ability by mastering both the rich empirical experience and the scientific explanation is a mirror of the reality that the boundary of the two domains of knowledge does not exist in farmers' minds once the combination of information is formed. "Hybrid in character" is what Dove (2000: 238) says about people's knowledge. The confluence of local and extra-local experience as argued by Dove (2000:235) is really happening. Farmers' experiments, named by them, "*studi-studi petani*" (farmers' studies), are a clear example of the confluence (also see Frossard 1998 on "Peasant Science"). My recent study among farmers in another part of Indonesia, in Central Lampung—who have benefited from a nongovernment agency's serious efforts to build up farmers' self-reliance—proves that once the farmers gained their self-confidence, their creativity and knowledge enrichment, acquired from various ways of learning, flourished (see Winarto *et al.* 2000).

It is now high time to seriously reconsider the disjuncture between "western" scientific knowledge and local knowledge in the real world of farmers' life (see Agrawal 1995), which has been underlying not only the analysis of the differences between the two worlds, but also the paradigm of development programs among various agrarian people (also see Nygren 1999). However, it is not easy to abandon entirely the conventional paradigm of development and the hegemony of scientific knowledge and technology. It is still a question to what extent the supporting and conducive environment for the ongoing intermingling knowledge to flourish will be seriously created. Farmers do not always experience consistent support to back up their struggles in creating and maintaining the new schemas of interpretation and practices.

When I returned to visit them in late 1996, the farmers' leader's complaint was: "We are like plants; the governments sow us, but they did not water us, so the plants will die." This was the simile he used to portray the existing situation and the spirits of the IPM "seeds of knowledge." The "seeds" have to keep struggling in the existing environment of recurrent outbreaks of pests and diseases, the continuing recommendation of pesticides use, without appropriate support and assistance in critical situations. Some of the "seeds" grew in the old tradition of controlling pests again whenever they felt that the IPM strategies would not save their harvests. Would these "seeds of knowledge" always experience hardships in their efforts to grow in a better and healthy niche in the future? It is time now to evaluate thoroughly the fundamental premises of the Green

Revolution with its strong emphasis on high productivity and the determinant role of scientific knowledge and technology. IPM has begun to shift the Green Revolution paradigm. But, a much stronger and thorough shift is still in a great demand. This is indeed necessary to enable the "seeds" to produce a fruitful harvest on the basis of their own talents to grow in "good ground and niche."

APPENDIX 1

The Brief History of the Green Revolution in Java

The Green Revolution was begun in the rice *sawah* of Java in 1965 with the program called BIMAS (*bimbingan massal* or mass guidance). This program involved a substantial effort in infrastructure rehabilitation, agricultural extension, and the distribution of fertilizers, high-yielding seed varieties, pesticides and credit (Hansen 1978; Birowo and Hansen 1981; Hardjono 1983; Fox 1991). The rice intensification effort was expanded in 1967 through the introduction of INMAS (*intensifikasi massal* or mass intensification). The introduced technological package of INMAS was similar to BIMAS, but without the government's provision of the operating credit for farmers. The rice-technology transfer was characterized by the exercise of power and a one-way communication process preempted by the government. Due to problems in the repayment of BIMAS credit and other factors, the initial BIMAS program was inevitably curtailed in 1968.

The government supplemented the BIMAS with a new approach, the so-called *Bimas Gotong Royong* (*Bimas GR*) Program (1968–1969–1970). Contracts were made with foreign firms from Europe and Japan to provide fertilizer, pesticides and credit to farmers through the village head. Cash allowances, seed and advice to extension workers were also supplied. The CIBA Company was responsible for applying organophosphate insecticide by aerial spraying (Badan Urusan Logistik 1976; Hansen 1978; Mears and Moeljono 1981; Nataatmadja et al. 1988). The BIMAS GR program eventually failed (see Hansen 1978; Hussein 1986; Nataatmadja et al. 1988, for problems following Bimas Gotong Royong). The government then introduced another program called the "Perfected (Improved) BIMAS Program" (Bimas Yang Disempurnakan) in 1970. Foreign firms were removed from the scene, and farmers could exercise choice, but with significant constraints from the government. Aerial spraying was abandoned in favour of hand spraying (Hansen 1978:331) and pesticides were made available in the market and at cooperative units at subsidized prices. Farmers then learned to apply pesticides regularly.

In 1979, another intensification program, INMAS (*Intensifikasi khusus* or special intensification) was introduced to overcome stagnation in the intensification campaign and to increase the cropping intensity in irrigated areas even further. The basis of INMAS was group farming rather than individual effort by each farmer to optimize their resources (Hardjono 1983; Sekretariat Badan Pengendali BIMAS 1991). The rice intensification program continued with the *Supra* INMAS (super special intensification) program in 1987 in selected areas because production was not keeping pace with the growth in demand. This program included not only a technological package, but also service and social/organizational packages (Sawit et al. 1988).

Toward the end of the 1990s, the government declared another food intensification program called GEMA PALAGUNG 2001, an abbreviation for *Gerakan Mandiri Padi, Kedelai dan Jagung Tahun 2001* (Self-help Movement of Rice, Soybean and Corn for the Year 2001). This is the main program in the 'Special Effort to Overcome the Food Production Crisis' (*Upaya Khusus Penanggulangan Krisis Produksi Pangan*) to increase food productivity (Departemen Pertanian 1998). The overall crisis in Indonesia in 1997 and 1998 was behind the drafting of this program. The main objective was to achieve high productivity in the year 2001 by increasing the crops-index-diversity, the cropping-areas, and the yields for three main commodities: rice, soybean and corn (Departemen Pertanian 1998).

APPENDIX 2

Integrated Pest Management in Rice

The Presidential Declaration (*Instruksi Presiden*) No. 3/1986 on the Improvement of Brown Plant Hopper Control on Rice Crop (*Peningkatan Pengendalian Hama Wereng Coklat pada Tanaman Padi*) defined the Integrated Pest Management as follows:

The integrated pest management system is the control system that involves various means of harmonious control that will not cause financial loss and damage to the environment.

The pest management control in rice should be based on the following integrated pest management systems:

1. management of cropping pattern;
2. planting of resistant high yielding varieties;
3. eradication and sanitation;
4. judicious use of pesticides.

The management of cropping patterns

1. The management of cropping patterns is directed toward uniform planting, rotation of food crops and varieties.
2. The local regional governments manage the cropping patterns according to technical guidance from the Ministry of Agriculture.

The planting of resistant high yielding varieties

1. Research in discovering resistant high yielding varieties should be improved.
2. High yielding varieties resistant to brown plant hopper should be managed well to prevent the development of new biotypes. The strategic reservation of high yielding varieties resistant to brown plant hopper should be provided in order to respond to the resistance breakdown of the current planted varieties.

3. The regions with widespread pest outbreaks should be given priorities in planting the resistant high yielding varieties that have yields and qualities close to *Cisadané* and *PB42*.
4. The Ministry of Agriculture decides the recommended resistant, high yielding varieties.
5. The timely provision of seeds of resistant high yielding varieties in sufficient quantity is under the responsibility of *Perum Sang Hyang Seri* and *PT. Pertani*.

Eradication and sanitation

Eradication/sanitation of heavily infested rice plants should be carried out and if necessary replaced by other food crops, secondary crops or others, or fallowed for one to two months period.

The judicious use of insecticides

1. Insecticides are to be used only when other methods of pest control have proven ineffective; specifically when the pest population exceeds established economic threshold levels.
2. Types of insecticides utilised and their application methods must take into account the preservation of natural enemies of brown plant hopper.
3. Types of insecticides that might cause pest resurgence, resistance, or other damaging side effects are therefore illegal and forbidden.
4. The banned insecticides for use on rice are:

    1. Agrothion 50 EC   Fenitrotion
    2. Azodrin 15 WSC   Monocrotofos
    3. Basazinon 45/30 EC   Diazinon + BPMC
    4. Basmiban 20 EC   Klorpirifos
    5. Basminon 60 EC   Diazinon
    6. Basudin 60 EC   Diazinon
    7. Bayrusil 250 EC   Kuinalfos
    8. Bayrusil 5 G   Kuinalfos
    9. Basudin 10 G: Diazinon
    10. Brantasan 450/300 EC Diazinon + BPMC
    11. Carbavin 85 WP   Karbaril

12.	Cytrolane 2 G:	Mefosfolan
13.	Dharmasan 60 EC	Fentoat
14.	Dharmathion 50 EC	Fenitrotion
15.	Diazinon 60 EC	Diazinon
16.	Dicarbam 85 S	Karbaril
17.	Dimaphen 50 EC	Fenitrotion
18.	Dimecron 50 SCW	Fosfamidon
19.	Dursban 20 EC	Klorpirifos
20.	Dursban 15/5 E	Klorpirifos + BPMC
21.	Dyfonate 5 G	Fenofos
22.	Ekalux 25 EC	Kuinalfos
23.	Ekalux 5 G	Etrimfos
24.	Ekamet 5 G	Etrimfos
25.	Elsan 60 EC	Fentoat
26.	Elstar 45/30 EC	Fentoat + BPMC
27.	Eumulthion TM	Triklorfon + Azinfosmetil
28.	Folimat 500 SL	Ometoat
29.	Fomadol 50 EC	Malation
30.	Gusadrin 150 WSC	Monocrotofos
31.	Hostathion 40 EC	Triazofos
32.	Karbathion 50 EC	Fenitrotion
33.	Lannate 25 WP	Metomil
34.	Lebaycid 550 EC	Fention
35.	Lirocide 650 EC	Fenitrothion
36.	Miral 2 G	Isasofos
37.	Monitor 200 LC	Metamidofos
38.	Nogos 50 EC	Diklorvos
39.	Nuvacron 20 SCW	Monocrotofos
40.	Ofunack 40 EC	Piridafention
41.	Padan 50 SP	Kartap Hidroklorida
42.	Pertacide 60 EC	Fentoat
43.	Petroban 20 EC	Klorpirifos
44.	Phyllodol 50 EC	Diklorvos
45.	Reldan 24 EC	Metil Klorpirifos
46.	Sematron 75 SP	Asefat
47.	Sevin 5 D	Karbaril
48.	Sevin 5 G	Karbaril
49.	Sevin 85 S	Karbaril
50.	Sumibas 75 EC	BPMC + Fenitrotion
51.	Sumithion 50 EC	Fenitrotion

52.	Sumithion 2D	Fentrotion
53.	Surecide 25 EC	Sianofenfos
54.	Tamaron 200 LC	Metamidofos
55.	Thiodan 35 EC	Endosulfan
56.	Trithion 4 E	Karbofenotion
57.	Trithion 95 EC	Karbofenotion

These insecticides are not to be used on rice, but may be used on secondary crops or other nonrice crops.

5. An insecticide that is now considered very effective in controlling brown plant hopper at the egg and nymph stage is Applaud 10 WP, which has buprofezin as its active substance.

6. If Applaud 10 WP is unavailable, insecticides with MIPC or BPMC as active ingredients can be used:

    1. Mipcin 50 WP   MIPC
    2. Hopcin 50 EC   BPMC
    3. Bassa 50 EC   BPMC
    4. Baycarb 50 EC   BPMC
    5. Dharmabas 50 EC   BPMC
    6. Kiltop 50 EC   BPMC

7. Beside brown plant hopper, other main pests that can be dangerous to rice crops are stem borers and green plant hoppers. Insecticides with carbofuran as their active ingredient can be used to control and eradicate these pests:

    1. Furadan 3 G   carbofuran
    2. Curaterr 3 G   carbofuran
    3. Dharmafur 3 G   carbofuran

8. The Ministry of Agriculture will decide additions to insecticides in points 4, 5, 6 and 7 on the basis of research.

Pest monitoring

1. Early and accurate pest monitoring to identify the possibility of pest outbreaks has to be improved by increasing the number of pest observers and improving their knowledge and skills.

2. The result of pest monitoring in point 1 becomes the basis for deciding the types and methods of insecticide application.

3. The Ministry of Agriculture defines the function and role of pest observers in the effort at brown plant hopper control.

The movement of pest control and extension

1. In the effort to control insecticide use in pest control, the pest observers are given authority to decide the types and dosages of insecticides and when to apply them.
2. The extension workers provide extensions to farmers' groups/farmers under the pest observers' guidance to enable farmers to know, desire and control pest immediately.
3. The extension workers and farmers' groups/farmers will be trained to improve their skills.
4. To support the success of pest control and extension movement, the extension workers and pest observers working in the field are technically and operationally under the coordination of *Dinas Pertanian Tanaman Pangan* (the Office of Agricultural Food Crops).

Source: Presiden Republik Indonesia. 1986. *Lampiran instruksi Presiden Republik Indonesia no. 3 tahun 1986 tanggal 5 Nopember 1986: Peningkatan pengendalian hama wereng coklat pada tanaman padi.*

APPENDIX 3

The Objectives and Organization of Integrated Pest Management Training

The ideas for a practical IPM training for rice had been developed in the early years of the FAO (Food and Agricultural Organization) Intercountry Rice Integrated Pest Control (IPC) Program. The first training course on IPM was held in the Philippines in 1978. The program was extended to other countries with financial support from Australia and the Netherlands. The Intercountry Program's founders, however, did not foresee that IPM would become the property of farmers, since IPM knowledge had only become the property of the entomological researchers and the pest surveillance systems' personnel. The Intercountry Program's experts perceived that farmers did not have the knowledge to recognise predators and their ecological role. As long as farmers had not developed these field skills, good crop protection techniques that were disseminated from research institutes would languish (FAO 1990:35–36).

The IPC experts believed that sufficient training for farmers was necessary as a prerequisite to developing methods for conserving hundreds of species of beneficial insects in the rice ecosystem. Decisions about whether an insecticide application was needed could only be made if farmers were able to identify key predator species and use information obtained from field monitoring techniques (Kenmore and Shepard n.d.:13). On the basis of this perspective and since IPM was, in fact, based on population and community ecology, the Indonesian IPM planners also believed that such concepts must be taught if farmers and those who support them are to understand the real meaning of an IPM program. Training on fundamental aspects of biology and ecology, therefore, were considered crucial to success in overhauling the Indonesian approach to pest management (FAO 1991:6; 43).

As a follow-up of the Presidential Declaration, in 1989, the Indonesian government initiated the design of a training program for 1,000 pest observers, 2,000 extension workers and 100,000 farmers for over three years. The Ministries of Agriculture, Education and Culture, Health, Population and Environment, and Economics-Finance and Industries

The Objectives and Orangization of IPM Training 373

(EKUIN) coordinated by the National Development Planning Board (BAPPENAS, Badan Perencanaan Pembangunan Nasional) organised a National Steering Committee to implement the IPM training and development program. This committee had the responsibility to identify and discuss general issues and outline policy guidelines for the implementation of IPM training. The Steering Committee was assisted by a Working Group to ensure that the daily program of IPM training went according to schedule (see figure in appendix 3.1). The FAO was invited to create a training team and form a separate bilateral agreement between FAO and BAPPENAS. USAID (United States Agency for International Development) supported the program with a special policy

Figure Appendix 3.1 *The organogram of the national IPM program of Indonesia*

```
                    Advisory Board
                    Steering Committee
                          |
        ┌─────────────────┴─────────────────┐
   Project Manager  <────────────>   Working Group
                                          |
                                    Central Secretariat
                          
                                          National Level
                          ─────────────────────────────
                                          Field Training
                                          Facility Level
                          
                          Head of
                          Field Training Facility
                          (I,II)
                          |
                          Field Training Facility
                          Secretariat
                          |
        ┌─────────────────┴─────────────────┐
   Project Administrator <──────────> Field Trainers
```

Source: FAO (1991, Annex 4:4).

Appendix Map 3.1 *Location of IPM field training facilities in six provinces in Indonesia*

Source: The Indonesian National IPM Program (n.d.).

support grant. Rice centres within six provinces (West Java, Central Java, East Java, Yogyakarta, North Sumatra and South Sulawesi) were given first priority in IPM training because of their contribution to the total rice food production (The National IPM Program n.d.; Oka 1991). Nine field-training facilities in these six provinces were formed to provide training and facilities to the trainers. One field-training facility in Central Java, Soropadan, was allocated to train the trainer-of-trainers (field leaders I and II) in rice and secondary crops IPM training sessions. These trainers-of-trainers then trained pest observers and extension workers in the nine field training facilities (FTF) disseminations (see Map Appendix 3.1).

The National IPM Program has now been placed under the responsibility of the Ministry of Agriculture.

APPENDIX 4

Integrated Pest Management Program Competency Objectives

Analysis and action in the IPM Farmer Field Schools are based on four principles: 1) growing a healthy crop; 2) conserving beneficial predators and parasites; 3) observing fields weekly to determine management actions necessary to produce a profitable crop; and 4) making farmers experts in their own fields. Directly related to these IPM principles are a set of competencies. At the completion of the Farmers' Field School, an IPM farmer growing transplanted flooded rice should be able to perform the following tasks:

Grow a healthy crop

1. Choose a rice variety resistant or tolerant to local disease and insect complexes that yields well under local soil and micro-climatic conditions.

2. Prepare a seedbed and grow seedlings that recover quickly after transplanting.

3. Apply correct amounts and combinations of organic manures and chemical fertilizers (N, P, K and Zn) based on soil conditions at transplanting and panicle initiation.

4. Correctly identify the panicle initiation stage of the crop.

5. Irrigate the fields for weed management and better fertilization during anthesis.

6. Remove weeds during the 2nd and 4th weeks after transplanting and before harvesting.

7. Drain field one week before harvest for more uniform maturation.

8. Determine correct harvest time for maximum production and quality after milling.

9. Dry grains for storage purposes and better prices.

Conserve natural enemies

1. Recognize natural enemies in the field.
2. Explain the effects of pesticides on natural enemies.
3. Promote survivorship of predators by managing habitats for their benefit: short grass on bunds, straw stacks after harvest, etc.

Observe fields weekly

1. Recognize phytophagous insects, diseases, and rat damage in the field.
2. Know that pests are defined by their population density.
3. Accurately gauge field conditions of insect populations, diseases, weeds, and rats.
4. Analyze the density of insects and natural enemies taking into consideration crop health, potential yield, water supply, and other factors affecting yield. The analysis should lead to a *field management decision*, including agronomic and pest control practices.
5. Take early season action against rats when previous season damage was high. Actions should include community organizing for rat control programs.
6. When insect densities must be reduced by insecticides, choose the proper insecticide for the specific insect and apply the insecticide with minimum exposure to self and nontarget species and with proper dosage and delivery.
7. When diseases or insect populations are high, adjust varietal choice for the following season.

Source: Program Nasional Pengendalian Hama Terpadu n.d. *The Indonesian IPM Program*:5–8.

APPENDIX 5

The National Curriculum: "A Day in a Farmers' Field School"

For 10 weeks from the beginning to the end of a planting season, the IPM Farmers' Field School was held once a week for 3–4 hour/sessions. The national curriculum for a day in Farmers' Field School was designed as follows:

Into the field:

Five-member teams observe general field conditions, sample plants, collect insects, make notes, and gather live specimens.

Agro-ecosystem analysis:

This is the core of the weekly process. Each team uses its field samples and notes to create a visual analytical tool combining key factors such as pest/predator densities, plant health, field conditions, weather, and current management treatments.

Decision making:

The output of analysis is a *field management* decision thoroughly discussed in small groups and defended in open discussion before the full group of participants. "What if ..." scenarios further hone analytical skills during the across group discussion.

Special topics:

Topics are linked to crop stage and/or specific local problems. This part of the curriculum is tailored for each field school from a larger selection of field guide activities mastered by facilitators during their extensive training. These exercises require more fieldwork. Topics covered include rat control, crop physiology, health and safety, economic analysis, and water/fertilizer management.

Group dynamics:

Activities in problem solving, communication, leadership, and team building are conducted weekly to strengthen group cohesion, maintain motivation, and help participants develop organizational skills.

Review and planning:

Each school maintains a 1,000 m²-season-long, head-to-head comparison of IPM field management versus a national intensification package scheme. Weekly summaries of developments in the field are conducted by reviewing results of the agroecosystem analysis. At the end of the season, final yield and economic analysis is done by the group. Other long-term activities are reviewed during this session. Such activities may include the development of "insect zoos" for learning about plant-insect and insect-insect interactions, dry insect collection, rat control trials, and defoliation studies. Planning Field School activities also take place at this time.

Source: Program Nasional Pengendalian Hama Terpadu, n.d. *The Indonesian IPM Program*:3–5.

APPENDIX 6

Table Appendix 6.1 *The Weekly Schedule of IPM Farmers' Field School in Ciasem*

No.	Week	Topic/Session	Trainer
1.	Week I	Ballot Box Pretest "What is this?"	Pest observer Extension worker
2.	Week II	Ecosystem I Parasites and imitating predators' behaviour	Pest observer Extension worker
3.	Week III	Ecosystem II Predator, carbofuran, and azodrin	Pest observer Extension worker
4.	Week IV	Ecosystem III Group dynamics	Extension worker[a]
5.	Week V	Ecosystem IV Life cycle and food web Group dynamics	Pest observer Extension worker
6.	Week VI	Ecosystem V Rat population	Pest observer Extension worker
7.	Week VII	Ecosystem VI Pesticides and health Group dynamics	Pest observer Extension worker
8.	Week VIII	Ecosystem VII Dialogue with visitors[b] Rat poisons	Extension worker[a]
9.	Week IX	Ecosystem VIII[c] Agroecosystem analysis Group dynamics	Pest observer Extension worker
10.	Week X	Ballot Box Posttest	Extension worker[d]

Source: The pest observer (the main trainer) in Ciasem and my own observation, 1990.

[a]The pest observer was absent due to his participation in a workshop among the IPM trainers at the field training facilities in Jatisari. The extension worker led the training assisted by the other BPP staff members.

[b]A group of visitors from Jakarta and Jatisari visited the training and conducted a dialogue with the farmers (see chap. 4). The pest observer (the main trainer) accompanied the visitors, but did not lead the training.

[c]A group of undergraduate and graduate students from the Department of Anthropology, the University of Indonesia visited the training led by Iwan Tjitradjaja. The extension worker from the other village, C. Tengah, participated in this session.

[d]The pest observer was absent due to illness. The extension worker was accompanied by the other BPP staff members to carry out the ballot box posttest. Following up the

test, a facilitator from Yogyakarta introduced to the farmers the idea of presenting a performance about IPM in the form of a drama. This was a part of the National IPM Program to disseminate IPM to the local people and officials. Several times practices followed this activity, but at the end, there was no audience to be invited to watch the performance. The facilitator only took pictures of farmers' performances.

Glossary

Bahu — farmers' measurement for land equivalent to 500 *bata* or approximately 0.71 ha.

Bapuk — farmers' term for extreme harvest failure, an acronym of *lo<u>ba</u>* (many) and *em<u>puk</u>* (soft) referring to empty white panicles

Bata — farmers' measurement for land equivalent to 14.3 m²

Bataan — dry land dug up to make bricks

Beluk — white heads; damage symptoms on paddy, which have formed panicles at the reproductive stage, caused by white rice stem borer larvae

Bupati — the head of a regency

Buruh tani, buruh — labourer

Camat — the head of a district

Desa — village

Gubernur — governor, the head of a province

Guntai, petani guntai — absentee landowner

Kabupaten — regency

Kampung — hamlet

Kecamatan — district

Kuintal — farmers' measurement for 100 kg of rice or fertilizers

Lurah, kepala desa — the head of a village

Nabur — broadcasting either fertilizers or carbofuran (granule insecticides)

Nyemprot — spraying insecticides or herbicides

Obat, "medicines" — pesticides, including various types of pesticides: insecticides, herbicides and fungicides

Pemilik, petani pemilik — owner, farmer-owner

Penggarap, petani penggarap — cultivator, farmer-cultivator

Penggerek batang — rice stemborer, a shortening of *penggerek batang padi putih* refers to white rice stemborer (*Scirpophaga innotata*)

Penyakit — "illnesses," "disease," damage symptoms on paddy caused by either pests or diseases

Petani — farmer

Propinsi — province

Racun, racun tikus — poison, term often used by farmers to refer to rodenticides

Sawah — wet rice field that receives water supply from (technical) irrigation

Sawah tegalan — dry rice field receiving water from rain or pumped water.

Sentra Peramalan Hama dan Penyakit Tanaman — Pest/Disease Surveillance Centre for Food Crops

Sundep — dead hearts: damage symptoms on young paddy, at the vegetative stage, caused by white rice stem borer larvae

Wakil, Kepala Dusun — hamlet leader, the head of a hamlet

Notes

1

Knowledge in the Making: An Introduction

1 The introduction of pesticides in the early years of the Green Revolution in Java was accompanied by an extension of the term previously used by farmers for true medicines to a new domain: chemical pesticides (see chap. 3).
2 See Barth (1981, 1984) on his notion of the generative model of processes. In his 1994 article, Barth raises again his argument about turning from totalizing cultural models to generative models of processes.
3 For example, see Boster (1985, 1986), Richards (1986, 1989a, 1994), Brosius et al. (1986), Rhoades (1987, 1989), Rhoades and Bebbington (1988), Dove (1993), Fairhead (1993), Long (1998(3a, 1993b), Arce and Long (1993), Long and Villareal (1994), Fairhead and Leach (1994), Stolzenbach (1994), Millar (1994).
4 In *Micromotives and Macrobehavior*, Schelling (1978) presents his analysis, which explores the relations between the behaviour characteristics of the individuals and the characteristics of the aggregate, the macrobehaviour.
5 For examples, Murtaugh (1980) did a study of the interaction between Mexican corn farmers and extension agents during one series of agricultural demonstrations in a tour of experimental stations. Goodell (1983) carried out an evaluation of the performance of the agricultural extension programs in 22 selected areas of Bangladesh and India and several Southeast Asian countries. Arce and Long (1992, 1993) examined in detail the impact of SAM (*Sistema Alimentario Mexicano*, Mexican Food System), which had the objective of producing a rural development program oriented to the needs of rain-fed agriculture. Bentley and Andrews (1991), an anthropologist and an entomologist, examined the MIPH (Integrated Pest Management in Honduras) project for maize and beans led by Andrews from 1983.

6 The course had five main sections; 1) insect reproduction, 2) entomopathogens, 3) parasitoids, 4) predators, and 5) manipulation of natural enemies (Bentley 1994:149–50).

7 Van de Fliert began her study in the 1989–1990 rainy season, a season before the introduction of IPM. She pursued her study during the time I did my fieldwork in Subang, West Java in the following 1990 dry season, 1990–1991 rainy season, 1991 dry season and 1991–1992 rainy season.

8 The more recent descriptions and information of IPM and the Farmer Field School in Asia and Africa can be found in Pontius, Dilts, and Bartlett (2002) and LEISA (2003).

9 Bottrell (1979:27–45) describes the various control techniques of IPM as follows: 1) biological control, 2) host resistance, 3) cultural control, 4) physical and mechanical control, 5) autocidal insect control, 6) chemical behavioural insect control, and 7) selective chemical control. Adapting from Pimbert (1991) Bentley and Andrews (1996:4) summarize the control techniques of IPM in six areas: 1) cultural pest control, 2) host plant resistance, 3) biological control, 4) the rational use of chemical pesticides with economic thresholds, 5) legal control, and 6) mechanical control. According to Reissig et al., (1986:24), the IPM control techniques in rice cover: 1) cultural practices, 2) varietal resistance, 3) the use of natural enemies (biological control), 4) monitoring and sampling techniques, and 5) the use of insecticides.

10 According to Bottrell (1979:22), "The economic threshold (N^*) is the pest density (or amount of plant damage) at which incremental costs of control just equal incremental crop returns. At N^* some crop income is sacrificed (CI [Crop Income]1–CI2). Above N^* the farmer would fail to get additional crop revenue in proportion to the greater cost of control. If controls are initiated successfully at the tolerance or damage threshold ($N1$), zero damage would occur but the costs of control would not be justified."

11 A severe brown plant hopper outbreak occurred in 1974 that disastrously damaged the new HYV *Pelita*, as well as the "local" rice varieties (Mears and Moeljono 1981; Hardjono 1983; Nataatmadja et al. 1988; Fox 1991). The government's response was to breed other HYVs with genes resistant to brown plant hopper such as *IR26* and *IR30* in 1975; *IR24, 28, 32,* and *34* in 1976. But another outbreak of brown plant hopper biotype 2 occurred in 1976–1977, and the government released further resistant HYVs (*IR36* and *38)* in 1977 and again in 1980 (*Cisadané, Cimandiri, Cipunegara, Krueng Aceh* and others). Another brown plant hopper outbreak occurred in 1985 in some places in Sumatra and Java (Bahagiawati and Oka 1987; Fox 1991), a year after Indonesia's declaration of self-sufficiency in rice production. Nevertheless, the breeding program continued with new HYVs such as *IR64*. *IR64*, which showed partial resistance to all known types of brown plant hopper, spread more rapidly and widely than other previous HYVs (Fox 1991:72).

12 Their ideas were strongly influenced by Knowles and his associates (1985; see also Knowles 1973) who developed the "andragogy" or the "adult-education" model; also by Paulo Freire with his philosophy of education, and the "liberating approach" to education in contrast to the "conventional" and the "progressive" approaches (Freire 1972; Program Nasional Pengendalian Hama Terpadu 1989). Dilts (1985:88–90) referred to this type of training as "Training for Emancipation" (see also Program Nasional Pengendalian Hama Terpadu 1989).

13 The training for the selected extension workers was carried out at the end of the IPM training for the pest observers and was called "Orientation for Rice IPM Training." This training had an effective six (6) days of training with two main activities: 1) learning the IPM objectives and principles, the andragogy method, "two-way communication system," and group dynamics; following the pest observers in their field activities in observing the comparative plots, the experimental and other field studies, and making reports; and 2) preparing the implementation of the IPM Farmers Field School: selecting farmers groups; making contact and coordination to *Balai Penyuluh Pertanian* (BPP, Rural Extension Centre or REC) and other related agencies; and designing the IPM Farmers Field Schools' schedules and activites together with the pest observers.

14 The IPM field training for pest observers consisted of three seasons: i.e., the rice-IPM training season, the IPM Farmers Field School season and the secondary crop IPM training season. From the "experiential discovery learning" method practised in the first and third training seasons, the pest observers were expected to know "where the recommendation for IPM comes from, namely, from a proper ecosystem management" (Gallagher, personal communication 1991). Explanations to the farmers could thus be based on what they had learned and found from their own experiences with strong confidence in and respect for farmers. Learning to train farmers by training farmers was the aim of the second season's Farmers Field School's training. Through this experience, the pest observers were expected to be capable of teaching what they knew to others and carrying out the follow-up program with the farmers. In the fourth term, the pest observers took courses at the university to complete their course in the university (Diploma I-Degree).

15 While carrying out my fieldwork in 1990, I had not been officially admitted as a Ph.D. student at the Australian National University. Therefore, I did not get an official permit to have study leave from my superior, the Head of the Department of Anthropology at the University of Indonesia. As a result, I still had to give lectures in the 1990–1991 academic year. Only after leaving my country to pursue my study at the Australian National University, was I able to carry out full time observation in the 1991–1992 rainy season (November 1991 to end of February 1992). Therefore, I acknowledge the help of my research assistants (in the 1991 dry season and the 1991–1992 rainy season), and the farmers who always assisted me with stories of what they had experienced during my absence.

2
The "Genuine" Rice Farmers in their "Unbounded Niche"

1 *Kampung* refers to a hamlet. Henceforth, I will only use the names of the hamlets, e.g., Marga Tani or Kebon Cau.
2 Henceforth, I will use the acronym BPP *(Balai Penyuluhan Pertanian)* to refer to the Rural Extension Centre in the district of Ciasem.
3 The regency of Subang belongs to *Strata Pesisir Utara*—the northern flat coastal region—of the Province of West Java (together with the other five regencies: Tangerang, Bekasi, Karawang, Indramayu and Cirebon) (Hussein 1986:93). In terms of the elevation, cropping index, and cropping pattern, the regency of Subang is divided into three parts: 1) the northern part with an elevation of 0–20 m above sea level, the cropping pattern of rice-rice and a cropping index of 200; 2) the southern part with an elevation of 20–200 m above sea level, the cropping pattern of rice-rice-*palawija* (secondary crops) and a cropping index of >200; and 3) the most southern part with an elevation of 200–1600 m asl, plantation and horticulture and a cropping index up to 300 (Josef, Dinas Pertanian Tanaman Pangan Kabupaten Subang, personal communication 1990).
4 Some residents in Marga Tani recalled four waves of migrants from central West Java. First was the period after independence confrontation against the Dutch and the English (1948–49); second was the Darul Islam rebellion led by Kartosuwiryo in the 1960s; third was the opening of the PERUM Sang Hyang Seri in 1968; and the latest was the evacuation of people from Saguling, the place where the Saguling Dam was constructed in the 1980s.
5 Also see other studies on landholding and landownership among farmers in the northern region of Subang or other parts of JALUR PANTURA, which show a larger size of *sawah* owned/held by a farmer as compared to the size of *sawah* in the southern part of Subang or other villages in central West Java (e.g., Hayami and Kikuchi 1982; Wiradi and Manning 1984; Fujimoto 1986; Pincus 1991, 1996).
6 Fujimoto (1986:83) reports that share tenancies can be divided into subcategories according to the rate of sharing of the produce between two parties: 1) *maro,* equal sharing; 2) *mertelu,* one-third retained by the tenant and two-thirds paid as rent; 3) *merapat,* one-quarter retained by the tenant and three-quarters paid as rent. In Marga Tani, only the *maro* system operates.
7 Farmers have their own idioms for rice field measurement, i.e., 1 *bahu* equals 500 *bata* and one *bata* equals 14.3m². In terms of hectares, one *bahu* equals 0.71 ha. "Hectare" is also used by the farmers in translating their own measurements to the formal one.
8 See Fox (1993b) for the use of the term "rice basket" in his article on East Java.

9 In the rest of this book I will use the term KUD to refer to the Village Cooperative Unit. Farmers use this acronym to refer to the cooperative institution dealing with the government's subsidized scheme, KUT (*Kredit Usaha Tani*), farmers' credit package. In the first three seasons (in the 1987-88 rainy season, the 1988 dry season and the 1988-89 rainy season), the number of applicants came to more than 70% (between 52 and 57) of farmers. In 1990, the number of applicants declined sharply to six farmers (8.1%), due to a bad debt problem in the local KUD. See the history of KUD in Winarno (1985).

10 These absentee landowners come from various cities and rural areas in West Java and from nearby places. Not all of the sharecroppers in the rice field areas surrounding Marga Tani are residents in this hamlet. The absentee landowners have sharecropping agreements with farmers from nearby places as well.

11 Hayami and Kikuchi (1982:183) report that the *ceblokan* system is an old system, but has been introduced into the Subang area rather recently. Underlying the adoption process of this system was, according to them (Hayami and Kikuchi 1982:184), the decline in the return to labour relative to the return to land and capital due to the growth of the labour force against limited resources. Pincus (1996:94-126) disagrees with Hayami and Kikuchi's assumption. On the basis of his findings in three villages in Subang, Pincus (1996) assumes that the class structure and the relative bargaining power of the various agrarian classes play a role in the development of this kind of labour arrangement. Pincus (1996) agrees that these factors are bound up with the unique pattern of village formation in each location. In Marga Tani, which resembles the portrait of the North Subang village in Pincus's study, the cultivators prefer this system for *sawah* close to their residences. Besides reducing costs in return to the labour for weeding, under this system, the harvesters have the obligation to carry the grain home. Even though the cultivators have to tolerate the extended time the harvesters need to complete their jobs, bringing paddy home increases the chance of having a better bargaining position with the rice traders, The cultivators also claim that this system secures the opportunity for *neighbour*s and relatives to have a share in harvesting through the exclusive harvesting rights provided to them. Even though the harvesters do not receive wages for their preharvesting work (e.g., weeding), as Hayami and Kikuchi (1982:189) say, the stronger patron-client relationship reduces the risk of not finding employment.

12 Hayami and Kikuchi (1982:186) mention that the shift from *bawon* to *ceblokan* in their study area was almost completed by 1978. Until 1992, the *bawon* system in Marga Tani continued to exist. The people call the system *brandangan* where every one from within or outside the village can participate and receive a *bawon*. Bringing the grain home is a problem for *sawah* distant from home. However, the bigger share the cultivators can have and the shorter time for reaping and receiving the cash by selling the grain directly to the traders are also the benefits the cultivators can

gain from this system. However, this choice increases the chance of losing a better bargaining position in determining retail price.

13 The monthly rainfall data collected from 1989 to early 1992 shows that less than 100 mm of rain were recorded during the six-month period from May to October each year. No rainfall fell in October 1990 and August–September 1991. The highest rainfall (>200 mm) occurred in November–December 1990 and February, March, and December 1991 (source: Kantor Pengamatan Pengairan Ciasem 1992).

3

Keep the Plants Healthy: Spraying "Medicines"

1 Farmers' inferences about the relationship between the application of fertilizer, the fertile growth of paddy and the increased BPH population is in fact, concomitant with the scientists' discovery. Litsinger (1985:499) says that, "Fertilizer usage has increased with the development of fertilizer responsive varieties which in turn has increased pest abundance. Weeds also take up the fertilizer and grow faster than rice. Insects multiply faster from better nutrition." Also see Conway (1985) and Fox (1991) for the factors inducing crop vulnerability to disease and insect destruction.

2 *Sangga* and *ikat* (*pocong*) are the measurements farmers used at the time when they cultivated long-stem traditional rice varieties with the traditional hand knife (*ani-ani*). The harvest labourers used to cut the stems at the middle, tie them with ropes and bring them home to be dried and threshed. One *ikat* is one bundle of rice (one *pocong*). Two *ikat* (two *pocong, kuncèn*) become one *gèdèng* (around 10 kg of rice). One *sangga* consists of five *gèdèng* and 40 *sangga* constitute one *caèng*, which is similar to 2 tons of rice. Today, farmers use the sickle (*arit*), cut the stems close to the ground, and thresh them directly in the field. The harvest labourers (in the case of *ceblokan*) bring the seeds home and leave the stalks in the field. Hence, the measurement that farmers use nowadays is kilogram, *kuintal* (100 kg) or ton/*bahu*.

3 Rhoades and Bebbington (1988:328; also see Rhoades and Bebbington 1995) identify three kinds of experiments with potatoes carried out by Peruvian communities: a) curiosity experiments; b) problem-solving experiments; and c) adaptation experiments. Adaptation experiments can be of two kinds: 1) when farmers are testing an unknown component technology within a known environment; and 2) when farmers are testing a known technology within an unknown environment, such as a zone of colonization.

4 Haji Nafi, who has been a farmer since the 1940s, mentioned various rice varieties planted by farmers in that period. His list included: a) awned paddy (*padi bulu* or *paré gedé*) consisting of *padi Ruyung, Jerah, Benong, Walèn, Mambang, Kopo, Putih; Banjar Patoman, Paré Bodas, Kuntulan, Gènjah Mlati; Ranté, Gènjah Kopo, Menurun* and *Solo*; b) awnless paddy (*padi céréh*) consisting of *Céréh Usen, Rakim, Gembol, Abang/Beureum, Banji, Pandan, Belut, Gampung, Brandul* and others. The varieties of glutinous rice varieties were, among others, *ketan Randakaya, Mas, Item, Nangka Odèng,* and *Putih*. By means of experiment, farmers also adopted the improved rice varieties released by the Dutch-Indonesian breeding program. They also classified these varieties as *padi gagangan* or *padi jangkung* (long-stem rice varieties) like their traditional rice varieties. These included: *padi Bengawan, Gadis (Sigadis), Dewi Shinta, Jembar, Srèndèt, Angkong, Cempak, Jelita, Blaster* and *Jaèr* (see Fox 1991, 1993a for the genealogy of rice varieties).

5 The first chemical fertilizer introduced to farmers was urea (N). This component was strongly rejected by farmers in the early stage of the BIMAS program because of their understanding that their paddy would grow well without any chemical fertilizer. They refer to the introduction of urea as the period known as *Jaman* SIBA (CIBA Period). CIBA was the chemical company responsible for distributing the new rice varieties and urea to farmers in the form of credit. In return, farmers had to give 1/6 of their yields to the company (see Hansen 1978). Through trial and error, they gradually adopted this component after gaining confidence in the benefits of urea. The second component introduced to farmers was triple superphosphate (TSP) in the 1970s followed by potassium chloride (KCl) and ammonium sulphate (ZA, another nitrogen fertilizer that supplies some sulphur) in the mid 1980s. Haji Nafi told me that in the early period of BIMAS, farmers rejected urea, e.g., by throwing the bags of urea into streams. Now, farmers seek chemical fertilizers even if they have to borrow money from moneylenders, pay in credit from the shop owners, or get them through whatever means available.

6 Adiningsih et al. (1989) mentioned that the use of TSP (P) in the mid 1970s increased nearly threefold from the early 1970s. The government introduced TSP following the introduction of urea in the early 1960s. Figures from the 1988 P status map of the lowlands of Java reveal the expansion of areas with high P status. Adiningsih et al. (1989) noted that of the + 3.65 million ha of lowland soils in Java, 1.45 million ha had a high P status. In the lowland rice soils in West Java the area with high P status was larger than those with medium P status (Adiningsih et al. 1989:70). According to Adiningsih et al. (1989:70), "Due to the fact that P in the soil is not mobile, the residual effect of applications of TSP made over more than 20 years at rates greater than the uptake by the crop, P may have accumulated in lowland soils." Fox (1991) also mentions the high residual effect of P in TSP on most soils to which it is applied. He (1991:78) further says that, "... the repeated application of TSP, as has already occurred for the past decade in Indonesia, generally creates a soil reservoir of P." Despite the scientific evidence, officials in the Ministry

of Agriculture maintain that P is still required in both agricultural intensification and extensification. Satari (1987:13) says: "The residual value of P fertilizer is so high and important, so that the application of P fertilizers can be considered as a capital investment. The subsidy of P fertilizers can be considered as an investment grant for the farmer." Industrial and other interests also play a role in defining this policy.

7 There were several reasons for the delay in fertilizer applications, e.g., the late arrival of credit packages, the inability of farmers to purchase inputs in cash, or labour scarcity.

8 Ammonium sulphate (ZA) is primarily a nitrogen fertilizer. The government recommended farmers to use this fertilizer because it also supplies sulphur. One farmer who had tried to apply ZA, Haji Ali, told me that ZA was good to make the leaves greener, much greener than without ZA. However, he claimed that he had never received any explanation from agricultural officials about the substance of ZA.

9 Nazarea-Sandoval (1995:117–21) also found the distinction between "harmless" and "harmful" arthropods among farmers in the Philippines. According to her, these are local conceptions and not equivalent to the way the arthropods are classified in applied entomology.

10 Van de Fliert (1993:98) rephrases the proverb "Have an umbrella ready before it starts raining" as "Use an umbrella even when it does not rain," to portray more accurately farmers' perceptions about pest control in Grobogan, Central Java.

11 Many farmers perceived *Applaud* as similar to other pesticides, i.e., to "kill" brown plant hoppers and not to retard the growth of the nymphs. This stage in the brown plant hoppers' life cycle (nymph) was unknown by farmers (up to the 1989–1990 rainy season). A few farmers, however, told me that *Applaud* had the function of "rotting" or "freezing" (*membusukkan, membungkeri*) the brown plant hoppers' eggs.

12 At this period of harvest failure, farmers heard rumours that two brands of pesticides—counterfeit products, well known as the favourite liquid insecticide (*Thiodan*) and the granular insecticide (*Furadan*)—were being illegally produced by unknown parties. According to these rumours, these false products did not have the same function and strength as the genuine ones. In farmers' interpretations, one cause of the ineffectiveness of their practices in controlling white rice borer was their use of these apparently false products.

4

Spraying "Medicines" Is Old-Fashioned

1. For several weeks of training, the farmers did not receive any "pocket money" as usual. First, the trainers said that they did not receive the funds on time for that particular week. Later, they promised the farmers to use the money to order special T-shirts marked with the IPM badge for each participant. Until the "school" ended and until I left the field, the shirts had never been provided to the farmers. The farmers got very upset at this treatment. "We will accept the fact if there is no money for us to attend the 'school.' But don't cheat the farmers by telling a lie," complained many farmers in both places (C. Baru and C. Tengah).

2. Not assisting the farmers to make the "insect zoos" was later found in other places as well, even in the period of almost one decade later when I did my research in Central Lampung.

3. Also see the economic interest of providing permission to the chemical company's dealer to introduce a new brand of herbicide in the neighbouring village, ch. 1.

4. Hobart (1993:12) uses the term "discourse" as adapted from Foucault's term for "... the regularities of what is said and done, including, importantly, the conditions of knowledge and power with its inevitable closures."

5. The story presented in this session was the event observed after the opening ceremony held in Kebon Cau. The farmers were the IPM participants in Kebon Cau.

6. Rp.9,000.- at the time of my fieldwork (1990–92) was equivalent to US$4.50.

7. By referring to the IPM handbook he had, the pest observer stated the economic threshold of the following pests:

1.	WRB—*sundep* (deadhearts)	10% and above
	WRB—egg clusters	bundle of egg/3 m² (0.3)
2.	brown plant hopper	20/rice hill or above 1/stem
3.	rice gall midge	if the infected stem was found under 40 days of age
4.	rats	if there was an indicator of rats including signs of attack or dung, although the damage had not occurred yet
5.	cutworm/army worm	more than two/m²
6.	leaf folder (*hama putih; hama putih palsu*)	25% damage symptoms

7.	rice seed bugs	$5/m^2$ or above at the flowering stage
8.	blackbug	12/rice hill or above

For disease, farmers had to control it—without counting—if an indicator of disease attacks occurred.

5

"Now Our Way of Thinking Is Differemt"

1 In a rice farmer's world, these contextual factors consist of manpower or labour availability, capital and technological resources and constraints, local leadership and extension activities, government policies, ecological and market conditions, other farmers' activities, as well as individual purposes, intentions, beliefs and confidences

2 Also see Johnson-Laird and Wason (1977:14–15 referring to Wertheimer 1961) about the failure of learning among children who have to work out the area of a parallelogram according to a formula.

3 In Kebon Cau, I found two IPM farmers who decided to continue spraying with *Thiodan* on the day of the IPM opening ceremony. One farmer sprayed his nursery preventively as he usually did, whereas another farmer, Ujan, decided to spray the "sick" seedlings attacked by *sundep* (see the case of Ujan in chap. 4). Another IPM farmer, who learned about Ujan's plan critically reminded him about the *Camat*'s speech in which he had told farmers to avoid the inappropriate use of "medicine" (see chap. 4).

4 In week VIII, the head of BPP Ciasem and the acting pest observer who visited the IPM training in both Kebon Cau and Marga Tani told me that the day's count of moths trapped at the BPP office was already up to 122 (on 27th June 1990). The number reached 200 on 23rd June 1990. In the beginning of the "moths' flight" (*penerbangan kupu-kupu*) on 1st June 1990, there had been 70 moths trapped.

5 According to Kalshoven (1981:103), the nymphs of rice seed bugs feed on the "milk" ripe grains (*masak susu*) and continue feeding as adults, moving from older fields to new rice fields. Reissig et al. (1986:225) mentioned that these pests "have sucking mouthparts. To feed, they secrete a liquid to form a stylet sheath that hardens around the point of feeding and holds the mouthparts in place. Both nymphs and adults feed on rice grains. They prefer rice at milk stage but will also feed on soft and hard dough rice grains."

6 Kalshoven (1981:106) also mentions other circumstances that may further aggravate this situation. One is "the growing of different rice

varieties having differing maturation period. This can postpone harvest for 30 days (also see Reissig et al. 1986:222 on staggered planting as a possible cause of outbreak)."

7 Ou (1973:10) says that this disease causes very heavy losses: "It causes poorly developed grains, increases underdeveloped grains, reduces the weight of grains." This disease is also spread quickly (Ou 1973:17).

8 On the basis of the printed materials provided by the National IPM Program, Ayim, on his own initiative, used these materials to introduce to his hamlet and rice-field neighbours the concept of natural enemies. He also taught them about insects that belonged to this category, various other pests and the WRB moths and eggs. Whenever he went to his *sawah*, he took these materials with him. Idham and other farmers also used these leaflets when discussing their own findings.

6

Voicing for Freedom, Striving for Harvests

1 When I visited the BPP office to find out about the follow-up processing of the farmers' requests, I found that the form had already been filled in completely by the extension worker. One of the BPP staff who had been recently placed in this BPP told me that it was the first time he had found that the extension worker had himself completed the form.

2 Van der Eng (1993:103) also mentions that the principle of persistent persuasion (*perintah halus*) in agricultural extension was gradually reintroduced after Indonesia's independence. In 1905 the colonial government had explicitly renounced the use of this principle in agricultural extension.

3 The KUD official in Sukamandi Jaya, Ciasem told me that for one hectare *sawah*, farmers would receive the complete credit package consisting of: 1) fertilizers: 200 kg urea, and 100 kg each of TSP, KCl and ZA; 2) carbofuran (granular pesticide: 20 kg); 3) carbamat (liquid pesticide: 1.0 l); 4) herbicide: 0.5 l; 5) foliar fertilizer: 1 kg; and 6) cash: Rp.30,000.- (A$20,00). In the 1990 dry season, the total value of KUT for 1 ha of *sawah* was Rp.230,000. (A$153,33). Rp.6,500 was deducted for the administrative fee. Farmers reported that the price of fertilizers at that time was Rp.18,000/100 kg for urea, Rp.21,000/100 kg for TSP and Rp.20,000/100 kg for KCl.

4 In October 1990, there was a zero (0) mm-monthly rainfall as observed by the *Kantor Pengamatan Pengairan Ciasem* (see data on rainfall, chap. 2). The Agricultural Research Station in Sukamandi (BALITTAN *Sukamandi*) reported that at the time of the early outbreak of WRB in several places in JALUR PANTURA was found in 1988–89, the rainfall was below normal

in September to November (<100 m/decade). These weather conditions were probably suitable for the reproduction of WRB. The diverse planting schedules in one water region, even in one rice field area, could also accelerate the population growth of this pest (Balai Penelitian Tanaman Pangan Sukamandi 1990:37; also see Suharto and Kertoseputro 1989). Sosromarsono (n.d:3) by referring to van der Goot (1925), says that two factors correlated quite well to bring about the outbreak of this pest, i.e., the planting schedule and the weather conditions in the beginning of the rainy season. Rauf (1990:11) also says that prior to 1940, the outbreak of WRB would occur if the previous dry season was too dry and the rainy season came late.

5 According to the Food and Agricultural Organization-Institut Pertanian Bogor (FAO-IPB) Field Laboratorium team who carried out studies on WRB population dynamics and its control strategies in Karawang (Panyingkiran—Rawamerta) in 1990–1991, WRB can only develop in one region if the number of insects at the end of a fallow period exceeds the minimum population threshold. To reach this, WRB must have a high population to go through the diapause period and the emergence of moths at the same time. The longer the period of diapause, the shorter the reaction time for moths to emerge (from the first rainfall until the emergence of moths). Even though the new generation of these moths has a relatively uniform age, the period from laying eggs up to the emergence of moths varies widely (from 24 to 45 days). Hence, the age distribution of WRB population in the next generation will be more diverse. The population entering the diapause period in the dry season is affected by the growth rate in the previous rainy season. In the recent agroecosystem conditions, the rapid growth rate of WRB is likely to be related to its relatively high life potential, particularly in the areas largely planted with *IR64* in which the life of third generation WRB is concomitant with the plant stage that provides a relatively high life potential to the insects. Other possible factors are the injudicious use of pesticides that can eradicate WRB predators and increase their fertility if used below the recommended dosage, and the increased use of foliar fertilizer that can accelerate population growth (Program Nasional Pelatihan dan Pengembangan Pengendalian Hama Terpadu 1991b:4–6).

6 Ayim raised the idea of providing rewards of Rp.500/moth and Rp.250/egg cluster at this early stage of white rice borer outbreak when farmers had not yet discovered a high number of moths and egg clusters. A year later (1991–1992), a farmer mentioned the idea of paying wages for collecting egg clusters with the price of Rp.25/egg cluster, one-tenth cheaper than Ayim's first idea.

7 The extension worker in the next village had introduced the stages of larvae (*instar*) in IPM training (Extension IPM Farmers' Field Schools) held in this season. The BPP staff had also been familiar with this knowledge, but no information had been transmitted to farmers in Marga Tani. Kalshoven (1981, 245) mentions that five larval stages are known. Sosromarsono (n.d.:4–7) describes in detail each stage of larva—in

which the larva changes its skins—in terms of length, form and colour, i.e., *instar one, instar two, instar three, instar four, instar five* and then pupae. For further discussion, see Sosromarsono (n.d) and van der Goot (1925). Rustam learned about these different larval stages accidentally from my conversation with him when I referred to the term used by the extension workers in other places.

8 Ayim's inference, in fact, corresponded to the pest observer's account of the moths trapped by the light-trap at the BPP office. On December 26, 1990 there were two moths trapped, but the next day the number increased to 28 and reached its peak on January 2, 1991 (317 moths). The population then reduced to seven on January 22, 1991 and then increased again. On January 28 the population reached 33 moths, but at the peak of the flight (on February 6, 1991) it multiplied to 6,031 moths. After that, the number declined gradually to 41 moths on February 28, 1991 (BPP Ciasem, 1990–1991).

9 At this period, many farmers (IPM and non-IPM farmers) came regularly in the evening for a couple of weeks during the Gulf War in the Middle East to watch the news on Haji Ali's television. Some of them came to play badminton in the yard. From Haji Ali and my activities in recording farmers' reports and findings, until 20 February 1991, the total recorded egg clusters collected by 20 farmers (IPM and non-IPM) amounted to 30,000 egg clusters from around 25 ha *sawah*.

10 Armin was the one who put the light trap on the floor of his terrace. The result of my counting of dead moths at Armin's house the next day (up to 4,500 moths) was then used by Armin to warn other farmers working in the mosque to control WRB in their fields, as Idham and Ayim had in warning of the need to control moths.

11 In one of the IPM sessions, the IPM trainers asked farmers to draw a food web with each group drawing the web of one pest. By drawing, farmers were expected to find the prey and the predators themselves. Different groups had different tasks as well. In such a training session based on "learning by doing," farmers did not receive a comprehensive explanation of the food webs of all pests found in the rice environment nor the life cycle of each predator and the duration of each stage in the cycle.

12 In one case, I brought home several egg clusters that, according to a non-IPM farmer, had already been sprayed with *Applaud* and hence would "freeze" (*jadi bungker, beku*). At home (Haji Ali's place) I put the egg clusters in the plastic bag as the farmers did. From Haji Ali's findings later, the egg clusters hatched. This evidence was used by Ayim and Haji Ali to prove that "freezing" egg clusters by spraying was invalid.

13 In fact, Kalshoven (1981:248) says that direct methods including hand collection of egg clusters and moths in the *sawahs* are not successful. On the other hand, collecting the egg masses in the seed beds is considered effective and feasible (see Oka 1991; Program Nasional Pelatihan dan Pengembangan Pengendalian Hama Terpadu 1991b).

14 In the 1991–1992 rainy season, I also discovered that some farmers in C. Tengah, the neighbouring village, practiced Islamic rituals and had recourse to God's assistance to combat the severe rat attacks after failing to prevent the outbreak.

15 For example, Sukim told me that "paddy transplanted in month eleven (*bulan sebelas*) were good, those transplanted in month twelve (*bulan duabelas*) on the 20th were bad, and those transplanted later than that, were good again. Thus, the most important thing was that the transplanting schedule should be in month eleven. If it has to be delayed, delay it totally. Don't transplant in the middle. I know this because I took notes. Those transplanted between the 20th–25th had the most severe damage, the 15th still escaped. I transplanted my paddy on the 15th of December and it was good." Instead of the date of transplanting, Armin referred to the date when panicles came out (*waktu padi ke luar*). He mentioned that paddy where panicles came out in the period between the 17th–25th of February 1991 had the worst performance. Armin's wife could also differentiate between the differences in yields according to transplanting schedule even though she was not able to give the dates as Armin did.

7

Recreating Knowledge and Persisting Paradigm

1 See van Dorp and Rulkens (1993:120) on farmers' varietal selection on four major mandate crops: soybean, maize, cassava and sweet potato among farmers in Lombok and Sumbawa. Although rice is different from these crops, some criteria in farmers' selection were similar to what I found among rice farmers, i.e., the agronomy aspects such as yield, maturity period and resistance to pests/diseases and the product quality, such as price at the market, taste, and texture.

2 When I returned in 1996, *Sido Muncul* replaced *IR64* as the dominant variety planted in the dry season. The yield production was similar to *IR64*. Since it has a longer maturity period than *IR64*, the farmers considered it more resistant to rat attack than *IR64*. However, farmers knew that *Sido Muncul*, a nonhigh-yielding variety, was not resistant to brown plant hopper, and hence, the majority of them planted *IR64* in the rainy season. Rotating variety instead of continuous planting of one variety became a common practice.

3 When I carried out my observation in Central Lampung in 1998, the farmers in this area were also enforced to receive the pesticide component in the subsidized scheme.

4 In 1995, the government introduced a new form of urea to replace the granules, in the form of tablets. The way the government forced the

farmers to use the new form of urea was memorized by the farmers as similar to the way the government forced them to use urea for the first time in the early years of the Green Revolution.

5 In 1998, a similar case was found in Central Lampung when the local extension worker sent the chemical substances to the farmers' leader's residence without his consent. The farmers' leader, who was also a local IPM facilitator, was forced to receive the chemical substances under the threat that if he refused, the credit-scheme would not be forwarded. Very conflicted, he accepted the forced delivery.

6 Not all farmers perceived *sundep* as originating from white moths and larvae that at the reproductive stage caused the symptoms of *beluk*. Some mentioned that they found larvae inside the stems, but those larvae were not WRB larvae. Instead, they came from inside or from above the ground. Some farmers interpreted *sundep* as a different kind of "illness," such as a kind of "red disease" caused by wind, rotten roots or illness from the ground. Since some farmers did not find any larvae while examining the stems, they said that there were no "pests" or, metaphorically, no "people" (*tidak ada orangnya*) inside the stems. In contrast to farmers' knowledge of *sundep*, a more common understanding was achieved about the cause of *beluk* or *penggerek batang*, namely the white moths, egg clusters and larvae boring inside the stems. Only the IPM farmers and those who had close communication with farmers, such as Idham and Ayim, had an idea that the pupa before the larva becomes a moth.

7 From the IPM project leader, I received information that the pest observers in West Java—after graduating from the university—should return to their main job in monitoring pests and disease in food crops. They were not allowed to assist farmers directly, contrary to those in the province of East Java (Dilts, personal communication 1992).

8 The common old phrase is: "Having an umbrella ready before the rain comes" (*Sedia payung sebelum hujan*).

9 The preventative measures explained by the scientist were: broadcasting carbofuran in its appropriate dosage in the nurseries as soon as the farmers found moths or egg clusters; changing the pattern of cultivation from rice-rice-fallow period (*padi-padi-bera*) into rice-rice secondary crops (*padi-padi-palawija*). The planting of secondary crops would cut the WRB life cycle. This was then contested by the farmers from C. Tengah who had practised soybean planting and yet were experiencing the outbreak.

10 When mentioning this insecticide (*Padan*), the expert asked me to keep this information "off the record." The use of this insecticide was still in the trial-and-error stage and had not been recommended to farmers. He also warned the farmers to use the safety measures to avoid direct contact with the substance.

8

Seeds of Knowledge

1 From 1993 onward, many more IPM follow-up activities were held in many places in Java and other provinces. These activities include other similar training financed by the National Program or other local regional sources, the building up of networks among the IPM alumni, or the conducting of workshops and seminars. Through these programs, many more farmers had the chance to gain access to IPM knowledge and principles. The dissemination of knowledge among farmers themselves is also supported by the formation of network and other activities. Unfortunately, up to the 1996–1997 rainy season when I visited my research sites again, there had been no follow-up activities held among the farmers' communities in both Ciasem Baru and Ciasem Tengah, the first villages to receive IPM in the district of Ciasem.

Bibliography

Adimihardja, K.
1989 Manusia Sunda dan alam lingkungannya: suatu kajian kes mengenai kehidupan sosiobudaya dan ekologi komuniti Kasepuhan Desa Sirnarasa Jawa Barat Indonesia. Ph.D. thesis. Bangi: Fakulti Sains Kemasyarakatan dan Kemanusiaan, University Kebangsaan Malaysia.

Adiningsih, J.S., D. Santoso, and M. Sudjadi
1989 The status of N, P, K and S of lowland rice soils in Java. In *Sulfur fertilizer policy for lowland and upland rice cropping systems in Indonesia*, edited by G. Blair and R. Lefroy. Proceedings of a seminar held at Jakarta 18–20 July 1989, 68–76. Burwood: Brown Prior Anderson.

Agrawal, A.
1995 Indigenous and scientific knowledge: some critical comments. *Indigenous Knowledge and Development Monitor* 3(1):3–6.

Arce, A., and N. Long
1992 The dynamics of knowledge: interfaces between bureaucrats and peasants. In *Battlefields of knowledge: The interlocking of theory and practice in social research and development*, edited by N. Long and A. Long, 211–46. London: Routledge.

1993 Bridging two worlds: An ethnography of bureaucrat-peasant relations in western Mexico. In *An anthropological critique of development: The growth of ignorance*, edited by M. Hobart, 179–208. London: Routledge.

Badan Urusan Logistik
1976 Special country studies on national rice policies: Indonesia. Jakarta. Manuscript.

Bahagiawati, A., and I.N. Oka
1987   Perkembangan biotipe wereng coklat *Nilaparvata lugens.* stal. di Indonesia. In *Wereng coklat,* edited by J. Soejitno, Z. Harahap, and H.S. Suprapto, 31–42. Bogor: Badan Penelitian Tanaman Pangan.

Balai Desa Ciasem Baru
1990   Report on white rice stem borer's damage on rice. Ciasem.

Balai Penelitian Tanaman Pangan Sukamandi
1990   Laporan tahunan 1989/90—Balittan Sukamandi. Sukamandi: Badan Penelitian dan Pengembangan Pertanian.

Barlow, C., and C. Condie
1986   Changing economic relationships in Southeast Asian agriculture, and their implications for small farmers. *Outlook on Agriculture* 15(4):167–78.

Barth, F.
1967   On the study of social change. *American Anthropologist* 69:661–69.
1981   *Process and form in social life: Selected essays of Fredrik Barth:* Vol. 1. London: Routledge & Kegan Paul.
[1966] 1984   *Models of social organization.* London: Royal Anthropological Institute of Great Britain and Ireland.
1987   *Cosmologies in the making: A generative approach to cultural variation in inner New Guinea.* Cambridge: Cambridge University Press.
1989   The analysis of culture in complex societies. *Ethnos* 54(1–2):120–42.
1990   The guru and the conjurer: Transactions in knowledge and the shaping of culture in Southeast Asia and Melanesia. *Man* 25:640–53.
1993   *Balinese worlds.* Chicago: The University of Chicago Press.
1994   A personal view of present tasks and priorities in cultural and social anthropology. In *Assessing cultural anthropology,* edited by R. Borofsky, 349–61. New York: McGraw-Hill.
1995   Other knowledge and other ways of knowing. *Journal of Anthropological Research* 51:65–68.
2002   Sidney W. Mintz lecture for 2000: An anthropology of knowledge. *Current Anthropology* 42(1):1–18.

Beek, W.E.A. van de
1993   Processes and limitations of Dogon agricultural knowledge. In *An anthropological critique of development: The growth of ignorance*, edited by M. Hobart, 43–60. London: Routledge.

Bentley, J.W.
1989   What farmers don't know can't help them: The strengths and weaknesses of indigenous technical knowledge in Honduras. *Agriculture and Human Values* 6(3):25–31.
1992   Alternatives to pesticides in Central America: Applied studies of local knowledge. *Culture and Agriculture* 44:10–13.
1994   Stimulating farmer experiments in non-chemical pest control in Central America. In *Beyond farmer first: rural people's knowledge, agricultural research and extension practice*, edited by I. Scoones and J. Thompson, 147–50. London: Intermediate Technology Publications.

Bentley, J.W., and K.L. Andrews
1991   Pests, peasants, and publications: Anthropological and entomological views of integrated pest management program for small-scale Honduran farmers. *Human Organization* 50(2):113–24.
1996   *Through the roadblocks: IPM and Central American smallholders*. Sustainable Agriculture Programme Gatekeeper Series 56. London: IIED.

Bentley, J.W., J. Castaño-Zapata, and K.L. Andrews
1995   World integrated pathogen and pest management and sustainable agriculture in the developing world. *Advances in Plant Pathology* 11:247–72.

Bentley, J.W., and G. Rodriguez
2001   Honduran folk entomology. *Current Anthropology* 42(2): 285–300.

Bentley, J.W., G. Rodriguez, and A. Gonzalez
1994   Science and people: Honduran *campesinos* and natural pest control inventions. *Agriculture and Human Values* 11(2/3):178–82.

Berger, P.L., and T. Luckmann
1966   *The social construction of reality: A treatise in the sociology of knowledge*. New York: Garden City.

Birowo, A.T., and G.E. Hansen
1981   Agricultural and rural development. In *Agricultural and rural development in Indonesia*, edited by G.E. Hansen, 1–27. Westview Special Studies in Social, Political, and Economic Development. Boulder: Westview Press.

Bloor, D.
1983   *Wittgenstein: A social theory of knowledge*. London: The Macmillan Press.

Borofsky, R.
1987   *Making history: Pukapukan and anthropological constructions of knowledge*. Cambridge: Cambridge University Press.
1994a   Rethinking the cultural. In *Assessing cultural anthropology*, edited by R. Borofsky, 243–49. New York: McGraw-Hill.
1994b   The cultural in motion. In *Assessing cultural anthropology*, edited by R. Borofsky, 313–19. New York: McGraw-Hill.
1994c   On the knowledge and knowing of cultural activities. In *Assessing cultural anthropology*, edited by R. Borofsky, 331–48. New York: McGraw-Hill.
1994d   Assessing the field. In *Assessing cultural anthropology*, edited by R. Borofsky, 468–91. New York: McGraw-Hill.

Bosch, R. van den
1978   *The pesticide conspiracy*. Garden City, NY: Doubleday.

Boster, J.S.
1985   "Requiem for the omnicient informant": There's life in the old girl yet. In *Directions in cognitive anthropology*. edited by J.W.D. Dougherty, 177–97. Urbana: University of Illinois Press.
1986   Exchange of varieties and information between Aguaruna manioc cultivators. *American Anthropologist* 88(2): 428–36.

Bottrell, D.R.
1979   *Integrated pest management*. Washington, DC: Council on Environmental Quality.

Boudon, R.
1982   *The unintended consequences of social action*. New York: St. Martin's Press.

Bourdieu, P.
1977   *Outline of a theory of practice*. New York: Cambridge University Press.

1990 *The logic of practice.* Cambridge: Polity.

Boyd, R., and P.J. Richerson
1985 *Culture and the evolutionary process.* Chicago: The University of Chicago Press.
1993 Rationality, imitation, and tradition. In *Nonlinear dynamics and evolutionary economics,* edited by R.H. Day and P. Chen, 131–49. New York: Oxford University Press.

Bratman, M.E.
1992 Practical reasoning and acceptance in a context. *Mind* 101(401):1–15.

Brewer, J.D.
1979 *Agricultural knowledge and cultural practice in two Indonesian villages.* Ph.D. diss., University of California, Los Angeles.

Brokensha, D., D.M. Warren, and O. Werner, eds.
1980 *Indigenous knowledge systems and development.* Lanham: University Press of America.

Brookfield, M.
1996 Indigenous knowledge: A long history and an uncertain future. *PLEC News and Views* 6:23–29.

Brosius, J.P., G.W. Lovelace, and G.G. Marten
1986 Ethnoecology: An approach to understanding traditional agricultural knowledge. In *Traditional agriculture in Southeast Asia: A human ecology perspective,* edited by G.G. Marten, 187–96. Boulder and London: Westview Press.

Bruner, E.M.
1993 Epilogue: creative persona and the problem of authenticity. In *Creativity/Anthropology,* edited by S. Lavie, K. Narayan, and R. Rosaldo, 321–32. Ithaca and London: Cornell University Press.

Cancian, F.
1967 Stratification and risk taking: A theory tested on agricultural innovation. *American Sociological Review* 23:912–27.
1980 Risk and uncertainty in agricultural decision making. In *Agricultural decision making: Anthropological contributions to rural development,* edited by P.F. Barlett, 161–76. New York: Academic Press.

Carson, R.
1962   *Silent spring*. New York: Fawcett Crest Books.

Chaiklin, S.
1996   Understanding the social scientific practice of *Understanding practice*. In *Understanding practice: Perspectives on activity and context*, edited by S. Chaiklin and J. Lave, 377–401. Cambridge: Cambridge University Press.

Chambers, R.
1992   Beyond traditional knowledge: enabling them and changing us. Note for the SAREC Workshop on People's Participation in the Management of Natural Resources—Research Needs and Research Priorities. Stockholm 5–6 October.

1994   Foreword. In *Beyond farmer first: Rural people's knowledge, agricultural research and extension practice*, edited by I. Scoones and J. Thompson, xiii–xvi. London: Intermediate Technology Publications.

Chambers, R., A. Pacey, and L.A. Thrupp, eds.
1989   *Farmer first: farmer innovation and agricultural research*. London: Intermediate Technology Publications.

Chambers, R., R. Longhurst, and A. Pacey, eds.
1981   *Seasonal dimension to rural poverty*. London: Frances Pinter.

Choesin, E.M.
2002   Connectionism: alternatif dalam memahami dinamika pengetahuan local dalam globalisasi. *Antropologi Indonesia* 26 (69):1–9.

Collier, W.L., A. Soentoro, G. Wiradi, E. Pasandaran, K. Santoso, and J.F. Stepanek
1982   Acceleration of rural development of Java. *Bulletin of Indonesian Economic Studies* 13(3):84–101.

Colson, E.
1984   The reordering of experience: Anthropological involvement with time. *Journal of Anthropological Research* 40(1): 1–13.

Conklin, H.C.
1957   *Hanunoo agriculture: A report on an integral system of shifting cultivation in the Philippines*. Development Paper 12. Rome: FAO Forestry Division.

Connerton, P.
1989   *How societies remember.* Cambridge: Cambridge University Press.

Conway, G.R.
1985   Agroecosystem analysis. *Agricultural Administration* 20:31–55.

Conway, G.R., and E.B. Barbier
1990   *After the green revolution: Sustainable agriculture for development.* London: Earthscan Publications.

Conway, G.R.,and J.N. Pretty
1991   *Unwelcome harvest: Agricultural pollution.* London: Earthscan Publications.

Crick, M.R.
1982   Anthropology of knowledge. *Annual Review of Anthropology* 11:287–313.

D'Andrade, R.
1987   A folk model of the mind. In *Cultural models in language and thought,* edited by D. Holland and N. Quinn, 112–48. Cambridge: Cambridge University Press.
1995   *The development of cognitive anthropology.* Cambridge: Cambridge University Press.

Departemen Pertanian
1987   Memantapkan kelestarian swasembada pangan tahun 2000 dan seterusnya. Jakarta.

Dilts, R., and S. Hate
1996   IPM farmers' field schools: Changing paradigms and scaling-up. *Agricultural Research & Extension Network* 59b:1–4.

Dilts, R.
1985   Training: re-schooling society? *Prisma* 38:78–90. (English ed.)

Dinas Pertanian Tanaman Pangan Propinsi Jawa Barat.
1991   Laporan tahunan 1990: buku II. Bandung: Pemerintah Propinsi Daerah Tingkat I Jawa Barat.

Dorp, M. van, and T. Rulkens
1993   Farmer crop-selection criteria and genebank collections in Indonesia. In *Cultivating knowledge: Genetic diversity,*

farmer experimentation and crop research, edited by W. de Boef, K. Amanor, K. Wellard, and A. Bebbington, 119–27. London: Intermediate Technology Publications.

Dougherty, J.W.D., and C.M. Keller
1985   A practical approach to knowledge structures. In *Directions in cognitive anthropology*, edited by J.W.D. Dougherty, 161–74. Urbana: University of Illinois Press.

Douglas, M., and A. Wildavsky
1983   *Risk and culture: An essay on the selection of technological and enviromental dangers.* Berkeley: University of California Press.

Dove, M.R.
1988   Introduction: Traditional culture and development in contemporary Indonesia. In *The real and imagined role of culture in development: Case studies from Indonesia*, edited by M.R. Dove, 1–37. Honolulu: University of Hawaii Press.

1993   Uncertainty, humility, and adaptation in the tropical forest: the agricultural augury of the Kantu. *Ethnology* 40 (2):145–67.

2000   The life-cycle of indigenous knowledge, and the case of natural rubber production. In *Indigenous environmental knowledge and its transformations: Critical anthropological perspectives*, edited by R. Ellen, P. Parkes, and A. Bicker, 213–54. Amsterdam: Harwood Academic Publishers.

Elster, J.
1983   *Explaining technical change: A case study in the philosophy of science.* Cambridge: Cambridge University Press.

1989   *Nuts and bolts for the social sciences.* Cambridge: Cambridge University Press.

Eng, P. van der
1993   *Agricultural growth in Indonesia since 1880: productivity change and the impact of government policy.* Rijksuniversiteit Groningen: Universiteitsdrukkerij.

Fairhead, J.
1993   Representing knowledge: The "new farmer" in research fashions. In *Practising development: social science perspectives*, edited by J. Pottier, 187–204. London: Routledge.

Fairhead, J., and M. Leach
1994   Declarations of difference. In *Beyond farmer first: Rural people's knowledge, agricultural research and extension practice*, edited by I. Scoones and J. Thompson, 75–79. London: Intermediate Technology Publications.

Fliert, E. van de
1993   *Integrated pest management: Farmer field schools generate sustainable practices: a case study in central Java evaluating IPM training*. Wageningen: Agricultural University Wageningen.

Fliert, E. van de, and Y.T. Winarto
1993   From technological packages to ecological principles. *ILEIA* 2:16–18.

Food and Agricultural Organization
1990   Mid-term review of FAO intercountry program for the development and application of integrated pest control in rice in South and South East Asia. Mission Report phase II. Jakarta.
1991   Mid-term review mission: Training and development of integrated pest management in rice-based cropping system. Mission Report. Jakarta.

Foucault, M.
1982/83   Afterword: the subject and power. In *Michel Foucault: Beyond structuralism and hermeneutics*, edited by H.L. Dreyfus and P. Rabinow, 208–26. Chicago: The University of Chicago Press.

Fox, J.J.
1991   Managing the ecology of rice production in Indonesia. In *Indonesia: Resources, ecology, and environment*, edited by J. Hardjono, 61–84. Singapore: Oxford University Press.
1993a   Ecological policies for sustaining high production in rice: Observations on rice intensification in Indonesia. In *South-East Asia's environmental future: The search for sustainability*, edited by H. Brookfield and Y. Byron, 211–24. Tokyo: United Nations University Press.
1993b   The rice baskets of East Java: The ecology and social context of *sawah* production. In *Balanced development: East Java in the new order*, edited by H. Dick, J.J. Fox, and J. Mackie, 120–57. Oxford: Oxford University Press.

Freeman, D.
[1955] 1992 *The Iban of Borneo.* Kuala Lumpur: S. Abdul Majeed. (Originally published. as *Report on the Iban of Sarawak*).

Freire, P.
1972 *Pedagogy of the oppressed.* Harmondsworth: Penguin Education.

Frossard, D.
1998 Peasant science: A new paradigm for sustainable development? *Research in Philosophy and Technology* 17:111–26.

Fujimoto, A.
1986 Share tenancy and rice production: Lessons from two village studies in West Java. In *An economic study of rice farming in West Java: a farm household survey of two villages in Bandung and Subang,* edited by A. Fujimoto and T. Matsuda, 81–99. Tokyo: Nodai Research Institute, Tokyo University of Agriculture.

Fujisaka, S.
1995 Incorporating farmers' knowledge in international rice research. In *The cultural dimension of development: Indigenous knowledge systems,* edited by D.M. Warren, L.J. Slikkerveer, and D. Brokensha, 124–39. London: Intermediate Technology Publications.

Gallagher, K.
n.d. *Pengendalian hama terpadu untuk padi: Suatu pendekatan ekologi.* Jakarta: Program Nasional Pengendalian Hama Terpadu.

Gardner, P.M.
1976 Birds, words, and a requiem for the omniscient informant. *American Ethnologist* 3(3):446–68.

Gatewood, J.B.
1985 Actions speak louder than words In *Directions in cognitive anthropology,* edited by J.W.D. Dougherty, 199–219. Urbana: University of Illinois Press.

Gladwin, H., and M. Murtaugh
1980 The attentive-preattentive distinction in agricultural decision making. In *Agricultural decision making: Anthropological contributions to rural development*, edited by P.F. Bartlett, 115–36. New York: Academic Press.

Goodell, G.E.
1983 Improving administrators' feedback concerning extension, training and research relevance at the local level: new approaches and findings from Southeast Asia. *Agricultural Administration* 13:39–55.

Goodenough, W.H.
1994 Toward a working theory of culture. In *Assessing cultural anthropology*, edited by R. Borofsky, 262–75. New York: McGraw-Hill.

Goody, J.
1987 Foreword. In *Cosmologies in the making: A generative approach to cultural variation in inner New Guinea*, edited by F. Barth, vii–xi. Cambridge: Cambridge University Press.

Goot, P. van der
1925 *Levenswijze en bestrijding van den witten rijstboorder op Java*. Mededeelingen van het Instituut voor Plantenziekten no.66. Wageningen: H. Veenman & Zonen.

Haliman, A., and G. Williams
1983 Can people move bureaucratic mountains? Developing primary health care in rural Indonesia. *Social Science Medicine* 17(19):1449–55.

Hanks, W.F.
1991 Foreword. In *Situated learning: Legitimate peripheral learning*, edited by J. Lave and E. Wenger, 13–24. Cambridge: Cambridge University Press.

Hansen, G.E.
1978 Bureaucratic linkages and policy-making in Indonesia: BIMAS revisited. In *Political power and communications in Indonesia*, edited by K.W. Jackson and L.W. Pye, 322–42. Berkeley: University of California Press.

Hardjono, J.
1983 Rural development in Indonesia: The "top-down" approach. In *Rural development and the state*, edited by D.A.M. Leam and D.P. Chaudhri, 38–65. London: Methuen.

Harker, R., C.Mahar, and C. Wilkes
1990 *An introduction to the work of Pierre Bourdieu: The practice of theory*. Hampshire: The MacMillan Press.

Harper, D.
1987 *Working knowledge: Skill and community in a small shop.* Chicago: University of Chicago Press.

Hayami, Y., and M. Kikuchi.
1982 *Asian village economy at the cross roads: An economic approach to institutional change.* Tokyo: University of Tokyo Press.

Healey, C.J.
1978/79 Taxonomic rigidity in biological folk classification: Some examples from the Maring of New Guinea. *Ethnomethodology* 5(3/4):361–83.

Hirschman, A.O.
1970 *Exit, voice, and loyalty: Responses to decline in firms, organizations, and states.* Cambridge, MA: Harvard University Press.

Hobart, M.
1993 Introduction: the growth of ignorance? In *An anthropological critique of development: The growth of ignorance,* edited by M. Hobart, 1–30. London: Routledge.

Holy, L., and M. Stuchlik
1981 The structure of folk models. In *The structure of folk models,* edited by L. Holy and M. Stuchlik, 1–34. London: Academic Press.
1983 *Actions, norms and representations: Foundations of anthropological inquiry.* Cambridge: Cambridge University Press.

Howes, M., and R. Chambers
1979 Indigenous technical knowledge: Analysis, implications and issues. *IDS Bulletin* 10(2):5–11.

Hull, T.H.
1976 *Almanak penanggalan Jawa-Masehi untuk penelitian sosial-ekonomi.* Yogyakarta: Lembaga Kependudukan Universitas Gadjah Mada.

Hunter, I.M.L.
1977 Mental calculation. In *Thinking: Readings in cognitive science,* edited by P.N. Johnson-Laird and P.C. Wason, 35–45. Cambridge: Cambridge University Press.

Hussein, S.
1986 An analysis of the agricultural knowledge system of Indonesia. Ph.D. diss. Cornell University.

Indonesian National IPM Program.
n.d. *Farmers as experts.* Jakarta.

Jarvie, I.C.
1969 *The revolution in anthropology.* Chicago: Henry Regnery Company.

Jay, R.R.
1969 *Javanese villagers: Social relations in rural Modjokuto.* Cambridge: The Massachusetts Institute of Technology.

Johnson, A.W.
1971 Security and risk-taking among poor peasants: A Brazilian case. In *Studies in economic anthropology,* edited by G. Dalton, 143–50. Anthropological Studies no. 7. Washington DC: American Anthropological Association.
1972 Individuality and experimentation in traditional agriculture. *Human Ecology* 1(2):149–59.
1974 Ethnoecology and planting practices in a swidden agricultural system. *American Ethnologist* 1(1):87–101.
1976 Individuality and experimentation in traditional agriculture. In *Human ecology: An environmental approach,* edited by P. Richerson and J. McEvoy III. North Scituate, MA: Duxbury Press.

Johnson-Laird, P.N., and P.C. Wason
1977 An introduction to the scientific study of thinking. In *Thinking: Readings in cognitive science,* edited by P.N. Johnson-Laird and P.C. Wason, 1–27. Cambridge: Cambridge University Press.

Kalshoven, L.G.E.
1981 *Pests of crops in Indonesia.* Jakarta: PT Ichtiar Baru—Van Hoeve.

Kearney, M.
1996 *Reconceptualizing the peasantry: Anthropology in global perspective.* Boulder: Westview Press.

Keesing, R.M.
1987 Models, "folk" and "cultural": paradigms regained. In *Cultural models in language and thought,* edited by D.

Holland and N. Quinn, 369–93. Cambridge: Cambridge University Press.

1994 Theories of culture revisited. In *Assessing cultural anthropology*, edited by R. Borofsky, 301–12. New York: McGraw-Hill.

Keller, C., and J.D. Keller

1993 Thinking and acting with iron. In *Understanding practice: Perspectives on activity and context*, edited by S. Chaiklin and J. Lave, 125–42. Cambridge: Cambridge University Press.

Kemp, J.

1988 *Seductive mirage: The search for the village community in Southeast Asia.* Dordrecht: Foris Publications.

Kenmore, P., and M. Shepard

n.d. Insecticides vs. biocontrol in an IPC programme: Rice in tropical Asia. Unpublished manuscript.

Kenmore, P.E.

1992 Indonesia's IPM—a model for Asia. In *Intercountry programme for the development of integrated pest control in rice in South and Southeast Asia: supplementary documents for project document.* Phase III. FAO.

Kern, J.R.

1986 The growth of decentralized rural credit institutions in Indonesia. In *Central government and local development in Indonesia*, edited by C. Mac Andrews. Singapore: Oxford University Press.

Knowles, M.S.

1973 *The adult learner: A neglected species.* Houston: Gulf Publishing Company.

Knowles, M.S. and Associates.

1985 *Andragogy in action: Applying modern principles of adult learning.* San Francisco: Jossey-Bass Publishers.

Kroeber, A.L.

1948 *Anthropology.* London: Harrap.

Kuhn, T.S.

1962 *The structure of scientific revolution.* Chicago: The University of Chicago Press.

1970 *The structure of scientific revolution*. Second edition, enlarged. Chicago: The University of Chicago Press.
1993 Metaphor in science. In *Metaphor and thought*, edited by A. Ortony, 533–42. Cambridge: Cambridge University Press.

Kuznar, L.A.
1997 *Reclaiming a scientific anthropology*. Walnut Creek: A Division of Sage Publications.

Lave, J.
1988 *Cognition in practice: mind, mathematics and culture in everyday life*. Cambridge: Cambridge University Press.
1996 The practice of learning. In *Understanding practice perspectives on activity and context*, edited by S. Chaiklin and J. Lave, 3–32. University of California, Berkeley: Cambridge University Press.

Lave, J., and E. Wenger
1991 *Situated learning: Legitimate peripheral participation*. Cambridge: Cambridge University Press.

LEISA
2003 *Magazine on low external input and sustainable agriculture. Learning with farmer field schools*. LEISA 19 (l).

Leonard, D.K.
1977 *Reaching the peasant farmer: Organization theory and practice in Kenya*. Chicago: The University of Chicago Press.

Lindstrom, L.
1990 *Knowledge and power in a South Pacific society*. Washington DC: Smithsonian Institution Press.

Litzinger, J.A.
1985 Integrated pest management for rice in Asia. In *Women in rice farming: Proceedings of a conference on women in rice farming systems*, 489–500. The International Rice Research Institute, 26–30 September 1983, Aldershot, Hants: Gower Publishing Company.

Long, N.
1993a Introduction. In *Battlefields of knowledge: The interlocking of theory and practice in social research and development*, edited by N. Long and A. Long, 3–15.London: Routledge.
1993b From paradigm lost to paradigm regained? The case for

an actor-oriented sociology of development. In *Battlefields of knowledge: The interlocking of theory and practice in social research and development,* edited by N. Long and A. Long, 16–43. London: Routledge.

Long, N., and M. Villareal
1994   The interweaving of knowledge and power in development interfaces. In *Beyond farmer first: Rural people's knowledge, agricultural research and extension practice,* edited by I. Scoones and J. Thompson, 41–52. London: Intermediate Technology Publications.

Longhurst, R., R. Chambers, and J. Swift
1986   Seasonality and poverty: Implications for policy and research. *IDS Bulletin* 17(3):67–71.

Marglin, S.A.
1996   Farmers, seedsmen, and scientists: Systems of agriculture and systems of knowledge. In *Decolonizing knowledge: From development to dialogue,* edited by F. Apffel-Marglin and S.A. Marglin, 185–248. Oxford: Clarendon Press.

Maurya, D.M.
1989   The innovative approach of Indian farmers. In *Farmer first: Farmer innovation and agricultural research,* edited by R. Chambers, A. Pacey, and L.A. Thrupp, 9–14. London Intermediate Technology Publications.

Mayer, R.E.
1993   The instructive metaphor: Metaphoric aids to students' understanding of science. In *Metaphor and thought,* edited by A. Ortony, 561–87. Cambridge: Cambridge University Press.

Mears, L.A., and S. Moeljono
1981   Food policy. In *The Indonesian economy during the Soeharto era.* edited by A. Booth and P. McCawley, 23–61. Kuala Lumpur: Oxford University Press.

Millar, D.
1994   Experimenting farmers in Northern Ghana. In *Beyond farmer first: Rural people's knowledge, agricultural research and extension practce,* edited by I. Scoones and J. Thompson, 160–65. London: Intermediate Technology Publications.

Moore, S.F.
1975 Epilogue: uncertainties in situations, indeterminacies in culture. In *Symbol and politics in communal ideology: Cases and questions.* Edited by S.F. Moore and B.G. Myerhoff, 210–39. Ithaca, NY: Cornell University Press.
1986 *Social facts and fabrications: "Customary" law on Kilimanjaro, 1880–1980.* Cambridge: Cambridge University Press.
1987 Explaining the present: theoretical dilemmas in processual ethnography. *American Ethnologist* 14(4):727–36.
1994 The ethnography of the present and the analysis of process. In *Assessing cultural anthropology.* edited by R. Borofsky, 362–76. New York: McGraw-Hill.

Murtaugh, M.
1980 See for yourself: Some problems in the use of demonstration tours to promote agricultural development (Mexico). In *Indigenous knowledge systems and development,* edited by D. Brokensha, D.M. Warren, and O. Werner, 29–36. Lanham: University Press of America.

Nataatmadja, H., D. Kertosastro, and A. Suryana
1988 Perkembangan produksi dan kebijaksanaan pemerintah dalam produksi beras. In M. Ismunadji. *Padi, buku I,* 37–53. Bogor: Badan Penelitian dan Pengembangan Pertanian: Pusat Penelitian dan Pengembangan Tanaman Pangan.

Navarro, R.L., J.R. Medina, and D.P. Callo, Jr.
1998 *Empowering farmers: The Philippine national integrated pest management program.* Los Baños: SEAMEO Regional Center for Graduate Study and Research in Agriculture.

Nazarea-Sandoval, V.D.
1995 *Local knowledge and agricultural decision making in the Philippines: Class, gender, and resistance.* Ithaca: Cornell University Press.

Nygren, A.
1999 Local knowledge in the environment-development discourse: From dichotomies to situated knowledge. *Critique of Anthropology* 19(3):267–88.

Oka, I.N.
1991 Kajian penanggulangan wabah hama penggerek batang padi berdasarkan konsepsi pengendalian hama terpadu. Manuscript. Jakarta: Program Nasional Pengendalian

Hama Terpadu, Badan Perencanaan dan Pembangunan Nasional.

1995 *Pengendalian hama terpadu dan implementasinya di Indonesia.* Yogyakarta: Gadjah Mada University Press.

Oldeman, L.R.
1983 Agroclimatic maps relation to rice based cropping systems. In *Peranan hasil penelitian padi dan palawija dalam pembangunan pertanian,* edited by M. Ismunadji, M. Syam, F. Bahar, A. Widjono, Sumarno, Suprapto H.S., I. Prasadja, M. Machmud, S.O. Manurung and P. Mundy, 271–85. Bogor: Badan Penelitian dan Pembangunan Pertanian, Departemen Pertanian.

Ortiz, S.R.
1973 *Uncertainties in peasant farming: A Colombian case.* London: The Athlone Press.
1979 Expectations and forecasts in the face of uncertainty. *Man* 14(1):64–80.

Ortner, S.B.
1984 Theory in anthropology since the sixties. *Comparative Studies in Society and History* 26:126–66.

Ortony, A.
1993 Metaphor, language, and thought. In *Metaphor and thought,* edited by A. Ortony, 1–16. Cambridge: Cambridge University Press.

Ou, S.H.
1973 *A handbook of rice diseases in the tropics.* Los Baños: International Rice Research Institute.

Palmer, I.
1978 *The Indonesian economy since 1965: A case study of political economy.* London: Frank Cass.

Pelto, P.J., and G.H. Pelto
1975 Intra-cultural diversity: Some theoretical issues. *American Ethnologist* 2:1–18.

Perkins, J.H.
1982 *Insects, experts, and the insecticide crisis: The quest for new pest management strategies.* New York: Plenum Press.

PERUM Otorita Jatiluhur
  n.d.   Perusahaan Umum Otorita Jatiluhur. Purwakarta. Manuscript.

PERUM Sang Hyang Seri
  n.d.   Perusahaan Umum (PERUM) Sang Hyang Seri. Sukamandi. Manuscript.

Pest/Disease Surveillance for Food Crops
  1991   Guidance for crash-programme of white rice stem borer control in JALUR PANTURA. Jatisari. Manuscript.

Petrie, H.G., and R.S. Oshlag
  1993   Metaphor and learning. In *Metaphor and thought*, edited by A. Ortony, 579–609. Cambridge: Cambridge University Press.

Philips, S.U.
  1982   The language socialization of lawyers acquiring the "cant." In *Doing the ethnography of schooling*, edited by G. Spindler, 177–209. New York: Holt, Rinehart and Winston.

Pimbert, M.
  1991   *Designing integrated pest management for sustainable and productive futures*. Sustainable Agriculture Programme Gatekeeper Series 29. London: IIED.

Pincus, J.
  1991   Third project report: preliminary analysis of village data: Agrarian institutions in three West Java villages. Section I. Manuscript. Cambridge University.
  1996   *Class power and agrarian change: Land and labour in rural West Java*. London: MacMillan Press.

Ploeg, J.D. van der
  1993   Potatoes and knowledge. In *An anthropological critique of development: The growth of ignorance*, edited by M. Hobart, 209–27. London: Routledge.

Pontius, J., R. Dilts, and A. Bartlett
  2002   *From farmer field school to community IPM: Ten years of IPM training in Asia*. Bangkok: FAO Community IPM Programme. Food and Agriculture Organization of the United Nations Regional Office for Asia and the Pacific.

Prawirasuganda, A.
  1964   *Upatjara adat di Pasundan*. Bandung: Sumur Bandung.

Pretty, J.N.
1995   *Regenerating agriculture: Policies and practice for sustainability and self-reliance.* London: Earthscan Publications.

Program Nasional Pelatihan dan Pengembangan Pengendalian Hama Terpadu.
1991a   Buku petunjuk lapangan untuk PHT padi. Jakarta.
1991b   Rangkuman hasil pertemuan sambung rasa laboratorium lapang PHT dan kasi Perlintan se-JALUR PANTURA Karawang, 29–31 Juli 1991. Jakarta.

Program Nasional Pengendalian Hama Terpadu
1989   IPM hand-out for training of trainers. Jakarta.
n.d.   The Indonesian IPM Program. Jakarta.

Pusat Penelitian dan Pengembangan Tanaman Pangan (*Central Research Institute for Food Crops*)
1991   *Varietas unggul tanaman pangan (High-yielding varieties of food crops).* Bogor.

Quinn, N., and D. Holland
1987   Culture and cognition. In *Cultural models in language and thought,* edited by D. Holland and N. Quinn, 3–40. Cambridge: Cambridge University Press.

Rauf, A.
1990   Analisis epidemi penggerek padi putih di jalur pantura. *Seminar pengendalian hama penggerek batang padi putih.* Bogor: Kerjasama Proyek Prasarana Fisik Bappenas dengan Jurusan Hama dan Penyakit Tumbuhan Fakultas Pertanian Institut Pertanian Bogor.

Redfield, R.
1960   *The little community and peasant society and culture.* Chicago: The University of Chicago Press.

Reissig, W.H., E.A. Heinrichs, J.A. Litsinger, K. Moody, L. Fiedler, T.W. Mew, and A.T. Barrion
1986   *Illustrated guide to integrated pest management in rice in tropical Asia.* Los Baños: International Rice Research Institute.

Resnick, L.B.
1991   Shared cognition: Thinking as social practice. In *Perspectives on socially shared cognition,* edited by L.B. Resnick, J.M. Levine, and S.D. Teasley, 1–20. Washington, DC: American Psychological Association.

Restle, F.
1975 *Learning: Animal behavior and human cognition.* New York: McGraw-Hill.

Rhoades, R.E.
1987 Farmers and experimentation. *Agricultural and Administration (Research and Extension) Network.* Discussion Paper 21. London: Overseas Development Institute.
1989 The role of farmers in the creation of agricultural technology. In *Farmer first: farmer innovation and agricultural research,* edited by R. Chambers, A. Pacey, and L.A. Thrupp, 3–9. London: Intermediate Technology Publications.

Rhoades, R.E., and A. Bebbington
1988 Farmers as experimenters. *ILEIA* 4(3):328.
1995 Farmers who experiment: an untapped resource for agricultural research and development. In *The cultural dimension of development: Indigenous knowledge systems,* edited by D.M. Warren, L.J. Slikkerveer, and D. Brokensha, 296–307. London: Intermediate Technology Publications.

Richards, P.
1980 Community enviromental knowledge in African rural development. In *Indigenous knowledge systems and development,* edited by D. Brokensha, D.M. Warren, O. Werner, 81–94. Lanham: University Press of America.
1985 *Indigenous agricultural revolution: Ecology and food production in West Africa.* London: Hutchinson and Boulder: Westview Press.
1986 *Coping with hunger: Hazard and experiment in African rice-farming system.* London: Allen & Unwin.
1989a Farmers also experiment: A neglected intellectual resource in African science,, *Discovery and Innovation* 1(1):19–25.
1989b Agriculture as a performance. In *Farmer first: Farmer innovation and agricultural research,* edited by R. Chambers, A. Pacey, and L.A. Thrupp, 39–43. London: Intermediate Technology Publications.
1992 Rural development and local knowledge: The case of rice in central Sierra Leone. Paper presented at Beyond farmer first: Rural people's knowledge, agricultural research and extension practice workshop. Brighton: The Institute of Development Studies, The University of Sussex.

1993 Cultivation, knowledge or performance. In *An anthropological critique of development: The growth of ignorance*, edited by M. Hobart, 61–78. London: Routledge.

1994 Local knowledge formation and validation: The case of rice production in central Sierra Leone. In *Beyond farmer first: Rural people's knowledge, agricultural research and extension practice*, edited by I. Scoones and J. Thompson, 165–70. London: Intermediate Technology Publications.

Robinson, K.
1989 Choosing contraception: cultural change and the Indonesian family planning programme. In *Creating Indonesian cultures*, edited by P. Alexander, 21–38. Sydney: Oceania Publications.

Rogoff, B.
1984 Introduction: Thinking and learning in social context. In *Everyday cognition: Its development in social context*, edited by B. Rogoff and J. Lave, 1–8. Cambridge: Harvard University Press.

Rogoff, B., and J. Lave, eds.
1984 *Everyday cognition: Its development in social context*. Cambridge: Harvard University Press.

Rola, A.C., Z.S. Provido, M.O. Olanday, with F.J. Paraguas, A.S. Sirue, M.A. Espadon, and S.P. Hupeda
1998 *Making farmers better decision makers through the farmer field school*. Los Baños: SEAMEO Regional Center for Graduate Study and Research in Agriculture.

Röling, N., and E. van de Fliert
1994 Transforming extension for sustainable agriculture: The case of integrated pest management in rice in Indonesia. *Agriculture and Human Values* 11(2/3):98–108.

1998 Introducing integrated pest management in rice in Indonesia: A pioneering attempt to facilitate large-scale change. In *Facilitating sustainable agriculture: Participatory learning and adaptive management in times of environmental uncertainty*, edited by N. Röling and M.A.E. Wagemakers, 153–71. Cambridge: Cambridge University Press.

Romney, A.K., S.C. Weller, and W.H. Batchelder
1986 Culture as consensus: A theory of culture and informant accuracy. *American Anthropologist* 88 (2):313–38.

Rosaldo, R.
1993   *Culture and truth: The remaking of social analysis.* Boston: Beacon Press.

Rosaldo, R., S. Lavie, and K. Narayan
1993   Introduction: Creativity in anthropology. In *Creativity/ Anthropology,* edited by S. Lavie, K. Narayan, and R. Rosaldo, 1–8. Ithaca and London: Cornell University Press.

Sankoff, G.
1971   Quantitative analysis of sharing and variability in a cognitive model. *Ethnology* 10(4):389–408.

Satari, G.
1987   Peranan fosfor dalam pembangunan pertanian di Indonesia [The role of phosphorus in agricultural development in Indonesia]. In *Prosiding lokakarya penggunaan pupuk fosfat,* edited by M. Sudjadi et al., 13–20. Bogor: Pusat Penelitian Tanah, Badan Penelitian dan Pengembangan Pertanian.

Saville-Troike, M.
1987   Dilingual discourse: The negotiation of meaning without a common code. *Linguistics* 25(1):81–106.
1989   *The ethnography of communication: An introduction.* Oxford: Basil Blackwell.

Sawit, M.H., and I. Manwan
1991   The New SUPRA INSUS rice intensification program: The case of the North Coast of West Java and South Sulawesi. *Bulletin of Indonesian Economic Studies* 27(1):81–103.

Sawit, M.H., A. Saefuddin, and I. Manwan
1988   Program intensifikasi pola SUPRA INSUS di JALUR PANTURA Jabar dan Sulsel: masalah, kendala dan saran perbaikannya. Paper presented at the Simposium Penelitian Tanaman Pangan II. Pusat Penelitian dan Pengembangan Tanaman Pangan, Badan Litbang Pertanian. Ciloto, Puncak. 21–23 March.

Schelling, T.C.
1978   *Micromotives and macrobehavior.* New York: Norton.

Schiller, B.L.M.
1980   The green revolution in Java: Ecological, socio-economic and historical perspectives. *Prisma* 18:71–93.

Scoones, I., and J. Thompson
- 1994a Introduction. In *Beyond farmer first: Rural people's knowledge, agricultural research and extension practice,* edited by I. Scoones and J. Thompson, 1–12. London: Intermediate Technology Publications.
- 1994b Knowledge, power and agriculture—towards a theoretical understanding. In *Beyond farmer first: Rural people's knowledge, agricultural research and extension practice,* edited by I. Scoones and J. Thompson, 16–32. London: Intermediate Technology Publications, pp.16–32.

Scott, J.C.
- 1976 *The moral economy of the peasant: Rebellion and subsistence in Southeast Asia.* New Haven: Yale University Press.

Sekretariat Badan Pengendali BIMAS.
- 1990 *Himpunan kebijaksanaan tatalaksana program intensifikasi.* Jakarta.
- 1991 *Sejarah perkembangan Bimas: dinamika proses gerakan partisipasi masyarakat tani dalam program Bimas menuju tahap tinggal landas.* Jakarta.

Shiva, V.
- 1988 Reductionist science as epistemological violence. In *Science, hegemony and violence: a requiem for modernity,* edited by A. Nandy, 232–56. Oxford: Oxford University Press.
- 1991 *The violence of the Green Revolution: Third world agriculture, ecology and politics.* London: Zed Books; Penang: Third World Network.
- 1993 *Monocultures of the mind: Perspectives on biodiversity and biotechnology.* London: Zed Books and Penang: Third World Network.
- 1997 *Biopiracy: The plunder of nature and knowledge.* Boston, MA: South End Press.

Shore, B.
- 1991 Twice-born, once conceived: Meaning construction and cultural cognition. *American Anthropologist* 93:9–27.

Sillitoe, P.
- 1983 *Roots of the earth: Crops in the Highlands of Papua New Guinea.* Kensington: New South Wales University Press.
- 1998 The development of indigenous knowledge: A new applied anthropology. *Current Anthropology* 39(2):223–252.

Smith, R.F., J.L. Apple, and D.G. Bottrell
1976   The origins of integrated pest management concepts for agricultural crops. In *Integrated pest management*, edited by A.J. Lawrence and R.F. Smith, 1–16. New York: Plenum Press.

Sosromarsono, S.
n.d.   Bioekologi dan strategi pengendalian terpadu penggerek batang padi putih, *Schirpophaga (Tryporyza) innotata Walker (Lepidoptera: Pyralidae)*. Bogor. Manuscript.

Sperber, D.
1984   Anthropology and psychology: towards an epidemiology of representations. *Man* 20:73–89.

Stolzenbach, A.
1993   Learning by improvization: farmers' experimentation in Mali. In *Beyond farmer first: Rural people's knowledge, agricultural research and extension practice,* edited by I. Scoones and J. Thompson, 155–59. London: Intermediate Technology Publications.

Strauss, C., and N. Quinn
1997   *A cognitive theory of cultural meaning.* Cambridge: Cambridge University Press.

Stuchlik, M., ed.
1981   *The structure of folk model.* A.S.A Monograph 20. London: Academic Press.

Suharto, H.
1989   Serangan hama padi beberapa waktu tanam di Purwokerto Jawa Tengah tahun 1988. *Kompilasi hasil penelitian padi 88/89*:288–91. Sukamandi: Balai Penelitian Tanaman Pangan.

Suharto, H., and D. Kertoseputro
1989   Fluktuasi hama wereng coklat dan penggerek batang di Pantai Utara Jawa Barat pada tahun 1988. *Kumpulan seminar Balitan Sukamand,* 1–9. Sukamandi: Balai Penelitian Tanaman Pangan.

Sweetzer, E.E.
1987   The definition of *lie:* An examination of the folk models underlying a semantic prototype. In *Cultural models in language and thought,* edited by D. Holland and N. Quinn, 43–66. Cambridge: Cambridge University Press.

Thomason, R.H.
1986 The context-sensitivity of belief and desire. In *Reasoning about actions and plans: Proceedings of the 1986 workshop*, edited by M.P. Georgeff and A.L. Lansky, 341–60. Los Altos, CA: Kaufmann Publishers.

Tim Survei Tanah Pusat Penelitian Tanah dan Agro Klimat
1990 *Penelitian kesesuaian lahan untuk intensifikasi tanaman pangan Propinsi Jawa Barat.* Bogor: Pusat Penelitian Tanah dan Agro Klimat, Badan Penelitian dan Pengembangan Pertanian, Departemen Pertanian.

Tjitradjaja, I.
1987 *Drawdown farming at Jatiluhur Dam, West Java: A case study of local responses to new conditions.* Ph.D. diss., Rutgers, The State University of New Jersey.
1989 Contextual explanations: A methodological examination. *Berita Anthropologi* 13(45):1–10.

Tyler, S.A.
1969 Introduction. In *Cognitive anthropology*, edited by S.A. Tyler, 1–23. New York: Holt, Rinehart and Winston.

Umbara, Ki
1978 *Dewi Sri: dongeng asal mulanya padi, diceritakan kembali oleh Ki Umbara.* Jakarta: Pustaka Jaya.

Vayda, A.P.
1983 Progressive contextualization: methods for research in human ecology. *Human Ecology* 11(3):265–81.
1986 Holism and individualism in ecological anthropology. *Reviews in Anthropology* 13:295–313.
1993 Ecosystems and human actions. In *Humans as components of ecosystems: The ecology of subtle human effects and populated areas*, edited by M.J. McDonnel and S.T.A. Pickett, 61–71. New York: Springer-Verlag.
1994 Actions, variations, and change: The emerging anti-essentialist view in anthropology. In *Assessing cultural anthropology*, edited by R. Borofsky, 320–30. New York: McGraw-Hill.

Vayda, A.P., B.J. McCay, and C. Eghenter
1991 Concepts of process in social science explanation. *Philosophy of the Social Sciences* 21(3):318–31.

Vayda, A.P., and I. Setyawati
1995   Questions about culture-related considerations in research on cognition and agro-ecological change: Illustrations from studies of agricultural pest management in Java. In *Cultural dynamics in development processes*, edited by A. de Ruijter and L. van Vucht Tijssen, 259–68. UNESCO Publishing/Netherlands Commission for UNESCO.

1998   Questions about culture-related considerations in research on cognition and agro-ecological change: Illustrations from studies of agricultural pests management in Java. *Antropologi Indonesia* 22(55):44–52.

Wallace, A.F.C.
[1961] 1970   *Culture and personality.* New York: Random House.

Wardhani, M.A.
1992   Developments in IPM: The Indonesian case. In *Integrated pest management in the Asia-Pacific Region*, edited by P.A.C. Ooi, G.S. Lim, T.H. Ho, P.L. Manalo, and J. Waage, 27–35. CAB International: Asian Development Bank.

Warren, D.M., L.J. Slikkerveer, and D. Brokensha
1995   Introduction. In *The cultural dimension of development: indigenous knowledge systems,* edited by D.M. Warren, L.J. Slikkerveer, and D. Brokensha, xv–xviii. London: Intermediate Technology Publications.

Warwick, D.P.
1986   The Indonesian family planning program: government influence and client choice. *Population Development and Change* 12(3):453–90.

Wassmann, J.
1995   The final requiem for the omniscient informant? An interdisciplinary approach to everyday cognition. *Culture and Psychology* 1:167–201.

Watts, M.
1983   *Silent violence: Food, famine, and peasantry in Northern Nigeria.* Berkeley: University of California Press.

Wessing, R.
1974   *Cosmology and social behaviour in a West Javanese settlement.* Athens: Ohio University Center for International Studies.

Wharton, Jr., C.R.
1971   Risk, uncertainty and the subsistence farmer: technological innovation and resistance to change in the context of survival. In *Studies in economic anthropology*, edited by G. Dalton, 154–61. Anthropological Studies no. 7. Washington, DC: American Anthropological Association.

White, B.
1976   Production and reproduction in a Javanese village. Ph.D. diss., Columbia University.

White, B., and G. Wiradi
1989   Agrarian and nonagrarian bases of inequality in nine Javanese villages. In *Agrarian transformation: Local processes and the state in Southeast Asia*, edited by G. Hart, A. Turton, and B. White with B. Fegan and L.T. Ghee, 266–302. Berkeley: University of California Press.

Winarno, B.
1985   The roles of village organizations in rural development: an analysis of the Indonesian experience. Ph.D. diss., The University of Missouri-Columbia.

Winarto, Y.T.
1993   Farmers' agroecological knowledge construction: The case of integrated pest management among rice farmers on the north coast of West Java. In *Rural people's knowledge, agricultural research and extension practice*. Research Series 1, vol. 3:68–90. London: IIED.

1994   Encouraging knowledge exchange: Integrated pest management in Indonesia. In *Beyond farmer first: Rural people's knowledge, agricultural research and extension practice*, edited by I. Scoones and J. Thompson, 150–54. London: Intermediate Technology Publications.

1995   State intervention and farmer creativity: Integrated pest management among rice farmers in Subang, West Java. *Agriculture and Human Values* 12(4):47–57.

1997a   Maintaining seed diversity during the green revolution era. *Knowledge and Development Monitor* 5(4):3–6.

1997b   Pengendalian hama terpadu: Pembentukan dan pengalihan pengetahuan di antara petani padi di Subang, Jawa Barat. In *Koentjaraningrat dan antropologi di Indonesia*, edited by E.K.M. Masinambow, 165–89. Jakarta: Antropologi Asosiasi Indonesia bekerjasama dengan Yayasan Obor Indonesia.

1998 "Hama dan musuh alami," "obat dan racun": Dinamika pengetahuan petani padi dalam pengendalian hama. *Antropologi Indonesia* 22 (55).

1999 Creating knowledge: scientific knowledge and local adoption in rice integrated pest management in Indonesia (a case study from Subang, West Java). In *Applied anthropology in Australasia*, edited by S. Toussaint and J.Taylor, 162–92. Perth: University of Western Australia.

Winarto, Y.T., E.M. Choesin, Fadli, A.S.H. Ningsih, and S. Darmono

2000 Satu dasa warsa pengendalian hama terpadu: Berjuang menggapai kemandirian dan kesejahteraan. Research report to Indonesian FAO Inter Country Program. Jakarta.

Wiradi, G., and C. Manning

1984 *Landownership, tenancy and sources of household income: Community patterns from a partial recensus of eight villages in rural Java*. Bogor: Studi Dinamika Pedesaan, Yayasan Penelitian Survey Agro Ekonomi.

Wittgenstein, L.

1958 *Preliminary studies for the "philosophical investigations" generally known as the blue and brown books*. Oxford: Basil Blackwell.

Wolf, E.R.

1957 Closed corporate communities in Mesoamerica and Central Java. *Southwestern Journal of Anthropology* 13:1–18.

1966 *Peasants*. Englewood Cliffs, NJ: Prentice-Hall.

Design, typography,
and production
by **H.G. Salome** of

Hamden, Connecticut USA